Doing Ethnography

Doing Ethnography

Studying Everyday Life

Edited by
Dorothy Pawluch
William Shaffir
Charlene Miall

Canadian Scholars' Press
Toronto

Doing Ethnography: Studying Everyday Life
Edited by Dorothy Pawluch, William Shaffir, and Charlene Miall

First published in 2005 by
Canadian Scholars' Press Inc.
180 Bloor Street West, Suite 801
Toronto, Ontario
M5S 2V6

www.cspi.org

Canadian Scholars' Press gratefully acknowledges financial support for our publishing activities from the Government of Canada through the Book Publishing Industry Development Program (BPIDP) and the Government of Ontario through the Ontario Book Publishing Tax Credit Program.

Library and Archives Canada Cataloguing in Publication

   Doing ethnography : studying everyday life / edited by Dorothy Pawluch, William Shaffir, Charlene E. Miall.

Includes bibliographical references and index.
ISBN 1-55130-245-4

   1. Sociology. 2. Ethnology. 3. Symbolic interactionism. I. Pawluch, Dorothy, 1953- II. Shaffir, William, 1945- III. Miall, Charlene Elizabeth Shaffir, William, 1945-

GN345.D65 2005   301   C2005-903219-7

Cover design by George Kirkpatrick
Cover image © Elsa Warnick/Images.com. Reproduced by permission of the illustrator and
   Images.com
Page design and layout by Brad Horning

05 06 07 08 09   5 4 3 2 1

Printed and bound in Canada by Marquis Book Printing Inc.

Canada

For

Alexandra
Dorothy Pawluch

Rivka, Yael, Motty, Elichai, and Ariel
William Shaffir

Andrew, Christopher, and Sarah
Charlene Miall

Table of Contents

Part 1C: Relating to Respondents

Part 1D: Writing about Social Life

PART 2: ETHNOGRAPHY IN PROCESS: CASE STUDIES OF EVERYDAY LIFE

Part 2A: Constructing Perspectives

Part 2B: Constructing Identities

Part 2C: Doing and Relating

Preface

Studying everyday life—how hard can it be? Or, as Don Cherry might say, "It's not rocket surgery." Alas, if studying everyday life were as simple, uncomplicated, and self-evident as it sounds, there would be no need for volumes such as this one. Only those who have tackled a study that aims to capture the experience of everyday life from the perspectives of the social actors who live it know how daunting, seemingly intractable, and gut-wrenching the problems can get. At the same time, only those who have tackled such studies can fully appreciate the intellectual payoffs to be reaped from persisting and trying to work through the problems. Our goal in this collection is to capture both sides of the experience—to present papers that address the challenges of doing ethnographies, but also papers that demonstrate the kinds of insights about everyday life that ethnographies can yield.

Our task was made easier because we were able to draw on the writing of colleagues who have participated in the Qualitative Analysis Conference. The Qualitative Analysis Conference began in the early 1980s as a relatively informal gathering of researchers who worked within an ethnographic tradition. Over the years the conference evolved into the premiere venue for qualitative research in Canada. In 2001 and 2002, the Qualitative Analysis Conference was held at McMaster University in Hamilton, Ontario. Each of the chapters in this volume started out as a paper presented there. Even as we were pulling the programs for the conference together, we recognized the significance of the ideas to be presented and the merit in giving this work broader exposure. A plan was hatched. As we wrapped up our hosting duties, we invited those who had joined us at the Hamilton meetings to submit their papers for possible publication. The response was enthusiastic. We received many more papers than we could possibly have hoped to include. Our greatest regret is that we were forced to turn so many excellent papers away. We were especially disappointed about the need for a second—and unexpected—round of cuts after the manuscript's focus shifted. We faced the disheartening task of having to inform colleagues and good friends that despite their laborious efforts to comply with our suggested revisions, their contribution would not be included. We trust that they understand the vagaries of the publishing process.

Collaborative efforts involving a host of contributors, and, directed by more than two editors, are almost always accompanied by frustrations, disagreements, and a host of experiences leading to firm resolutions that undertakings of this nature will never be repeated. However, contrary to Simmel's observations about conflicts generated by triads, our interpersonal experiences as colleagues and editors were overwhelmingly positive and, perhaps, truly exceptional. We met fairly regularly to monitor the work's progress and to share our concerns and even anxieties about the volume's directions, but such emotions, we understood, came with the territory. To our credit and relief, our respective senses of humour served as reliable guides to situate our task within a proper perspective. Though attending to our editorial responsibilities conscientiously, more than equal time was allocated to reporting on family matters, to new and unexpected twists at the university, and to first-hand reports about the quality of apple picking in the Hamilton area.

We have a number of people to thank for assisting us in bringing this volume to life. We are grateful to each of our contributors for their submissions, for complying with our numerous requests, and for working so co-operatively and patiently with us to prepare their papers for publication. We thank several sets of reviewers for their thoughtful comments. Megan Mueller, Senior Editor at Canadian Scholars' Press, was a pleasure to work with. She steered the manuscript through its various permutations with an expert hand and helped us to sharpen its focus. Althea Prince, Rebecca Conolly, and Renée Knapp at Canadian Scholars' Press were also helpful. Gail Coulas and Tony Christensen assisted with the preparation of the manuscript and the pedagogical material. Two grants, provided by the Social Sciences and Humanities Research Council, made it possible for us to bring the Qualitative Analysis Conference to McMaster University. The grants also allowed us to follow through with this volume.

A NOTE FROM THE PUBLISHER

Thank you for selecting *Doing Ethnography: Studying Everyday Life*, edited by Dorothy Pawluch, William Shaffir, and Charlene Miall. The editors and publisher have devoted considerable time and careful development (including meticulous peer reviews) to this book. We appreciate your recognition of this effort and accomplishment.

Teaching Features

This volume distinguishes itself on the market in many ways. One key feature is the book's well-written and comprehensive part openers, which help to make the readings all the more accessible to undergraduate students. The part openers add cohesion to the section and to the whole book. The themes of the book are very clearly presented in these section openers.

The general editors have also greatly enhanced the book by adding pedagogy to close and complete each section. Each part ends with critical thinking questions and annotated related websites.

The contributors have done a great deal to ensure that chapter pedagogy is quite rich. Each chapter contains formal introductions and conclusions, as well as glossary terms and detailed references. The art program is equally rich, with over 60 boxed inserts. Some chapters also include figures and tables. Each subsection opens with a carefully selected photograph.

Introduction to
Doing Ethnography: Studying Everyday Life

Dorothy Pawluch, William Shaffir, and Charlene Miall

All first-year sociology students—at least those who are paying attention—learn that there are three main theories or perspectives that sociologists use in studying society. Structural functionalism and conflict theory are usually said to be focused on the macrosociological or large-scale dimensions of society, such as its institutions (the economy, marriage and the family, education, religion, government, health care systems, etc.) and its power relations. Symbolic interactionism's interests, in contrast, are characterized as microsociological. Symbolic interactionism is typically described as a perspective interested in face-to-face interactions, in how people work out their relationships and make sense of life and their place in it. This description of sociology is all too often understood by students and sociologists alike to mean that, while structural functionalists and conflict theorists study the "big" questions, symbolic interactionists deal with more mundane, picayune concerns. While symbolic interactionist research might be fascinating, or even titillating when it ventures into the underside of life, the suggestion is that it somehow misses the most critical part of the story and is oblivious to the larger forces that are really shaping society.

The starting point for this book is that symbolic interactionism has received a bum rap. In truth, *any* question about society, "big" or "small," is ultimately about people interacting with each other. Whether the issue is changing gender relationships, corporate deeds and misdeeds, class structures, or the school performance of children from cultural minorities, it all comes down to one thing—people doing things together. Some sociologists already know this. More and more of them are figuring it out. There has been a move in recent years away from talking in reified terms about "social structures"—divorce rates, divisions of labour, racism—as if these were mysterious forces capable somehow of exercising agency or acting on human beings. More and more sociologists, whether they see themselves as symbolic interactionists or not, are appreciating that it is human beings who act and who, through the ways in which they define situations and construct lines of action for themselves, create and constantly recreate social structures. In fact, the discipline of sociology seems to be moving towards an integration of theoretical perspectives, with the premises of symbolic interactionism and its focus on people doing things together at the centre of that convergence. Sociology is becoming more interactionist in its approach. Symbolic interactionism is no longer the "aside" or, as Mullins (1973) once called it, the "loyal opposition" among sociological perspectives, but a perspective around which the entire discipline is converging.

This is essentially the argument that David Maines makes in a book called *The Faultline of Consciousness* (2001). Maines argues—and demonstrates—that, both in their theorizing and in their empirical analyses, sociologists of all stripes are employing the central tenets of symbolic interactionism. Attention to human action as a proper focus of sociological analysis has "spilled over from the boundaries of [symbolic interactionism] where it has rested almost exclusively for decades and into the consideration of general sociology" (Maines, 2001, p. 17). The importance of situations and context for understanding human conduct, the necessity to consider the meanings or definitions that social actors attach to things and situations around them, the utility in understanding social structures as an expression of social processes are being recognized in every area of sociology. The outcome of these developments is that the old dichotomies that once characterized sociological discourse are breaking down. "The distinctions of structure and process, macro and micro, materialism and idealism are giving way to more mature and realistic depictions of human group life that better serve the scholarly and practical interests of sociologists" (p. 25).

The irony that has given Maines the title of his book, however, is that, even while sociology is increasingly drifting in the direction of a more interactionist sociology, many sociologists seem unaware of the fact. Symbolic interactionism as a perspective continues to suffer from serious image problems. An example comes from Maines's own experience at a certain university where he was regularly called the "symbolic interactionist." He writes that these references "never occurred as blatant instances of name-calling, as in 'you dirty interactionist!' but as quieter and more effective forms of dismissive labelling and indifference" (Maines, 2001, p. 1). Most symbolic interactionists can relate. Maines argues that there is a false consciousness within the discipline about the impact that symbolic interactionism has had both on how sociologists frame their questions and how they go about trying to answer them. While its contributions may not yet have been recognized nor acknowledged, Maines insists that symbolic interactionism has tenaciously developed "the best hope yet for a credible general sociology."

Maines's argument provides a good context for the collection of papers in this book. Both in their content and in the story of how these papers came to be included in one volume, the papers demonstrate Maines's point about the increasingly interactionist face of sociology and perhaps even the social sciences more broadly. The papers are culled from the proceedings of the Qualitative Analysis Conference held at McMaster University, Hamilton, Ontario, in May of 2001 and May of 2002. The Qualitative Analysis Conference goes back 20 years to 1983. In its early years, the conference attracted mostly sociologists who identified themselves as symbolic interactionists and worked within an interactionist tradition.

Early participants also shared in common a particular view about how best to capture the human group activity that is at the core of an interactionist analysis, favouring an ethnographic approach. An ethnography describes the process of intensively studying a social group by immersing oneself in the day-to-day lives of people in the group (Pawluch, 2005, p. 231). They used methods such as intensive, non-directive and naturalistic interviewing, participant observation, and documentary analysis.

In more recent years, presenters have come from, or have at least received their academic training in, departments of anthropology, psychology, history, nursing, social work, geography, public health, and education. Not all of the book's contributors would describe themselves as symbolic interactionists or even sociologists. Yet all do ethnographic work and have found, at a conference that continues to be defined largely by symbolic interactionist principles and an interactionist-inspired methodology, a comfortable venue within which to present and receive feedback on their research.

In content, the papers in this book make contributions to virtually every area of study within sociology—organizations, the family, deviance, religion, work, health, the military. Whether the papers are avowedly symbolic interactionist or framed in more poststructuralist, feminist, or political economy terms, they are essentially about people doing things together or about how to study such people. While the book may have a decidedly interactionist thread running through it, then, and is based on ethnographic approaches to studying social life, it is not a specialized book of interest only to those who want to know more about symbolic interactionism and its applications. It provides a good introduction to sociology more generally, demonstrating the vast range of issues that one might address and the insights one might glean about the fundamental processes of social life.

The book starts with a chapter by one of Canada's foremost sociologists and symbolic interactionists. Robert Prus (1996) is best known for his work on generic social processes (GSPs). By GSPs, Prus means those elements of interaction that occur across diverse contexts and those activities that are involved in "doing" or accomplishing human group life in the various situations in which it occurs. Among the GSPs he has identified are processes such as acquiring perspectives, developing identities, doing activities, making commitments, and generating relationships. One might think about GSPs as what it is that people are doing when they are doing things together. Prus's goal in trying to get sociologists to think in terms of GSPs is to create a basis for analytical comparisons across cases of ethnographic research so that, for instance, those studying bikers, priests, or elite athletes have something to say to each other. While the groups they study may be diverse and appear to share little in common, their members are all engaged in the same sorts of social processes. Sharing and comparing insights gleaned from individual studies creates the possibility of saying something more generally about human group life and to formulate interpretations that would have relevance and applicability in a broad range of social situations.

In Chapter 1 ("Studying Human Knowing and Acting: The Interactionist Quest for Authenticity"), Prus provides for the uninitiated—or for those who may not have been paying close attention in that first introductory sociology course—a comprehensive and thoroughly readable introduction to symbolic interactionism. The paper includes a discussion of its roots, premises, and methods. It ends with a useful set of guidelines and instructions for those who might want to try their hand at systematically studying what people do and how they do it.

The papers in Part 1 are methodologically focused, addressing how best to do ethnographies or study people doing things together. Sociologists tend to concentrate their writing efforts on reporting the results of their investigations. Though the ways in which their studies were conducted—the groups they studied, the people they observed or interviewed, how their observations were recorded—may be described, not much attention is generally paid to the actual experience of doing social research with all its trials and tribulations. (For some exceptions, see Ferrell & Hamm, 1998; Shaffir, Stebbins, & Turowetz, 1980.) These papers offer a refreshing corrective. Each paper gives readers a sense of what it is like to study human group activity ethnographically. Rarely do things go as smoothly as our final research reports or published papers suggest. As the paper titles in Part 1 show, there are endless challenges and pitfalls, but also charms, payoffs, and rewards.

The papers in Part 2 report the findings of completed ethnographic studies. They are organized loosely around several of the generic social processes that Prus identifies in his paper—constructing perspectives, constructing identities, doing and relating.

A common theme in many of the papers is the concern that qualitative researchers have for the integrity and well-being of their respondents and the ethical dimensions of their research. There has been much attention paid of late to the ethics of ethnographic or qualitative research, spurred by the demands of formal ethics review processes throughout North America. Any medical, scientific, or social research involving human beings needs to meet rigorous ethical standards. These standards, however, have been largely designed with quantitative, hypotheses-driven research in mind where it is possible to obtain informed consent and to specify in advance precisely what will be done or asked of the subjects (individuals) being studied. It is more difficult for qualitative researchers, whose methods are likely to include simply hanging around a particular social setting (overtly or covertly) or chatting informally and in ways that cannot always be predetermined, to meet some of the existing standards. The situation has put qualitative researchers at a disadvantage when it comes to getting ethics clearance for their studies and has raised eyebrows in some circles about the ethics of qualitative research. More seriously, it may be gagging qualitative researchers and effectively stifling the kind of research that does not lend itself to the constraints of the review process. Ferrell and Hamm (1998, p. xiv) describe the current climate as the "dark ages" in the history of ethnographic research.

The irony, as Will van den Hoonaard (2002) has observed, is that no other group of researchers has so explicitly, so persistently, or so conscientiously reflected on the ethics of their studies. There is a long tradition among qualitative researchers of attending to one's responsibilities and obligations to those one is studying (Adler

& Adler, 1993; Fine, Weis, Weseen, & Wong, 2000). Van den Hoonaard (2002, p. 13) argues that qualitative researchers have always had a "sanguine and more nuanced view" of ethical matters than their quantitative counterparts. Even now, he insists, it is qualitative researchers who are "opening up new perspectives and sensibilities about the ethical dimensions of [academic research]" (p. 3).

The papers in this volume confirm the abiding commitment to ethical research among ethnographic researchers. Whether the issue is deciding how to handle emotionally sensitive topics, how much or how little of oneself to reveal, how to ensure that respondents' voices come through loudly and accurately, there is a persistent preoccupation with not only "getting it right" but "doing it right."

REFERENCES

Adler, P.A., & Adler, P. (1993). Ethical issues in self-censorship: Ethnographic research on sensitive topics. In C.M. Renzetti & R.M. Lee (Eds.), *Researching sensitive topics* (pp. 249–266). Newbury Park, CA: Sage.

Ferrell, J., & Hamm, M.S. (Eds.). (1998). *Ethnography at the edge: Crime, deviance and field research.* Boston, MA: Northeastern University Press.

Fine, M., Weis, L., Weseen, S., & Wong, L. (2000). For whom? Qualitative research, representations and social responsibilities. In N.K. Denzin & Y.S. Lincoln (Eds.), *Handbook of qualitative research* (pp. 107–132, 2nd ed.). Thousand Oaks, CA: Sage.

Maines, D.R. (2001). *The faultline of consciousness: A view of interactionism in sociology.* New York: Aldine de Gruyter.

Mullins, N. (1973). *Theory and theory groups in contemporary American sociology.* New York: Harper and Row.

Pawluch, D. (2005). Qualitative analysis, sociology. In K. Leonard (Ed.), *Encyclopedia of social measurement* (pp. 231–236). New York: Elsevier.

Prus, R. (1996). *Symbolic interactionism and ethnographic research: Intersubjectivity and the study of human lived experience.* Albany, NY: University of New York Press.

Shaffir, W.B., Stebbins, R.A., & Turowetz, A. (Eds.). (1980). *Fieldwork experience: Qualitative approaches to social research.* New York: St. Martin's Press.

Van den Hoonaard, W.C. (Ed.). (2002). *Walking the tightrope: Ethical issues for qualitative researchers.* Toronto: University of Toronto Press.

Chapter 1

Studying Human Knowing and Acting: The Interactionist Quest for Authenticity

Robert Prus

One of the most consequential tasks facing social scientists is the problem of developing theory that adequately represents the nature of human knowing and acting. Although anyone who has acquired language may strive to make some sense of people and the things they do, there is much difference of opinion on how the study of human group life ought to be pursued both among people within the community at large and those in the social sciences more specifically.

First, it should be recognized that some people discourage the study of human knowing and acting, insisting instead that people should concentrate their efforts on matters of religion, morality, activism, political and military affairs, making money, getting their work done, being entertained, or simply "being happy." Second, even those who have tried to explain human behaviour (and community life) in more sustained terms have taken notably different approaches to their human subject matter.

Not uncommonly, thus, people have invoked a wide assortment of explanations to account for the things people do. For our purposes, these may be categorized as "internal," "external," and "associational" explanations. Explanations that assume notions of "internal causation" generally attribute people's behaviour to (a) people's physiological conditions, requirements, and dysfunctions and/or (b) people's psychological makeup and dispositions. Another set of explanations invokes "external forces" of various sorts to account for people's behaviours and experiences. These include (a) astrological or cosmological elements, (b) climatological or physical environment-related explanations, and (c) non-human agents such as deities, demons, and other supernatural essences, as well as physical objects and other life forms thought to control or otherwise induce certain kinds of human behaviour. A third broad set of explanations may be designated as "associational" or group-related. Here, people contend that human behaviour is a product of one or other aspects of community life.

Whereas associational explanations have a more distinctive sociological quality, immense differences still exist among these. Thus, although some people invoking associational explanations focus more directly on the ways that humans make sense of their situations and develop their behaviours in conjunction with others in the community, others who adopt associational explanations argue that certain kinds of structures (variables, factors, forces) act on people to produce certain kinds of behaviours and/or broader social patterns.

Given this great diversity of viewpoints and emphases, it is important that students of the human condition not only be mindful of the more basic variations these explanations assume but also develop a means of sorting through these notions in questing for a theory and methodology that represents human knowing in more genuine or authentic terms.

In what follows, I address six topics: (1) the problematic nature of human knowing and acting; (2) a set of interactionist assumptions or conceptual coordinates for studying human group life; (3) morality and deviance as a consequential feature of community life; (4) the centrality of ethnographic research for learning about human lived experience; (5) the necessity of developing generic or transcontextual concepts; and (6) pursuing quality in qualitative representations of human life-worlds. Each of these matters merit much more attention than can possibly be developed in the present statement, but a consideration of each is essential for developing a more viable social science.

THE PROBLEMATICS OF HUMAN KNOWING AND ACTING

As minded creatures who experience the currents and uncertainties of change, as well as the intrigues and dilemmas of diversity, amid senses of continuity, people often assume that their situations are unique or at least are substantially different from those of their predecessors. Relatedly, people often assume that they require a radically new and different theory to account for their particular experiences.

However, as a closer examination of recorded history indicates, the matters of human ambiguity, change, and diversity of circumstances are far from unique to the present era. Thus, although the particular people may differ in each instance, as also may their times and places, activities and associates, religions and moralities, and costumes and physical appearances, the matters of ambiguity, change, and diversity are the more or less constant companions of all humans. Likewise, whereas the circumstances in which specific people find themselves may differ notably, even with very short time spans, one finds considerable parallels in the broader challenges that people face, both in their quests for survival and in striving for desired circumstances and experiences within their respective communities.

Relatedly, whereas disciplines such as sociology, psychology, and anthropology may be seen as comparatively recent (19th and 20th century) innovations, the study of human group life has a much longer intellectual legacy. Thus, the written texts that have survived the ravages of time from Mesopotamia (c. 2000 B.C.E.; see Dalley, 1989) and especially the classical Greek era (c. 700–300 B.C.E.) clearly attest to human encounters with diversity, change, and ambiguity, as well as the struggles and challenges that humans more routinely encounter in the lived instances of "the here and now." Relatedly, issues pertaining to matters of human agency, action, character, and interpersonal relations have received noteworthy analytic attention in the classical Greek literature, as also have considerations of religion, poetics, history, philosophy, morality, crime and deviance, policy, government, and international relations and conflict.

Still, the development of Western social thought has been far from systematic, cumulative, or comprehensive. Ironically, too, while great advances have been made in the areas of science and technology, our understanding of the human condition does not appear to have advanced substantially since the classical Greek era (c. 700–300 B.C.E.)—if one uses the existing texts of Thucydides (c. 460–400 B.C.E.), Plato (c. 420–348 B.C.E.), and Aristotle (c. 384–322 B.C.E.) as reference points.

Some extremely good scholars have attended to human knowing and acting in fairly direct terms in the intervening centuries. Among others, this includes Cicero (106–43 B.C.E.), Augustine (354–430), Thomas Aquinas (1225–1274), Niccoló Machiavelli (1469–1527), Thomas Elyot (1490–1560), Thomas Hobbes (1588–1679), John Locke (1632–1704), David Hume (1711–1784), and Wilhelm Dilthey (1833–1911). However, the study of human knowing and acting often has received only sporadic attention over the years as people became absorbed (variously) by concerns with physical survival, political and military ventures, religion, morality, and the somewhat related quests for the control and reformation of human behaviour. Thus, only in the last century or so have Western scholars begun to examine the ways that people make sense of and engage the world about them in more sustained fashions.

Still, this more recent humanist, pragmatist, or interpretivist emphasis was far from a singular or dominant concern in the fledgling social sciences of the 19th and 20th centuries. Indeed, in their attempts to match the successes of those in the physical sciences, the scholars who were most central in developing the social sciences on a more contemporary plane almost completely disregarded the study of human knowing and acting (and relatedly, the uniquely human matters of speech, thought, activity, and interaction).

Accordingly, people such as Auguste Comte and Emile Durkheim in sociology and John Stuart Mill and Wilhelm Wundt in psychology insisted on imitating the methods used by those in the physical sciences. Taking a "structuralist" or "positivist" approach, their predominant emphasis was on finding ways of predicting and controlling human behaviour. Great stress was placed on finding causes (i.e., factors, structures, conditions, forces, and the like) for people's behaviours and situations (i.e., viewing these outcomes or events as dependent variables).

Thus, whereas sociology would become known for survey research and psychology for experimentation, the primary emphasis would be on defining issues in ways that would foster quantification of the human condition (i.e., obtain data readily amenable to statistical analysis). Accordingly, things that do not readily lend themselves to measurement tend to be dismissed as peripheral, if not more completely irrelevant, to the broader social science venture.

Taking exception to these (structuralist or positivist) attempts to reduce the study of the human condition to sets of variables or factors, other philosophers and social scientists insisted on the importance of attending to the human qualities that most differentiated people from other non-living and living entities. Although much diversity also exists among this latter set of scholars (who often describe themselves as interpretivists, humanists, pragmatists, constructionists, and interactionists), the general argument is for the necessity of attending to the matter of people interpreting or making sense of their circumstances and intentionally entering into the process as agents.

To be sure, one finds much variation within both structuralist and interpretivist approaches to the study of the human condition. However, because their baseline assumptions and approaches are so different, it is important to be mindful of these two broader (structuralist vs. interpretivist) sets of emphases in the human sciences.

In what follows, I will be outlining the central features of a *symbolic interactionist* approach to the study of human lived experience. As part of a broader pragmatist (also humanist, constructionist, or interpretivist) tradition, the material following focuses on the ways that people engage the world as minded, deliberating, interacting, and adjusting agents.

From an interactionist viewpoint, the study of community life is very much the study of human knowing and acting. The emphasis is on the ways that people actually do any and all of the activities that constitute human group life.

Envisioned as having capacities to act in meaningful, reflective, or deliberative manners, people are seen to invoke agency in developing their activities and engaging in interchanges with others. The objective is to examine the ways in which people, as living, breathing, thinking, acting, interacting, and adjusting essences, deal with the particular situations in which they find themselves.

AN INTERACTIONIST APPROACH: BASIC ASSUMPTIONS

Focusing on the *enacted features* of the human group, the interactionists (see Mead, 1934; Blumer, 1969; Strauss, 1993; Prus, 1996, 1997, 1999; Prus & Grills, 2003) work with assumptions of the following sort:

(1) Human behaviour is to be explained from *within the human group* rather than on the basis of individual characteristics or subjectivities. Thus, although people have physiological capacities for wide ranges of sensation and motion, things only become known and are made meaningful within the context of community interchange. That is, while human all knowing (as Aristotle observes) is enabled by people's physiological senses and capacities for differentiation, memory, and mobility, people are to be understood as community creatures. It is only as participants in the human community that people learn notions of "what is" (and "what is not"). This is achieved on the basis of linguistic and behavioural interchange with others. Accordingly, meaningful human behaviour cannot be reduced to individual characteristics or qualities.

(2) Since it is words (and other agreed-upon signs or symbols) that allow people to make indications to others or "signify things" that are potentially knowable

to others (i.e., allow people to establish mutually designated reference points), *language or speech* is the essential enabling mechanism for all meaningful human knowing and acting. Relatedly, as people's speech is apt to vary from community to community as well as from group to group within specific communities, we may expect to find somewhat different notions of reality (as in what is known and what is considered important).

(3) People act towards objects *mindfully of the meanings* that they give (linguistically assign) to those things. Indeed, it might be stressed that because people act towards things in linguistically meaningful terms, notions of objects, activities, and speech are to be understood as central, interrelated components in the developmental process of "being human" (socialized, participating in community life).

Further, because people act within a world of objects, human group life cannot be reduced to speech. Using terms such as "objects," "items," or "phenomena" to refer to any of the particular essences to which people may attend, experience, or act towards, people live, think, and act mindfully of the *world of objects*. All of these objects are known (and not known — as in ambiguity) through and within the limits of people's language. Whereas some humanly referenced items (a) may be entirely linguistic or symbolic (as in ideas or concepts) in constitution and (b) some other phenomena may be encountered and recalled essentially as "images," people still come to know about aspects of these objects through linguistic definitions of the sensations (and resistances) that they encounter as they contemplate these objects both in more direct personal terms and discuss these and related matters with other people. Thus, it is in acting towards things (both in more defined terms and only vaguely known images or other sensations) and dealing with other people with respect to those objects that people test out, assess, and reassess their images, intentions, activities, earlier physiological sensations, and memories of all items of their awareness (see Blumer, 1969; Prus, 1996).

(4) Whereas people know things only in linguistic terms, language is to be understood within the context of activity. Viewed thusly, people's *activities* represent the central point of human existence and scholarly analysis. As Aristotle observed, all animal life is characterized by capacities for sensation and internally generated motion. However, human activity is more than an organic feature of living and surviving. People also give meanings to things by the particular ways that they act towards those objects and talk about those things both with others and themselves. Not only does speech (encompassing communication and thought) denote a realm of activity but speech is also the activity that provides humans with the means of meaningfully or knowingly engaging, testing, and assessing situations in more immediate terms and developing one's notions of knowing in a more comprehensive sense.

Likewise, whereas all sensations presuppose some capacity for physiological activity, so do all modes of attending to things, engaging objects, and participating in situations. Still, it is important to recognize that, in contrast to organic motion more generally, human activity is made meaningful primarily in reference to the knowingly intentional or purposive matter of "doing something" or "getting something done." People need not be successful in their ventures, but meaningful activity implies some purpose or sense of pursuing or accomplishing some end or objective.

(5) As people acquire speech (and learn about things within the human community), people develop capacities to act as *deliberative, purposive* agents. This appears to be a tentative, developmental process wherein, after establishing some notions of differentiation, people begin attending to others and start to assume the viewpoints of other people with respect to other objects and their own essences, sensations, and motions. As people use the terms (language) of the other in referencing particular things (as in material objects, sensations, other people, or aspects of their own being) and strive to do specific things or produce particular effects, we may speak of them as assuming some degree of agency.

It is this process of taking the role or adopting the standpoint of the other (Mead, 1934) that is essential to people developing notions of themselves as objects. Relatedly, only when people start to "act towards themselves an objects" can one speak of people "having a sense of self" or being "self-reflective" in even a more rudimentary sense. Quite directly, as Mead (1934) observes, there can be *no self without the other*. The self is predicated on adopting the viewpoint of the other and applying these notions to aspects of one's essences as an object (i.e., an object to the other). Approached thusly, acting with intention or assuming agency occurs when people take others and/or themselves into account in doing things. In more comprehensive terms, this also implies the further capacities on the part of people (a) to take the viewpoint of the other in the absence of the other; (b) to knowingly act in conjunction with others; and (c) to monitor and make meaningful adjustments to their own activities even as they are in the process of doing things (either in their role or in combination with others).

(6) Group life is *negotiable*. In the process of achieving senses of self and the abilities to take themselves and others into account in developing particular lines of activity, people also acquire capacities for engaging in influence work or persuasive endeavour. Not only may people attempt to shape the behaviours of others in a wide variety of manners but they also may attend to attempts of others to shape their behaviours and resist as well as acknowledge and co-operate with those other people.

(7) Group life has a *relational* quality. Not only does most early socialization as well as most people's more intimate associations take place in small group settings, but people also only know themselves relative to or in relationships with others. Indeed, people's behaviours and senses of self and other (identities) are meaningful only with respect to those with whom they associate in more direct terms and/or those with whom they can identify in categorical (i.e., as "one of") terms. It is in this sense that we may speak of people's "self-other identities" as the foundations of

social structure for it is by defining oneself in relation to the other that one achieves a sense of the prevailing social order. Still, because people's associations exist and take place in process terms, all relationships (along with people's identities and activities within) are best seen as matters "in the making."

In addition to the more immediate bonds, affiliations, and networks that people develop in association with others on a more specific basis, humans also develop and sustain a much broader range of understandings, organizational arrangements, governing practices, policies, and the like. As with smaller (e.g., dyads and triads) groupings, more encompassing social arrangements, procedures, or "structures" do not exist as "givens" or objective states, but also are problematic in their initial formulation and continuity. Consequently, the emergence, direction, and continuity of all existing modes of organization are contingent on people acting in ways that affirm these earlier forms and patterns of association.

(8) Human group life is *processual*. As suggested in the earlier premises, the interactionists attend to the emergent, ongoing nature of human lived experience. Not only are the things that people do more extensively on their own best envisioned in emergent terms, but so also are all of people's associations and interchanges, as well as all of the features of community life in which people participate, to be acknowledged as developmental flows.

On a methodological level, the interactionists stress the necessity of studying *the instances* in which people do things in the "here and now" of ongoing group life. This they do by means of sustained interactive contact with the particular people involved in the situations under study. As well, while attentive to the ways that people interact with others in *all levels of association*, from dyadic and triadic encounters to more extended instances of community, regional, and international relations, the interactionists also are concerned about studying *all of the forms of association* (e.g., cooperation, conflict, competition, loyalty, friendship, deception, playfulness) in which people engage.

Relatedly, the emphasis is not on what people should or should not do but more centrally on *what* people actually do and the ways in which they go about these activities. In contrast to those adopting structuralist approaches, the interactionist concern is not why or what makes or causes people to do things. Instead, the interactionists ask *how* people enter into the process or developmental flows of human group life as minded, intentioned, adjustive agents. The objective is to learn about the ways that people, as reflective beings, live and interact with others in the broader community.

To locate the development of this theoretical viewpoint in a historical context, it might be observed that symbolic interactionism began to take shape at the University of Chicago in the early 1900s. Building directly on the pragmatist philosophy of John Dewey and George Herbert Mead, interactionism reflects the pragmatist emphasis on attending to the ways that people make sense of and act towards the world as thinking, purposive, goal-oriented beings. Thus, whereas people are seen as acting with various biological capacities and limitations, as well as attending to the cultural traditions and organizational motifs of the particular communities in which they are embedded and their more immediate sets of associates, people are seen to knowingly and meaningfully engage the world as agents. Still, symbolic interaction differs from pragmatist philosophy primarily because of the more focused ethnographic approach that the interactionists take to the study of human group life.

A large number of people contributed to the development of ethnographic research and symbolic interaction at the University of Chicago. Still, Herbert Blumer emerges as a particularly consequential contributor to this venture. While working centrally with the social behaviourism of George Herbert Mead, Herbert Blumer (1928) also insisted on the necessity of incorporating Charles Horton Cooley's method of "sympathetic introspection" (i.e., ethnographic inquiry) into an authentic social science.

We will be addressing some other methodological practices and conceptual emphases of symbolic interaction in subsequent sections of this chapter, but because people's concerns with moral order or "good" and "evil" pervade community life so extensively, a brief consideration of deviance or wrongdoing *as activity* may be instructive for understanding the central emphases and relevance of symbolic interaction for the study of community life.

DEVIANCE AND MORALITY AS COMMUNITY ESSENCES

Although a discussion of deviance and morality may seem diversionary in some respects, an adequate theory of human group life requires recognition of these fundamental features of the human community.

For our purposes, *morality* refers to the values, ideals, standards, or other preferences that groups (large or small) invoke in providing direction for their members, as well as evaluating and regulating the circumstances and activities of people more generally. Reflecting the differing notions of what particular groups define as good and bad, as well as the things members do to promote and regulate particular kinds of behaviour, morality assumes a relative quality.

Relatedly, *deviance* refers to any activity, appearance, or thought that *some audience defines* in negative terms—as in bad, wrong, immoral, evil, troublesome, disruptive, sinful, and the like. Viewed thusly, deviance is not an objective state of affairs, but takes place in more relative and situated terms as people invoke particular notions of morality in the settings at hand.

Viewed thusly, nothing is inherently deviant, right or wrong, or good or bad in itself. Instead, deviance reflects the *perspectives* of the particular people who *invoke definitions* of deviance or *impute negativities* of sorts to some target or targets. Whereas much deviance (as sin, evil) may be defined in religious terms, wherein images of the holy or divine are invoked as reference points for defining troublesome matters, morality is a more encompassing term than is religion.

Denoting people's notions of what is appropriate (as in customary, fair, or desirable), each group not only may be seen to have its own sense of *moral order* but each group of people also is likely to face the tasks of maintaining their senses of propriety and dealing with those who are seen to threaten or offend those moralities in some manner. Things deemed deviant or immoral, thus, may be seen to jeopardize the ideals, purpose, honour, well-being, or even survival of the group at hand. It is within these terms that deviance is defined and assumes such consequential dimensions for human group life.

Instead of defending, condemning, encouraging, remedying, or otherwise interfering with the natural sequence of events of community life, the interactionists approach morality and deviance as *natural aspects* of human group life. Hence, the life-worlds, activities, and associations of those involved in deviance are studied in much the same way that one would examine people's involvements in religion, politics, friendship, education, and entertainment. Likewise, the interactionists make a concerted effort to see how *all* of the people involved in instances of deviance make sense of their own situations and those of the others in the setting.

This is not to deny the mystique, intrigues, fascinations, or the fears, resentments, anger, or injuries and losses that people may associate with particular instances or types of wrongdoing. However, it is essential that researchers not become caught up in particular moralities lest these evaluations and emotionalities interfere with their ability to study people's activities in a more careful, sustained, and scholarly manner.

Envisioning deviance as a quality assigned to some activity or someone by some audience, interactionists attending to deviance would follow the processes along to see how particular activities might be defined in positive or negative terms; how specific people might be defined as deviants, criminals, sinners, and such; how people attempt to regulate instances of deviance; and how the targets of control efforts of various sorts as well as others in the settings at hand deal with these matters (Prus & Grills, 2003 provide a more extended consideration of the deviance-making process).

Recognizing that one does not require one theory for "the deviants" and another for "the normals," or one for "the good people" and another for "the evil people," we turn to a more generic emphasis on studying human group life as it takes place in all of the instances in which people do things.

THE ETHNOGRAPHIC QUEST

While sharing the pragmatist emphasis on human knowing and acting as "something in the making," the interactionists are intensely concerned about examining human group life in the particular instances in which people do things with others. We cannot deal with ethnographic research in detail in this statement, but the ethnographic quest of "achieving intersubjectivity or a conceptual oneness with the other" involves such things as making contact with the other, interacting with the other, managing oneself in the ethnographic context, and recording information about the life-worlds of the other.

As social scientists, the interactionists consider it essential to directly venture into the life-worlds of those they study. In addition to (a) observing the things that people do, the interactionists also (b) assume participant-observer roles in the setting, and (c) conduct extended, open-ended interviews with people whose life-worlds they are studying. The objective is to achieve *intersubjectivity* with those one studies; to access the viewpoints and experiences of the other and become *intimately familiar* with these people's situations, deliberations, activities, interchanges, and the like.

Observation

Beyond materials of more direct visual and auditory sorts, researchers employing observational procedures also may make use of any documents, diaries, records, products, technologies, and the like that they may access in the settings at hand. Still, despite the overall value of these (observational) materials, it is essential that researchers attend to the ways that these things are defined, experienced, and acted towards by the particular people in the settings at hand. Not only may other people view things in different ways but the very same people also may envision and act towards particular items (including other people and themselves) in different ways over time.

Because researchers do not know what will be important, or in what ways things may develop over time, it is essential that researchers make careful, detailed observations and notes about the things that people actually do. Relatedly, it is especially important that researchers guard against preoccupations with what they personally might consider to be the more unique aspects of the setting (as in physical settings, personal appearances, and personal styles that might be associated with the individuals whose life-worlds are being studied). Because the focus is on the other, all aspects of the situation are important primarily in terms of the ways in which (and only to the extent to which) they are deemed consequential to the participants in those settings. And, it is precisely in this respect that observational data is so limited.

Observations may alert researchers to particular things that might be investigated more thoroughly in other ways. Observational data also may be used to assess and test out things that researchers may have learned about in other ways. Still, observational materials are particularly limited when one intends to learn more about the viewpoints, deliberations, and strategic adjustments of the other. Observational data clearly are not viable substitutes for more sustained inquiries into people's capacities to act and interact as agents.

Participant-Observation

Whereas observers normally remain somewhat removed from the activities at hand, the *participant-observer* role allows researchers to more directly experience aspects of the situation at hand and the people involved therein. However, it should be emphasized that researcher experiences as a participant-observer need not correspond with the experiences of other participants in the setting. Indeed, researchers must especially guard against the tendency to draw inferences about things from their own perspectives as opposed to the standpoints of the participants in the setting at hand.

Also, in pursuing the dual roles of researcher and participant, it is important that participant-observers maintain a distinct research focus. In addition to occasions in which the participatory role is so demanding or otherwise engrossing that the research role may well subside into the background, participant perspectives often are notably partisan (vs. pluralist) in nature and may interfere with the analysis. Nevertheless, by spending more time in the setting and listening and interacting with others in a variety of inquisitive manners, researchers may be able to uncover materials that otherwise might escape their attention.

Still, researchers might appreciate that the other people in the setting not only can observe them but that these other people also may make inferences of any sort they might wish. As well, these other people need not share the participant-observer's enthusiasm for research and, at times, may deliberately obstruct these endeavours. Nevertheless, in contrast to straight observation, the participant-observer role offers researchers more sustained contact with the people in the setting and generally provides valuable opportunities for researchers to learn about and inquire into the viewpoints, practices, and adjustments of others in the setting.

Interviews

Because interviews can be such an effective means of learning about the life-worlds of the ethnographic other, extended, open-ended interviews generally are the most instructive means of gathering ethnographic data.

Still, rather than denoting a magical technology, interviews are to be recognized as problematic, collectively achieved ventures. Not all interviewers are equally adept at approaching people, establishing trust and openness, making inquiries, probing for depth, and the like. Likewise, despite their best efforts, not all interviews conducted by the same person are of equal worth. As instances of human interchange in the making, the eventual quality of the interview materials are contingent on the interactive contributions of both the interviewers and the participants. Thus, researchers may approach and pursue these matters with widely varying levels of knowledge, degrees of interest, attentiveness and care, quests for detail, openness to respondents, and persistence in learning more about people's lived experiences. Likewise, participants may be differentially attentive, knowledgeable, thoughtful, sincere, relaxed, open, distracted, and the like.

As well, because the interview is an emergent process, both researchers and participants may find that their sense of focus, openness, and comprehensiveness varies over the course of the interview as well as from one topic or subtheme to the next. Still, from an interactionist standpoint, the researcher's objective is to be as thorough and comprehensive in coverage as possible and to let the other explain things as fully, openly, and candidly as possible.

Relatedly, without aggressively emphasizing contradictions to the other, it is most instructive for researchers to seek respondents' assistance in explaining any ambiguities or inconsistencies that researchers encounter. In addition to asking participants for more detail on more unusual or improbable incidents, it also is essential to inquire fully into more routine, possibly taken-for-granted, practices. Thus, patience, perseverance, and diplomacy are highly consequential in this setting, as also are the matters of maintaining a focus on the instances in which things take place and encouraging the other to explain situations in extended detail.

In more general terms, the ethnographic objective is to gather as much detailed and reliable observational, participant-observation, and interview data as possible. Hence, those who more fully immerse themselves in the research setting in all three respects are apt to be greatly advantaged in learning about the life-worlds of the other (see Dietz, Prus, & Shaffir, 1994; Grills, 1998).

Because of its openness, ethnographic research and analysis can be extremely demanding, if not notably perplexing at times. It entails a great deal of ambiguity, and if it is to be done well, it requires an exceptional degree of thought and effort, as well as considerable courage and perseverance.

Still, the interactionist research agenda asks more of its researchers. While it is essential to develop one's ethnographies as fully and carefully as possible, the further objective is to develop more comprehensive understandings of community life from these more specific studies. Thus, a related emphasis revolves around the matter of developing generic concepts or terms that have a transhistorical or transcontextual relevancy.

ATTENDING TO THE GENERIC FEATURES OF HUMAN GROUP LIFE

> To speak of a science without concepts suggests all sorts of analogies—a carver without tools, a railroad without tracks, a mammal without bones, a love story without love. A science without concepts would be a fantastic creation. (Blumer, 1931, p. 515)

However interesting it may be to examine particular things in the field, speak with specific people about their experiences, or deal with certain kinds of topics, the intellectual payoff of ethnographic research is intensified when people develop concepts or terms of a more general or transcendent nature. This enables people to learn about things in a more encompassing sense, to know about wider ranges of things than just the more immediate cases.

Indeed, without concepts of some sort, human knowing would so limited that one might ask whether the term "knowing" would still be appropriate. Likewise, in the absence of concepts of a more transsituational or transcontextual sort that enable scholars to compare, contrast, and define the things that people do in a variety of settings, even ethnographic research is of limited value for comprehending the human condition. Further, as Blumer (1928, p. 349) observes, rather than destroying the unique features of human group life, concepts enable people to define and better comprehend their uniqueness.

In what follows, the term "generic social processes" (GSPs) refers to:

> the transsituational elements of interaction—to the abstracted, transcontextual formulations of social behavior. Denoting parallel sequences of activity across diverse contexts, generic social processes highlight the emergent, interpretive features of association. They focus our attention on the activities involved in the "doing" or accomplishing of human group life. (Prus, 1996, p. 142)

Whereas the term *generic* refers to the abstracted or general features of the phenomena under consideration and *process* draws attention to the ongoing, emergent, or natural sequencing of things, the notion of *social* (as used herein) encompasses the entire set of matters referenced in the interactionist premises introduced earlier. Further, although it will not be apparent in the highly compacted discussion that follows, the GSPs referenced here have been developed by examining a much broader range of ethnographic materials pertinent to these processes. For more extended discussions, references, and related resources pertaining to these and other GSPs, see Prus (1996, 1997, 1999) and Prus and Grills (2003).

Although the prominence (e.g., development, emphasis) of particular GSPs may be expected to vary from one group setting to the next, the following six generic social processes (Prus, 1996, pp. 149–186) appear highly instructive for comprehending people's experiences in all manners of community life-worlds. These are: (1) *acquiring perspectives*; (2) *achieving identity*; (3) *doing activity* (performing activities, influencing others, making commitments); (4) *developing relationships*; (5) *experiencing emotionality*; and (6) *achieving linguistic fluency*.

Each of the preceding six GSPs entails an extended set of sub-processes. Still, by focusing more specifically on one GSP, that of *developing relationships*, readers may achieve a better understanding of the conceptual emphasis implied in the broader set of GSPs identified here.

Abstracted from the ethnographic literature, the following sub-processes seem central to the ways that people generally engage relationships with others, regardless of context. In the material presented here (drawn extensively from Prus & Grills, 2003, p. 133), three features of the relationship process are delineated: (1) anticipating encounters with others; (2) attending to particular relationships; and (3) dealing with distractions and disaffections. Readers are encouraged to consider these matters mindfully regarding their own relationships, asking whether, to what extent, and in what ways the sub-processes identified here might correspond with their own experiences in dealing with other people in both more general and specific terms.

Anticipating encounters with others refers to people's preliminary preparations for, contacts with, and assessments of others. This would include such things as (1) *getting prepared for encounters with people more generally*; (2) *envisioning oneself as available for association with others*; (3) *defining particular others as potentially desirable associates*; (4) *approaching potential associates and/or receiving indications of receptivity from others*; (5) *encountering and indicating acceptance and resistance with respect to other associates*; and (6) *assessing self and others as viable associates for desired relationships*.

Attending to particular relationships focuses on people's more distinctive interactive encounters with specific others. Assuming that people already have had some contact with specific others, matters of the following sort become more consequential in dealing with particular others: (1) *developing styles of interaction with respect to and in conjunction with the other*; (2) *managing openness and secrecy in associations with the other*; (3) *developing shared understandings, joint preferences, and loyalties relative to the association at hand*; and (4) *intensifying closeness (as through expressing affection, developing dependencies on others, fostering reliance of self by others, embarking on cooperative ventures, and collectively dealing with threats and opposition)*.

Since all relationships are problematic in their formation as well as their continuities, the matter of *dealing with distractions and disaffections* represents another set of sub-processes central to understanding and studying the relationship process. Hence, it appears instructive to consider the ways that people deal with more disruptive and disenchanting features of their associations. This includes: (1) *the kinds of things that participants define as problematic or that emerge as points of contention among the participants;* (2) *the ways that people attempt to deal with these troublesome situations;* (3) *when and how these episodes continue, intensify, dissipate, and possibly become renewed and extended among members of the group;* (4) *when and how other people (other insiders or outsiders) become involved in these interchanges, and what sorts of directions the ensuing interchanges may take;* (5) *how these interchanges are worked out with respect to any longer term relationships between the members of the particular group under consideration;* and (6) *when and how particular relationships become severed and, possibly, reconstituted.*

While denoting analytic focal points, and summary statements of sorts, it should be stressed that these GSPs (and the sub-processes within) are envisioned as tentative, working formulations rather than definitive claims or statements of fact. Thus, whereas the GSPs listed here have been developed mindfully of a much larger interactionist/ethnographic research literature, they represent approximations of more complex features of human group life and are to be tested out and assessed for validity on every occasion possible. Indeed, the objective is to develop more accurate, more precise, more carefully qualified versions of any existing GSPs, using all instances (and studies of) human activity as reference points.

As a set, these GSPs represent a conceptual grid with which researchers might approach the study of people involved in any group or arena of human endeavour (e.g., religion, deviance, family relations, science). As well, by acknowledging a number of (analytical) themes that the participants may invoke in any arena, these GSPs enable social scientists to make considerably more precise and thorough comparisons across otherwise seemingly disconnected studies of human group life.

Although GSPs may suggest valuable lines of inquiry for subsequent research and serve as instructive comparison points for analysis, the data (i.e., actual instances) encountered in the field is to maintain priority over the concepts. Rather than searching for examples that might fit these notions, the task is to examine these concepts mindful of the data generated in specific ethnographies with the explicit purpose of assessing, qualifying, and extending our understandings of these foundational aspects of human group life.

PURSUING QUALITY IN THE QUEST FOR AUTHENTICITY

As students of the human condition, readers will be faced with a number of tasks. These include the matters of making sense of the things that one encounters in the literature, assessing the relative worth and authenticity of the materials and claims encountered from others, and striving for quality in one's own work. Since these are fundamental and long-standing concerns, points of the following sort are often mentioned when people try to assess the quality of particular pieces of research and theory or try to generate more quality in the works that they, themselves, are doing. Still, it may be helpful to address these in more direct and explicit terms. Although these are presented primarily "as things to consider in developing one's work as a qualitative researcher," these notions can be used to assess the contributions and viability of the materials developed by others as well as highlight some themes introduced earlier.

1. *Focus on Activity*—Because human group life revolves around activity, it is especially instructive to attend to the things that people do and the ways in which they do things. As researchers, it is important to provide detailed accounts of people's anticipations, deliberations, acts, interchanges, obstructions, and adjustments.

2. *Concentrate on the Other*—Since the objective of qualitative research is to learn about people's lived experience, it is essential to maintain focus on the ethnographic other. This means emphasizing the standpoints and activities of those people whose life-worlds one is studying (vs. using studies to express self or promote particular moralities external to the other).

3. *Be Mindful of One's Assumptions or Premises*—Because all studies build on particular assumptions about human group life, it is extremely important not only to attend to your own "conceptual home base," but also to be able to clarify your theoretical position and methodological emphases both for the reader and yourself. When encountering materials that others have developed, it is instructive to ask about the premises and procedures on which these other statements have been generated. When these are unclear, messy, mixed, or obscure, this should serve as a warning to proceed with considerable caution (and skepticism).

4. *Strive for Openness and Authenticity*—This is important in learning about, developing an analysis of, and representing the ethnographic other. Carefully attend to the viewpoints, meanings, experiences, and practices of the other and try to convey these to the reader as fully, carefully, and accurately as possible. Further, when encountering materials in the field, as well as reading other people's accounts, it is instructive to ask about the fuller range of possibilities that one might expect in situations of that sort as well as to consider the probabilities or likelihood that things are as they are claimed to be. More generally, it is important to pursue as much detail as you can and try to see how all of the features of particular situations fit together or achieve a developmental flow.

5. *Develop a Comparative Analysis*—As a researcher, this means attending to the similarities and differences between one's current study and other studies in the field. Whereas the interactionist quest for generic social processes routinely entails a comparative analysis, it is in building theory from the instances and engaging in comparative analyses that people develop knowledge of a more general and broadly

relevant sort. This is why it is so helpful to become acquainted with the literature, particularly those studies that deal with processes (e.g., GSPs) of parallel sorts. Thus, whereas many people limit themselves to the substantive literature in which a particular topic is embedded, it generally is much more productive to locate one's projects in more generic conceptual terms.

6. *Write (and Rewrite) to Communicate with the Reader*—When developing your statements, define your terms of reference and try to write directly, clearly, and precisely. Expect your sources to do the same. Be cautious of authors who do not define their central terms of reference. Also, when doing research in the field, pursue clarification of a related sort. The more you learn about the ethnographic other, the more completely and accurately you can develop and convey these notions to your readers. In developing your text, the goal is to enable the reader to achieve a greater sense of "oneness" (i.e., more completely share meanings) with the author.

7. *Write Things to Last Forever*—Try to develop your material in ways that would be relevant to the long-term study of human knowing and acting. Rather than writing for the ever-fleeting present, or in manners intended to entertain or excite your readers, develop your materials as resources that other scholars could use for all times. When reading texts, look for a careful sustained, pluralist analysis (vs. more superficial, moralistic, dramatized, or playful accounts).

8. *Try to Stay Focused*—In "staying focused," I am not just talking about completing particular projects, but rather about being attentive to the primary objectives of the study throughout the duration of the project.

Because ethnographic studies generally take considerable time to develop and there are so many things that take place in research sites as well as researchers' own lives—both of intellectually interesting and other diversionary natures—it is not uncommon for people to lose focus on the more specific and central social science emphasis of the project at hand.

Indeed, because of the comparatively less structured, more ambiguous, developmental flow of qualitative work, the matter of maintaining a consistent conceptual focus and methodological approach for a period of months or years may be one of the greatest and yet most elusive, or taken-for-granted, challenges that researchers encounter.

9. *Pursue All Opportunities to Learn about People*—By this I mean listening to, learning from, and striving to understand people wherever and whenever one encounters others. Whether one is watching people, listening to others talk, or is involved in reading texts, it is important to be attentive to what these people have to say and to be inquisitive, questing for more detail and fuller explanations. Still, it is no less important to consider carefully the things (events, incidents, instances) one encounters in everyday life, to see how things develop and do (or don't) fit together, to assess things for their typicality, to compare these things with the other things one

has encountered and experienced, and to be mindful of the matters of possibility and authenticity in the quest to connect theory with actual instances of human knowing and acting. Indeed, it is important to more or less continuously ask if one's theory matches with the things encountered and to inquire into any discrepancies. The objective is not to make the data fit the theory but to develop theory that more closely approximates human knowing and acting.

These suggestions will not guarantee success, nor will they eliminate most of the obstacles, frustrations, or dilemmas associated with the study of human lived experience. Still, if one attends to matters of this sort, one's projects likely will be stronger as a result. Clearly, as well, these emphases will not destroy creativity or thinking. Instead, these notions draw attention to the importance of making one's work more valuable to the scholarly community at large—and that is the sort of quality for which we should be questing.

REFERENCES

Barnes, J. (Ed.). (1984). *The complete works of Aristotle*. Princeton, NJ: Princeton University Press.

Blumer, H. (1928). *Method in social psychology*. Unpublished doctoral dissertation, University of Chicago, Chicago, Illinois.

Blumer H. (1931). Science without concepts. *American Journal of Sociology, 36*, 515–533.

Blumer, H. (1969). *Symbolic interaction*. Englewood Cliffs, NJ: Prentice-Hall.

Cooper, J.M. (1997). *Plato: The collected works*. Indianapolis, IN: Hackett.

Dalley, S. (1989). *Myths from Mesopotamia: Creation, flood, Gilgamesh, and others*. New York: Oxford University Press.

Dietz, M.L., Prus, R., & Shaffir, W. (1994). *Doing everyday life: Ethnography as human lived experience*. Toronto: Copp Clark Longman.

Grills, S. (1998). *Doing ethnographic research*. Thousand Oaks, CA: Sage.

Mead, G.H. (1934). *Mind, self and society*. Chicago: University of Chicago Press.

Prus, R. (1996). *Symbolic interaction and ethnographic research: Intersubjectivity and the study of human lived experience*. Albany, NY: State University of New York Press.

Prus, R. (1997). *Subcultural mosaics and intersubjective realities: An ethnographic research agenda for pragmatizing the social sciences*. Albany, NY: State University of New York Press.

Prus, R. (1999). *Beyond the power mystique: Power as intersubjective accomplishment*. Albany, NY: State University of New York Press.

Prus, R., & Grills, S. (2003). *The deviant mystique: Involvements, realities, and regulation*. Westport, CN: Praeger.

Strauss, A. (1993).*Continual permutations of action*. Hawthorne, NY: Aldine de Gruyter.

Thucydides. (1972). *History of the Peloponnesian war* (R. Warner, Trans.). New York: Penguin Putnam.

PART 1

DOING ETHNOGRAPHY: CHALLENGES AND STRATEGIES

Sociologists undertaking fieldwork using a symbolic interactionist perspective share many of the following understandings. The social world to be studied is conceptualized as emergent and processual, and importance is placed on the meanings individuals attach "to situations, others, things, and themselves through a process of interpretation" (Taylor & Bogdan, 1984, p. 9). Depending on these processes of interpretation, individuals will act in certain ways as they move through different situations.

> From a symbolic interactionist perspective, all organizations, cultures, and groups consist of actors who are involved in a constant process of interpreting the world around them. Although people may act within the framework of an organization, culture, or group, it is their interpretations and definitions of the situation that determine action. (Taylor & Bogdan, 1984, p. 10)

In studying a social world, the challenge facing the researcher is to learn to appreciate the distinctive concerns and ways of behaving in the world that is being observed and "to comprehend and to illuminate the subject's view and to interpret the world *as it appears to him*" (Matza, 1969, p. 25). Wax (1967) identifies the process of acquiring an appreciation of the meanings attributed to objects and events in a given society as follows:

> The student begins "outside" the interaction, confronting behaviours he finds bewildering and inexplicable: the actors are oriented to a world of meanings that the observer does not grasp ... and then gradually he comes to be able to categorize peoples (or relationships) and events. (p. 325)

According to Lofland's vision, the researcher aims to attain an "intimate familiarity" with a sector of social life (1976, p. 8).

Achieving an intimate familiarity with a social world necessarily involves "learning the ropes"—a phrase commonly used to identify how researchers learn to negotiate their way in a social setting. This begins as soon as the researcher sets out to examine the people and their activities in the research setting, about his or her relationship to the setting and its people, and continues until he or she exits the field. And much like accessing a setting, learning its normative requirements is affected by the characteristics of the setting itself, the self-presentation of the investigator, and the group members' feelings and responses to the researcher and the project.

Given that there are no magic formulas for learning the ropes, the researcher typically begins by participating in the subjects' daily lives—talking to them, observing what they do, and listening sympathetically to what they say. As the accounts of seasoned field researchers attest, during this process, loosely described as "hanging around," different research roles are assumed that may shift as the research progresses. The particular roles that are claimed and/or to which the researcher is assigned are critical for learning the ropes. A basic problem revolves around the delicate balance required between involvement, or the attempts to acquire an insider's perspective, and the possibility of "going native" (Miller, 1952), or the danger that excessive involvement may thwart the ability to conduct dispassionate research. The literature concerning this topic indicates that field research is characterized by a combination of engrossment and distance, both of which are necessary to gain an appreciation of the actor's perspective. The dynamics of this balance, however, are not determined by the researcher alone but are shaped by the demands and expectations of the researched.

The student wishing to become acquainted with the practices and challenges of field research can consult a variety of texts and readers on the subject. In the introduction to this section—"Doing Ethnography"—we attend to a number of issues that, while not exclusive to field research, are typically associated with this methodological approach. More precisely, we touch on matters of the credibility of the research, or its validity, the challenge of accessing the research setting or a population within it, concerns about research ethics, establishing and maintaining rapport with informants, and writing up the research findings.

The problem of validity in field research concerns the difficulty of gaining an accurate or true impression of the phenomenon under study. The companion problem of reliability centres on the replicability of observations; it rests on the question of whether another researcher with similar methodological training, understanding of the field setting, and rapport with the subjects can make similar observations. McCall and Simmons (1969) have observed that in field research these two problems include: (1) reactive effects of the observer's presence on the phenomena being observed; (2) distorting effects of selective perception and interpretation on the observer's part; and (3) limitations on the observer's ability to witness all relevant aspects of the phenomena in question (p. 78).

Reactive effects are the special behavioural responses subjects make because the observer is in the setting, responses that are atypical for the occasion. Webb, Campbell, Schwartz, Lee, and Grove (1981, pp. 49–58) include in their consideration two particular reactive effects that frequently invalidate social science data—the guinea pig effect and role selection. In the first, subjects are aware of being observed and react by putting their best foot forward; they strive to make a good impression. In the second, which is closely related, they choose to emphasize one of several selves that they sense is most appropriate given the observer's presence.

Researcher biases are certainly not unique to practitioners of field methods even though this problem, at first blush, appears to characterize field research most prominently while, by contrast, hardly affecting methods relying upon surveys, laboratory experiments, and formal interviews. H.S. Becker presents a convincing case for the very opposite: That despite the absence of strict procedural rules guiding the field researcher's data-gathering activities, the conclusions resulting from data gathered by field research are highly credible. The thrust of his argument is contained in the following:

> Because it [fieldwork] gives us information on people acting under the very social constraints whose operation we are interested in, and because its numerous items of information and flexible procedures allow us to test our conclusions repeatedly and in a variety of ways, we need not fear that its unsystematic character will distort our findings in ways that we, our readers, or the people we study will find convenient, congenial, or expectable. (1970, p. 62)

Observers also selectively perceive and interpret data in different ways and sometimes seriously bias their investigations. The most celebrated of these is "going native," or so thoroughly embracing the customs and beliefs of the focal group that one becomes incapable of objective work. Special orientations towards subjects, whether of love, hate, friendship, admiration, respect, or dislike, can influence our views of these people and their behaviour.

A related fieldwork predicament that can cut off researchers from events of great importance to them concerns the status of the researcher. A particular thorny status problem is the exclusiveness of sex: being male, for instance, may bar one from direct observation of female activities. Rosalie Wax (1971), for example, describes the exclusiveness of certain age and sex categories she encountered as a woman scientist who has worked in several different groups, and Shaffir (1974) has attended to this problem in his writings on Hassidic—ultra-Orthodox—Jews.

The ethical issues that plague social scientists, in general, are vitally germane to the social experience of fieldwork. Issues surrounding the ethics of concealment have received particular attention, notably the matter of being a covert observer, or social scientific investigator whose professional aims are unknown to the subjects. They take the individual for someone else, usually one of them. Even where the observer's true role is known, ethical considerations may arise when there is concealment of certain aspects of the project. Occasionally, the project's very aims are kept secret, or concealment may be more subtle but no less questionable in the eyes of some scientists, when data are gathered by means of a hidden tape recorder, inadvertently overheard remarks, or intentional eavesdropping. These clandestine methods add tension to the conduct of fieldwork because there is always the risk that what is hidden will somehow be uncovered. Finally, individual researchers may question the propriety of concealing opinions that are diametrically opposed to those held by their subjects.

Although all field researchers are faced with ethical decisions in the course of their work, there is no consensus concerning the researcher's duties and responsibilities either to those studied or to the discipline itself. As Roth (1960) has so aptly argued, the controversy between "secret research" and "non-secret research" is largely misguided, for all research is secret in some way. A more profitable line of investigation is to focus on "how much secrecy shall there be with which people in which circumstances" (p. 283). Most field researchers hold that some measure of responsibility is owed the people under study, though the extent of this conviction and its application are left to each researcher's conscience.

Although the contributions in Part 2, "Doing Ethnography," are grouped around four subheadings, these are meant to highlight the particular themes around which the material is organized rather than identifying them as the most salient issues confronting practitioners of qualitative research or matters exclusive to this methodology. Just the same, however, matters relating to the merits of qualitative research, the choice of tactics employed during the course of interviews, how best to relate to respondents, the impact of this relationship and its consequences both for self and others, and how best to organize and present one's findings when writing about social life are issues that, in one form or another, merit careful consideration and resolution.

In one of the earliest, and most insightful, statements about ethnographic research, Rosalie Wax (1971) cautions about the uniqueness of research settings, emphasizing that because situations differ both across and within all settings, "the honest and experienced fieldworkers frequently tell beginners ... that there is not much they can tell them" (p. 20). Along this line, the reader will quickly discover that the concerns addressed by the contributors, while generic to qualitative research, are best understood within the context of their particular research project.

Each of the contributions in this section attend to a dimension of the qualitative research experience that, in some way, impacted upon the research and required attention. In the remainder of this introduction, we focus on the general and particular concerns that, when examined in their totality, enable us to understand the range of dynamics comprising the field research experience. Though easily overlooked, it is important to underscore that since field research differs from other research methods in that the researcher serves both as an observer and participant in the lives of the people studied—he or she "becomes an *instrumentality* or *medium* of the research" (Lofland & Lofland, 1995, p. 3)— it is understandably challenging to identify a set of fixed rules or conventions by which the research is conducted. It is not surprising, therefore, that the authors are somewhat tentative about the strategies they pursued, knowing, however, that they proved useful in their particular situation to resolve a problem or dilemma.

CONSIDERING THE MERITS OF QUALITATIVE RESEARCH

While the methodological orientation of this volume is qualitative research techniques, the positivist model remains the dominant research paradigm in sociology. In it, quantitative sociologists, relying on methods that generate a "positive science"—data collection that is "clear, rigorous, and reliable ... and permit the testing of empirical hypotheses in a logically consistent manner" (Schwartz & Jacobs, 1979, p. 5)—eschew those seemingly unreliable methods of qualitative researchers that try to discover things about a social world that those within it may not know, and which is based on the understandings of insiders. As Charlene E. Miall and Karen March's contribution illustrates, the positivist and interpretive research paradigms focus on their subject matter through different research lenses.

Reporting on a Canada-wide survey conducted on adoption issues, they demonstrate how attention to issues through qualitative research modified their understanding of their survey results. This finding is hardly inconsequential if we wish to understand social phenomena beyond trends and general patterns. More specifically, in the matter of adoption and adoptive kinship, the authors' work underlies the importance of qualitative research for appreciating the meanings relating to fixed alternative responses to questions about motherhood. Thus, while male and female respondents' survey responses to issues of motherhood and its importance for women were not significantly different, attention to their qualitative data enabled Miall and March to conclude that the meanings underlying the "biology is destiny" claim are, in fact, gender differentiated: women, more than men, focused more on actual mothering behaviour and how it impacts on their sense of self-worth. Sensibly, the authors recommend that quantitative and qualitative research strategies, where appropriate, may profitably be used in tandem.

While the underlying advantages of qualitative methods for investigating slices of social life are shared by researchers, the practices employed in the field reflect not only situational contingencies but an understanding of how research subjects are best involved in the research enterprise. The contribution by Karen Szala-Menoek and Lynne Lohfeld introduces the reader to a research strategy that, at first blush, appears to contradict how academic/scientific research ought to be conducted. The strategy they outline, PAR (Participatory Action Research), involves a tight collaborative relationship between the researcher and those studied, thereby blurring, if not effectively eliminating, the distinctions between them. One discovers that a PAR project is not merely a different way of doing research but, as fundamentally, a distinctive approach to thinking about how research may be accomplished. In a PAR project, not only do selected members of the community become actively involved in matters of decision making, and data collection and analysis, but, ideally, also in determining if, and when, the research should be undertaken in the first place. The ground rules governing PAR clearly fluctuate, reflecting, among other considerations, the participants themselves and how a problem is identified. As such it is best to conceptualize PAR as a model along a continuum whose practitioners, noting its essential departures from the scientific research model, contend that its supreme value lies as an effective agency of social change. By contrast, skeptics contend that the goal of scientific research, notably generating theoretical models of social interaction, must remain within the preserve of trained professionals, though conceding that latitude may be exercised for drawing upon informants' knowledge and areas of expertise.

INTERVIEWING STRATEGIES

As research settings enjoy unique features, researchers may modify their data-gathering approach to ensure the collection of kinds of data that might otherwise remain undisclosed. A challenge common to field researchers for collecting relevant data centres around establishing and maintaining rapport with informants. At issue for the researcher is balancing the urge to probe for information typically concealed in everyday interaction, especially to an outsider, with a self-presentation of graciously accepting any and all responses at face value. As the researcher becomes more familiar with the social world under investigation, and realizes that informants are withholding information, or steering the conversation away from particular lines of inquiry, the issue over whether and how to maintain the delicate balance typically requires re-evaluation. Along this line, the strategy of relying upon the co-operation of the research subjects, expecting them to act naturally while studied and to assume that once the relationship of trust is secured the truth about what some members are up to would surface, may be called into question (Douglas, 1976). In their contribution to the volume, Andrew Hathaway and Michael Atkinson suggest that researchers may be overly accommodating informants' responses, and propose a more active strategy when interviewing informants: Issuing overt challenges of the kind used by the police, journalists, and other professionals. Recognizing that one must know when to probe and where to draw the line, they draw upon their studies of drug advocates and tattoo artists respectively, demonstrating how their more active interviews yielded kinds of information that may not otherwise have been acquired.

Although the ideal research setting is conceptualized as "one in which the observer obtains easy access, establishes immediate rapport with informants, and gathers data directly related to the research interests" (Taylor & Bogdan, 1984, p. 19), such settings rarely exist. Rather, as we have suggested, the field researcher is constantly engaged in processes of interpretation about how best to carry out the research, particularly when contingencies arise in the research setting that challenge taken-for-granted assumptions about how the research will or should proceed.

Totten and Kelly's contribution deals with young offenders convicted of murder. Though youth homicide is relatively rare, there is a public fascination with youth who kill. Drawing on interviews with 19 young people, Totten and Kelly try to "put a human face" on statistics about youth homicide by allowing these young people to tell their own stories—about their experiences in early childhood and adolescence, about the circumstances surrounding the homicides they committed, and about their lives in custody (see Kelly & Totten, 2002). Their paper in this volume focuses on the issues involves in doing a study of this type. Totten and Kelly discuss problems in gaining access to these young people, dealing with the risks, establishing the kind of rapport that they needed in order to elicit accounts from them, and finally, ascertaining the truthfulness of the accounts they provided. They describe a strategy for separating truthful from untruthful accounts.

Berg (2001, p. 152) has noted that, whereas most research methods books consider the potential harm that can befall subjects of research, the problem of personal or emotional harm to *researchers* is rarely considered. The papers by Anne Wright, Gillian Ransom, and Scott Kenney focus most squarely on the processes whereby interpretive processes accompanying the research endeavour can impact, not only on data collection, but also on personal understandings of the self and others. As well, these contributions attend to unanticipated developments as the research unfolds.

In her study of homeless people with combined mental health and substance misuse problems, Anne Wright documents how the practice of conducting fieldwork with this population was different to that originally planned. Noting that access to the homeless was blocked by powerful official "gatekeepers," she documents first how it was necessary for her to invest considerable time negotiating with these gatekeepers. Her perceptions of what the organization wanted from her led her to adopt certain identities and roles, and to make bargains that facilitated her acceptance as a researcher.

Further, at each stage in her research, Wright describes how she was confronted with methodological, ethical, and practical issues that required her to "rethink" her approach to her research with the homeless. These processes of interpretation, or definitions of the situation, resulted in her changing her approach and establishing basic principles that shaped the nature of the emergent data and her patterns of interaction with her research subjects. First, Wright limited or stopped her data collection if the well-being of any participant was in doubt, despite the importance, theoretically, of obtaining complete life histories from her subjects. Second, she became aware that, from an organizational point of view, she was expected to act as a helper to her subjects, but not as a worker—in fact, it was important not to come between a worker and his or her client. Third, she remained aware that people's vulnerability in relation to potential exploitation needed to be considered at all times.

Shaffir, Stebbins, and Turowetz (1980) and Shaffir and Stebbins (1991) have compiled anthologies of research studies that document in some detail the problems qualitative researchers can experience in getting in, learning the ropes, maintaining relations, and leaving the field. The compromises made by researchers in the field, however, are frequently "glossed over" within the final research presentation, and sanitized versions of studies can obscure the very real difficulties encountered in ethnographic research. Further, according to Berg (2001, p. 143), "in their attempt to objectify their research efforts, many investigators ignore, omit, or conceal their feelings," giving rise to the perception that field researchers are devoid of human emotion and/or manipulative (Johnson, 1975).

Wright, however, documents how her research impacted on her personally in a way she hadn't anticipated. Her ethnographic study with the homeless meant that she spent most of her time with street people. Making observations often required waiting in day centres for people to arrive for an interview, and conducting the interviews themselves was often emotionally draining. She found that she had to strike the right balance between emotional engagement and distance. It seemed that the stronger her personal engagement, the more draining the fieldwork became.

This, in turn, had a negative impact upon her ability to carry out her research. In the end, Wright was compelled to set up a support network, a contingency she had not anticipated at the beginning of her research.

RELATING TO RESPONDENTS

In her paper on female engineers and engineering work, Gillian Ransom describes the tensions and challenges she encountered as her perceptions of the research in progress underwent changes. Specifically, as a feminist scholar studying gender, Ransom began her research intending to study the retention of female engineers in male-dominated workplaces. As she notes, a very clear set of assumptions initially informed her research: given the gender differences that exist between men and women, it was important to encourage women to become engineers, and to retain them in engineering workplaces. Over time, however, Ransom began to think critically about these issues, observing that, rather than differing from their male counterparts, female engineers appeared to readily embrace the masculine work culture. These women succeeded by becoming "one of the boys," up to and including disparaging other women.

Ransom also began to consider the links between the engineering companies she was studying and the energy industry in Calgary. She perceived that the uses to which engineering knowledge was being put had serious environmental and social consequences. As a result, Ransom became concerned about her uncritical willingness to give tacit support through her research to the engineering companies themselves and the women working there.

These changing processes of interpretation created personal difficulties for Ransom, who documents her concerns that she was somehow deceiving her research subjects and "distancing" herself from them. On the other hand, she felt uncomfortable giving apparent support to the gender stereotyping the female engineers themselves engaged in. To resolve these tensions, Ransom discusses how she made use of a research strategy that enabled her simultaneously to be critical, but also to "understand and humanize" her research participants.

Attention to the more personal and emotional dimensions of the field research experience are addressed by Scott Kenney, who documents the impact on the researcher of studying emotionally upsetting topics, in this case, the coping strategies of families of murdered children. He discusses how he gained access to research participants by sharing his own experience of a murder of a cousin. Despite this shared experience, Kenney notes that the interview process was fraught with personal anxiety as he and his research subjects discussed upsetting and sensitive topics. He also documents how he used verbal and non-verbal cues from respondents in deciding when to take a break from the interview itself, shutting off the tape recorder and chatting about other topics until he perceived that the interview could continue.

Kenney also observes that, despite the emotional difficulty of conducting the interviews, the transcription and analysis of the data were also personally upsetting, not only to himself, but to the student transcriber he hired, and to his

Ph.D. committee. Paradoxically, however, as the analysis continued, Kenney felt himself becoming more detached from the data, and ultimately desensitized as he worked to complete his dissertation. Kenney concludes by noting that his own coping strategies for dealing with his feelings about the data paralleled those of the participants he studied. In order to deal with his feelings, Kenney balanced his analysis with other life activities—a strategy of emotion management that enabled him to handle the emotional upset his research engendered.

WRITING ABOUT SOCIAL RESEARCH

The subtext of this book is the symbolic interactionist imperative to acquire the insider's perspective and capture the lived experience of social actors. Symbolic interactionists are committed to the view that, if we want to understand human behaviour, we have to put ourselves in the position of those engaging in these behaviours so as to grasp the meaning that they attach to what they do. Once grasped, however, the work of the symbolic interactionist has not ended. Moving beyond description to analysis, symbolic interactionists synthesize what they see, interpret it, consider it within a broader context, and relate it to sociological concepts and social processes they are exploring.

Of course, the process of capturing, interpreting, and presenting the lived experience of any social group raises the question of whose "voice" is represented and heard in our analyses—that of the social actors we study, our own, or both? Over the past two decades, qualitative researchers have spent increasingly more time reflecting on their role as observers and analysts of social life and on the implications of using their own lived reality to make sense of the feelings and actions of those they study. Some writers (Hertz 1997; Richardson, 1990) have suggested that analysts do not simply report "facts" or "the truth" about respondents' lives, but are actively constructing interpretations of those lives and experiences. Laurel Richardson (1990, p. 12) claims that researchers are not just speaking *about* the social actors they study, but are speaking *for* them. Researchers do the staging in the story that emerges. They order and construct the social reality presented in their analyses. The lived experiences of respondents are refracted through the analyst's lens, never captured in any pure sense.

The final two papers in this section reflect an interest in "voice" in qualitative research. Linda Snyder begins with the premise that in any qualitative study, there are two perspectives present—that of the researcher/self and that of the participants/ other. While it is important to capture participants' perspectives, researchers have the responsibility, she insists, to interpret and analyze data. How much relative emphasis should each perspective receive? And where participant and researcher may not see things in the same way, whose perspective should take precedence?

Using her own experiences studying Chilean women involved in an employment program, Snyder attempts to identify factors that may come into play as a researcher decides whose perspective to emphasize or whose voice to privilege. Snyder suggests that, in situations where the voices of a particular group, particularly powerless groups, have not often been heard or their experiences well understood, one might want to prioritize the perspective of participants. This is also the case when the analysis is about the lived experience of participants. They know best what that experience entails.

However, in other instances, it is legitimate to prioritize the researcher's voice. The researcher, she argues, may have the broader perspective or expertise that participants are lacking. The researcher may be making general observations rather than commenting on anything raised directly by participants. While it may be preferable to work out an interpretation of what is happening in any given social setting with participants, there are good reasons in some instances for not doing so. If the analyst's observations are sensitive or critical, for example, one may not want to risk causing harm to participants' self-esteem or relationships. Snyder insists that, however a researcher manages these decisions, reflexivity and transparency are paramount.

Finally, Katherine Bischoping provides an interesting discussion of how voice—both that of respondents and that of researchers—becomes an issue in the apparently simple act of deciding who to quote and how to edit quotes. Qualitative researchers take for granted that not everyone can be quoted in a study and that entire transcripts cannot be reproduced in an analyses. They assume that, in their selection of quotes, they are looking for the clearest and pithiest, those that best demonstrate the analytical point they are making. Moreover, it often comes as a surprise to those who have never worked with verbatim transcriptions of everyday speech just how messy and fragmented talk can be. In incorporating quotes in their writing, most qualitative researchers, again, take for granted that there will be a certain amount of "cleaning up." The intention is to get the reader to see the point and not be distracted by the messiness of the talk. Bischoping questions the taken for granted and asks: "What is it that is left on the ethnographer's cutting room floor and why?"

Her candid account of a study involving interviews with undergraduate students shows that a range of considerations factored into her decisions around the use of quotes. In some cases, she admits, she edited in order to make a quote more vivid and to make respondents sound more intelligent, coherent, or sympathetic. Of course, lack of editing or light editing can create for readers the opposite impression about respondents. In one case, involving a respondent that Bischoping did not much like, she let the respondent pretty well speak for herself and wonders how much this had to do with getting revenge. When she reflects on who she quoted and whose words were omitted from her writing, she found that she did not use the words of one respondent with whom she strongly connected, fearing that she might have gone too far in revealing herself to her respondent and influenced what she got back. Nor did she use any quotes from a tense interview with a respondent with whom she felt no rapport at all, though she concedes he had relevant things to say.

Bischoping concludes that what gets left on the cutting room floor tells a story, in fact many stories, about our respondents and about ourselves as researchers. Too often these stories are overlooked. She encourages qualitative researchers to be more reflexive about their editing experiences and to begin sharing them with others.

REFERENCES

Becker, H.S. (1970). *Sociological work: Method and substance*. Chicago, IL: Aldine.

Berg, B. (2001). *Qualitative research methods for the social sciences* (4th ed.). Toronto: Allyn & Bacon.

Douglas, J.D. (1976). *Investigative social research: Individual and team field research*. Beverly Hills, CA: Sage.

Hertz, R. (1997). *Reflexivity and voice*. Thousand Oaks, CA: Sage.

Johnson, J.M. (1975). *Doing field research*. New York: Free Press.

Kelly, K.D., & Totten, M. (2002). *When children kill: A Socio-psychological study of youth homocide*. Orchard Park, NY: Broadview Press.

Lofand, J. (1976). *Doing social life: The qualitative study of human interaction in natural settings*. New York: John Wiley & Sons.

Lofland, J.A., & Lofland, L.H. (1995). *Analyzing social settings: A guide to qualitative observation and analysis* (3rd ed.). Belmont, CA: Wadsworth.

Matza, D. (1969). *Becoming deviant*. Englewood Cliffs, NJ: Prentice-Hall.

McCall, G.J., & Simmons, J.L. (Eds.). (1969). *Issues in participant observation*. Reading, MA: Addison-Wesley.

Miller, S.M. (1952). The participant observer and "over-rapport." *American Sociological Review, 17*, 97–99.

Richardson, L. (1990). Writing: Reaching diverse audiences. Thousand Oaks, CA: Sage.

Roth, J. (1960). Comments on secret observation. *Social Problems, 9*, 283–284.

Schwartz, H., & Jacobs, H. (1979). *Qualitative sociology: A method to the madness*. New York: The Free Press.

Shaffir, W. (1974). *Life in a religious community: The Lubavitcher Chassidim in Montreal*. Toronto: Holt, Rinehart and Winston of Canada.

Shaffir, W., Stebbins, R., & Turowetz, A. (Eds.). (1980). *Fieldwork experience: Qualitative approaches to social research*. New York: St. Martin's Press.

Shaffir, W., & Stebbins, R. (Eds.). (1991). *Experiencing fieldwork: An inside view of qualitative research*. Newbury Park: Sage.

Taylor, S., & Bogdan, R. (1984). *Introduction to qualitative research methods: The search for meanings* (2nd ed.). Toronto: John Wiley & Sons.

Wax, M.L. (1967). On misunderstanding *verstehen*: A reply to Abel. *Sociology and Social Research, 51*, 323–333.

Wax, R.H. (1971). *Doing fieldwork: Warnings and advice*. Chicago, IL: University of Chicago Press.

Webb, E.J., Campbell, D.T., Schwartz, R.D., Lee, S., & Grove, J.B. (1981). *Nonreactive measures in the social sciences* (2nd ed.). Boston: Houghton Mifflin.

PART 1A

CONSIDERING THE MERITS
OF QUALITATIVE RESEARCH

Chapter 2

Interpretive Practices and the Role of Qualitative Methods in Informing Large-Scale Survey Research

Charlene Miall and Karen March

INTRODUCTION

In social research, **paradigms** guide the production of knowledge by specifying the nature of reality, how it can be known, and the methodologies needed to conduct research (Guba & Lincoln, 1994, p. 107). Sociological knowledge production is diverse both in the theoretical and substantive interests of researchers and in the methodologies they employ. However, positivism has taken precedence over other paradigms, and is generally viewed as superior in producing knowledge about the world (cf. Denzin & Lincoln, 1994; Jackson, 1999). Sociologists using a positivist paradigm model their research approach after the natural sciences. They argue that the accurate measurement of social phenomena and statistical analysis of that data are required to discover and confirm laws of probability, using these to explain and predict general patterns of human behaviour (Taylor & Bogdan, 1984). Thus, **quantitative research** strategies emphasize researcher objectivity, deductive reasoning, hypothesis testing, rigorous measurement techniques, and precision in data analysis.

The interpretive paradigm, on the other hand, adopts a phenomenological worldview that assumes the existence of multiple realities emerging from "intangible mental constructions, socially and experientially based, local and specific in nature" (Guba & Lincoln, 1994, p. 110). Sociologists using an interpretive approach consider how people make sense of their world, emphasizing the study of meaningful, symbolic communication, patterns of interaction among individuals, and the importance of *verstehen*. According to Patton (1990, p. 57), "the *verstehen* tradition stresses understanding that focuses on the meaning of human behaviour, the context of social interaction, an empathetic understanding based on personal experience, and the connections between mental states and behaviour" [italics in the original]. **Qualitative research** strategies, therefore, emphasize a subjective, inductive, holistic, and process-oriented approach in which people are seen as behaving in orderly but not necessarily predictable ways (Reichardt & Cook, 1979, pp. 9–10).

Positivists seek the causes or *facts* of social phenomena and show little interest in the personal states of individuals (Taylor & Bogdan, 1984, p. 1). Thus, quantitative methodologies routinely used in survey studies measure assessments of issues to establish the *facts* of a situation; for example, to what extent, in statistical terms, a general population supports or doesn't support a particular issue. Reports of results are usually presented, in a seemingly unproblematic way, as tables derived from statistical analysis. Interpretive sociologists, however, are concerned with the understanding of human behaviour from the actor's own point of view. Qualitative methodologies, therefore, provide a framework within which people can reveal "the ways in which they have organized their world, their thoughts about what is happening, their experiences, and their basic perceptions" (Patton, 1990, p. 24). This requires the researcher to watch, listen, ask, record, and examine everyday life (Prus, 1996).

Quantitative and qualitative data also differ markedly. According to Patton (1990, p. 24), quantitative data are "succinct, parsimonious and easily aggregated for analysis ... systematic, standardized, and easily presented in a short space." Qualitative data are "longer, more detailed, and variable in content; analysis is difficult because responses are neither systematic nor standardized" (p. 24). Further, qualitative data may consist of "direct quotations from people about their experiences, opinions, feelings and knowledge"; descriptions of events, people or situations; and the use of personal diaries, government documents, and reports (p. 10).

In this chapter, we report on a Canada-wide survey conducted on adoption issues and discuss how qualitative research on these same issues altered our understanding of the survey results obtained. We consider how male and female respondents' apparent agreement on fixed alternative (yes/no) questions was, in fact, accompanied by different explanations of why they answered the way they did. We will begin by presenting an overview of the research topic.

BIOLOGICAL VERSUS ADOPTIVE KINSHIP

In Western society, the kinship system is based on *blood* or biological relationships, understood as indissoluble and *mystical* in nature, transcending legal and other kinship arrangements (Kirk, 1981; Schneider, 1980). Non-relative adoption, however, clearly separates the biological from the social nurturing part of parenting (March & Miall, 2000). Through traditional practices of adoption, birth parents relinquish their right to raise their biologically related children. Adoptive parents assume this social parenting role. As an institution, adoption challenges constructions of parenting as a process of child-bearing and child-rearing (Kirk, 1981).

Further, changes in the social context have challenged the traditional family form. The use of reproductive technologies, such as donor sperm, donor ova, donor embryos, and surrogates to form families, challenges notions of *real* biological kinship. Increased divorce rates and remarriages create families where a step-parent may replace a biological parent. Same-sex couples form families where only one partner may have a biological relationship to the children. "As whatever remains to the meaning of kinship becomes more voluntaristic, the symbolic representation of family is likely to be in flux" (Edwards, 1991, p. 358). Given changes in the social context, we were interested in examining how the wider community currently viewed kinship, whether biological or adoptive.

In this chapter, we discuss a portion of our larger research study on adoptive kinship. We consider assessments of the nature of motherhood as instinctive, learned or both; the importance of motherhood as a role for women; and assessments of biological and adoptive mothers' feelings for their children. A complete discussion of our research can be found in Miall and March (2003, 2005a, 2005b).

METHODOLOGY

Research on community attitudes towards adoption has either been qualitative, with little **generalizability** to the larger community (Miall, 1996, 1998; Ryburn, McCaulay, & Powell, 1997/98); or quantitative, in the form of survey research, with no exploration of the meanings underlying responses (Dave Thomas Foundation for Adoption, 2002; Evan B. Donaldson Adoption Institute, 1997; Rompf, 1993). Methodologically, we had decided to use a two-stage research design—a Canada-wide survey to establish quantitatively the prevalence of social constructs of adoption established in our previous qualitative research, and intensive qualitative interviews with a sub-sample of this population to document *meanings* underlying their responses. The funding agency reviewing our proposal, however, directed us to adopt a more traditional design—the exploratory qualitative study followed by a quantitative survey—as a condition of funding and we complied.

Box 2.1

While most studies using qualitative methods tend to be exploratory in nature, qualitative methods can be used to add detail and depth to quantitative studies where patterns of response have emerged that are generalizable across populations and settings (Patton, 1990, p. 130). This is usually accomplished by drawing a sub-sample of respondents from the surveyed sample population and conducting in-depth interviews to "help make sense out of and interpret survey results" (Patton, 1990, p. 132). This research design facilitates comparisons of the two samples, drawn as they are from the same population.

Two samples were drawn from the Canadian population in 2000. In phase one, 82 qualitative interviews (41 males and 41 females) were conducted in two eastern Canadian cities. We used a pre-tested, semi-structured interview schedule. Respondents were asked first to answer a fixed alternative question (for example, *agree/disagree*) on the relevant issue and then asked to explain their answer (*Why do you feel this way?*). This use of open-ended questions enabled us "to understand and capture the points of view of other people without predetermining these points of view through prior selection of questionnaire categories" (Patton, 1990, p. 24). We coded the qualitative data into categories according to themes and frequency of theme responses noted (Berg, 2001; Lofland & Lofland, 1984).

Box 2.2

In sample 1, respondents selected randomly from the city directory were sent a letter informing them of the study and then telephoned to arrange an in-home interview. Despite a low response rate (below 50%), 94 interviews were conducted. Twelve respondents identified as birth parents, adoptive parents, or adoptees were eliminated from the study. Sociology graduate students conducted in-depth interviews in respondents' homes. The interviews, which lasted from one to two hours, were taped and transcribed. Nine participants were interviewed by telephone.

In sample 2, 766 telephone interviews were conducted by The Institute for Social Research at York University in Toronto, Canada, between May and June 2000. The interviews took from 15 to 20 minutes to complete. Sixty respondents identified as birth parents, adoptive parents, or adoptees were eliminated from the sample. The final response rate was approximately 56%. Given disparities in population sizes in each of the regions, weights were provided to compensate for unequal probabilities of selection at both the provincial and household levels using the 1991 Canadian Census, the one most recently available. For results based on the total sample and with a confidence level of 95%, the error attributable to sampling and other random effects was plus or minus 3.5 percentage points.

In phase two, a sample of 706 respondents (287 males and 419 females) 18 and older was randomly selected from across Canada using Computer Assisted Telephone Interviewing (CATI) methods. A standardized questionnaire with 45 fixed alternative questions was pre-tested to review question wording and ordering effects, and modified accordingly. Most fixed alternative questions were replicated from phase one interviews or addressed themes emerging in the open-ended responses. For quantitative analysis, we used the SPSS Base 9.0 software package (SPSS Inc., 1999).

Table 2.1 presents the socio-demographic characteristics for both samples. Although we don't claim equivalency, given the different sampling methods, the close similarity between these two samples in terms of most socio-demographic characteristics, and the general pattern of agreement in majority responses found for the fixed alternative questions, lent support to our decision to examine the relevance of insights identified in the qualitative responses for the larger survey.

In analyzing our qualitative and quantitative data, we highlighted the role of gender as a variable. This approach challenges "the unexamined, often unstated, assumption that the meanings of attitudinal and behavioral measurement items (such as Likert-type questions) are the same for all male and female respondents" (Fox & Murry, 2000, p. 1164). By using a design that considered the meaning underlying responses and the prevalence of social constructs by gender, we avoided problems associated with assuming gender neutrality in data sets (p. 1165).

Table 2.1: Socio-Demographic Characteristics of the Samples

Socio-demographic Characteristics+	Sample 1 N = 82		Sample 2 N = 706	
Gender				
Male	50%	(41)	41%	(287)
Female	50%	(41)	59%	(419)
Age				
29 years or younger	9%	(7)	24%	(161)
30 to 49 years	46%	(37)	47%	(323)
50 years or older	45%	(36)	29%	(202)
Education				
Elementary school or less	10%	(8)	4%	(27)
High school or less	16%	(13)	37%	(260)
Post-sec./univ. or less	64%	(52)	52%	(359)
Post-graduate	10%	(8)	7%	(49)
Income				
Under $20,000	8%	(6)	15%	(83)
$21,000 – $59,000	47%	(36)	45%	(258)
$60,000 – $100,000	37%	(29)	27%	(154)
Over $100,000	8%	(6)	13%	(74)
Marital Status				
Married/common law	67%	(55)	62%	(436)
Widowed/separated/divorced	12%	(10)	14%	(96)
Single	21%	(17)	24%	(166)
Parental Status				
Yes	72%	(58)	67%	(469)
No	28%	(23)	33%	(233)
Language				
English	100%	(82)	75%	(529)
French			25%	(177)

+ Missing cases not included in calculations.

> ### Box 2.3
>
> Family scholars are increasingly examining the role of gender in research on the nature of motherhood and fatherhood, stressing the importance of viewing gender as a social construct embodying cultural meanings about masculinity and femininity (Arendell, 2000; Fox & Murry, 2000; Marsiglio, Amato, Day, & Lamb, 2000). When gender is conceptualized as a socio-cultural construction, and sex as a biological given, they become distinguishable from one another. Although gender and sex are correlated in some ways, observed empirical differences between men and women are not solely "evidence of biological or 'essential' differences between the sexes but also as reflective of sociocultural and political processes of gender" (Fox & Murry, 2000, p. 1165).
>
> Researchers are directed to view mothering and motherhood as "dynamic social interactions and relationships, located in a societal context organized by gender and in accord with the prevailing gender system" (Arendell, 2000, p. 1193). Mothering, as it is defined and practised, should be understood not as "natural, universal, and unchanging" (Glenn, 1994, p. 4), or the product of biological reproduction, but as historically variable. The problem to be explored, according to Arendell (2000), is not the capacity of women to biologically reproduce, but rather how mothering activities are given meaning in culturally organized ways.

INTERVIEW AND SURVEY RESULTS FOR FIXED ALTERNATIVE QUESTIONS

In Table 2.2, the results of the two samples are presented for males and females on assessments of the nature of motherhood as instinctive or learned; the importance of motherhood as a role for women; and whether maternal feelings for adopted and biological children are the same or different. There were no statistically significant differences in responses between the male and female respondents in either sample on the nature of motherhood and its importance as a role for women. A significant difference in gender response was noted in both samples, however, on the sameness of feelings of biological and adoptive mothers for their children. Women were significantly more likely than men in both samples to consider adoptive mothers' feelings to be basically the same as biological mothers' feelings.

While these responses would justify our concluding that males and females in our samples shared the same values in terms of the nature of motherhood and its importance, they differed in their assessments of biological and adoptive mothers' feelings for their children. This divergence could not be explained on the basis of fixed alternative answers alone. The open-ended responses to the sample 1 interview questions, however, yielded subtle yet important differences between the male and female respondents that helped us to understand why their assessments on other issues diverged. We will now consider these open-ended responses.

Table 2.2: Comparison by Gender of Assessments of Motherhood and Biological and Adoptive Parenting

Assessments of Motherhood/Kinship	Sample 1 Males (N = 41)	Sample 1 Females (N = 41)
Motherhood Instinctive	53% (21)	50% (20)
Motherhood Very Important	76% (31)	76% (31)
Adoptive Mother Feelings Basically the Same	59% (20)*	78% (29)*
Assessments of Motherhood/Kinship	Sample 2 Males (N = 287)	Sample 2 Females (N = 419)
Motherhood Instinctive	60% (164)	54% (217)
Motherhood Very Important	88% (249)	88% (364)
Adoptive Mother Feelings Basically the Same	68% (178)*	83% (312)*

Note: Missing cases not included in calculations.
* $p < .01$ using difference-of-proportions tests.

THE NATURE OF MOTHERHOOD AS A ROLE FOR WOMEN

In our qualitative interviews, respondents were asked to assess whether motherhood was instinctive or learned or both and the importance of motherhood as a role for women. The majority of male and female respondents felt that motherhood was *instinctive* in women and that it was also a *very important* role for women. Males who responded that motherhood was instinctive were more likely to present it as an article of faith, so to speak. It was a matter of biological determinism, or just the way women are. "I would probably say it's instinctive. If you compare humans to other species or other animals, there is a certain instinctiveness with respect to the raising of, of young children" (Respondent 61). Another male respondent observed, "Biologically, I don't think that the race would have continued if it hadn't been … I think it's an inborn instinct. I think in all of the animal species" (Respondent 65).

Female respondents considering the desire to mother as instinctive also explained it as a natural part of being a woman, although many also noted that not all women had the instinct. "I think it's in our blood. That's my opinion. It's in a woman's blood, the desire to have kids or take care of kids. I know me, it's in my blood. That's what makes us women" (Respondent 29). However, females were also more likely to emphasize the nurturing and socializing aspects of motherhood, and the importance of this role in instilling values and morals, and teaching responsibility, discipline, and skills to children. As one female respondent observed, "I can only go by how I felt like, I mean, the closeness of the child and I knew it'd need to be taken care of and washed and cleaned and loved" (Respondent 23). Another noted, "I feel you've got these lives that you're … you're … moulding for the future. And you have to prepare them. And you have to give them security and teach them a few things" (Respondent 13).

Further, while males focused on the role of *female biology* in predisposing women to motherhood, female respondents also stressed motherhood as an important part of their *self-development*—motherhood made them feel worthwhile, gave them a new perspective on life that was beneficial, rewarding, and built character. As one female respondent observed, "I think it helps to foster patience, understanding. Well I think that would of course help in any other thing that a woman wanted to do, the fact that she had to put somebody else ahead of herself" (Respondent 33). Another noted, "I find it forms our character … think it makes us softer" (Respondent 41). A third revealed that "it's just something I've always wanted. I don't know, that bond … something that always made me feel like, worthwhile" (Respondent 12).

To conclude this section, while the notion of "biology is destiny" continued to be evident in fixed alternative questions on the nature of motherhood, the meanings underlying this assertion were demonstrated, in the qualitative data, to be gender differentiated. Women focused more on actual mothering behaviour and its impact on their sense of self-worth. Men, on the other hand, regarded motherhood as natural or biologically inherent in women. This differentiation in meaning based on gender standpoint was most clearly seen in this sample in assessments of (a) how adoptive mothers feel about their children versus biological mothers' feelings; and (b) how a biological or birth mother might feel about a child placed for adoption versus one she parented herself.

MATERNAL FEELINGS OF BIOLOGICAL AND ADOPTIVE MOTHERS

In terms of maternal feelings, the majority of respondents in the Canada-wide survey felt that an adoptive mother's feelings for her child would be basically the same as a biological mother's feelings for her child. As in the interview data, females were significantly more likely to respond this way than males. The analysis of the qualitative interviews revealed that male respondents felt that the same *maternal instinct* was there for women regardless of a biological tie. "Well, if, if we accept that there's a maternal instinct, whether the child is adopted or natural one, both are the same" (Respondent 61). "The maternal instinct is so strong in people and I think it's there. And I think that babies and children deliberately have built-in mechanisms to pull all the right strings, particularly in mothers" (Respondent 73).

Males responding that maternal feelings were *different* also focused on the importance of biological instinct. However, the biological act of reproducing was felt to induce feelings unrelated to the actual parenting of a child. "I think of a, a natural parent particularly when they're talking about the birth and delivery of their, their young child … it still seems to be that fundamental bonding time … But I, I think those are maternal feelings that would be absent in an adopted mother" (Respondent 48). As another male put it, "The biological mother is obviously giving birth and living with this child for nine months whereas, where, you know, it's a longer time to attach themselves to. But adoptive parents kind of, although you're, I'm sure, happy to get an adopted child, you kind of just … one day you have it" (Respondent 60).

Female open-ended responses revealed that maternal feelings were the same because adoptive mothers had a strong desire to *parent* a child that transcended a biological relationship to it. Tied to this was the notion that adoptive mothers chose to be parents, unlike many women who became pregnant unintentionally or didn't really want to be mothers. "If you really want a child, you're out there to adopt a child … It's like you really love that child because you want that child in your life" (Respondent 24). "I think they're basically the same because that woman would have absolutely wanted that child … Some people get pregnant accidentally and they don't really want that child but they'll keep it" (Respondent 32). Another respondent observed, "I think you would just develop that bond if, if you're having a child with you 24 hours a day … you're gonna develop the same bond as you would with your own birth child" (Respondent 25). Female respondents who felt there was a difference in maternal feelings between biological and adoptive mothers, like males, emphasized the importance of biological reproduction in loving or bonding with a child.

To conclude, a majority of males and females indicated through fixed alternative responses that an adoptive mother's feelings for her child were the same as a biological mother's feelings. Males, however, were more likely to link these maternal feelings and mothering practices to a natural instinct in women regardless of their biological relationship to a child. In assessing adoptive mothers, males referred to the desire and natural instinct of a woman to be a mother to the adopted children. Females, on the other hand, were more likely to link the sameness of maternal feelings to the actual parenting behaviour of the mother, whether the child was adopted or not. Given that adoption separates the biological from the social aspects of parenting, it is not surprising that more females supported the sameness of feelings for biological and adoptive mothers because of their stronger association of motherhood with actual parenting behaviour.

We will now consider how these gendered meanings about motherhood impacted on assessments of how a biological or birth mother might feel about a child placed for adoption versus one she parented herself.

ASSESSMENTS OF BIRTH MOTHERS, PARENTING EXPERIENCES, AND BONDING

In our qualitative study, a number of open-ended questions were asked that did not easily translate into the fixed alternative questions required for survey research. We report here on one such question because it illustrated, again, the importance of studying the meanings underlying fixed alternative responses to questions about motherhood. The question asked focused on whether birth mothers would feel the same way about biologically related children they hadn't raised (relinquished for adoption) as those they had. In other words, did the experience of parenting a child make a difference in a birth mother's feelings for a biologically related child?

A majority of males (57%) felt that a birth mother's maternal feelings for a child she hadn't raised would be *basically the same* as for a child she had raised. A majority of females (62%), however, felt that the feelings would be *basically different*. In their open-ended responses, males again emphasized the biological connection as a factor that would influence a birth mother's feelings for her children whether she raised them or not. As one male respondent put it, "I would say basically the same because … in a way, there, there would be some sort of bonding, of knowing that that person belonged … You gave them life and brought them into the world" (Respondent 52). Another observed, "I don't think because you've given up a child that you have necessarily lost those feelings … I would say they biologically are the same … and the maternal feelings are the same." (Respondent 61).

The minority of males who felt the birth mother's feelings would be different stressed the importance of actual parenting behaviour with or without maternal instinct. "I think they'd be basically different. And their family relationship is based on the history and, and everything they've, they've done. And they wouldn't have that relationship" (Respondent 48). Similarly, another observed, "In addition to the basic maternal instincts, there are emergency trips to the hospital through the upbringing and things like that that create a much deeper and firmer bond than someone stepping off a bus and saying, 'Hi, I'm your kid.'" (Respondent 73).

The majority of females who felt that the feelings would be different also linked it to parenting behaviour and its importance in bonding with children. "Because I think once you've raised a child, with each, let's say milestone in their life, you grow to love them more. If you don't have those experiences while they're growing up, you can't have the same level of feeling" (Respondent 16). As another respondent noted, "Although she may have some very strong feelings and connections, there is still that huge span of time where she hasn't been a mother to the child and it's not her fault or anybody's fault. It's not a good thing or bad thing. It's just that you don't have the first steps. You don't have the first day of school and all of those issues. A mother isn't someone who gives birth to somebody. A mother is somebody who raises them and she hasn't had that. And although I believe she can have very, very strong feelings for this person, it is different" (Respondent 39).

The minority of female respondents who felt birth mother feelings would be the same linked them, like male respondents, to the biological connection and giving birth. As one woman observed, "I think once you've given birth to a child, you will always have those feelings no matter whether they're with you or not" (Respondent 10). As another put it, "I think regardless of the reasons why they gave it up, you still have that bond, whether you chose to accept it or not. There's still that bond there and I don't think any mother who's had a child can take that away" (Respondent 34).

To conclude this section, in supporting the sameness of a birth mother's feelings for a child placed for adoption, a majority of the males again focused on the significance of the biological bond. Females, on the other hand, continued to focus on the importance of nurturing and parenting behaviour for birth mothers, concluding that a birth mother's lack of parenting behaviour would result in her feeling differently about a biological child relinquished for adoption.

THE ROLE OF QUALITATIVE METHODS IN INFORMING LARGE-SCALE SURVEY RESEARCH

In terms of our own data sets, if we had relied solely on the fixed alternative responses to our questions on the nature and importance of motherhood, we would have been unable to explain the significant gendered differences that emerged when our respondents were asked to assess the sameness of feelings of adoptive mothers and birth mothers for their children. The use of a qualitative research approach that attended to *meanings* underlying responses to questions provided us with a more complete picture of why respondents answered these questions differently, despite seeming agreement on the nature and importance of motherhood.

As noted earlier, qualitative research methods differ markedly from quantitative research methods and yield different kinds of data. Qualitative methods are traditionally used in exploratory studies and/or in the study of actor perceptions, personal meanings, and social worlds of interaction. As the viewpoint of the actor is stressed, *discovery* rather than the testing of well-defined hypotheses is the goal of this research (Patton, 1990). According to Blumer (1970, pp. 32–33), "the purpose of exploratory investigation is to move toward a clearer understanding of how one's problem is to be posed, to learn what are the appropriate data, to develop ideas of what are significant lines of relation, and to evolve one's conceptual tools in light of what one is learning about the area of life."

On the other hand, when statistical results indicate "global patterns generalizable across settings or populations," qualitative data can be used to fill in the meanings underlying these patterns (Patton, 1990, pp. 131–132). Despite the traditional tendency of researchers to claim allegiance to one methodological approach over another, many research studies combine both quantitative and qualitative research strategies (Jackson, 1999; Palys, 1997). According to Glaser and Strauss (1967, pp. 17–18) "there is no fundamental clash between the purposes and capacities of qualitative and quantitative methods or data … We believe that each form of data is useful for both verification and generation of theory, whatever the primacy of emphasis." Further, apart from a commitment to a particular theoretical paradigm, the choice of a quantitative, qualitative or combined research method should also depend on the demands of the research situation at hand (Reichardt & Cook, 1979, p. 16).

Little attention has been paid, however, to how these research strategies, particularly when combined, guide investigative processes, the evaluation of data, and how such data are interpreted (Jackson, 1999). Further, while researchers acknowledge their membership in a larger scientific community of scholars, they rarely examine how their own allegiance to particular research paradigms actually contributes to the continuation of a qualitative-quantitative divide (Guba & Lincoln, 1994). Our experience with the funding agency that required us to reshape our research design to reflect a more "traditional" use of qualitative methods reflects this allegiance in practice. In the end, we were left to justify the use of our qualitative data in interpreting our survey responses, given the requirement placed on us to draw two separate samples rather than a sub-sample of the survey population, our original intention.

CONCLUSION

As demonstrated in this paper and others, differences in quantitative and qualitative research strategies, methods, and data do not preclude their use together. Indeed, their relationship might be better conceptualized as *symbiotic* where symbiosis is defined as "the living together of two kinds of organisms to their mutual advantage" (Webster, 2002, p. 641). For example, the oft-cited lack of generalizability of results generated through qualitative research can be addressed when this method is utilized as part of a representative random sampling design. On the other hand, Denzin (1970, p. 9) has argued that the **"fallacy of objectivism"** in quantitative research might be avoided with the concomitant use of qualitative methods. The fallacy of objectivism has been defined as the researcher's belief that if "formulations are theoretically or methodologically sound they must have relevance in the empirical world." As our research has clearly demonstrated, these formulations can sometimes yield misleading "social facts" about the empirical reality under review.

GLOSSARY

Fallacy of objectivism: Refers to the researcher's belief that if "formulations are theoretically or methodologically sound they must have relevance in the empirical world" (Denzin, 1970).

Generalizability: Refers to the extent to which a researcher can come to some conclusion about a population based on information derived from a sample (Vogt, 1999).

Paradigms: Basic belief systems made up of ontological assumptions (what really exists), epistemological assumptions (how we can know it), and methodological approaches used to study reality (Guba & Lincoln, 1994).

Qualitative research: Characterized by a subjective, inductive, holistic, and process-oriented approach in which people are seen as behaving in orderly but not necessarily predictable ways. Examples of qualitative methodologies are participant-observation and intensive interviewing with open-ended questions.

Quantitative research: Characterized by an emphasis on researcher objectivity, deductive reasoning, hypothesis testing, rigorous measurement techniques, and precision in data analysis. Examples of quantitative methodologies are the use of scaling techniques and surveys with fixed alternative questions.

REFERENCES

Arendell, T. (2000). Conceiving and investigating motherhood: The decade's scholarship. *Journal of Marriage and the Family, 62*, 1192–1207.

Berg, B.L. (2001). *Qualitative research methods for the social sciences* (4th ed.). Boston: Allyn & Bacon.

Blumer, H. (1970). Methodological principles of empirical science. In N.K. Denzin (Ed.), *Sociological methods: A sourcebook* (pp. 20–39). Chicago, IL: Aldine.

Dave Thomas Foundation for Adoption. (2002). *National adoption attitudes survey*. Harris Interactive Market Research. In co-operation with the Evan B. Donaldson Adoption Institute.

Denzin, N.K. (Ed.) (1970). *Sociological methods: A sourcebook*. Chicago, IL: Aldine.

Denzin, N.K., & Lincoln, Y.S. (Eds.). (1994). *Handbook of qualitative research*. Thousand Oaks, CA: Sage Press.

Edwards, J. (1991). New conceptions: Biosocial innovations and the family. *Journal of Marriage and the Family, 53*, 349–360.

Evan B. Donaldson Adoption Institute. (1997). *Benchmark adoption survey*. Princeton Survey Research Associates.

Fox, G.L., & Murry, V. (2000). Gender and families: Feminist perspectives and family research. *Journal of Marriage and the Family, 62*, 1160–1172.

Glaser, B., & Strauss, A. (1967). *The discovery of grounded theory: Strategies for qualitative research*. New York: Aldine Publishing Company.

Glenn, E.N. (1994). Social constructions of mothering: A thematic overview. In E.N. Glen, G. Chang, & L.R. Forcey (Eds.), *Mothering: Ideology, experience, and agency* (pp. 1–29). New York: Routledge.

Guba, E.G., & Lincoln, Y.S. (1994). Competing paradigms in qualitative research. In N.K. Denzin & Y.S. Lincoln (Eds.). *Handbook of qualitative research* (pp. 105–117). Thousand Oaks, CA: Sage.

Jackson, W. (1999). *Methods: Doing social research* (2nd ed.). Scarborough, ON: Prentice-Hall.

Kirk, D. (1981). *Adoptive kinship*. Toronto: Butterworths.

Lofland, J., & Lofland, L. (1984). *Analyzing social settings: A guide to qualitative observation and analysis*. Belmont, CA: Wadsworth Publishing.

March, K., & Miall, C. (2000). Adoption as a family form. *Family Relations, 49*, 359–362.

Marsiglio, W., Amato, P., Day, R., & Lamb, M. (2000). Scholarship on fatherhood in the 1990s and beyond. *Journal of Marriage and the Family, 62*, 1173–1191.

Miall, C. (1996). The social construction of adoption: Clinical and community perspectives. *Family Relations, 45*, 309–317.

Miall, C. (1998). Community assessments of adoption issues: Open adoption, birth reunions, and the disclosure of confidential information. *Journal of Family Issues, 19*, 556–577.

Miall, C., & March, K. (2003). A comparison of biological and adoptive mothers and fathers: The relevance of biological kinship and gendered constructs of parenthood. *Adoption Quarterly, 6*, 7–39.

Miall, C., & March, K. (2005a). Social support for changes in adoption practice: Gay adoption, open adoption, birth reunions and the release of confidential identifying information. *Families in Society, 86*, 83–92.

Miall, C., & March, K. (2005b). Open adoption as a family form: Community assessments and social support. *Journal of Family Issues, 26*, 380–410.

Palys, T. (1997). *Research decisions: Quantitative and qualitative perspectives* (2nd ed.). Toronto: Harcourt Brace.

Patton, M. (1990). *Qualitative evaluation and research methods* (2nd ed.). Newbury Park, CA: Sage.

Prus, R. (1996). *Symbolic interaction and ethnographic research*. New York: State University of New York Press.

Reichardt, C., & Cook, T. (1979). Beyond qualitative versus quantitative methods. In T. Cook & C. Reichardt (Eds.), *Qualitative and quantitative methods in evaluation research* (pp. 7–17). Beverly Hills, CA: Sage.

Rompf, E.L. (1993). Open adoption: What does the "average person" think? *Child Welfare, 72*, 219–230.

Ryburn, M., McCaulay, D., & Powell, J. (1997–98). Public attitudes to post-adoption contact. *Adoption and Fostering, 21*, 57–59.

Schneider, D. (1980). *American kinship: A cultural account*. Chicago, IL: University of Chicago Press.

SPSS Inc. (1999). *SPSS base 9.0*. US: SPSS Inc.

Taylor, S., & Bogdan, R. (1984). *Introduction to qualitative research methods: The search for meanings*. New York: John Wiley & Sons.

Vogt, W.P. (1999). *Dictionary of statistics and methodology* (2nd ed.). Thousand Oaks, CA: Sage.

Webster. (2002). *Webster's new world dictionary and thesaurus* (2nd ed.). New York: Hungry Minds Inc.

Chapter 3

The Charms and Challenges of an Academic Qualitative Researcher Doing Participatory Action Research (PAR)

Karen Szala-Meneok and Lynne Lohfeld

INTRODUCTION

Participatory action research (**cPAR**) is a research strategy whereby the community under study defines the problem, analyzes it, and solves it. The people own the information and may contract the services of academic researchers to assist in this process. In classic principal investigator research (**cPIR**), the professional or academic researcher sets the research agenda, makes all decisions about the research question to be pursued, data collection, methods of analysis, and how and where to disseminate findings. The goals of PAR and academic PIR are intrinsically different, making it particularly challenging for academic researchers to use the PAR framework when pursuing a university career. A modified PAR (**mPAR**) model, in which both community and academic members' needs are addressed, can help bridge this gap.

Before writing this paper, we asked ourselves where participatory action research (PAR) fits in a collection of essays on the qualitative analysis of social life, and what applied anthropologists doing community-based health research can add to this discussion. We found several answers to this question. First, participatory action research, a term coined by Whyte (1991), like other types of community-based research uses qualitative methods to increase public participation in health and social change programs (Hall, 1977; Lindsey & McGuinness, 1998). Therefore, information about PAR might help qualitative researchers working to improve the quality of life of specific groups (cf. Law, 1993; Lindsey & Stajduhar, 1998; Ryan & Robinson, 1990). Second, applied anthropologists help people solve problems; we record and share their often-silent voices. Third, the term itself embodies much of what we believe: that research should be as participatory as possible, that it should help communities solve problems they target, and result in new knowledge that is meaningful and empowering (Freire, 1970, 1982; Hall, 1992; Ryan & Robinson, 1996). Fourth, we believe that many qualitative researchers are deeply committed to the principles of collaborative research. PAR takes that commitment one step further by enabling study participants to become research partners and co-learners

(Elden & Levin, 1991) and create lasting change that can restore power and voice to communities (Freire, 1993; Smith & Williams, 1993).

We also faced other questions associated with PAR: How can academic researchers do this type of work? Can they meet professional goals set by their peers and still work alongside community members within the PAR framework? Is there only one way to do PAR?

In this paper we discuss what PAR is, how PAR is done, the role of the PAR researcher, and suggest a new model of PAR that may help academic researchers interested in doing this type of work. We draw on examples from one of our PAR projects to illustrate key points.

WHAT IS PAR?

In most PAR projects, community members participate actively with a professional researcher from inception and design, to data collection and analysis, through to dissemination of results and beyond. While doing a PAR study, community members often find themselves able to express more clearly concerns and seek solutions for them, and reduce long-standing power differentials that exist between trained researchers and themselves. This is different from the more conventional model of research in which community members are often treated as passive subjects. In that role, their participation is limited to authorizing and possibly funding a project, providing data, and/or receiving the results (Whyte, Greenwood, & Lazes, 1991).

PAR is one of several transformative practices that combine research, popular education, and action designed to benefit a disenfranchised group (Hall, 1981, 1993; Park, 1993). By engaging people in meaningful dialogue about a problem they face, a PAR project provides opportunities for people to speak in full voice. Park (1993, p. 12) explains that problems faced by marginalized people "must be understood in the hearts and the guts as well as in the heads, and the people with the problems must talk to each other as whole persons with feelings and commitment as well as facts." Taking part in a PAR project provides people with opportunities to reveal their views about problems as well as coming to know themselves better both as individuals and as a collective. This results in a better understanding of the problem within the unique context of a particular community. It can also galvanize people to make the commitment to solve a problem that can become a call to action. As Hall (1993, p. xvii) powerfully states, "participatory research fundamentally is about the right to speak."

Community members are also "co-investigators" in PAR projects, pursuing answers to questions they raise about their daily lives (Tandon, 1988). In this way, PAR helps break down the distinction between formally trained researchers and other research partners (Gaventa, 1988). In anthropological terms, PAR projects combine the **emic perspective**, or the insider's knowledge and views, with the skills and perspectives of the outside researcher, or the **etic perspective**. PAR projects are based on the premise that solutions make more sense and are more likely to be implemented when the people directly involved devise and pursue them. Rahman

(1991, p. 15) states that the goal of PAR is "to return to the people the legitimacy of the knowledge they are capable of producing through their own verification systems as fully scientific ... as a guide in their own action."

When community members and researchers share decisions and outcomes, they establish more egalitarian relationships. For many academics, this is an about-face and an unanticipated opportunity for growth (or as some might call it, a humbling experience). In part, this is possible because PAR works best when careful attention is paid to fostering respectful, attentive, sincere, and open communication among partners (Stringer, 1999). These should be the goals of all qualitative research, as exemplified by the wide use of member checking (the practice of asking study participants if the researchers have interpreted their stories correctly), as a standard technique to increase the rigour of a qualitative study. Two-way communication, decision making and feedback are important in PAR projects because all decisions related to the project have to be negotiated by the researchers and those community members most actively involved.

HOW PAR IS DONE

The first step in a PAR project is the point when people who are facing a problem become aware that there is an issue that should be addressed. This awareness, however, may not be widely shared throughout the community. Therefore, opinion or community leaders are likely to contact a researcher on behalf of their larger community to help formulate the research problem, and design and conduct a project to solve it. In this way, consultants (researchers) become *de facto* community members, and community members become active research partners (Park, 1993).

In a PAR project, key members of the community are actively involved in decision making, data collection, and analysis. This is becoming more familiar to qualitative researchers. In the PAR studies, however, it is the community members and not the formally trained researcher who have (or should have) the loudest voice when deciding what to do. This may even include "releasing" the professional researcher. Ervin (2000) gives the example of a PAR project where an anthropology doctoral candidate was the trained researcher. Before data collection was completed, her community partners asked her to withdraw from the project because they were capable of carrying out the work themselves. Although all professional researchers will eventually sever formal ties with their PAR community partners, this case clearly shows how vulnerable academic PAR researchers can be—a theme we return to later in this paper.

PAR researchers generally serve as advisors, facilitators, and resource persons rather than "sole researchers." They may, at times, have a stronger vote in joint research decisions because they have technical skills that many community members do not (Park, 1993) to ensure that the study is rigorously done. However, the aim of the researcher is to introduce community partners to data collection and analysis methods that both facilitate the expression of community voice and meet the canons of ethical and careful scholarship. For these reasons, typical PAR projects use multiple data sources and types collected with a variety of methods such as: participant observation, library research, investigating archival or historical materials, life history documentation, surveys, focus groups, and individual interviews (Park, 1993; Ryan & Robinson, 1996) in order to offset weaknesses of a single method (a process known as triangulation). Given the need to explain and negotiate methodological decisions during a PAR project, such work is typically more time-consuming and is at risk of lengthy interruptions or premature closure than more purely academic research.

To further compound the difficulties faced in a PAR study, many funding agencies and peer-reviewed journals still expect that all research team members have advanced degrees and considerable research experience. Therefore, even though funding agencies increasingly call for community partners, many studies are rejected because too few core team members have academic credentials or extensive research experience. A countervailing trend is slowly emerging whereby local community members are being trained by researchers to carry on that role themselves in future studies (cf. Ryan, 1996).

PAR studies are also different from conventional social science research in that the PAR-linked research process doesn't end once the data have been analyzed, patterns of social causation identified, and contractual obligations to funding agencies met. PAR projects are ongoing educational processes that often continue beyond the funded lifespan of a specific study. This is because successful PAR projects live on in the critical consciousness and renewed action of a community. As such, they can propel people towards further research in their own communities (Park, 1993), giving rise to spin-off projects where outside researchers may be invited back to the community to become involved in other local initiatives.

THE ROLE OF THE PAR RESEARCHER

We can think of three models that describe how professional or academic researchers who predominantly use qualitative methods work. Each model is predicated on a particular role or set of roles that researchers should fill. The most common model is the traditional or career-builder research model. Professional researchers develop a working hypothesis or research question that is likely to add to a their track records (i.e., funded by a prestigious granting agency and later appearing in a peer-reviewed journal). In this model, people who are under study are either treated as sources of data or asked to verify the accuracy of raw data or analytical products through member checking (Whyte et al., 1991). Rarely are they invited to make decisions about the design, implementation, or ways of using results from a study because this would shift control out of the hands of the professional researcher.

The second model, also common in the health and social sciences, is the professional expert or consultant model. Researchers are asked by a sponsor to study a problem, identify facts, and recommend a course of action. As hired consultants, they usually control the research process unless the client decides to veto a proposed course of action. Although this model may be suitable when the aim is to collect facts and examine their implications for future action, it is highly inappropriate if the aim is to support a group or organization undergoing a process of change and self-determination (Whyte, 1991).

In the third model, researchers are not outside experts conducting a study. Rather, they are specialized team members, bringing skills that serve as catalysts that can help community members clarify problems and develop effective solutions. One of their jobs is to demystify the research process and put as much control as possible over a project into the hands of community partners. This shifts responsibility for a project's success to the community members who may choose to ask for guidance from the professional researcher (Stringer, 1999).

In today's academic world, collaborative research with non-academics in a community setting is a relatively new and growing phenomenon. Increasingly funding agencies require that the principal investigators indicate who their community partners are and identify the roles filled by professional researchers and community agencies or individuals listed in a grant proposal. Despite this recognition of the value of collaborative community-based research, granting agencies still expect that a proposal will include an *a priori* research question, a clearly outlined methodology for collecting and analyzing data, and a fully specified timeline, budget, and dissemination plan. Little room is made for the possibility that the research design or process will change as a consequence of the community-researcher partnership.

Career academics working in the community partnership or PAR model are still judged by the number of peer-reviewed publications and conference presentations under their names, not by how valuable a project has been to its community partners. Academics face severe economic and career pressures to produce high-quality work that fits within current expectations held by funding agencies and by the tenure and promotion committees in the colleges and universities where they work. This means that the roles and expectations imposed on them are at odds with the very principles that guide PAR research.

How can the academic researcher committed to contributing to social change through research carry out this type of work? Just as there are different models under which qualitative researchers conduct their work, there are also different ways to conduct PAR studies. We will introduce the concept of a continuum of PAR next.

THE PAR CONTINUUM

For reasons presented above, there are many academic researchers or students who feel they are unable to work in the PAR model even though they believe in the principles underlying collaborative social science research in general, and in PAR specifically. We believe that, even if a researcher cannot completely adhere to the principles of PAR, it is possible to conduct a modified project rather than following the more traditional style of social science research that is principal-investigator driven. In other words, it is possible for an academic researcher to apply several of the PAR principles, creating opportunities for community members to be research partners taking the lead in many aspects of conducting the study rather than serving as participants or sources of data.

As shown in Figure 3.1, we can think of social science research as existing along a continuum ranging from classic or full PAR model (**cPAR**), to the classic Principal Investigator Research (**cPIR**) model at the other extreme, with modified PAR (**mPAR**) somewhere in between these two approaches. Key differences among these three models of practice are shown in the figure. An example of a modified Participatory Action Research (mPAR) project, the Hamilton CaReS Project, may help illustrate what this type of work entails.

THE HAMILTON CaReS PROJECT, A CASE STUDY IN mPAR

The Hamilton Caregiver Respite and Support (CaReS) Project was one of eight Canadian projects funded by the J.W. McConnell Family Foundation of Montreal, with additional funding provided by the Hamilton Community Foundation. This work took place from 2000 to 2003 in Hamilton, Ontario, a city of nearly 500,000 people located approximately 68 kilometres west of Metropolitan Toronto. The mandate of the project was to help improve the quality of life of family *caregivers* by helping people find ways to augment caregivers' voice and increasing their choices about respite (a term used in all the McConnell projects that meant whatever support or services that a caregiver identified as bringing peace of mind and rejuvenation).

The CaReS Project was developed and managed by a core group of community members and academics working collaboratively with family caregivers and other people advocating for or providing direct services to caregivers. From the outset, the researchers clearly stated a commitment to ensure that the project would be community-driven with caregivers as full partners, some serving as advisory group members and others providing information about what local caregivers most needed and how to meet those needs.

The CaReS Project consisted of two parts. First we collected qualitative and quantitative (survey) data to learn about the experiences and needs of caregivers and the views of other community members who work with them. We designed and implemented a computer-assisted telephone survey that was administered to 300 caregivers. We also faxed a brief version of the survey to local family practitioners, geriatricians, faith leaders, parish nurses, and other service providers in order to compare their views with those of family caregivers.

In the second phase of the study, we used this information to develop four deliverables that would help members of key stakeholder groups hear the voice of local caregivers. This included various health and social service agencies, caregiver support and advocacy groups, as well as local policy-makers. We were very conscious of the need to bring the voice of caregivers to "the powers that be," as one caregiver described our mandate. The four products included a how-to toolkit that describes ways to conduct a modified PAR project for communities interested in doing a similar project; a local resource guide for caregivers; four pre-recorded public health messages accessible by calling a toll-free telephone number; and a website linking caregiver needs to local resources <www.stjosham.on.ca/cares>.

Figure 3.1: The Differences between Classic PAR (cPAR), Classic PIR (cPIR), and Modified PAR (mPAR) Projects

Research Issue	Models of Community-Based Social Science Research		
	Classic Participatory Action Research (cPAR)	Modified Participatory Action Research (mPAR)	Classic Principal Investigator Research (cPIR)
Research question	Community driven	Researcher developed, community approved	Knowledge/ theory driven
Control	In hands of community	In hands of community (unless related to a methodological issue; then shifts to researcher)	In hands of researcher and/or funders
Successful project	Leads to action as directed by community	Meets outcomes that community and researcher identify as important	Leads to new knowledge or theory
Method	May not be fully rigorous	Rigorous when possible (unless interferes with community goals and needs)	Highly rigorous
Dissemination and use of results	Community decides when, how, and to whom results are shared; mostly for local use, possibly by policy-makers	Joint decision by community and researcher	Researcher decides when, how, and to whom results are shared; key audience is other professional or academic researchers, possibly policy-makers
Ownership of results	Local community	Community agencies or groups and researcher	Researcher

Inception and Design

When drafting our letter of intent to the McConnell Foundation, we convened our community advisory team (comprising local caregivers and representatives from agencies advocating and/or providing services for caregivers). The proposal was a direct result of discussions from that meeting. After receiving funds to develop the full grant proposal, we reconvened our team. To our surprise, the full proposal was summarily rejected by our community partners who felt that a different focus was in order. We then took the rest of the meeting to draft the outline of a new proposal, one that they felt more clearly reflected their concerns and views of the problems facing Hamilton caregivers. This became the core of the proposal, which was ultimately awarded three years of funding and a mandate to continue the work. What struck us as particularly relevant was that many advisory team members later confessed to having been very surprised about the tone of that pivotal meeting. For the non-academic partners, it was the first time that many of them felt their opinions and views were both welcomed and integrated into a research proposal. In other research projects, community members reported feeling they had only token involvement, that they were often told after the fact about decisions or actions already made by the academic researchers heading up a project. For the academic team members, it was the first time that such a clear mandate from community partners was heard and acted upon within the confines of an academic, methodologically rigorous study. This set the tone for our advisory team, one that was very active, personally invested, and proud to be involved in the CaReS Project.

Data Collection and Analysis

When we designed our main data collection instrument (a computer-assisted telephone interview protocol), all members of the community advisory team were involved in the multiple rounds of revision that were needed. We held caregiver focus groups to verify that key questions about caregivers' needs would help identify the concerns of Hamilton family caregivers in readily understood language. After the data were collected, we held a "coding PARty" with 16 advisory team members (caregivers and academics) as well as other community-dwelling caregivers who wanted to be involved actively in the study. A caregiver and academic were paired together to pile sort the responses to one of the open-ended telephone survey questions (e.g., "What word best describes how you feel about being a caregiver today?") listed individually on slips of paper. The principal investigator and project coordinator later reviewed and modified the results of each team's thematic pile sorts. In this way, the voice of the local caregiver was built into the data collection and analysis processes in a way that was highly transparent and accountable to community members. This process is also an example of how member checking, a commonly used technique to increase rigour in qualitative research, can take on an even stronger PAR flavour. In keeping with the principles of PAR, our coding party also served to strengthen community ownership and participation in the creation of new knowledge and an opportunity to learn first hand about careful scholarship. We also noticed that several of the academic researchers on the team were deeply impressed by the ability of laypersons to fully engage in a highly abstract research task, and have reported that their views about community research have become more participatory as a result.

Knowledge Transfer

We have used traditional academic venues to share findings from our study (i.e., peer-reviewed journals, international conferences, academic rounds at local teaching hospitals, and poster presentations at regional and national congresses). We have also presented information about our methods and findings in several community-based settings (i.e., booths at local health and safety fairs, a home care information fair, Hamilton Caregiver Week celebrations, at a one-day caregiver workshop and information fair, and at meetings of community organizations, service clubs, and church groups). The CaReS Project has been described by community partners and other academic researchers as having successfully broken down the traditional "town-gown barrier" by bringing academics into the public eye and the community voice to academia. Both academic and community audiences have expressed surprise at how actively involved our community partners were. Several people also were amazed that academic researchers would make presentations within the community at a factory health fair or at an information booth as part of a public health campaign in a shopping mall.

One of our main achievements from the project is a website designed in consultation with several of Hamilton's family caregivers. We struck a working group so that caregivers could describe the types of information they needed and how to create a website that would help overcome the barriers commonly faced by caregivers when trying to seek information and help. Another group of caregivers reviewed the website during the design phase and advised the project coordinator and web designer (who was also a caregiver) on final changes.

Subsequent Action Based on New Knowledge

One example of how our community partners took the lead in using knowledge gained from the project is the one-day workshop and information fair we held. Caregivers were actively involved in all aspects of the workshop, from planning and development, to implementation and post-workshop feedback. We are including this example in our how-to toolkit so that other communities wanting to raise awareness about the needs of their own family caregivers can profit from our experience. This how-to toolkit will be a living blueprint or modifiable by any user to make it more applicable to a wide range of community issues raised by caregivers, service providers, academics, and policy-makers. It will also explicitly point to the value of adopting a modified participatory action research (mPAR) approach in order to highlight the roles and activities of both community and research partners while rigorously seeking answers needed to develop meaningful action that community members can endorse and ultimately own.

Caregiver Voice and Choice

As noted earlier, participatory research is about a community's right to speak (Hall, 1993). In the CaReS Project, two of our stated aims were to amplify caregiver voice and increase the choices available for meeting the need for rejuvenation with peace of mind, or respite, as outcome. This requires active listening to local caregivers, documenting their views and experiences, and translating what we hear into project practices and outcomes. Caregivers, as well as policy-makers and academic researchers, are interested in these messages. Ultimately, if service providers and advocates at the local, provincial, and federal levels act on what they hear, filtered through projects like ours, then we may see an increase in caregivers' choices for respite-as-outcome. This clearly reflects our belief that collaborative research (including PAR) enables people to create lasting change through action.

CAN THE CAREER ACADEMIC BE A PAR PRACTITIONER?

The question still remains: can career academics also be PAR practitioners? We believe they can if they use a modified PAR (mPAR) approach. Classic PAR is not well accepted in academia. A modified PAR model can help merge the ideals of PAR with the practical issues facing academics today and straddle two very different worlds: the community and academia. Both faculty and students face incredible pressures to conform to academic requirements when conducting PAR projects. Dissertations and funded research projects need to meet pre-established timelines. Data collection and analysis must be rigorous enough to warrant publication in peer-reviewed journals. Research must be attributable to an individual or small group of investigators, not owned by an entire community. But in classic PAR projects, the community sets the timetable and aims of a project, and lays claim to the outcomes as their own. The success or failure of a project is inextricably tied to a collaborative process that the academic researcher can participate in but certainly not direct. The goal is for community members to identify a problem, learn how to document and solve it, and then take appropriate action based on that new knowledge. Certainly this can form the core of good, solid academic research, but only if standard research practices are allowed to evolve, and canons of "good research" are re-examined in light of the needs of our community partners.

CONCLUSION

We strongly believe that academic researchers can work alongside relatively powerless or marginalized groups to help them better understand and change their world. We can collaborate with them based on our expertise, our community membership (researchers are also members of a community-at-large), and a sense of professional and personal purpose. However, we can do this only if we relinquish the expectation that we should be in the driver's seat because we're the only ones with a license.

We are aware that the classic PAR (cPAR) model can place academic researchers at risk because it forces them to turn their attention away from their immediate needs (e.g., completing a Ph.D., working towards tenure, successfully competing for prestigious grants) in favour of helping meet the needs of their community partners. We know that it is hard to explain to a thesis committee or an editor why a piece of work is progressing slowly or in unanticipated directions, and that the actual goal is to collect good-quality data under existing conditions in order to help others better understand and address problems they face rather than testing hypotheses or answering predetermined research questions.

Researchers who use a modified PAR (mPAR) approach can more easily follow the rules of academic research and still get the job done in a way that fits within the PAR framework. The mPAR model may, in fact, be highly acceptable to communities where a more structured approach, including a predetermined timeline and outcomes, along with opportunities to learn about how to do rigorous research, is welcomed.

The charm of PAR, for those of us who choose to follow this path, is that it is a way to promote social change and justice using the skills, talents, and training that we have. This is not to de-legitimize the work of researchers who are not interested in PAR and yet aim to improve others' quality of life, such as by conducting a randomized clinical trial to assess the efficacy of a new and potentially life-saving drug). Rather, PAR, and in particular mPAR, is an underutilized means of bridging the gap between pursuing a career as an academic or professional researcher and helping improve the quality of life of communities we are associated with.

The challenge of PAR is how to straddle the two worlds many of us face: the community we are in "PAR" with and our professional home world—academia, research consulting, or a combination of the two. Over time, we expect that there will be more PAR-proficient role models in the academic world as the message that PAR does not have to be an "all or nothing" high-stakes career gamble is more widely heard. To that end, modified PAR (mPAR) can be a respected, rewarding, and useful way to conduct applied research in the spaces where university and community meet.

GLOSSARY

cPAR: Classic participatory action research occurs when the community under study defines the problem, analyzes it, and solves it. The people own the information and may contract the services of academic researchers to assist in this process.

cPIR: Classic principal investigator research model. The professional or academic researcher sets the research agenda, makes all decisions about the research question to be pursued, data collection, methods of analysis, and how and where to disseminate findings.

Emic perspective: The research strategy that focuses on the local person's explanations, categories, and criteria of significance.

Etic perspective: The research strategy that emphasizes the observer's rather than the local person's explanations, categories, and criteria of significance.

mPAR: Modified participatory action research blends elements of classic participatory research with classic principal investigator research.

REFERENCES

Elden, M., & Levin, M. (1991). Cogenerative learning: Bringing participation into action research. In W.F. Whyte (Ed.), *Participatory action research* (pp. 127–142). Newbury Park, CA: Sage Publications.

Ervin, A. (2000). Participatory action research. In *Applied anthropological tools and perspectives for contemporary practice* (pp. 199–210). Boston: Allyn and Bacon.

Freire, P. (1970). *Pedagogy of the oppressed.* New York: Seabury Press.

Freire, P. (1982). Creating alternative research methods: Learning to do it by doing it. In B. Hall, A. Gilliette, & R. Tanden, *Creating Knowledge: A Monopoly? Participatory Research in Development* (pp. 29–37). New Delhi: Society for Participatory Research in Asia, and Toronto: International Council for Adult Education.

Gaventa, J. (1993). The powerful, the powerless, and the experts: Knowledge struggles in the information age. In P. Park, M. Braden-Miller, B. Hall, & T. Jackson (Eds.), *Voices of change: Participatory research in the United States and Canada* (pp. 21–40). Westport, CT: Begin & Harvey.

Hall, B.L. (1977). *Creating knowledge: Breaking the monopoly.* Toronto: Participatory Research Project of the International Council for Adult Education.

Hall, B. (1981). Participatory research, popular knowledge and power: A personal reflection. *Convergence, 14*(3), 6–19.

Hall, B. (1992). From margin to centre? The development and purpose of participatory research. *The American Sociologist, 26*(1), 15–27.

Hall, B. (1993). Introduction. In P. Park, M. Braden-Miller, B. Hall, & T. Jackson (Eds.), *Voices of change: Participatory research in the United States and Canada.* (pp. i–xxii). Westport, CT: Begin & Harvey.

Hall, B., Gillette, A., & Tandon, R. (Eds.). (1982). Creating knowledge: A monopoly? *Participatory Research in Development.* New Delhi: Society for Participatory Research in Asia, pp. 29–37.

Law, M. (1993). Changing disabling environments through participatory action-research: A Canadian experience. In S.E. Smith & D.G. Willms (Eds.), with N.A. Johnson, *Nurtured by knowledge: Learning to do participatory action-research* (pp. 34–58). Ottawa: International Development Research Centre.

Lindsey, E., & McGuinness, L. (1998). Significant elements of community involvement in participatory action research: Evidence from a community project. *Journal of Advanced Nursing, 28*(5), 1106–1114.

Lindsey, E., & Stajduhar, K. (1998). From rhetoric to action: Establishing community participation in AIDS-related research. *Canadian Journal of Nursing Research, 30*(1), 137–152.

Park, P. (1993). What is participatory research? A theoretical and methodological perspective. In P. Park, M. Braden-Miller, B. Hall, & T. Jackson (Eds.), *Voices of change: Participatory research in the United States and Canada* (pp. 1–19). Westport, CT: Begin & Harvey.

Rahman, M.A. (1991). The theoretical standpoint of PAR. In O. Fals Borda & M.A. Rahman (Eds.), *Action and knowledge: Breaking the monopoly with participatory action research* (pp. 13–23). New York: Apex Press.

Ryan, J., & Robinson, M. (1990). Implementing participatory research in the Canadian North: A case study of the Gwich'in language and culture project. *CULTURE, 10*(2), 57–73.

Ryan, J., & Robinson, M. (1996). Community participatory research: Two views from Arctic Institute practitioners. *Practicing Anthropology, 18*(4), 7–11.

Smith, S., & Williams, D. (Eds., with N. Johnson) (1993). *Nurtured by knowledge: Learning to do participatory action-research.* Ottawa: International Development Research Centre.

Smith, S.E. (1993). Deepening participatory action-research. In S.E. Smith & D.G. Williams, (Eds., with N. Johnson), *Nurtured by knowledge: Learning to do participatory action-research* (pp. 173–263). Ottawa: International Development Research Centre.

Stringer, E.T. (1999). *Principles of community-based research.* Thousand Oaks, CA: Sage Publications.

Tandon, R. (1988). Social transformation participatory research. *Convergence, 21*(2–3), 5–18.

Whyte, W.F. (Ed.). (1991). Introduction. In *Participatory action research* (pp. 7–15). Newbury Park: Sage Publications.

Whyte, W.F., Greenwood, D.J., & Lazes, P. (1991). Through practice to science in social research. In W.F. Whyte (Ed.), *Participatory action research* (pp. 19–55). Newbury Park: Sage Publications.

PART 1B

INTERVIEWING STRATEGIES

Chapter 4

Self-Presentation and Social Poetics: Active Interview Tactics in Research with Public Figures

Andrew D. Hathaway and Michael F. Atkinson

INTRODUCTION

The need to establish and maintain good rapport with interviewees is supported by most social scientists, and especially qualitative field researchers. Researchers often inhibit themselves unnecessarily, however, by overly accommodating informants' responses during interview sessions (Becker, 1954, 1970). Such a non-reflexive approach to interviewing undermines our contribution to the research process. More innovative methods are needed to lay bare hidden agendas, ideologies, and other information that would not otherwise have been uncovered by "passive" interviewing (Dexter, 1970; Douglas, 1976; Miller & Tewksbury, 2001; Tourangeau & Smith, 1996). Studies involving "public figures" (Spector, 1980), in particular, present a research challenge of this nature. Public figures often are compelled to participate in research to voice a worldview "on the record" (Levy & Hollan, 1998). An additional task in such cases becomes to examine critically the accounts of interviewees, and work towards further disclosure. This may involve overt challenges of the type used by journalists, police, and other professionals (see Altheide, 2002; McKenzie, 2002; Roth, 1962; Zoppi & Epstein, 2002) as a way to gain more fully rounded narratives.

Elsewhere we describe an approach to interviewing that is modelled on a strategy of police interrogation (Hathaway & Atkinson, 2003). Playing "good cop" during an interview facilitates candour and trust while setting the stage for more aggressive "bad cop" tactics. These sorts of **"active interviews"** (Gubrium & Holstein, 1997), more generally, ideally resemble the informal structure of everyday talk and interaction. Obtrusiveness and disagreement are natural tools of conversation (Schwalbe, 2002). Thus, we ought to go beyond the role of accommodating listener to sometimes issue challenges and coax more information. This works best, in our experience, when the researcher shares with the informant an intimate familiarity with the subject of investigation. In the following case studies, we drew on our status as insiders in two very different communities. In the studies undertaken—on drug reform advocates and tattoo artists, respectively—active interviews provided the kind of information that may not otherwise have been imparted.

Box 4.1: Classic Case Studies in Cultural Anthropology

In his study of witchcraft in the Azande tribe of Sudan, Evans-Pritchard (1937) provided an early description of how preliminary knowledge and deception might be used to gather information from informants. Working in league with his research confederate (a local witchdoctor-in-training named Kamanga), the anthropologist played on the jealous pride of two rival practitioners to trick them into revealing their most closely guarded secrets. *Behind Many Masks* (1962) details Berreman's research among the Paharis of India. His Indian research confederate Sharma possessed different social statuses than Berreman. Thus, he was able to approach and extract from the Paharis views that reflected these multiple standpoints. Instead of two or more distinct characters playing off one another and their different interactions with the subject, the range of interview tactics outlined in this chapter are enacted by a single researcher working to gain undisclosed information.

Box 4.2: Note on Ethics

"Conflict methodologists" (see Christie, 1976; Lundman & McFarlane, 1974; Young, 1976) go so far as to assume that research informants are inevitably deceptive. Interviewers are accordingly justified, they argue, in using deception to secure valid data. The method we describe is not based on deception, but rather a more natural (and ethical) adherence to the dynamics of everyday talk and interaction. This involves changing the context of interviews so as to elicit new insights from informants by issuing challenges and engaging in debate. The people we interviewed were public figures accustomed to being questioned intently on controversial viewpoints and activities. A strategic approach to interviewing need not be seen as deceptive or coercive, although power imbalances between research participants may in part determine the propriety of certain tactics. None of the questioning styles outlined in this chapter were socially, personally, or emotionally destructive. In our experience, moreover, the researcher-informant relationship was actually strengthened. We apparently gained more respect from our informants by openly engaging in debate through conversation.

TWO CASE STUDIES

Claims Making by Drug Reform Advocates

Hathaway (1999) interviewed 13 Canadian drug reformers, most of whom are well-known in drug policy circles. The fact that the participants are recognizable public figures made the sampling procedure and preparation for interviewing quite different from most other field studies (Spector, 1980). Interviews came later on in the research, and were geared to exploring interpretations of informants that do not appear in public documents (e.g., academic publications, court and legislative transcripts, media reports, editorials, and activist literature). Use of the research interview as a **"claims making"** (Spector & Kitsuse, 1977) forum takes on new significance when informants' prior assertions are on the public record.

Unlike in most other types of field research, names and affiliations are especially relevant to the analysis and presentation of the data. Indeed, the standard guarantees of anonymity and confidentiality may be neither desirable nor necessary in research involving public figures (Odendahl & Shaw, 2002; Rainwater & Pittman, 1967). Well-known informants expect to be quoted and hold the interviewer responsible for quoting them directly. A neglected complication of such research is the problem of penetrating the public performances of informants who know that they will be identified by name with their statements. Many of the participants were themselves researchers, which tended to facilitate the course of interaction. Often asked where he stood on the issues in question, Hathaway employed whatever knowledge he possessed as a "lubricant" (Klassen & LeBlanc, 1993) to gain more revealing exchanges and garner further insights from informants.

Put otherwise—in terms long familiar to cultural anthropologists (see Box 4.1)—the interviewer sought to interactively explore the cultural intimacy, or **social poetics** (Clifford & Marcus, 1986; Herzfeld, 1997), embedded in this form of open-ended talk. Strategic application of cultural discourse is open to researchers as well as research subjects. Interviewers may thereby employ their own tactics to strategize around what we share with informants, and what sets us apart as outsiders. Where **dramaturgical analysis** (see Goffman, 1959, 1974) essentially separates performative and everyday social interaction, the fluidity of social poetics suggests an analytical approach along the lines of a continuum (see Figure 4.1). To illustrate this process, the interviewer initially encouraged elaboration of perspectives already on the record.

A book by drug reform advocate, Bruce Alexander, for example, theorizes the continuance of a "temperance mentality" (Alexander, 1990). The interviewer sought to gain a fuller description of this notion through accommodating questions phrased in the first person. Thus, he asked the interviewee: [Hathaway] "Are we seeing changes in the temperance mentality over time?" [Alexander] "I don't know ... the temperance movement has changed its content ... But still the essential content of the temperance movement is that there are two classes of drugs, the demonic ones and the beneficial, wonderful ones ... That concept is alive today as it ever was. It's just that the drugs on both sides have shifted ..." [Hathaway] "So despite all that's written about rational reform, we must continue to work to make small differences

Figure 4.1: Active Interview Continuum

Neutral to Active → Skepticism, Playing Dumb, → Direct Personal Challenges and Accommodation → Other Indirect Challenges →   Outright Confrontation

→→→ Researcher's level of engagement with the views of the respondent →→→

within the same basic framework?" [Alexander] "Exactly, and I think it needs to be understood in this larger way, because I don't think we can do much about it."

Accommodating follow-up questions facilitate a rapport-building sense of mutual perspective, and set the stage for more tactical, active engagement. These tactics may range from mild skepticism to more confrontational challenges. Examples of first steps along the continuum were long ago outlined by Becker (1954). He reported that he had coerced his informants into being more candid than they had intended. Becker did so by assuming a skeptical air and "playing dumb" about facts that were taken for granted. This invokes from informants a fuller account of their opinions and presses for further disclosed information. While Professor Alexander's conception of "temperance" was initially accepted, for example, his view is later called into question in the interest of clarification. With a skeptical air, the interviewer asked him: "Isn't temperance more about moderation than prohibition?" [Alexander] "No, it's all about prohibition. Temperance is just a misnomer for it ... The initial temperance people really were in favour of moderational temperance. But ... by 1830, they were all about prohibition."

Another illustration is drawn from an interview with Dr. Diane Riley, an advocate for harm reduction. This public health perspective on drug policy favours a value-neutral approach to drug abuse problems, addressing them in pragmatic rather than moral terms (Erickson, Riley, Cheung, & O'Hare, 1997). Harm reduction is widely supported by experts and officially endorsed by the Government of Canada. Yet, in the broader scheme of global drug politics, the perspective is largely marginalized and has been disavowed by the United Nations. Seeking further insights, the interviewer questioned Riley about a UN meeting on the global drug problem (June 1998) that neglected harm reduction groups outright. Hathaway asked: "Why wouldn't a harm reduction group like yours be granted official standing at this meeting?" [Riley] "Because of the name; the UN is very opposed to harm reduction." [Hathaway] "Is this not a widely accepted paradigm today?" [Riley] "Oh no, absolutely not! No, the accepted paradigm by the UN is prohibition. And there is no funding whatsoever; they will not fund countries that do harm reduction ... No, it's quite the opposite."

As a way to pursue undisclosed information or merely to clarify prior ambiguities, assuming a skeptical tone with informants can provoke the kind of statements that often go unsaid. The ambiguity in this case concerns the extent to which harm reduction has gained official acceptance as a viable drug policy alternative. Extended skeptical inquiry also provided insight into Riley's undisclosed ideological position. When she brought up the issue of rights and drug policy, the interviewer asked, "Is more ground being made on the human rights side of drug use than in harm reduction?" Dr. Riley replied: "No ... because in most countries, trying to sell anything on a human rights platform is useless ... you have to find some other way in ..." [Hathaway] "So despite your earlier comments on the overall lack of acceptance for harm reduction principles, it's still the best prospect for changes in policy?" [Riley] "Well yes ... I think it's the answer, and it's a stepping stone towards broader policy reform. The end's got to be much more than harm reduction but it's a good stepping stone, and for the moment I think it's the solution to many problems."

Skepticism is used to probe beneath the informant's value-neutral position to reveal a humanistic underlying moral standpoint. Another ploy of Becker's (1954) proved useful in exploring the so-called "American influence" on Canadian drug policy. Law professor Alan Young brought up the issue as follows: "The only reason why Canada is not moved by this issue is our geographical proximity to the United States, which for their own bizarre and perverse reasons believe that the war on drugs is an important part of their domestic policy ..." [Hathaway] "So Canada and the US are very much linked in respect to drug policy?" [Young] "Of course they are! What, you don't think the United States doesn't flex their muscle around the world on their drug policy? ... They have troops in Bolivia, they have troops in Colombia. They use the drug war as an excuse to infiltrate other countries and influence their national policy."

Despite his earlier exposure to similar perspectives, the interviewer played dumb in order to elicit a more detailed and forceful response. Such tactics run the risk of antagonizing informants, who may become impatient with an uninformed researcher. The exercise of due discretion is thereby required, based on the interviewer's reading of the circumstances and observed temperament of his or her informant. Although a knowing nod may at times be more appropriate, these tactics and the more aggressive ones that follow enriched the range and quality of data we recorded.

Tattoo Art and the Business of Tattooing

Atkinson's (2003) research on tattoo enthusiasm in Canada included interviews with 27 artists encountered in tattoo studios, local hangouts, at conventions, and through friendship networks. The artists ranged widely in terms of their professional experience and the extent to which they were known in the Canadian tattoo figuration. With most of them having participated in media interviews on the practice, the majority had some level of experience as public spokespersons for tattooing. Although their anonymity was upheld by the researcher, many expected and specifically requested to be identified in final reports of the study.

Early interview questions explored artists' narratives about the art and business of tattooing. Atkinson later adopted a more aggressive tone to challenge certain aspects of these narratives. Initial accommodation was found to be useful for eliciting "**front work**" (Douglas 1972) performances from the artists about the cultural meaning(s) of tattooing. They promoted tattooing as a form of cultural difference, often in terms of personal empowerment, bonding with others, or symbolizing commitment to a certain lifestyle. The interviewer used questions such as the following to encourage elaboration of this view of tattooing as personally meaningful artwork: "A lot of people talk about tattooing as an art. What does the term art mean to you, and how do you see tattooing as an art?"; "Is there a difference between how you view the art as a person who wears tattoos and how you see it as a person who does tattooing?"; "How do you see your roles in shaping the way people view the art of tattooing? Do you keep this in mind when talking to people about tattoos?"

Since the researcher shared the social status of a tattoo enthusiast, his use of the first person served to reinforce mutual understandings and create a more amiable interview context. For example, he asked informants: "Do you think there is something we [tattoo enthusiasts] can do to make people more tolerant of tattooed bodies?"; "Is there an effective way to get our perspectives across so that people might better understand the meanings we associate with the art?" Establishing himself in this way as an empathetic listener and confidant, the interviewer facilitated further development and articulation of these front-stage narratives. The "involvement-detachment" (Goudsblom & Mennell, 1998) pendulum is swung towards personal involvement as a technique to build rapport, generate trust, and refine taken-for-granted cultural understandings.

Integral to the staging of this performance is the researcher's ability to converse with interviewees in their own terms, assuming the experiential knowledge needed to discuss their activities with insight and conceptual direction. By declaring involvement and personal interest in the subject, Atkinson fostered a context of mutual identification that facilitated more in-depth conversations (see Ellis & Berger, 2002). Playing the standard role of non-judgmental listener, he established a context of friendly interchange to encourage elaboration by informants. Later on more skeptical and confrontational questions were used to probe beneath perceived front-work performances. Atkinson's transition to more aggressive lines of inquiry was based on his impression that unstated motivations informed the artists' promotion of tattooing as culturally meaningful artwork.

Initially, the change in tactics consisted of indirect challenges to what the interviewer saw as an idealized construction of the practice. He asked, for example:

Atkinson: "What do you say to people who claim that tattooing isn't really an art, or even a low-class art?"

Artist: "Some of the best artists I know do tattoos, and just because their art isn't hanging in some gallery, it doesn't mean it's crap. Who is anybody, really, to criticize what I do for a living and say it isn't worth much? I don't jump around saying all lawyers are scumbags or all postmen are lazy ... As long as my work is respected by my clients, that's fine with me."

Atkinson: "A recent newspaper article claimed that the contemporary boom in tattooing is nothing more than a fad among youth in Canada ... Do you see yourself as someone who is cashing in on a popular trend right now but who will need to move on to something more socially useful in the future when people don't think tattoo art is cool anymore?"

Artist: "Tattooing has been around for a long time, and my main concern is to appeal to the people who are serious about tattooing ... I have to run my business with them in mind, not the posers who aren't committed ... And if all the recent attention given to tattooing solidifies a loyal client base, that's the best thing that can come out of it for all of us [tattoo artists]."

Appeals of this nature, to the assumed business sense of the researcher, comprised "narrative clues" (Weiss, 1994) as to the disparity between art-centred ideologies and later emphasis on profits. Making earlier challenges more forthright and personal served to highlight the noted discrepancy. Two examples of this tactic are as follows:

> Even though tattoo artists have cleaned up their studios in recent years and are trying to attract more middle-class, discerning, and artistically inclined clients, I've noticed that artists still revel in the image of the rebel or the outsider and use this to sell the practice. Why, then, should we [non-tattoo artists] believe that artists are really trying to make this into a respectable art form? Wouldn't it really hurt the business of tattooing if it ever became a fully respectable form of expression?
>
> If you ... do what you do in order to expand cultural understandings of the body, why are your service fees so high? I mean, the whole spiel about individuality, creativity, and meaningfulness ... isn't that just a neat way of carving out a lucrative way of doing what you love?

In response to such questions, artists typically denied commercial exploitation. At the same time, however, they acknowledged promoting New Age views of the body (see Demello, 2000; Featherstone, 2000) as a way to sustain their clientele and long-term profits. This "back-stage" (Goffman, 1959) view of the practice may have never come to light had the artists' front work not been met by challenges.

DISCUSSION

By approaching the interview as a kind of performance, we provided examples of ways by which to probe behind the scenes. Qualitative research is often judged by the researcher's ability to uncover information concealed in everyday interaction (Berreman, 1962; Prus, 1980). Failure to account for what is undisclosed impedes a fuller understanding of the lives of our informants. Although they often adopt a value-neutral position, the political stance of many drug reform advocates owes much to the moral philosophy of liberalism with its emphasis on choice and personal freedom (Hathaway, 2001, 2002). Although tattoo artists readily impart their ideologies of art and free expression, the profit motive behind these promotions emerges with deeper probing of their narratives. As public figures, with prior media experience, both groups of informants were accustomed to interviewers challenging their views and activities. Accordingly, on our part, a more benign approach to interviews seemed unwarranted.

Use of the described tactics stimulated production of interpretive standpoints that would have been neglected in a strictly empathetic interview. Rather than steering away from such critical lines of inquiry, we sought to extend the occurrence of everyday confrontations and challenges to the scientific realm of data collection. In Bauman's (1978) terms, a shift in verbal performance is required to disrupt the standard flow of information in an interview, allowing active exploration of alternative narratives. While mediating the performance and responses of the other, one draws on shared understandings of the subject matter to access what lies behind the framework of appearances projected. Seemingly embedded norms or regularities are subject to negotiation, requiring a skilled appreciation of what others consider the regularities to be in practice.

Refusing to engage our commonalities and differences is both inconsistent and condescending when we expect respondents to speak openly with us (Herzfeld, 1997). It should come as no surprise when such engagement is lacking that interviewees merely respond to us rather than converse with us. In heeding Prus's (1996) call to pursue intersubjectivity, we contend that disagreement and confrontation can be fruitfully injected into the interview process. There is a need for due discretion based on our intuition or cost-benefit appraisal of pursuing the more confrontational approaches (see Box 4.2). While highly sensitive issues are sometimes beyond our grasp, however, shared life experience may facilitate probing into difficult areas. A wider range of options is certainly available as we gain familiarity with others and vice versa. Extended participant observation thereby makes asking challenging questions more feasible (Dewalt & Dewalt, 1998).

CONCLUSION

Opting to pursue a more critical line of inquiry in interviews is ultimately contingent on the social poetics, or cultural understandings, that contextualize the relationship between research participants. While this tactic is not appropriate in each and every situation, the standard kid-glove treatment of most social scientists neglects the social insight of intimate familiarity while tacitly encouraging superficial front work by informants. By venturing beyond these often well-rehearsed performances, to recognize and confront them with presentations of our own, we can more fully grasp the research interview's potential for mutual exchange and exploration.

GLOSSARY

Active interviews: An unstructured approach to interviewing that implies full participation and attention by interviewers to their own reactions and responses.

Claims making: The analytical focus of social constructionists, who contend that objective conditions, or "facts," are secondary to what people say about the putative conditions.

Dramaturgical analysis: Employs the metaphor of theatre with particular reference to the front and backstage (i.e., behind-the-scenes) activity that contributes to staging a social performance.

Front work: Viewing social interaction as a kind of performance, front work refers to the selective presentation of views and experience to establish or maintain a particular appearance.

Social poetics: An interpretive approach in the social sciences and humanities to the intersubjective, relational understandings created in everyday conversation.

NOTE
This chapter is adapted from "Active interview tactics in research on public deviants: Exploring the two cop personas," by A.D. Hathaway & M.F. Atkinson, 2003, *Field Methods*, *15*(2), pp. 161–185.

REFERENCES

Alexander, B. (1990). *Peaceful measures: Canada's way out of the war on drugs*. Toronto, ON: University of Toronto Press.

Atkinson, M. (2003). *Tattooed: The sociogenesis of a body art*. Toronto, ON: University of Toronto Press.

Altheide, D. (2002). Journalistic interviewing. In J. Gubrium & J. Holstein (Eds.), *Handbook of interview research: Context and method* (pp. 411–430). Thousand Oaks, CA: Sage.

Bauman, R. (1978). *Verbal art as performance*. Rowley, MA: Newbury House.

Becker, H. (1954). A note on interviewing tactics. *Human Organization, 12*(winter), 31–32.

Becker, H. (1970). *Sociological work: Method and substance*. Chicago, IL: Aldine.

Berreman, G. (1962). *Behind many masks*. Ithaca, NY: Society for Applied Anthropology.

Christie, R. (1976). Comment on conflict methodology: A protagonist position. *Sociological Quarterly, 17*(4), 513–519.

Clifford, J., & Marcus, G. (1986). *Writing culture: The poetics and politics of ethnography*. Berkeley, CA: University of California Press.

Demello, M. (2000). *Bodies of inscription: A cultural history of the modern tattoo community*. Durham, NC: Duke University Press.

Dewalt, K., & Dewalt, B. (1998). Participant observation. In R. Bernard (Ed.), *Handbook of methods in cultural anthropology* (pp. 259–299). Walnut Creek, CA: Altamira.

Dexter, L. (1970). *Elite and specialized interviewing*. Evanston, IL: Northwestern University Press.

Douglas, D. (1972). Managing fronts in observing deviance. In J. Douglas (Ed.), *Research on deviance* (pp. 93–115). New York, NY: Random House.

Douglas, J. (1976). *Investigative social research*. London, UK: Sage.

Ellis, C., & Berger, L. (2002). Their story/my story/our story: Including the researcher's experience in interview research. In J. Gubrium & J. Holstein (Eds.), *Handbook of interview research: Context and method* (pp. 849–876). Thousand Oaks, CA: Sage.

Erickson, P., Riley, D., Cheung, Y., & O'Hare, P. (1997). *Harm reduction: A new direction for drug policies and programs*. Toronto, ON: University of Toronto Press.

Evans-Pritchard, E. (1937). *Witchcraft, oracles and magic among the Azande*. Oxford, UK: Clarendon Press.

Featherstone, M. (2000). *Body modification*. London, UK: Sage.

Goffman, E. (1959). *The presentation of self in everyday life*. Garden City, NY: Doubleday.

Goffman, E. (1974). *Frame analysis*. Cambridge, MA: Harvard University Press.

Goudsblom, J., & Mennell, S. (1998.) *The Norbert Elias reader*. Oxford, UK: Basil Blackwell.

Griffen, C. (1991). The researcher talks back: Dealing with power relations in studies of young people's entry into the job market. In W. Shaffir & R. Stebbins (Eds.), *Experiencing fieldwork: An inside view of qualitative research* (pp. 109–119). Newbury Park, CA: Sage.

Gubrium, J., & Holstein, J. (1997). *The new language of qualitative method*. New York, NY: Oxford University Press.

Hathaway, A. (1999). *Harm reduction, human rights, and Canada's cannabis controversy.* Unpublished doctoral dissertation, McMaster University, Hamilton, Ontario, Canada.

Hathaway, A. (2001). Shortcomings of harm reduction: Toward a morally invested drug reform strategy. *International Journal of Drug Policy, 12*, 125–137.

Hathaway, A. (2002). From harm reduction to human rights: Bringing liberalism back into drug reform debates. *Drug and Alcohol Review, 21*(4), 397–404.

Hathaway, A., & Atkinson, M. (2003). Active interview tactics in research on public deviants: Exploring the two-cop personas. *Field Methods, 15*(2), 161–185.

Herzfeld, M. (1997). *Cultural intimacy: Social poetics in the nation-state.* New York: Routledge.

Klassen, T., & LeBlanc, S. (1993). Methodological issues in sociological research on public policy: Utilizing interviews. *Society, 17*(2), 21–26.

Levy, R., & Hollan, D. (1998). Person-centred interviewing and observation. In R. Bernard (Ed.), *Handbook of methods in cultural anthropology* (pp. 333–364). Walnut Creek, CA: Altamira.

Lundman, R., & McFarlane, P. (1974). Conflict methodology: An introduction and preliminary assessment. *Sociological Quarterly, 17*(4), 503–512.

McKenzie, I. (2002). Forensic investigative interviewing. In J. Gubrium & J. Holstein (Eds.), *Handbook of interview research: Context and method* (pp. 431–452). Thousand Oaks, CA: Sage.

Miller, J., & Tewksbury, R. (2001). *Extreme methods: Innovative approaches to social science research.* Needham Heights, MA: Allyn & Bacon.

Odendahl, T., & Shaw, A. (2002). Interviewing elites. In J. Gubrium & J. Holstein (Eds.), *Handbook of interview research: Context and method* (pp. 299–316). Thousand Oaks, CA: Sage.

Prus, R. (1980). Sociologist as a hustler: The dynamics of acquiring information. In W. Shaffir, R. Stebbins, & A. Turowetz (Eds.), *Fieldwork experience: Qualitative approaches to social research* (pp. 132–145). New York, NY: St. Martin's Press.

Prus, R. (1996). *Symbolic interaction and ethnographic research: Intersubjectivity and the study of human lived experience.* Albany, NY: SUNY Press.

Rainwater, L., & Pittman, D. (1967). Ethical problems in studying a politically sensitive and deviant community. *Social Problems, 14*, 357–366.

Roth, J. (1962). Comments on "secret observation." *Social Problems, 9*(3), 283–284.

Schwalbe, M. (2002). Obtrusiveness as a strategy in ethnographic research. *Qualitative Sociology, 25*(1), 49–61.

Spector, M. (1980). Learning to study public figures. In W. Shaffir, R. Stebbins, & A. Turowetz (Eds.), *Fieldwork experience: Qualitative approaches to social research* (pp. 98–109). New York, NY: St. Martin's Press.

Spector, M., & Kitsuse, J. (1977). *Constructing social problems.* Menlo Park, CA: Cummings.

Tourangeau, R., & Smith, T. (1996). Asking sensitive questions: The impact of data collection mode, question format, and question context. *The Public Opinion Quarterly, 60*(2), 275–304.

Weiss, R. (1994). *Learning from strangers: The art and method of qualitative interview studies.* New York, NY: Free Press.

Young, T. (1976). Some theoretical foundations for conflict methodology. *Sociological Inquiry,* 46(1), 23–29.

Zoppi, K., & Epstein, R. (2002.) Interviewing in medical settings. In J. Gubrium & J. Holstein (Eds.), *Handbook of interview research: Context and method* (pp. 355–384). Thousand Oaks, CA: Sage.

Chapter 5

Conducting Field Research with Young Offenders Convicted of Murder and Manslaughter: Gaining Access, Risks, and "Truth Status"

Mark Totten and Katharine Kelly

INTRODUCTION

This chapter reports on a Canadian qualitative study on **youth homicide** (Kelly & Totten, 2002). Youth homicide is not common in Canada. While homicide rates have risen, the overall number of homicides remains low. In 1975, 18 youth (0.69 per 100,000) were charged with homicide (there are no data on youth convicted); by 1999, this number had risen to 45 youth (2.23 per 100,000). Between 1989 and 1998, a yearly average of 52 young people (the vast majority are male) were charged, ranging from a low of 36 youth in 1987 to a high of 68 youth in 1995 (Statistics Canada, CCJS, 1999, 2000). Putting a human face on youth who commit homicides can provide us with valuable insights into causal factors and enhance services.

The research involved **in-depth interviews** with 19 subjects who were convicted of homicide (homicide includes murder [first and second degree] and manslaughter) while under the age of 18. We wanted to uncover the participant's world from his or her own viewpoint, so we allowed participants to tell us their accounts as they emerged and to guide the sequencing of issues if they so chose. We supplemented these accounts with the interview guide to ensure consistent information from all informants. Each interview was tape recorded and handwritten notes were kept as a backup. The research explored the intentions, meanings, and motives young people ascribe to their actions within the context of having them recount their life experiences. Our theoretical position suggested that involvement with the criminal justice system and in high-risk activities was the result of a lifetime of events that, in turn, contributed to the risk of committing homicide. Using **life course analysis**, experiences in childhood and adolescence, communities, schools, peer groups, families, and the justice and social welfare systems were explored. Contextual factors (those immediate to the homicide) also contributed to the commission of murder.

Conducting qualitative research on youth homicide posed a number of challenges. In-depth interview methodology is susceptible to specific problems regarding interpretation and evaluation (Silverman, 1993; Totten, 2000). A number of issues emerged while conducting this research: **gaining access**, risks (to participants, other individuals, and researchers), and evaluating **account "truth status"** (Silverman, 1993) of accounts. There is limited Canadian research on these issues.

GAINING ACCESS

Researching youth homicide places a number of constraints on researchers. There is no easily accessible list from which to select participants. While convictions are part of the record, under the *Young Offenders Act* (YOA) the names of youthful offenders are sealed. We did not have names of individuals prior to their agreeing to participate. So, we contacted facilities in selected sites and asked if there were any youth convicted of homicide in custody or recently discharged, and if the institutions could contact these young people to explain the study. We used a similar process with parole/probation officers and non-profit organizations. Not all the institutions and individuals we contacted were able and/or willing to identify contacts for us and not all those contacted were willing to participate.

Even after offenders had consented to take part in the study, gaining access to conduct the interviews was not easy. Two offenders were on probation and working full time; two were on parole. These four interviews in the community were relatively simple to set up and conduct; they took place in offices and homes. Accessibility was much more difficult in correctional facilities. Gaining entrance, even with the offender's consent, was a lengthy process and was sometimes denied. Access was easier when our request was supported by a non-profit agency, due to their working relationship with the institution.

Although interviewing under the surveillance of youth workers or guards was difficult, Young Offender (YO) facility staff were generally flexible and supportive. Interviews in penitentiaries, however, were interrupted by inmate "counts" and had to be fit around meal times and guard shift changes. These interviews were more controlled and took place in secure rooms.

Interviews were often volatile, due to the behavioural and emotional difficulties of many offenders. Two examples are illustrative. Both young men had difficulty sitting still, were illiterate, and had serious learning disabilities. They were visual learners and responded best when imagery and drawings were used to illustrate questions. In one case, the interview was split into three sections and took place over a seven-day period. One offender had serious childhood trauma and, at the age of 23, still sucked his thumb. The other young man had a serious stutter. At one point, he asked if he could go to his cell and get his art folder. The guards reluctantly agreed. He showed us his remarkable work. Following this, he was much more engaged and forthcoming about events in his life.

A final aspect of gaining access was reviewing the YO records of participants, which provided documentary accounts of life history, the homicide, and experiences with the justice system. We knew that such records would be useful to compare against the accounts that the offenders provided. Gaining access was challenging. None of the offenders who had served time in the YO system had copies of their predisposition reports, assessments, or any other records (records are the property of the provincial/territorial Probation Service). Relevant professionals had to be contacted directly, using the required consent forms, to initiate access to these records. This took time and in some cases access to these records was denied due to YO administrators' concern regarding liability issues (lawsuits by victims' families).

Access to records was much easier for those in the federal system. We obtained these directly from participants or through their parole officers. We were able to get copies of records for all the participants, but not complete files.

RISKS

The study posed particular risks for our sample, other individuals associated with these offenders, and for ourselves. We went through several ethical reviews and a judicial review to obtain a youth court judge's order. Each of these reviews required us to establish a number of protections for participants and other persons involved in their lives: voluntary participation, informed consent, no harm to participants and others, anonymity and confidentiality.

To prevent harm to offenders, we were careful in our selection process. Those assessed by referral sources as being emotionally or mentally unstable were not interviewed. We worked with local agencies and institutions to provide all participants with follow-up support. We informed participants of what we were required to report in terms of their admission to involvement in life-threatening criminal activity, and cautioned them that if they did reveal such information we would report it.

Two other issues posed risks and limited confidentiality: disclosures of child abuse/neglect and suicidal behaviour. Legislation requires that any professional having suspicion of child maltreatment must report this immediately to the local child welfare agency. As well, we expected that some of the participants would have significant mental health issues. The informed consent form indicated that confidentiality would be breached should any of these issues arise during the interview (Kelly & Totten, 2002).

We had an ethical and a legal obligation to ensure the anonymity and confidentiality of the participants, victims, and their families. However, we were also concerned that if the homicide events were identifiable, the victims' families might be further traumatized. To ensure that participants remained anonymous, we used pseudonyms, did not identify in what region of the country the homicides had occurred, excluded particular details that would identify cases in publications (e.g., weapons used, details on the victims, dates), and removed any names mentioned in the course of the interviews and all personal identifiers from the transcripts.

Both of us suffered vicarious trauma as a result of hearing the accounts of the homicides, reading the records, and learning of the abuse in the lives of some of our participants. This presented a number of concerns. First, from a research perspective, such trauma can negatively impact on data analysis. Second, on a personal level, it can lead to emotional stress and distress (Totten & Kelly, 2004).

TRUTH STATUS OF ACCOUNTS

How truthful were the accounts of the homicides? Norman Denzin notes that interview situations are not unlike conversations between strangers. Because it is difficult to tell if a person is lying, there is a tendency to fabricate in order to present oneself in a positive light. Offenders interacted with us in the interviews. Their responses must be put into the context of our questions and within the context of the whole interview. The level of rapport with participants varied. In some cases, it was quite good, and participants openly shared their experiences, emotions, and behaviours. These participants provided a wealth of unsolicited details and were willing to entertain critical questions about their accounts, behaviours, and experiences. We could confront offenders on inconsistencies and obvious inaccuracies. In other interviews, rapport was low. While participants agreed to answer questions, they were not forthcoming with information and rarely provided accounts on unsolicited issues. When we probed for details, they refused to provide them, changed the subject, or simply shrugged and waited for the next question.

Triangulation of participants' accounts against official records (parole, probation, psychiatric, psychological assessments; YO facility/Correctional Services Canada reports) and media reports provided us with some sense of accuracy, yet these latter documents may have been biased. So, we also used the technique of "investigative discourse analysis" (Rabon, 1994). This allowed us to ascertain whether participants were attempting to *convey* information or *convince* us of a particular position. Don Rabon developed this approach for analyzing accounts of suspects being interviewed by police.

Rabon's argument is that *truthful accounts seek to convey while deceptive accounts seek to convince* the interrogator of a particular interpretation of events. Rabon offers guidelines on how to assess whether an account is truthful independent of triangulation. A narrative has three components: what the subject actually relates; what the subject meant to relate; and what interpretation the investigator makes of the account. The goal of interpretation is to align the first and third components. Accounts are likely to be deceptive when:

(1) The speaker demonstrates a *lack of conviction about his or her own assertions* by using a variety of techniques: modifying or equivocating terms, denial or negation, abjuration, weakened assertions, and stalling. *Modifying or equivocating terms* allow the speaker to "evade the risk" of commitment and indicate that she/he is having difficulty admitting to what is being said. Examples include: "I guess," "I believe," "kind of," "sort of," "hopefully," "I think." *Denial or negation* is "a defense mechanism that disavows or denies thoughts, feelings, wishes, or needs that cause anxiety." In negation, the speaker avoids speaking about what did happen or what she/he does know and instead talks about what she/he did *not* do, what she/he does *not* know, what she/he did *not* observe, what did *not* happen, and so on. *Abjuration terms* serve to withdraw an assertion that was made in the previous clause or sentence. Abjuration terms are usually conjunctions such as "but," "if," "when," "nevertheless." *Weakened assertions* are used when the speaker is attempting to produce additional support for what she/he said. The most common verbs used in weakened assertions are "tried" and "started." Other examples include "to tell you the truth" and "as a matter of fact." *Stalling* allows a speaker to hold back and use pauses, and includes terms like "um," "oh," "uh," "well," "okay now."

(2) Accounts are likely to be untrue when they are *vague or general*. These include temporal lacunae, which mark a blank space or missing details. They indicate that something has been left out or passed over. This includes statements such as "later on," "after that," "by and by," "next thing you know." We felt it was important

to be cautious about such gaps in accounts. Accounts may also be vague because of repression, "a mental process in which anxiety producing mental content is forcefully removed from consciousness and prevented from re-emerging" (Rabon, 1994, p. 18). A general lack of details can indicate that an account is untrue or some other mechanisms are limiting recall.

(3) Accounts that have *limited use or an absence of self-references* may also indicate lack of truth. The absence of the term "I" indicates that the speaker has a lack of commitment to the narrative or to what is being asserted. Use of the possessive pronoun "we" is common in narratives where the speaker is attempting to downplay his or her role in events. While the use of "we" may be difficult to avoid, heavy use of it may indicate that the person sees or wishes to portray him or herself as a passive object of external events or actions that she/he has no control over. Distorted accounts may also have second-person referencing, where the speaker refers to him or herself with the second-person pronoun "you." It suggests that the speaker feels no personal accountability or responsibility for whatever happened. Changes in the use of terms are also important. When and understanding why a speaker shifts from the use of "I" to the use of "we" when referring to her or his actions during particular aspects of events is significant.

(4) Finally, Rabon argues that *shifts in verb tense are important*. In particular, when a speaker uses the present tense to refer to past events, this is a signal that the account is not truthful. The speaker is constructing the account in the moment and uses the correct verb tense for this process, but an incorrect tense for describing events in the past.

First, we used Rabon's approach to assess the truth status of accounts for those participants for whom we had gained access to official records. If this method proved useful for accounts we could triangulate, we assumed that it would also be useful for accounts with limited supporting documentation.

Below, we assess the truth status of homicide accounts from two interviews. In both cases, the participants had been convicted and admitted some involvement. However, Scott's account suggests that he was being deceptive; he lied about the brutality of the murder. Phillip's account suggests that he was being honest. This analysis is in line with official records.

SCOTT: AN UNTRUTHFUL ACCOUNT?

Scott had been diagnosed as a sadistic psychopath and was in a medium-security facility. He had been convicted of first-degree murder and was serving a consecutive sentence for two torture-beatings. He was 27 years of age and had already spent 10 years in prisons. Scott was a victim of extreme abuse as a child and had experienced severe head trauma at age two. His father was an abusive alcoholic. Scott was illiterate, learning disabled, and had been addicted to crack cocaine and alcohol since age 14. He claimed to have been clean since his incarceration. Scott attempted to manage the interview and came with binders full of art work and newspaper clippings of his crimes.

Scott's account has a number of features that suggest he lacked conviction. He used abjuration to justify his involvement in the second (fatal) assault. Scott

BOX 5.1: Lines 1–35: Scott's Homicide Account

1. **Scott:** "This guy comes walking up and wants a drink at the water fountain and *I'm like okay,*

2. go ahead. Then my (co-accused) and my (friend) start bothering the guy."

3. **Int:** "When you say they were bothering the guy …"

4. **Scott:** "Yeah, … he was a street individual. (They were) laughing at him and hassling him. And

5. *I'm like* what happens if you end up being like that one day, and *um, I guess* they got a hold of

6. something in his pocket—to me it looked like a handkerchief 'cause *I wasn't that close* to him

7. and my (friend) says well there's a woman's underpants in your pocket, like what do you got

8. them for … I don't know why they're there … if that's your fetish, that's your fetish … *But*

9. *anyways* my son's mother ended up going to the water fountain to get a drink and he was

10. mumbling some words to her, you know, like what are you doing with these losers, ah, I took

11. an insult to that … so I started a conflict with him like who the fuck are you calling a loser?

12. They're pestering you, I'm not bothering you … He turned around and I'm yelling at him like

13. you know, why are you calling me a fucking loser, I didn't do anything you know what I

14. mean? So he says if you want to deal with it, we'll deal with it. So I ended up being in a

15. fistfight with this guy I don't even know. It was like I don't want to fight you. First of all,

16. I'm just not going to sit there while you're calling me a loser—why are you telling her that

17. I'm a loser? *Anyways it ended up* being a fistfight and *I knew right before I was getting into it*

18. *that you don't stand a chance. I'm a lot younger than you first of all, second of all you're*

19. *clearly out of shape—I'm not, and third of all I don't know what your past history is, but I*

20. *can take one hell of a beating. So … it was a mistake.* I should have known better and to stop,

21. but I didn't stop. *So,* and I kept telling the guy "stay down, stay down" and he kept trying to

22. get back up and he kept taking swings and everything else … It was really embarrassing

23. because a cat and dog fight you know like who's gonna win—you know the dog's gonna

24. win. *So it ended up we* left, he was alive and my (co-accused)—he just got out of jail and

25. he's getting all nervous—oh the guy's going to identify us and blah, blah, blah and I said

26. listen—we'll go back and see how he's doing—that's it. So we go back and see how the guy's

27. doing and the guy's lying on a bench and we say hey, are you all right? And he's like fuck

28. this. I'm not looking at why the guy's mad, but now you look at it ten years later—the guy

29. just got punched, of course he's gonna be pissed off, you know. So, but I'm not thinking of

30. that, *as a kid*, you know, and *I'm like* "you haven't had enough," you know what I mean … my

31. (co-accused) started beating him. *Next thing you know*, the next morning I find out the guy's

32. dead … My son's mother went to the store to buy cigarettes and she brought back the

33. newspaper."

34. **Int:** "So you didn't know this guy at all. The second altercation—did you take part in it at all?"

35. **Scott:** "Yeah I did, I did. I kicked him, punched him."

qualified his actions (line 29) with a whole string of terms in an attempt to justify his behaviour. He said: "So, but, I'm not thinking of that, as a kid, you know, and …" He insisted that at the time of the fatal assault, he was not aware that the victim had every reason to be angry with him and his co-accused. Scott also used the abjuration term "but" when he linked his assertion that the victim's alleged sexual perversion was not important with the escalation of the incident into a physical assault (lines 7, 8).

Scott also used negation in his description of the initial encounter. He insisted that he did not know why the victim had underwear in his pocket, and that he did not care. He did not describe what was actually going on. He again used negation when he said, "I didn't do anything" (line 13), though we still don't know what was done. When describing the beginning of the first assault, he insisted that he did not want to fight (line 15), suggesting that he was forced to fight the victim. He also used negation when describing the second assault ("I'm not thinking") to explain why he assaulted the man again when the victim neither insulted nor attacked him.

Scott used a modifying term ("as a kid") to attempt to convince us that his involvement in the second (unprovoked assault) "made sense" at the time. He made references to cultural understandings of factors that might explain "bad" behaviour. While Scott described himself as a kid, he was 17 years old at the time of the killing.

There is a weak assertion (note the use of "started" at line 31) with reference to the start of the assault. The co-accused simply began beating the victim. There is no explanation of why, or what he does. Scott only acknowledged his own involvement after probing. Although there were some instances of stalling in the account, we need to be cautious here. Pauses may reflect memory problems recalling events.

Scott used vague words to attempt to cover up what really happened. Instead of telling us how the assault began by describing who struck the first blow, Scott glossed over this by using the phrase "So I started a conflict with him ..." (line 11). It appears from what follows that there was an argument. While Scott reported what he himself said, he was silent on what the victim said, except to insist that the victim invited a fight (lines 14, 15): "So he says if you want to deal with it, we'll deal with it." Note the use of the abjuration term "so" in this account. Scott attempted to get us to see the victim as provoking the assault.

Another attempt to gloss over details is found in Scott's account of the taking of the article from the victim's pocket. Scott said he "guessed" they got hold of something from the victim's pocket (lines 5, 6). How did they get the article from the victim? Had an assault already begun? These details are missing, rendering the account suspect. Scott distanced himself further from these events with the use of a negative (line 6), where he said he "wasn't that close to him [victim]." When Scott described the final assault, there was a temporal lacuna instead of specific details: "Next thing you know, the next morning I find out the guy's dead."

Scott's account uses self-references when describing verbal exchanges. He used the possessive "my" when referring to the other people he was with (and to his son). This suggests possessiveness and a self-centred view of the world. Scott's use of the term "I" vanishes when he referred to the assaults. While details are missing, Scott's removal of himself from the account portrays the assault as something he witnessed rather than took part in; alternately it was something he was compelled to do because of the actions of others. He refers to his own actions only on direct questioning (line 35). The absence of self references conveys to the listener that Scott had no, or only a minor, part in the assaults.

Scott's account switches between the past and present tenses at critical junctures, such as when he described his estimation of the victim's disadvantage in a fight (lines 18–20). He used the present tense to say "the victim does not stand a chance" and to assert the advantages he had. This switch is apparent again when he described their second encounter. Details about how many and what types of blows are absent.

Overall, the application of Rabon's method suggests that Scott was lying. We found through triangulation with official records that the final assault was more brutal than Scott described (there was no accounting of the initial assaults). For example, the fatal blows were the result of Scott and his co-accused jumping off a bench onto the victim's chest.

PHILLIP: A TRUTHFUL ACCOUNT?

At the time of the interview, 22-year-old Phillip was in a minimum-security facility, having served six years of a seven-year sentence for manslaughter. Institutionalized as a child in "too many psychiatric facilities to count," his parents were supportive but clearly overwhelmed. There was no abuse at home, but Phillip had significant problems coping with school and serious substance abuse issues. He described himself as a "loner" and "social outcast." He was 17 at the time of the homicide.

Phillip's account contains some lack of conviction, and there are instances of negation. When these are considered in context, however, they do not simply suggest that the account is untrue. The first occurrence (lines 5–7) is when he was not sure why his girlfriend was yelling the victim's name. They were both high, and this might have affected her behaviour. The second assertion suggests an attempt at social desirability. At line 15, he insisted that killing the victim really "wasn't an option" in his mind and that he drew the line at murder. He followed this with an abjuration term, "But on the other hand …", where he tried to justify continuing to talk about killing the victim with his girlfriend. He explained that he would have been lost without her and so he continued the mind game, hoping that she was not serious. Phillip said that he wanted her to see him as loving because he had agreed to kill the victim. He used negation when he noted that "nothing seemed to break it up" (lines 23, 24). There is another negation where he insisted "rage really had nothing to do with it" (line 26), but this may refer back to an earlier dialogue in the interview regarding his frequent rages in childhood. There is no stalling in this account. This may be because Phillip did not use these techniques in day-to-day speech, or because he had clear recall of the events. It may also reflect the truthfulness of the account.

This account is not detailed, but it is also not simply vague. There are vague terms used. These include "whatnot" (lines 2 and 9), "on occasion" (line 2), "the whole fluke" (lines 3, 4) and "this and that" (line 10). They refer to the drug use—what they took and how much—to details of the sexual assault on Phillip's girlfriend by the victim, and to what the girlfriend wanted Phillip to do to the victim. The absence of some of these details is not problematic. This is because they are not important to the homicide account. The absence of sexual assault details may indicate that the assault did not occur. There are also some temporal lacunae. At line 28, Phillip noted, "So anyway, it was somewhere from the game to becoming a reality." He passed over the process by which he actually decided to kill the victim, and moved from the bedroom down the hall to the victim's room. There is a second lacuna at line 31, where Phillip said, "Then what evolved …" He glossed over the details of the assault. This loss of detail does not (contrary to Scott's case) suggest that Phillip was not taking responsibility but rather suggests a social desirability factor.

On the other hand, the description of the assault itself contains some clear (and chilling) details. Phillip noted that the assault began with his hitting the victim with a baseball bat and that the first blow was very hard. He then gave some information that he hit the victim several more times. He attempted to explain why he did this. Finally, he described getting a knife and slitting the victim's throat. While the details are few, they are in sharp contrast to the details provided by Scott. Phillip reported what he did, and placed himself as an actor in the homicide.

Unlike Scott, Phillip used self-references throughout. Approximately two-thirds of the lines contain the self-referent "I" at least once. These referents are present in

BOX 5.2: Lines 1–37: Phillip's Homicide Account

1.　"Basically what happened, was that I had been living there and the girlfriend would come over

2.　all of the time, and we'd do our drugs *and whatnot*. I had went out on occasion to the store,

3.　and she stayed behind at the apartment. The night after, we were using LSD, coke, *the whole*

4.　*fluke*, and we went to the bedroom and were having sex. In the process of that, she had

5.　basically started calling out his name, saying, "No ***, no ***." I said, "I'm not ***, what are

6.　you talking about?" Of course, there's the confusion of the LSD here too, so I'm not sure if

7.　she's *just, you know, or whatever*. Anyway, she started crying, and broke down and told me

8.　that the night before, when I had been away at the store, that (the victim) had forced her to

9.　give him head *and whatnot*. That she wanted him dead, 'cause she couldn't stand him

10.　anymore, and that basically, she wanted him dead *and this and that*. It went from there where

11.　she was telling me she wanted him dead and this is how she wanted it done. Sort of like a

12.　mind game that she was playing, you know. I wasn't perceiving it as serious or what, but,

13.　this is what she was saying. I, at the time, wasn't sure of what I even felt. I was confused and

14.　everything. In my mind, I had no intention of killing him, I wasn't going to kill him. That

15.　sort of was where I drew the line. It wasn't an option as far as I was concerned. But on the

16.　other hand, we were very co-dependent, and I felt without her I was as good as dead anyway,

17.　so I felt obligated to play along with the game anyway. At least convince her I was capable

18.　of doing something like that, that if she wanted it done, that I would do it. But the thing was,

19.　I figured she'd come out and say she's not serious, or someone's going to come over, you

20.　know, that I could play this game right up to the point that she would do it, but that

21.　something would interrupt it. Then my ass would be covered, and I could say, "Well, you

22. know, I would've done it for you, baby, but this happened." That would've been the break,

23. right? Somewhere in the process of acting it and playing along with it, of course, nothing

24. seemed to break it up, but also, *I lost track of reality*, in the sense that I'm playing a game,

25. that I'm playing along with her. It goes to that no emotion thing where you can just do

26. anything. That's why I say rage really had nothing to do with it, because it wasn't because I

27. blew up and flew off the handle, when I heard this and went out and killed him. It was like a

28. blankness of no emotion. So anyway, it was somewhere from the game to becoming a reality.

29. I struck him with a baseball bat, and then from the first blow that I hit him, it sort of snapped

30. me into reality of what was happening. I just struck this guy and it was a pretty bad blow to

31. start with. I went into a panic from there, where I was hitting him more. *Then what evolved*

32. *from there*, is that I felt he was going to die from the injuries he had sustained, and there was

33. nothing I, couldn't call an ambulance or something that, 'cause he was already basically

34. going to die, but that he was suffering on the way to there. At that point, I got a knife and cut

35. his throat. That was, the purpose of that was, because I felt he was going die, but I couldn't

36. handle watching him suffer while he was going there. So that was really the essence of the

37. plan."

both the preamble to the description of the homicide and in the homicide account itself. Phillip was engaged in the account and believed in it. Phillip's use of verb tense was also in contrast to that used by Scott. Phillip used the past tense throughout, which suggests truthfulness.

Phillip's account suggests that he was being generally honest. Missing details and vague sections reflect his effort to increase social desirability rather than an attempt to lie. He took responsibility for the killing, and the account is supported by the official records.

Rabon's method was useful for both triangulated interview accounts and those where we did not have access to official records. The 19 accounts were neither completely truthful nor completely deceptive. Rather, these offenders moved between deceptive and truthful utterances. Deception was most commonly used to present themselves in a socially desirable light. Many attempted to portray themselves as less responsible than they actually were.

Ultimately, we cannot know for certain how accurate the accounts were. We note where we have evidence that suggests inaccuracies. When we do not have direct contradictory evidence, but there are indicators of inconsistencies, we accept with critical skepticism the account (Kelly & Totten, 2002). The transcribed accounts are mirrors of the interview conversations. Our handwritten notes also provide important details regarding body language, voice cue messages, physical and mental health issues.

CONCLUSION

Conducting in-depth interviews with offenders convicted of youth homicide poses many risks. Harm can potentially be brought upon offenders and their associates, victims' families, and researchers. For this reason, it is very difficult to gain access to participants. Universities, social agencies, governments, YO institutions, and federal correctional officials are reluctant to facilitate research in this area. Interviewing and analyzing the data are no less difficult. The accuracy of many participants' accounts is of concern. Does this mean that qualitative researchers should not study extreme youth violence? No. There is a dearth of Canadian literature on this topic. We know little about the life courses of adolescents who kill, or the immediate circumstances surrounding these homicides. Nor do we have good information on offenders' experiences following arrest: court, rehabilitation (or lack thereof), and community reintegration.

The first step in preventing youth homicide is to understand the life courses of offenders. In Canada, there is no such data apart from our study. Multidisciplinary intervention approaches, based upon a risk/resiliency model and targeted at key developmental stages of high-risk children and youth, have the best outcomes for violence prevention (Totten, 2003). Effective prevention programs work on individual risks and environmental conditions, using strategies that develop individual skills and competencies, train parents, enhance the school climate, and address peer group problems.

GLOSSARY

Account "truth status": Accuracy of a participant's verbatim report during an in-depth interview with a researcher.

Gaining access: Doing qualitative research on young offenders convicted of homicide poses serious problems, including: finding potential and willing participants (due to confidentiality provisions of youth justice legislation); obtaining the consent of ethical bodies, government, and institutions; gaining entrance to open and secure correctional facilities for interviews; gaining consent of various professionals to obtain correctional and other official records.

In-depth interviews: Face-to-face, lengthy, free-flowing conversation with participants, usually recorded verbatim and based upon a set of questions. The primary goal is to understand better the subject's viewpoint from his or her own perspective.

Life course analysis: Using life-time events, biological/psychological/social makeup, and immediate contextual factors to explain murder.

Youth homicide: The culpable killing of another person (first- and second-degree murder, manslaughter) by an adolescent aged from 12 to 17 years.

REFERENCES

Hammersley, M. (1992). *What's wrong with ethnography: Methodological explorations.* London: Routledge.

Kelly, K., & Totten, M. (2002). *When children kill: A social-psychological study of youth homicide.* Peterborough, ON: Broadview Press.

Rabon, D. (1994). *Investigative discourse analysis.* Durham, NC: Carolina Academic Press.

Scott, M., & Lyman, S. (1968). Accounts. *American Sociological Review, 33,* 46–62.

Silverman, D. (1993). *Interpreting qualitative data.* London: Sage.

Statistics Canada, Centre for Justice Statistics. (1999). Homicide in Canada. *Juristat, 19*(10).

Statistics Canada, Centre for Justice Statistics. (2000). The Justice Fact Finder. *Juristat, 20*(4).

Totten, M. (2000). *Guys, gangs and girlfriend abuse.* Peterborough, ON: Broadview Press.

Totten, M. (2003). Girlfriend abuse as a form of masculinity construction among violent, marginal male youth. *Men and Masculinities, 6*(6), 70–92.

Totten, M., & Kelly, K. (2004). Vicarious trauma suffered by researchers studying youth who kill. *Critical Criminology.*

Chapter 6

Complex Needs and Complex Issues: How Responding to Ethnographic Fieldwork Contingencies Shaped a Study of Homelessness

Anne Wright

INTRODUCTION

People suffering with co-morbid psychological and substance misuse problems are widely referred to as having "dual diagnosis"—something of a "chicken and egg" conundrum (Tucker, 1994). Dual diagnosis is a generic term referring to "the presence of more than one specific disorder in a person in a defined period of time" (Wittchen, Perkonigg, & Reed, 1996, p. 57). However, in this context it refers to "people with different types of mental disorder of varying severity, who are using psychoactive substances with varying frequency and in varying amounts" (Franey & Quirk, 1996, p. 2). The demographic and clinical predictors of substance abuse in severe mental illness are shown in Table 6.1.

Table 6.1: Demographic and Clinical Predictors of Substance Abuse in Severe Mental Illness	
Variable	Correlate with Substance Abuse
Gender	Male
Age	Young
Education	Low
Pre-morbid social-sexual adjustment	Good
Age of first hospitalization	Early
Treatment compliance	Poor
Relapse rate	High
Symptom severity	Higher suicidality

Source: From *Toolkit for Evaluating Substance Abuse in Persons with Severe Mental Illness* (p. 12), by K.T. Mueser, R.E. Drake, R.E. Clark, G.J. McHugo, C. Mercer-McFadden, & T.H. Ackerson, 1995, Concord: New Hampshire-Dartmouth Psychiatric Research Center.

As well as presenting diagnostic, assessment, and treatment difficulties (Farrell et al., 1998), associated problems include high resource utilization, poor prognosis, low social support, increased risk of violence, self-harm, suicide, prostitution, police contact, and homelessness (Merikangas et al., 1998; Mueser et al., 1995).

Many people with mental illness end up on the street following the closure of large psychiatric institutions and introduction of frequently inadequate "**care in the community**" provisions. These individuals are often unable to cope with life outside of an institution, slipping through the net of service provision (Mamodeally, McCusker, & Newman, 1999). People may also obtain housing but lack sufficient skills to retain it, ending up on the streets (Bebout & Harris, 1998). Some young people drift onto the streets following childhood mental illness, trauma, and/or institutional care. To conclude, homeless people with combined mental health and substance misuse problems are notoriously difficult to engage and retain within treatment programs, demonstrating mistrust of people and services, and resistance to accepting help (Blankertz, Cnaan, White, Fox, & Messinger, 1990). Their high numbers indicate that further research is warranted.

To address these issues, I conducted an ethnographic study in a British city to provide insight into where interventions could be targeted in the **career** of the homeless person with dual diagnosis to stop lifestyle entrenchment. The actual fieldwork process, however, was different from that originally planned, involving me in continuous compromise and negotiation—sometimes seemingly at the expense of data collection. In this chapter, I discuss these contingencies of the research process and how I responded to them.

NEGOTIATING ACCESS TO PARTICIPANTS

Anderson and Calhoun (1992, p. 496) comment that access to street people "*in situ*, tends not to be blocked by powerful official gatekeepers, as is often the case with more formal settings." However, I did not find this "deviant street population" to be "readily accessible for observation" either. For example, even when access to fieldwork settings was obtained, I was often unable to arrive at the fieldwork setting and "wait for conversational openings" (Anderson & Calhoun, 1992, p. 492). Instead, ethical and safety factors made it necessary for me to invest considerable time negotiating with various official gatekeepers. To facilitate this process, I designed a project information pack.

Specifically, I needed homeless shelter, drug agency, and Local Health Authority staff to refer clients to the project and allow me access to their premises for purposes that included getting to know people, hanging out, and conducting interviews. Thus, my research proposal needed to meet the strict criteria of the local ethics committee, which included having a participant consent form. This process of becoming a participant in the study introduced an air of formality to interactions that deterred one or two street people from full participation. As Irvine (1998, p. 168) points out, the requirements of the research proposals can themselves "constitute a force" that can shape the research "according to a formality that does not exist in ongoing social interaction." I also needed a baseline assessment of the complex needs of individuals, which also limited participation.

Even when the **local research ethics committee** had accepted my proposal, access to participants occurred only after I had been fully "vetted and tested" by agencies and services. For example, one organization met and eventually granted me full access to their client group. However, on arrival at the facility, staff requested that I not recruit anyone until they themselves were satisfied my presence would not deter clients from using the facility. Two agencies said that they wanted to know not only that my research was not deleterious to their clients, but also that my personal demeanour and professional attitude were suitable for work with street people. For example, the presence of someone with an overly officious demeanour might have deterred some people from using the shelter facilities that served as their home.

Box 6.1: Participant Tracking System

Ethnographic data collection was enhanced by using a participant tracking system that was originally developed and successfully employed (Bootsmiller et al., 1998) in order to ensure high follow-up rates during a longitudinal study of people with co-morbid mental health and substance use problems. This enabled tracing and tracking people who had become otherwise non-contactable, for example, because of unexpected hospitalization or imprisonment. It was a useful way of maintaining contact and monitoring participant's activities. Participants were encouraged to provide contact details of friends, family, and professionals. It was made clear that no information concerning other contacts or the participant's whereabouts would be revealed to the contacts provided. The researcher was, however, allowed to pass appropriate messages and letters on to the participant. If a participant needed tracing, a letter and "Consent and Nominated Contact" form was sent to each contact. The homelessness aspects of the study were emphasized, so that people's mental health and substance misuse problems were not disclosed. The sending of each form was followed by a phone call and courtesy letter, and was successful on each occasion.

Source: From *My Glittering Career: Development of a Career Model of Homelessness, Substance Misuse and Mental Health Problems*, by A. Wright, 2004, Unpublished doctoral dissertation, University of Bath, Bath, UK.

Anderson and Calhoun (1992) point out that, although access to some public settings may be restricted, special entry qualifications are not generally required. However, I found that: (a) ethical approval was needed; (b) I had to be perceived to have the appropriate skills, attributes, and attitude for the research; and (c) I was expected to show consideration for people's well-being. Specifically, I was not to cause distress to anyone and to use discretion when recruiting people and conducting fieldwork. I was also bound by the confidentiality requirements of the *Data Protection Act*, which enjoined me not to reveal to others any information I might have about the substance misuse or mental health problems of the clients.

Finally, participants were to be informed that, should they reveal any information pertaining to child abuse, it would be passed on to the relevant authorities.

Once all the city services and agencies were satisfied that their conditions of entry to the field had been met, I found many unexpected fieldwork settings and other opportunities became available. For example, I was able to accompany workers on their rounds and when operating alone in informal settings could take advantage of their "worker safety" systems—phoning base when arriving and leaving new settings, for example. Eventually I found myself blending in as an accepted part of the street scene, secure in the knowledge that other workers knew who and where I was.

GUIDING PRINCIPLES FOR DATA COLLECTION

As fieldwork progressed, a number of entwined methodological, ethical, and practical issues arose. Addressing these issues led to the emergence of what can be considered as four basic data collection principles that shaped the nature of the emergent data.

Don't Wobble Participants!

A clinician warned me that participating in research might "wobble" some people—that is, upset the balance of someone's psychological well-being. Many participants had severe mental illnesses and histories of deliberate self-harm and suicide attempts, and as the study unfolded, the extreme vulnerability of this client group became increasingly apparent. For example, during a conversation with a shelter worker, a participant suddenly became highly emotional and, pulling a knife from his pocket, sliced through the veins in his arm. It was, therefore, necessary to always be prepared for the unexpected.

This was challenging because, in addition to general observation of current functioning, I needed to collect from participants their life history data extending from early childhood to the onset of complex needs. Further, many participants had histories of regular sexual, emotional, and physical abuse reaching back into childhood. I found that some people immediately began to disclose their troubles at our initial introduction, and that it was necessary to anticipate and prepare for unexpected states of high emotion. Interviews, therefore, were often highly sensitive and had the potential to become intense. It was also possible that recounting personal issues might bring on a bout of serious mental illness, or a self-harm attempt. Further, after our interview, the only places to which people could usually go were back onto the street or to the chaotic night shelter.

Thus, ethical decisions to limit or even stop data collection had to be made if someone's equilibrium ever appeared threatened. Safeguarding the participant's welfare, however, required me to continuously modify my data collection methods. This, in turn, affected the type and quantity of data collected in that different methods of charting life history data and conducting interviews had to be developed. Alternative methods of data collection were also necessary in those cases where people were considered too unstable to be interviewed in depth. This meant that I was unable to collect some of the data mandated by my research.

For example, several months' work in trying to locate and engage "Jane" was finally rewarded. However, she tended to volunteer personal information and then become highly emotional. She asked me to accompany her to a clinical appointment, and at a preliminary courtesy meeting with the clinician, I was advised against conducting life history interviews with her, directed instead to a focus on more general topics. It was felt that confronting her past without intensive support might lead to serious adverse consequences for Jane's psychological functioning, as she often went through weeks of serious distress and was slow to recover.

I was also advised to contact those professionals with whom participants might be engaged, and to find out if there were any similar issues to be aware of. In order to counter the problem of "wobbling" people by probing sensitive issues, I designed an Information Release Form, approved by the local ethics committee, which enabled me to gather life history data from documents held by these other professionals. This revised method provided useful information that helped address problems of the reliability of the data. Thus, my initial private dismay at finding that I was unable to probe some people's histories was alleviated. However, as this client group was extremely vulnerable, I not only modified data collection methods, but, on occasion, also made the decision to limit or stop data collection altogether.

Box 6.2: Case Study—Ben's Experience of Mental Illness

Ben was a child when he first started hearing voices in his head, but attributed the onset of chronic schizophrenia to his later drug use: "First of all, I used to take cannabis all the time twenty-four-seven, for years …" and when he reduced this, the voices receded. "When I (was) taking speed … they *really* started … hallucinating, and thinking trees were talking to me and things, and then it would come for days, when the voices wouldn't go away, and I didn't take any drugs, and … the voices were shouting at me, saying 'You're thinking too loud' … I went into hospital three times—I tried to kill myself a second time …" The hospital had "said I could go—basically they stabilize schizophrenics on medication, and then send them (home)." He eventually learned to "put up with the voices" through "heroin … It was the only thing that really seemed to stop the voices … Other people had to inject for me for five years, so I'm being injected at least twice a day usually … My dad didn't take speed, so that didn't cause his schizophrenia … I am scared of taking speed and cannabis … the voices come back worse ... The long-term effects, is to make the illness worse … It just seemed to like, put me in a shadow world … I was at the end of the world, or really cut off from everything, from everyone else …"

Source: From My Glittering Career: Development of a Career Model of Homelessness, Substance Misuse and Mental Health Problems, by A. Wright, 2004, Unpublished doctoral dissertation, University of Bath, Bath, UK.

Roles in the Field: "It's okay to be a helper, but don't adopt the role of *worker.*"

Working as a researcher in a fieldwork setting that provides service engagement presented several challenges. The clear explanation of my role to participants was important to ensure that participants fully understood that I was a research psychologist, not a clinician, and that participation in my project was not a substitute for service engagement. This was achieved by (a) giving repeated verbal reminders, and (b) setting up the research as a discrete entity called "The Street Project." Through the use of information materials, business cards, headed notepaper, and a contact address, I attempted to define my role as a researcher and ensure that people did not confuse the research project with other service organizations.

Like other researchers (Carey, 1972), I found the question "Exactly what is it that you do then?" was often asked and, like Carey, I found that I had to teach participants what the role of "researcher" is. Carey (1972, p. 76) has pointed out that this process raises issues about what type of participant-researcher relationships are "(a) most advantageous for obtaining optimal information, and (b) most desirable in terms of ethical and humane considerations." I personally found that teaching people what a researcher is often initiated long and interesting group discussions, as it appeared novel for people to have informal social access to a "research psychologist." These discussions also became an interesting source of data regarding people's perceptions of health professionals, services, labelling, and the different processes by which professions could "find things out."

Role Conflict: "I'm a researcher, not a helper,"

In general, I was regarded as a student health researcher linked to various organizations, a perception partially reinforced by the formality of the initial assessment process, and by my links with agencies and services. However, as I had worked as a volunteer for a local drugs advice agency during fieldwork preparation, some participants were already familiar with me as a drugs worker. As a result, this worker role, which involved both encouraging service engagement and the assertive promotion of **harm minimization**, began to conflict with my current role as a passive observer. The role conflict also began to extend to agency staff and clients alike, and so I terminated all but one worker role—that of **assertive outreach** worker. This enabled me to spend evenings on the streets with the rough sleepers, in the company of another worker.

However, I still found myself in conflict when people continued to ask for personal advice, often prefacing their questions with "I know you are not a counsellor, but ... " Similarly, Henslin (1972) reported conflict between the roles of researcher and helper, and I found myself asking the same questions as he did. Specifically, when interviewing and interacting with people in need of professional guidance or intervention, should I refuse to step outside the researcher role? Should I simply ask my questions, then quietly leave and forget my participants, even though, because of my position and situation, I felt that I could offer key help? I canvassed several researchers and found their opinions to be sharply divided.

Henslin (1972) has suggested that should an individual decide *not* to step outside the researcher role, the problem is considerably reduced. Non-involvement is legitimated as one can simply say "That isn't my role" or "They would have been in the same situation if I hadn't appeared on the scene" (p. 57). He pointed out, however, that whether or not it was the role he wanted, he *did* appear on the scene. Thus, like Henslin and Carey (1972), I adopted Sarbin's (1954) tactic of "role segregation" (Henslin, 1972). This meant that I played the role of researcher first, and the role of professional helper when necessary. As Henslin concluded, each researcher "must deal with such moral dilemmas according to the ethics into which they have been socialized" (p. 58). In the end, I decided what to do depending on what I felt to be ethical in any given circumstance.

There was an unexpected payback to this approach, as I was often asked to accompany people to various appointments that I had recommended and helped them to make. Permission was also given to record and use this data, which meant that the process of service engagement and, sadly, disengagement could be closely observed. This provided far richer insight into the experience of people's lives than anticipated during project planning.

In addition, I also offered other types of help (such as a meal or transport) as payback for participation or, occasionally, as an interview "trade." This could, however, bring me into conflict with the agencies. For example, after helping move someone's belongings in my car from a temporary hostel to a newly acquired government-owned apartment, one agency informed me that I had performed the task of the staff responsible for that client. Additional concerns included insurance, legal, and safety issues. This experience contrasted with other situations where help was sanctioned and welcomed. The situation was quickly and amicably resolved, however, and an important lesson was learned.

Maintenance of Role Segregation: "Don't adopt the role of worker."
In this regard, it was also critical to segregate the roles of helper and worker. For example, Jane had begun to seek me out as a friend and ally. Her clinician phoned me to say that Jane had started missing appointments, possibly in part because she now felt enabled to temporarily cope, having sufficiently "offloaded" her troubles to me. However, engagement with me only provided "crisis intervention," not long-term meaningful intervention, and from then onwards, I actively encouraged Jane to make and keep her appointments, sometimes accompanying her. Thus, the components of the second principle included the following: it was acceptable to be a helper but not a worker; and it was important not to come between a worker and a client.

As noted in Table 6.2, however, the advantages of forming strong working relationships with organizations were also found to far outweigh the disadvantages.

Be Careful to Avoid Exploiting Vulnerability
It was important not to mislead people about any gains that could be made through participation. The formality of the initial assessment process, and my

Table 6.2: Perceived Advantages and Drawbacks of Developing Working Relationships with Professional Organizations During the Process of Conducting Fieldwork

	Advantages		Drawbacks
1	Maintenance of client well-being	1	Client suspicions of confidentiality breaches
2	Provision of urgent and general information	2	The occasional worker trying to elicit confidential information
3	Joint working and information pooling with client's consent	3	Being occasionally used as go-between client and worker, and between different organizations
4	Someone there if something goes wrong	4	Sense of answerableness and responsibility to these organizations
5	Maintenance of researcher safety		

Source: From *My Glittering Career: Development of a Career Model of Homelessness, Substance Misuse and Mental Health Problems*, by A. Wright, 2004, Unpublished doctoral dissertation, University of Bath, Bath, UK.

organizational relationships, lent a powerful "medical" tone to the project. As Carey (1972) observed, "the medical service relationship seems to be one that is generally understood in our society," and I did find it helpful in building trust (p. 75).

Defining the Role of the Participant

Discussing the role of researcher with participants simultaneously helped to define the role of the project participant. This led to interesting data concerning motivations for project participation. Henslin (1972) asserted that, in order to understand and evaluate information given by participants, "one must have an understanding of their motivations to conceal and reveal information ... the motivations themselves become part of the data." People gave a number of reasons as to why they were taking part in the project. Primarily, the participants appeared to engage in an exchange with the researcher for altruistic reasons (Henslin, 1972), but also because they felt that the experience empowered them, provided them with companionship, and held the potential for the improvement of prospects (p. 65).

However, these individuals were also vulnerable and often extremely lonely people, many of whose most constant relationships were with workers. Two people declared that they had become attached to me in ways that were clearly inappropriate, and I had suspicions about another. For example, I heard from a worker that John, who suffered from chronic schizophrenia, had said that I had asked him on a date, and that we were in telepathic communication. Unravelling this misunderstanding revealed that I had arranged with John a time and place (the community café) for our next interview. When writing it in my diary, I had said, figuratively, "Okay, it's a date. See you then!" I was also told that another man tended to develop obsessions with women he felt close to.

Miller (1952) has pointed out that it is difficult to prevent participant-researcher rapport from developing to the extent that it becomes a hindrance. He described rapport as "more than a technique of acceptance. It involves a sensitive understanding of individuals, so that one is able to make insightful analyses of behaviour." Miller also argued that, in order to guard against the potential development of "over rapport," the researcher needs to ask: "At what point does the closeness to the subjects limit the research role?" Following Miller's advice, I made it clear to participants that I was interested in many people who were homeless with mental health and substance misuse problems, and that the prime reason that I was present was related to my research interest and activity (p. 98).

It also transpired that two participants had experienced past sexual relationships with workers (in different cities), and I was witness to the lasting effects of these reported boundary transgressions and exploitation of vulnerability. People were also vulnerable in other ways. For example, individuals were harassed and threatened with violence by a drug dealer if seen talking to me in one instance. In another, the partner of a participant in a co-dependent relationship threatened violence. Accordingly, I developed a "tricky situation protocol" whereby clinicians were discretely notified about such events and professional boundaries discussed with the participants in a way that was sensitive to their feelings. Contact could be either curtailed or discontinued—one solution involved visiting the person only in the company of his regular worker. Care was also taken to avoid inadvertently giving people the "wrong message."

Anderson and Calhoun (1992, p. 494), have suggested that deviant populations are deprived of attention, and that some deviant individuals seek attention from "almost any available source." The need for attention thus provides the "responsive and strategic" researcher with a window of opportunity. However, I had to ensure that taking this window of opportunity was not, in fact, exploiting a person's vulnerability. Specifically, it was possible that, for some people, participation in the research became a means of continuing to keep me, as the researcher, engaged.

The emergence of these particular situations instigated the natural beginning of the end of the fieldwork year. Carefully decreased intensity of participant contact meant my stepping outside of the field, and gradually, a distance between myself and participants set in. In this regard, I explained to all that I soon had to write up my study and would therefore be around only infrequently. To sum up, it was necessary to define the role of participant and ensure that people were clear about the actual gains from participation. I also felt it was unethical to continue to collect data if I was in some way exploiting people's vulnerability.

The Researcher Role in Retrospect: "Look after number one!"

I was new to the field, which had numerous advantages in relation to having analytic insight in novel situations (Anderson & Calhoun, 1992). However I did not initially have much insight into my own well-being! Several agency sources had reported workers becoming jaded and acclimatized to the distressing phenomena encountered daily. Clients, however, spent much time complaining about the negative attitude of some staff and their being excluded from services if they missed more than three appointments. I began to see things from both sides as I had spent consecutive days waiting for participants to show up, and had sat alongside workers doing the same thing. On the other hand, I had also spent consecutive days with participants and observed how their combined problems rendered keeping appointments difficult. Kuhlman (1994) comments that practitioners structure most of their day around appointments, and so are provided a "measure of temporal control over the parameters of distress that one is exposed to" (p. 57).

However, conducting an ethnographic study meant that I was spending most of my time with the street people, carrying out observations that often combined with waiting in day centres for people to arrive for an interview, and conducting the interviews themselves. As Carey (1972) reported, "fatigue was a constant problem," and observing the chaotic drug lifestyle posed practical difficulties. These included "conventional commitments" having to be put aside in order to "adapt more realistically to the scene" (p. 82).

Anderson and Calhoun (1992, p. 497) have suggested that, within limits, researchers should take the opportunity to become "personally engaged" in the social world of their participants "rather than struggling to maximize their emotional distance," as this approach may result in increased "rigor and attention to detail." I found, however, that I had to strike the right balance between emotional engagement and distance. It seemed that the stronger my personal engagement, the more draining the fieldwork became, which, in turn, had a negative impact upon my professional practice.

Although I have concluded that it is possible to conduct a study like this one as an individual researcher, it is important to ensure that appropriate support is in place, an issue I did not fully appreciate during project planning. For example, my fieldwork led to the development of 20 detailed case studies comprised of observation, multiple interviews, psychological assessment, medical records, and other documentation. Twenty case studies also meant that there were 20 relationships to manage. These intense relationships could reasonably have required "resources and time beyond the means of a single student or independent research investigator" (Yin, 1994, p. 45).

Further, homelessness workers pointed out to me that they have daily team meetings and regular personal supervision. I, on the other hand, did not have these supports, yet I was often having more direct client contact than the workers. To address this discrepancy, I recruited two personal supervisors to whom I could talk on a personal level about the distressing phenomena I was witnessing in my daily routine. This proved to be an effective way to alleviate my feelings about what I was encountering. If it had not been possible to obtain this kind of appropriate support, then I would have had to agree with Carey (1972, p. 45) that "more than one fieldworker is required in this type of research." To conclude this section, researcher support is vital in studies of this nature for ensuring the well-being of both the researcher and the study participants, good professional practice, and effective data collection.

CONCLUSION

The ethical compromises made by researchers in the field are most frequently "glossed over in 'the smooth methodological appendix' of the research report" (Irvine, 1998, citing Bell & Newby, 1977). Irvine argues that such sanitized presentations "contradict the reflexive involvement that is part of the ethnographic tradition" (1998, p. 167). Like Irvine (1998), I found that data collection in the field was different from that anticipated during project planning. The process was subject to compromise and negotiation throughout due to the emergence of entwined methodological, practical, and ethical issues.

Addressing these issues led to the emergence of four basic principles that formed a framework within which the entire fieldwork process was conducted and shaped. First, that data collection would be limited or stopped if the well-being of any participant was in doubt. Second, it was considered acceptable to be a helper but not a worker—and it was important not to come between a worker and his or her client. Third, people's vulnerability in relation to potential exploitation was considered at all times. Finally, I ensured that I had appropriate personal support to help me cope with fieldwork demands. Therefore, reflecting upon, addressing, adapting to, and accepting the presenting issues changed the nature of the data collected. In fact the rich data collected from analysis of these emergent issues became part of the findings that directly helped to address the research objectives. These included identifying factors that maintained the career of being homeless, with combined mental health and substance misuse problems.

GLOSSARY

Assertive outreach: A service designed for people with complex needs who have difficulty engaging with traditional services, consequently requiring hospital admissions. Mental health clinicians and other workers go out into the community in order to build relationships with people, encourage engagement with treatment services, provide intensive support, care coordination, and intervention delivery.

Career: A psycho-socio construct used to represent the analysis of "a person's course or progress through life (or a distinct portion of life)" (Hughes, 1997, p. 389). For example, using this concept, the life course of a drug user can be traced from inception of the role, through its enactment, to its end. Just as in analytical terms there are a number of roles that individuals can play, there are also careers that intersect.

Care in the community: Care that followed legislation that saw many British psychiatric hospitals close, with patients, instead, receiving care in community settings. Aims of the approach included providing services that enabled people to be independent, live in their own homes, and receive services tailored to individual needs.

Harm minimization: An approach to substance misuse intervention that aims to decrease the harm to the individual and society (e.g., HIV, DVT) that is associated with drug use, until such a time that the individual is able to work towards abstinence. This can include providing education about reducing drug-related harm, offering counselling, treatment referral, needle and syringe exchanges.

Local research ethics committees: Work to a framework of standards, and are responsible to Health Authorities for assessing that all proposed research is appropriate, safe, and of sufficient quality that research participants and researchers are protected.

REFERENCES

Anderson, L., & Calhoun, T.C. (1992). Facilitative aspects of field research with deviant street populations. *Sociological Inquiry, 62*(4), 490–498.

Bell, C., & Newby, H. (1977). *Doing social research* (1st American ed.). New York: Free Press.

Bebout, R.R., & Harris, M. (1998). *Housing solutions: The community connections housing program.* Washington, DC: Community Connections.

Blankertz, L.E., Cnaan, R.A., White, K., Fox, J., & Messenger, K. (1990). Outreach efforts with dually diagnosed homeless persons. *Families in Society: The Journal of Contemporary Human Services* (September), 387–395.

Bootsmiller, B.J., Ribisl, K.M., Mowbray, C.T., Davidson, W.S., Walton, M.A., & Herman, S.E. (1998). Methods of ensuring high follow-up rates: Lessons learned from a longitudinal study of dual diagnosed participants. *Substance Use & Misuse, 33*(13), 2665–2685.

Carey, J.T. (1972). Problems of access and risk in observing drug scenes. In J.D. Douglas (Ed.), *Research on deviance* (pp. 71–92). New York: Random House.

Farrell, M., Howes, S., Taylor, C., Lewis, G., Jenkins, R., Bebbington, P., et al. (1998). Substance use and psychiatric co-morbidity: An overview of the OPCS national psychiatric morbidity survey. *Addictive Behaviours, 23*(6), 909–918.

Franey, C., & Quirk, A. (1996). Dual diagnosis. *Executive summary, 51*(July). London: The Centre for Research on Drugs and Health Behaviour.

Henslin, J.M. (1972). Studying deviance in four settings. In J.D. Douglas (Ed.), *Research on deviance* (pp. 35–79). New York: Random House.

Hughes, E. (1997). Careers. *Qualitative Sociology, 20*, 389–397.

Irvine, L. (1998). Organizational ethics and fieldwork realities: Negotiating ethical boundaries in codependents anonymous. In S. Grills (Ed.), *Doing ethnographic research: Fieldwork settings* (pp. 167–183). Thousand Oaks, CA: Sage.

Kuhlman, T.L. (1994). *Psychology on the streets: Mental health practice with homeless persons.* New York: John Wiley & Sons.

Mamodeally, A., McCusker, M., & Newman, M. (1999). *Rainbow project: Proposals to address the mental health and substance misuse needs of the homeless population in the West End of London.* The Riverside Mental Health Trust.

Merikangas, K.R., Mehta, R.L., Molnar, B.E., Walters, E.E., Swendsen, J.D., Aguilar-Gaziola, S., et al. (1998). Comorbidity of substance use disorders with mood and anxiety disorders: Results of the international consortium in psychiatric epidemiology. *Addictive Behaviours, 23*(6), 893–907.

Miller, S.M. (1952). The participant observer and "over rapport." *American Sociological Review, 17*, 97–99.

Mueser, K.T., Bennett, M., & Kushner, M.G. (1995). Epidemiology of substance use disorders among persons with chronic mental illnesses. In A.F. Lehman & L.B. Dixon (Eds.), *Double jeopardy: Chronic mental illness and substance use disorders* (pp. 9–26). Chur, Switzerland: Harwood Academic Publishers.

Mueser, K.T., Drake, R.E., Clark, R.E., McHugo, G.J., Mercer-McFadden, C., & Ackerson, T. H. (1995). *Toolkit for evaluating substance abuse in persons with severe mental illness*. Concord: New Hampshire-Dartmouth Psychiatric Research Center.

Sarbin, T.R. (1954). Role theory. In G. Lindzey (Ed.), *Handbook of social psychology: Vol. 1. Theory and method* (chap. 6). Reading, MA: Addison-Wesley.

Tucker, P. (1994). Substance abuse and psychosis: Chicken or the egg? *Australasian Psychiatry, 2*(6), 272–273.

Wittchen, H.U., Perkonnigg, A., & Reed, V. (1996). Co-morbidity of mental disorders and substance disorders. *European Addiction Research, 2*, 36–47.

Wright, A. (2004). *My glittering career: Development of a career model of homelessness, substance misuse and mental health problems*. Unpublished doctoral dissertation. The University of Bath, Bath, UK.

Yin, R.K. (1994). Case study research: Design and methods. *Vol. 5. Applied Social Research Methods Series* (2nd ed.). Thousand Oaks, CA: Sage Publications.

PART 1 C

RELATING TO RESPONDENTS

Chapter 7

"I'm Looking Forward to Hearing What You Found Out": Reflections on a Critical Perspective and Some of Its Consequences

Gillian Ranson

INTRODUCTION

This chapter describes some of the tensions and challenges I encountered in a four-year study of engineers and engineering work in Calgary. The tensions were political, theoretical, and ethical. In a practical sense, and at a personal level, they played out as dilemmas of representation: how I represented myself and my research project to the research participants; how I represented them to others outside their community; and how I represented research "findings" to (at least two) different audiences, with different claims, expectations, and interests.

These personal challenges connected my research to broader debates over ethics and qualitative research. In particular, they pushed me to join the scholarly engagement with the meaning of **informed consent**. They also led me to the scholarly discussions of **rapport** and representation. What follows is an account of this research "journey."

BACKGROUND

My research project began in 1997 as an examination of the interface of gender, paid work, and family life among engineers. I was interested in exploring the ramifications of increasing female participation in one of the last bastions of male professional domination. And in a climate of considerable optimism, fuelled by growing numbers of women graduating from faculties of engineering across the country, I was particularly interested in whether these women would remain in engineering for the long haul. This interest, linked to ongoing research concerns about the gendered, and reciprocal, impacts of work and family, framed the first phase of the study. This phase involved tracking women and men who had graduated from the Faculty of Engineering at the University of Calgary between 1980 and 1990. I picked this time period because it would yield a sample of graduates aged roughly from 30 to 40—in other words, the prime age for career establishment and family formation. Between June 1997 and August 1998, 317 graduates were located and surveyed. Of these, 63 took part in face-to-face interviews. These interviews, all of which I conducted myself, were intended to contextualize the survey data. But they rapidly became, for me, the most interesting and the richest source of material and have provided the basis for most of the work I have done on this phase of the project.

The first phase revealed a significant retention problem for women, and also the possibility that they might do better in large, bureaucratic organizations. So in 1999, with these findings in mind, I started the second phase of the project, a study of engineers in a large oil company with headquarters in Calgary. Of approximately 100 engineers in the company's upstream division, 64 of them completed a survey. During the summer of 2000, I also conducted 27 semi-structured interviews. The survey material provided useful background for a report to the company as a *quid pro quo* for access and support. In this phase, too, it was the interview material that was my personal research focus.

WORKING WITH ENGINEERS

The engineering community, and particularly the community of women engineers, took a lively interest in the project almost from the beginning. This interest was spurred by the establishment, at about the time my project started, of the NSERC/Petro-Canada Chair of Women in Science and Engineering (Prairie Region) at the University of Calgary. This chair is part of a network of five endowed chairs across the country aimed at promoting women's participation in science and engineering. The University of Calgary incumbent, with the other chairs in the network, saw the need for social research to facilitate this goal, and energetically promoted the efforts of anyone, like me, perceived to be working in the area.

This support had some interesting consequences. I was encouraged to present papers at two conferences, one in 1998, one in 2000, organized by the Canadian Coalition of Women in Science, Engineering and Technology (CCWEST). These conferences were intended largely as professional development for working engineers, with presentations of research papers (later published in conference proceedings and put on the website) as one part of a diverse, workplace-oriented conference agenda.

I was interviewed, also, by the newspaper produced by the Association of Professional Engineers, Geologists and Geophysicists of Alberta about the first phase of the study. This widespread dissemination of my work to an engineering audience produced more invitations to talk to engineers. I was invited to address some version of women's professional networks in three major oil companies in Calgary. I also presented some findings from the oil company study to a session in the company attended by women engineers, human resources officials, and the vice-president of engineering. And I have been a guest speaker at other professional gatherings of engineers.

A very clear assumption informed all this support and interest: that it was important to encourage women to become engineers, and to retain them in engineering workplaces. The tacit expectation of all the invitations extended to me was that I would shed some (more) light on how to make it happen. I doubt whether it would have occurred to anyone that the basic assumption might be open to any question at all.

I accepted the invitations out of a **feminist** commitment to give back to those who had supported and participated in the research and, for the most part, was able to package some dimension of the material in ways that seemed to resonate with the engineering audience. For example, in the first CCWEST conference (Ranson, 1998), I talked about some early findings of the first phase of my study concerning retention, and the strategies employed by women in order to keep working in engineering. At the second conference, in July 2000 (Ranson, 2000a), I talked about gender differences in family circumstances among working engineers in my study who were also parents. (Most of the working mothers had partners who were also in full-time careers; most of the working fathers had partners who worked part-time or were not in paid employment). I also shared work I had done with some of the men in the study on fatherhood and careers (later published as Ranson, 2001a).

CHANGING DIRECTIONS

The changes in direction were on two fronts, the first of which was scholarly and theoretical. As my reading and thinking about gender issues proceeded, I was no longer as willing as I once was to think in unproblematic, undifferentiated categories of "women" and "men" in engineering. This meant I was less willing to focus on the kinds of issues that could readily be shared with audiences interested in knowing how "the women" differed from "the men." I was actually growing very interested in the ways in which "the women" did *not* differ from "the men." For example, it became pretty clear that the **masculinist** work culture pervading many engineering workplaces was enthusiastically embraced by some of the women, and caused discomfort to some of the men (Ranson, 2003).

I was also becoming aware of the ways I could work with my interview data that made the engineering component incidental. For example, many of my interviewees had entered the labour market during the 1980s, a time of tremendous restructuring in the energy industry in Alberta. Many experienced layoffs, sometimes with extended periods of unemployment. (See Ranson, 2001b.) I started to read about narrative analysis as I listened to the different kinds of stories they told to make sense of their experiences. Instead of engineers who happened to be telling stories, they became, for me, storytellers who happened to be engineers.

Another example of engineering itself becoming decentred appears in a paper I recently completed, using the interviews with the women. My claim, in this paper, is that women can succeed in strongly male-dominated professional and organizational workplaces to the extent that they become "one of the guys," and that this strategy fails when they blow this cover in order to have children. Here I use engineering as a proxy for any male-dominated occupation. I am really interested in the construction of gender in masculinist work cultures, rather than among engineers.

A second change in direction was political. As a feminist scholar studying gender relations in a male-dominated profession, I had always recognized that my work had a political dimension. But politics of a different order came into play as the research proceeded. Engineering covers a vast spectrum of activities, from the delivery of clean water to the design of artificial limbs, that most would agree make the world a better place. But engineering knowledge is also used to make weapons, and vehicles that pollute the environment, and dams over wild rivers.

My project and I were both based in Calgary, where the energy industry dominates the economy, and directly or indirectly employs most engineers. Their work contributes to the process of extracting, as cheaply as possible, a diminishing supply of fossil fuel from the ground—sometimes in parts of the world where indigenous populations are harmed by their activities. This is work with serious environmental and social consequences. Concerns about the uses to which engineering knowledge is put began to emerge in earnest as I entered the second phase of the project, which involved interviewing engineers in a major oil company.

As a consequence, I included questions about ethics and values in the interviews, and alerted participants that I was doing so on the consent form (about which I will say more shortly). But I also began to wonder about my uncritical willingness to enter what environmental opponents of the oil industry would call "the belly of the beast," to give my talks to women engineers with the tacit aim of helping them improve their working lives within the company and "succeeding" there.

Box 7.1

My discomfort about the ideological differences between me and the engineers with whom I was working became particularly acute during the summer of 2000, when, at the time I was carrying out interviews with the women engineers for my oil company study, Calgary was hosting the World Petroleum Congress. This was an international gathering of corporate and government representatives to discuss petroleum resource exploitation and management. It inspired an energetic protest movement, including a remarkable conference that appropriated the WPC acronym for its title, "Widening People's Choices." The conference drew an array of international environmental activists who spoke passionately of environmental and human rights violations associated with the global petroleum industry, and discussed alternatives to what conference organizers called the "oil paradigm"—the extent to which our lives are dependent on fossil fuels. The protest movement of which the conference was a part was well organized, peaceful, and relatively small-scale. But since it happened fairly soon after the watershed World Trade Organization protests in Seattle, it provoked disproportionately extensive security precautions. I attended the "Widening People's Choices" conference, and took part in the march through Calgary on the Sunday before the World Petroleum Congress started. It was very hard to reconcile these activities, the outcome of my personal political commitment, with my commitment to interview oil company engineers who had a very different view of the protest. One engineer wondered aloud, during a pre-interview phone conversation, whether there would be "blood on the streets," and whether I would be able to get into the city to meet with her. She assumed that the protest would be for me, as for her, merely an inconvenience ...

I wondered, as a politically concerned citizen and an activist of sorts, if this was a worthy goal. And I worried as a researcher about the values conflict that could potentially distance me from the research participants.

This was a dilemma that I took up in another paper, and presented at a conference put on by the Institute of Gender Studies and Women's Studies at the University of Toronto in November 2000 (Ranson, 2000b). In this paper I applied to engineering Sandra Harding's critical analysis of science. Harding (1991) distinguishes between "the Woman question in science" and "the question of science in feminism." The "Woman question" focuses on women as a special interest group, and asks that their special needs and interests be met. This question links to the concern with removal of barriers to women's full participation. The "question of science in feminism" asks instead how feminist thinkers, with interests and perspectives echoed by other "countercultures" of science (for example, in anti-racist, ecology, and peace movements) might re-orient conventional science towards "emancipatory ends" (Harding, 1991, p. 49).

Applied to engineering, this question moves from a preoccupation with attracting and retaining women in engineering to ask what it is that women in engineering are being retained *for*. If, as is the case in Calgary, many are being retained to work for "Big Oil," the emancipatory possibilities did not loom large, and I remained troubled.

INFORMED CONSENT

From the foregoing, it becomes clear that I was starting to tell stories from my research that were not the stories my study participants necessarily thought I would be telling. Should they, *could* they, have been informed about my shifting interests? Or was the consent they originally gave sufficiently inclusive to cover the changes that took place? And how do I know they were well enough informed to give such global consent in the first place?

Box 7.2

Informed consent is now considered an ethical requirement in most research involving human subjects. But Thorne (1980) asks whether all potential research subjects should be equally entitled to the protection offered by the informed consent requirement. She points out two categories of people from whom informed consent might not be required. The first contains figures like government officials, physicians, police officers, and teachers. In their professional lives at least they are publicly accountable, and people have "a right to know what they are up to." The second category contains people whose behaviour is "so reprehensible or immoral that it warrants exposing." This group would include individuals like Hitler and Stalin, who may have forfeited their rights to privacy because they have "renounced membership in a moral community."

Source: From "'You Still Takin' Notes?': Fieldwork and Problems of Informed Consent," by B. Thorne, 1980, *Social Problems, 27*(3), p. 294.

The question of informed consent introduces a lively and ongoing debate on ethics review in qualitative research (e.g., Thorne, 1980; Van den Hoonaard, 2001). Much of this debate addresses the requirement to obtain consent from research participants in the formal and coercive way required by ethics review boards. But my particular interest here is with another dimension of the debate: the broader moral question of whether researchers ever tell the whole story of what they are proposing to do, even supposing they know ahead of time anyway. Opening a discussion about covert methods in social research, one writer claims: "It is a truism in fieldwork that there is often only apparent separation between the honest, open study and the 'covert' or deceptive one. This holds true because social research, particularly fieldwork, exhibits a continuum of concealment and disclosure" (Herrera, 1999, p. 331).

We all use cover stories to explain and justify our research, and to gain access to research participants. Gary Alan Fine distinguishes between "Deep Cover" (when the researcher does not disclose his/her research role), "Explicit Cover" (when the researcher makes as complete an announcement of the goals of the research as possible), and "Shallow Cover" (the middle ground, where the researcher announces the research intent but is vague about the goals). Fine notes that "[t]hese divisions, and the grey areas between them, remind us forcefully that the line between being 'informed' and 'uninformed' is not clear … and that all research is secret in *some* ways" (Fine, 1993, p. 277).

The consent form for the first phase of my study conformed squarely to my original research interests, as outlined above. I told participants that the purpose was "to examine the way career paths develop over time for men and women whose educational background is in engineering." I told them that a particular aim of the study was "to find out how some of the changes and transitions of adult life, like getting married, having children, or moving to another province, affect women's and men's careers." There is a certain coyness about the gender dimension, but the letter certainly "covered" my intentions at the time. There was enough public interest in the question of "women in engineering" that most participants assumed gender was a big part of the study anyway, especially given that the researcher was a woman. But they often had a different view of how the gender question should be addressed. I asked them questions about their experiences in order to be able later to make comparisons and have something to say about gender. They were expecting to be asked for their opinions about gender issues, and how women in engineering were doing. They weren't always expecting their lives to become my data.

This links to two major problems for those grappling with informed consent issues. The first is that social research like mine is academic research, which uses a specialized language and particular methodologies that are not always directly accessible by research participants. As Springwood and King (2001) ask, "Must a neo-Marxist ethnographer explicitly share his understandings of people, place and power? If so, how?" (Springwood & King 2001, p. 410; see also Daniels, 1983; Lerum, 2001). Linking to the academic language question, I would add that terms such as "gender" and "feminism" are liable to be taken up by potential interviewees in ways not anticipated or intended by the researcher. These are terms with a bad rap, and for this reason, some wariness about their use in consent forms is legitimate. The second problem is that, however painstaking the researcher is about disclosing research goals, research participants will have their own views of both the research and the researcher. Warren (2002) points out the "many indications in the literature on qualitative interviewing" that the respondent's understanding "may not match the interviewer's from the start, may shift over time, or may be 'confused'" (Warren, 2002, p. 89; see also Thorne, 1979, 1980).

My changes of direction exemplify yet another problem faced by qualitative researchers: that it is the very nature of qualitative research to be open-ended. Researchers at the start of a project usually do not know where they will end up, so how can they adequately inform respondents ahead of time? Writers such as Thorne (1980) distinguish between interview projects and other supposedly more long-term ethnographic research, suggesting that ethnographic research goals are more liable to change than are those of an interview project. But this is not the case. I suggest that the moral dilemma for interview researchers is actually more acute, since direction changes can happen long after contact with the original informants is lost. As Gubrium and Holstein (1990) have effectively demonstrated, different perspectives can be brought to bear on interviews conducted years earlier and with completely different research goals in mind. When I began my engineering research, I was interested in women's and men's career paths, and that's what I told them. I didn't know I would develop, along with a heightened awareness of environmental issues, a more sophisticated theoretical interest in (as I put it above) "the construction of gender in masculinist work cultures," which the original interview data actually opened up. And—back to the academic language question—I'm not sure how I would have framed that interest in a consent letter, even if I had known about it ahead of time.

POLITICS, RAPPORT, AND REPRESENTATION

The debate about informed consent intersects with other equally contentious matters. How much, or how little, to disclose about the research affects relationships with informants, especially in cases where full disclosure would expose a clash of values. Rapport creates expectations among informants about the story the researcher will tell, and (implicitly) how they will appear to others.

Dilemmas about the light in which research participants will appear may be more acute in the case of disadvantaged or subordinated groups (e.g., Armstead, 1995; Fine, Weis, Weseen, & Wong, 2001). Well-educated, well-paid, predominantly white middle-class engineers may seem less in need of special protection and concern. But, as Fine points out, our informants have given us a "gift"—of their time, their interest, and their words. The question is, "How have we returned the favour?" (Fine, 1993, p. 272) How indeed? With almost all my interviewees, I had excellent rapport. But did that mislead them?

The need to think differently about rapport in critical ethnographic research was the subject of a special issue of the journal *Qualitative Inquiry*. As the editors pointed out, rapport is unproblematic when ethnographers share the political and social

Box 7.3

There are two sides to the relationship between researcher and those who are the "subjects" of the research. As Rosanna Hertz comments: "Most of us think a lot about the people we study. After all, our careers are built on what we know and write about them. But what do our respondents think about what we write? What if they showed up in our classrooms or at our front doors looking for an accounting?" (Hertz, 2003, p. 473).

Hertz had a taste of what this might be like when, 20 years after she ended a field study in an Israeli kibbutz, a son of the family with whom she had lived while on the kibbutz appeared at her front door with "a backpack, a duffel bag, and plans to stay for a year." His arrival raised questions for Hertz about the real nature of the relationships she had contracted in the field. In particular, she recognized that, while she had seen her guest's parents as friends, they had seen her as family. Revisiting her experiences with them in the kibbutz, she came to agree with their view. So hosting their son became an opportunity to "cement our mutual obligations and responsibilities as family members."

Source: From "Paying Forward and Paying Back," by R. Hertz, 2003, *Symbolic Interaction, 26*(3), p. 475.

commitments of those they study. But, they added, "the emotive and intellectual bonds facilitating rapport, trust and identification have collapsed as ethnographers have increasingly **studied up**, returned home, and otherwise twisted the gaze ... Ethnographers have not asked themselves often or reflexively enough about the ideo-epistemological, ethical and interpersonal implications of using the words and actions of their informants against them" (Springwood & King, 2001, p. 404).

My experience of this values clash, and the temptation I have felt to use my informants' words against them, occurred in two main ways in my engineering research. First, as a feminist scholar, I found it painful to listen to the gender stereotyping and machismo that emerged in some of my interviews. (It wasn't pervasive, but it was certainly there—not for nothing does the term "cowboy engineering" have some meaning in Calgary.) It was also difficult to hear some of the women disparage other women and deny the existence of the structural barriers against women in engineering that were so apparent to me.

The second area concerned the environmental issues noted above. I became increasingly uncomfortable about studying engineers at all. My discomfort was probably not as extreme as that of Schacht (1997) who, as a pro-feminist man studied the misogynist world of rugby players, or of Gusterson (1993) who, as an anti-nuclear activist, studied a nuclear weapons laboratory. But social scientists have traditionally identified with the underprivileged and the disenfranchised (Hertz & Imber, 1993). I was no exception. As Katz (1997) would ask, what could be my warrant for researching this relatively privileged group?

Box 7.4

As an example of the way political and personal agendas complicate the way a researcher interacts with those being studied, US ethnographer Gary Alan Fine writes of his work on the deflection of stigma and presentation of self in social movements. As part of this research, he attended the national conference of Victims of Child Abuse Laws, a group organized to support adults accused of child abuse and to limit the powers of social workers. He writes:

"As a parent of two young children, this was a group with which I had some qualms about being associated, both meeting these 'creeps' and in having my good name associated with theirs. Although the research was not designed to debunk the organization, I assumed that members had to defend themselves. Through a relatively brief research sojourn, I found myself convinced that some of these activists were unfairly accused and others justly labelled and that the movement as a whole had a severe problem of boundary maintenance. Although I was not a hostile researcher, I was less sympathetic than I led others to believe. Should I have confessed my suspicions, or simply have made neutral and seemingly positive statements about understanding the legal system and social service agencies from their perspective? The identity that I presented was different from the one I felt."

Source: From "Ten Lies of Ethnography," by G.A. Fine, 1993, *Journal of Contemporary Ethnography,* *22*(3), p. 271.

LOOKING FOR RESOLUTION

To answer the last question first, Gusterson (1993) makes the argument that when researchers study *only* the marginalized, or the activists, they run the risk of making these groups appear problematic, and implicitly "normalizing" the dominant culture. In fact what is needed is the same critical and deconstructive approach among elites. They should not be exempt from scrutiny, and the people most likely to scrutinize are those whose political views are different.

The dilemma is how to present the results of such scrutiny in a way that *is* critical, but that skirts the kind of "condemnatory option" that is more the domain of activists or partisan journalists. This option usually draws on what Gusterson calls the *objectivist* strategy of writing about elites, in which the writer is positioned as the ultimate authority (Gusterson, 1993, p. 70). Adapting Clifford's (1983) terminology, Gusterson cites two other strategies—the *dialogic* and the *polyphonic*—that renounce this privilege, but in different ways.

Those who use the *dialogic* strategy, according to Gusterson, use their own perspective as a "partial but hospitable vantage point" from which to study other perspectives. Gusterson notes a good example of this approach in Cohn's (1987) article on the "defence intellectuals" who analyze and develop strategies for using nuclear weapons. Cohn presented herself as a feminist who was both "appalled and fascinated" by this particular masculine world, and her article is an extended personal engagement with it.

The *polyphonic* strategy, as Gusterson points out, depends for its critique less on the voice of the author than on others within the range of informants. Gusterson cites Ginsburg's use of this strategy in her 1989 book on the abortion debate in an American community. In the book, Ginsburg even-handedly includes the voices of both pro-choice and pro-life activists. Gusterson claims that polyphonic writing "can still have the critical effect achieved by objectivist and dialogic writing," but it does so by juxtaposing different positions within the text, rather than "invoking the formal authority of the author to condemn or problematize particular points of view" (Gusterson, 1993, p. 74).

I have emphasized Gusterson's work here because, like me, he wants simultaneously to be critical and also to "understand and humanize" research participants. Dialogic and polyphonic writing strategies allow for the writing of stories that can do both. Because they can do both, they go a long way towards resolving the ethical dilemmas of informed consent and representation noted earlier.

I discovered Gusterson too late to help me with my own representation dilemmas. So how did I do without him? Did I betray the trust of my informants? To what extent did I "use their words against them"? As it turned out, in one area of concern and conflict I solved the problem by abandoning the topic. The environmental issues turned out to be too complex, and too removed from my comfort zone of interest and expertise. Apart from the conference presentation I described above, I did no further work in this area. But the gender analysis remained lively, and appeared in several conference presentations and publications.

Lerum (2001) suggests that the trust and representation questions I have raised here are answered by the "gossip test"—could I say what I said to their faces? I think about this question with reference to one well-aired piece of my research on engineers who were also fathers. I had looked at this subset of my interviews to explore the ways men working in strongly masculinist professional work environments balanced expectations about themselves as employees and as fathers. What emerged was an interesting continuum of responses to the demands of a "workaholic" work culture. At one end were those who bought in completely, and delegated all family responsibilities to their partners. At the other end were those I called the "challengers," who were committed to balance, and consistently resisted workplace claims to more of their time than they were willing to give. It was clear, however, that all the fathers, even the challengers, had considerable discretion in terms of their family obligations. In almost every case, their jobs were the privileged ones in the family, and there was a woman available to pick up any slack. This turned out to be a story about men who were clearly advantaged, but who responded to that advantage in nuanced and interesting ways. I don't think I would have had any problem telling this story to their faces. But like Ceglowski (2000), I would probably continue to worry about what they might think.

CONCLUSION

I am moving on to different kinds of work. Some of it, as noted above, will make use of the interview material from the engineers to look at issues more incidental to engineering. This work will be less "shareable" with the community of engineers—but I have paid my dues in terms of sharing what *has* interested them, and I don't think they would begrudge me the opportunity now to pursue some interests that are more mine than theirs. My newest project is also an interview study, so the questions of informed consent, rapport, and representation will continue to engage me. But in one way at least, I am giving myself a break. The new project involves a group of people (parents going "against the grain" of normative gender expectations in their families) whose values I share. I am discovering, with relief, that it makes a big difference.

GLOSSARY

Feminist: The theoretical position that women should have political, economic, and social equality with men (also the activist movement aimed at bringing about gender equality).

Informed consent: The agreement by a potential participant to take part in a research study on the basis of advance information about the study.

Masculinist: Associated with masculine values, beliefs, and practices.

Rapport: In research contexts, refers to the quality of the relationship between researcher and participant (particularly with respect to the establishment of trust and its implications for the disclosure of information).

"Studying up": The practice among researchers of studying elites, or those in positions of power and influence.

REFERENCES

Armstead, C. (1995). Writing contradictions: Feminist research and feminist writing. *Women's Studies International Forum, 18*(5/6), 627–636.

Ceglowski, D. (2000). Research as relationship. *Qualitative Inquiry, 6*(1), 88–103.

Clifford, J. (1983). On ethnographic authority. *Representations, 1*(2), 118–144.

Cohn, C. (1987). Sex and death in the rational world of defence intellectuals. *Signs, 12*(4), 687–718.

Daniels, A.K. (1983). Self-deception and self-discovery in field work. *Qualitative Sociology, 6*(3), 195–214.

Fine, G.A. (1993). Ten lies of ethnography. *Journal of Contemporary Ethnography, 22*(3), 267–294.

Fine, M., Weis, L., Weseen, S., & Wong, L. (2001). For whom? Qualitative research, representations, and social responsibilities. In N.K. Denzin & Y.S. Lincoln (Eds.), *Handbook of qualitative research, 2nd ed.*, (pp. 107–131). Thousand Oaks, CA: Sage Publications.

Ginsburg, F. (1989). *Contested lives: The abortion debate in an American community.* Berkeley: University of California Press.

Gubrium, J.F., & Holstein, J.A. (1990). *What is family?* Mountain View, CA: Mayfield.

Gusterson, H. (1993). Exploding anthropology's canon in the world of the bomb. *Journal of Contemporary Ethnography, 22*(1), 59–79.

Harding, S. (1991). *Whose science? Whose knowledge?* Ithaca: Cornell University Press.

Herrera, C.D. (1999). Two arguments for "covert methods" in social research. *British Journal of Sociology, 50*(2), 331–343.

Hertz, R. (2003). Paying forward and paying back. *Symbolic Interaction, 26*(3), 473–486.

Hertz, R., & Imber, J. (1993). Fieldwork in elite settings: Introduction. *Journal of Contemporary Ethnography, 22*(1), 3–6.

Homan, R. (1992). The ethics of open methods. *British Journal of Sociology, 43*(3), 321–332.

Katz, J. (1997). Ethnography's warrants. *Sociological Methods and Research, 25*(4), 391–423.

Lerum, K. (2001). Subjects of desire: Academic armour, intimate ethnography, and the production of critical knowledge. *Qualitative Inquiry, 7*(4), 466–483.

Ranson, G. (1998, May). *Retention of women in engineering: Good news and bad news from Alberta.* Paper presented at the 7th conference of the Canadian Coalition of Women in Science, Engineering and Technology, Vancouver, B.C.

Ranson, G. (2000a, July). *The best of both worlds? Work, family life and the retention of women in engineering.* Paper presented at the 8th conference of the Canadian Coalition of Women in Science, Engineering and Technology, St. John's, Nfld.

Ranson, G. (2000b, November). *The long journey towards transformation of male professional turf: A case study in engineering.* Paper presented at the Institute of Gender Studies and Women's Studies Conference, University of Toronto, Toronto, Ont.

Ranson, G. (2001a). Men at work: Change—or no change?—in the era of the new father. *Men and Masculinities, 4*(1), 3–26.

Ranson, G. (2001b). Engineers and the western Canadian oil industry: Work and life changes in a boom-and-bust decade. In V.W. Marshall, W.R. Heinz, H. Krueger, & A. Verma (Eds.), *Restructuring work and the life course* (pp. 462–472). Toronto: University of Toronto Press.

Ranson, G. (2003). Beyond gender differences: A Canadian study of women's and men's careers in engineering. *Gender, Work and Organization, 10*(1), 22–41.

Schacht, S.P. (1997). Feminist fieldwork in the misogynist setting of the rugby pitch. *Journal of Contemporary Ethnography, 26*(3), 338–363.

Springwood, C.F., & King, C.R. (2001). Unsettling engagements: On the ends of rapport in critical ethnography. *Qualitative Inquiry, 7*(4), 403–417.

Thorne, B. (1979). Political activist as participant observer: Conflicts of commitment in a study of the draft resistance movement of the 1960's. *Symbolic Interaction, 2*(1), 73–88.

Thorne, B. (1980) "You still takin' notes?": Fieldwork and problems of informed consent. *Social Problems, 27*(3), 284–297.

Van den Hoonaard, W.C. (2001). Is research-ethics review a moral panic? *Canadian Review of Sociology and Anthropology, 38*(1), 19–36.

Warren, C. (2002). Qualitative interviewing. In J.F. Gubrium & J.A. Holstein (Eds.), *Handbook of interview research* (pp. 83–101). Thousand Oaks, CA: Sage Publications.

Chapter 8

Conducting Qualitative Research on Emotionally Upsetting Topics: Homicide and Those Left Behind

J. Scott Kenney

INTRODUCTION

Doing research on emotionally troubled (and troubling) participants has been little mentioned in the qualitative analysis literature. Yet, qualitative sociologists frequently deal with serious topics and troubling individuals. One immediately thinks of the many classic studies of deviance that have been conducted through ethnographic inquiry. However, the topic is much broader and includes areas such as medical sociology, criminology, victimology, feminist studies, and media analysis. This chapter attempts to take a preliminary look at the issues raised for qualitative researchers by emotionally troubling topics.

My research project dealt with murder. I personally dealt with 53 respondents, 32 of whom involved face-to-face interviews. The other 22, in a less direct fashion, filled out surveys (one person completed both). Respondents included parents and family members of children who had been murdered. I also accessed 108 homicide files at the Ontario Criminal Injuries Compensation Board (which included detailed psychiatric reports and victim impact statements), and conducted participant observation with an Ontario victims' support/advocacy organization. While my initial goal was to examine gender differences in active coping among such **homicide survivors**, it quickly became apparent that this was a group troubled by far more than the crime itself. Indeed, there were a wide variety of troubling issues to investigate (e.g., the often hurtful reaction of family, friends, and the community; upsetting encounters with various "helping" agents and the criminal justice system). Until this research, relatively little attention had been paid to such matters in this context (Kenney, 1998).

Doing qualitative research on such emotionally sensitive and explosive issues seemed the most appropriate research strategy for several reasons. First, there has been very little research done in the past on such subjects, so it was felt necessary to explore the respondents' own meanings and experiences through flexible, semi-structured interviews, ethnographic observation, and content analysis. I wanted to know their perspectives on these devastating experiences, not what others thought or assumed was important (Berg, 1995; Denzin, 1989). Second, there was a difficulty in identifying the population because of the isolation and secrecy that surrounds emotional and sensitive issues, particularly in relation to the death of children. As such, it would have been very difficult to conduct a large, quantitative study (Berg, 1995; Lee, 1993). Third, due to the sensitive nature of the issues, many respondents at first questioned my trustworthiness. I had to earn their trust, and face-to-face communication was the most appropriate way to do this.

ETHICS REVIEW

The literature shows that there are increasing difficulties faced by researchers in the face of ever more stringent ethics review policies (Lee, 1993; Van den Hoonaard, 2000). With particularly emotional and sensitive topics, such as battered women, such difficulties are even greater due to concerns about exposing subjects to stressful moments (Chatzifotiou, 2000). Hence, in studying homicide, I found the difficulties even more pronounced. As is standard, I obtained university ethics approval. In doing so, I initially faced the difficulty of creating instruments that were both sufficiently structured and sensitively worded to satisfy the ethics review board, but open enough to enable flexibility and for participants to speak their own words.

Given the uniqueness of the issues being explored, it was initially quite difficult to get in touch with potential participants (Lee, 1993). It was thus necessary to access organizations and their representatives that acted as **gatekeepers** (e.g., victim's organizations, support and bereavement groups). This also included submitting a detailed plan of proposed research and the questionnaire to a US victims' association for review by a staff physician before the research was approved. As for the content analysis of the Criminal Injuries Compensation files, it goes without saying that the provincial government would not allow the viewing of such sensitive documents unless confidentiality was to be respected. A detailed written agreement was carefully negotiated between the researcher and the board, ensuring just that.

In seeking ethics approval to deal directly with victims, it was very important for me to emphasize that data would be collected only from willing respondents who would be informed in advance about the sensitive nature of my research. Thus, detailed written notices were prepared for each organization regarding the nature of my study. I made it clear that research subjects, whether those being observed or individuals later agreeing to interviews or mail-back surveys, would be well aware of my role. Indeed, immediately prior to conducting each interview, I noted that each participant would again be informed that there would be personal, potentially upsetting questions asked. I indicated that respondents would be advised that they could decline any questions and withdraw from the interview at any time. They were further advised that their comments were confidential, that any records would be confidentially stored and destroyed following completion of the research, and that neither their names nor potentially identifying details would be used in any publication. Finally, before proceeding, I indicated that participants' written permission to tape record interviews would be required on a form that reiterated all of the above matters.

One final note in this regard. I have conducted several other victim-related projects since obtaining ethics approval for this research in the mid-1990s (e.g., on public and private victim support services and restorative justice programs). My experiences with research ethics policies and the inevitable political elements in these contexts have sometimes left me wondering whether I would be able to have my homicide project approved were I beginning this work today.

ISSUES IN THE DESIGN OF RESEARCH INSTRUMENTS

With reference to interview schedules and questionnaires, the organizational structure primarily centred around thematic topics while including many open-ended questions and opportunities for participants to speak about their own concerns. Both the interview schedules and the survey instrument followed the same basic structure. Following initial questions documenting demographic characteristics, participants were asked to describe in their own words their unique experiences.

Specifically, respondents were asked to describe their reactions, feelings, and how, if at all, they would be able to describe what it was like to lose a loved one in this manner. They were also asked what meanings this event disclosed for their current life. They were then questioned about what they viewed as helpful and unhelpful encounters with: (1) immediate family; (2) extended family and friends; (3) help agents, such as self-help organizations and the medical profession; and (4) various legal institutions. The issue of gender was examined in each of these contexts, particularly with regard to subjects' coping responses.

Possible threats to validity in the construction of these instruments were dealt with by having both academic colleagues and key members of the organizations read and comment before they were used. With regard to reliability, rather than rely on only one question per issue, these instruments were constructed in such a manner that they generally utilized several different questions to measure the same thing. As such, problems with consistency in responses were reduced or negated.

ACCESSING SUBJECTS

It has long been noted that locating subjects and gaining their co-operation are problems when researching sensitive subjects (Lee, 1993; Gelles, 1978). I recognized this and, as a result, started by volunteering with a national victims' rights organization. This offered me the opportunity to participate and conduct fieldwork on many key events crucially bearing on "victims'" concerns. Not only did I learn a great deal about victims' issues by helping with some of this organization's current projects, but I eventually worked myself into a position where I was able to (a) act as a delegate, distribute surveys, and conduct interviews at two national conferences; and (b) obtain information from courtroom observers and volunteers on the progression of a notorious murder trial. More than anything else, however, volunteering with this organization enabled me to have regular contact and to network with many potential respondents.

It quickly became apparent that closer access to many key respondents would not have been gained were it not for my ability to empathize or share a personal story. As a result, I shared my own experience of a murder in the family. This helped to establish a trusting relationship with my first well-connected respondent. The goodwill and word-of-mouth endorsements that followed not only enabled me to get personal accounts from many key individuals, but it rapidly snowballed. As a result of this success, I continued to share personal accounts with subsequent respondents.

Indeed, without my prior knowledge and experience with this topic, many participants indicated that they would not likely have felt comfortable enough to share the details of their experiences for fear that I would not be able to understand or handle many of the shocking details (i.e., I'd simply be seen as one of the detached, less-than-sensitive "ologists" often dismissed by many of my respondents).

INTERVIEWING AND OBSERVING RESPONDENTS

This was the core area where emotional upset on the part of respondents and the researcher was most notable. By and large the individuals I spoke with were glad to talk to someone about their experiences. Many respondents had become socially isolated, lost friends, and maintained little contact with family (Kenney, 2002b). This was often considered the result of others' misunderstanding, uncertainty of how to act, or because of blame, indicating that **labelling** was at work (Kenney, 2002b). Indeed, many felt as though they were being avoided. As one woman stated, "It's been two years and I think you are the third person that's been in this house."

The interviews were very emotional for respondents as well as for myself. Still, I found that carefully gauging questions and responses to the mood of participants helped to avoid upsetting them too much and prevented me from becoming visibly upset. Nevertheless, as the literature suggests (Chatzifotiou, 2000; Kinard, 1996), interviewer anxiety was an issue, and there were many times when the interviews were very tense. In the cases where showing upset was appropriate or where the subject matter rendered it unavoidable, I personally found that the empathetic experience of mutual upset actually helped both the respondents and myself.

Indeed, respondents were able to express emotions that they hadn't often had an opportunity to express before because people were avoiding them. There were a few interviews where I was especially concerned about having upset the respondents, but was reassured that it was not my fault: it was their situation. In the words of one woman: "My friends are afraid to keep bringing it up, and they shy away because they're afraid they're going to 'say something that's going to hurt you.' So they shy away. 'Cause, maybe they don't know that you want it. That it's all right to talk about it. They're afraid to. They don't understand that you can't be hurt any more than you already have been" (Female, age 45).

Being able to share these emotions generally strengthened my rapport with respondents. However, in situations where they were very upset, I turned off the tape recorder, and we would chat for a few minutes before resuming. There were a few exceptions that involved older men who adhered to more traditional gender roles and wouldn't show their upset. In these cases I took non-verbal cues such as finger tapping on the table as a sign to change the nature of the dialogue or to wrap up the interview. Yet, there was never a time where either a participant or the researcher could not finish an interview.

Because of the intensity and sensitive nature of the subject matter, I found that I had to plan the interview times carefully. I didn't face the problem of doing many emotionally gruelling interviews in a short time as I rarely did more than a couple of interviews a week. Nevertheless, I found it necessary to accommodate carefully respondents' time preferences such that interviews were held at, not only the most convenient time, but also when respondents felt it most helpful to talk.

Use of language was a constant challenge. I faced the problem of framing questions in such a way that it would be less likely to upset respondents. For example, I was informed that the seemingly innocent demographic question "How many children do you have?" can be quite upsetting in this context.

Perhaps more significantly, asking people to either describe (a) what it was like to lose someone like this, or (b) whether they personally saw themselves as victims, tended to provoke strong responses. While certainly evocative of a great deal of key data, these questions could be a touchy matter with some respondents. Some of their responses could be quite graphic. On the one hand, many simply stated that the experience was indescribable, but went on to use a variety of disturbing **metaphors of loss** (Kenney, 2002a) to convey, insofar as it was possible, their lived experiences. On the other hand, others, if they felt their victim status was in question, responded in a similar fashion to interactionally reinforce their position. One way or another, this metaphorical language was emotionally gripping.

Centred around the idea that "when you lose someone you love, you lose a part of yourself," expressions such as having one's "heart torn out," experiencing an

---

Box 8.1: Metaphors of Loss

"Metaphors of loss" are phrases that individual victims use to accomplish three things: (1) To convey, insofar as possible, the damage to their selves, to who they are, as the result of victimization; (2) to express the meanings of victimization as conveyed to them by their emotions; and (3) to reinforce the interpersonal definition of themselves as victims, particularly in order to exercise a form of practical control when challenged.

Rooted in the idea that "When you lose someone you love, you lose a part of yourself," respondents fleshed out various dimensions to this root metaphor, including: (1) permanent loss of future; (2) violating devastation; (3) being a "different person now"; (4) loss of control; and (5) lost innocence.

Interestingly, while women predominated in the expression of all of these, men tended to more fully emphasize loss of control—not surprising given traditional male gender roles, as well as the fact that many respondents were older adults.

Source: From "Metaphors of Loss: Murder, Bereavement, Gender, and Presentation of the 'Victimized' Self," by J.S. Kenney, 2002, *International Review of Victimology, 9*, pp. 219–251.

"amputation," feeling "dead inside," "violated," "broken," and having "no future" were delivered with an emotional punch that nearly left me reeling. For example:

"When they shot my son, they shot me. I felt such an emptiness. They killed my boy and they killed me inside. I'm not the same and I never will be" (Female, age 45).

"This was the most traumatic, violating event that I think could happen to anybody. I cannot imagine ever being more violated—not even by rape. My mother was a suicide, the rest of my family died of heart attacks and other various related things. There's no comparison. Absolutely no comparison" (Female, age 51).

"How does it feel? Well, it feels like someone reached into my heart, cut out a nice big chunk, filled it with blackness, and left me cold on the sidewalk" (Male, age 24).

"It's like sinking in quicksand, but never quite suffocating and dying oneself" (Female, age 53).

I particularly recall one interview in which I interviewed the father of a young woman who had been murdered by her boyfriend. This man was evidently in a very emotionally fragile condition, particularly due to the fact that he had previously saved the life of the offender and now felt it was "his fault" that his daughter had been killed. Many such comments were made throughout the interview, evidence that he was deeply embedded in a cyclical **grief cycle** (Kenney, 2003). This interview required considerable discretion, attention to the respondent's non-verbal cues, and **emotion management** on my part to navigate the interview to a successful conclusion (Hochschild, 1983).

Upon experiencing such difficulties in the interviews, I found that there needed to be added safeguards for those respondents farther afield who filled out mail-back surveys. Thus, before sending out questionnaires, I informed all such respondents in a cover letter about the subject matter of the survey, the nature of the questions, and confidentiality. I also gave them an opportunity to ask questions of me by phone before proceeding. Indeed, I spoke at length to many of these individuals on the phone before sending out questionnaires, and fielded several calls for clarification as these were being completed by respondents.

But perhaps most disturbing for me during the data collection was the fact that several respondents used the term "my baby" with reference to the deceased. I particularly recall one incident early in my research when I was volunteering and conducting fieldwork at a victims' organization. I had been asked to help type up a handwritten letter to the parole board for my "gatekeeper." In that letter she used the phrase "My baby was dead" in relation to her murdered daughter—something that triggered memories of my own cousin's emotionally intense funeral. "My baby" were the words that my aunt was screaming over and over as she was being escorted out of the funeral home after viewing his body. It was the saddest thing I'd ever seen in my entire life, and hearing such words from another mother in a similar context was very difficult for me, necessitating a break for the day.

TRANSCRIPTION AND DATA ANALYSIS

Personally, I feel that the emotionally difficult part of this research for me was only beginning once data collection was complete. There were times in transcribing and reviewing the data where my own upset was triggered. Respondents noted emotionally upsetting encounters in a number of contexts, things that shocked even this jaded sociological researcher, who thought he had heard it all. For example, in addition to the common avoidance by others, one mother spoke of highly disturbing forms of telephone harassment.

Box 8.2: The Upsetting Harassment of Victims

"Like, we got obscene phone calls to the house. The minute that we became public, I got phone calls that 'If you and your family had belonged to the right religion, these horrible things wouldn't happen to you. God is punishing you.' We'd get phone calls like that. One day this guy phoned and asked if I was the mother of one of these children that had been murdered. I said I was, and he says, 'Well, would you stay on the line while I masturbate?' And like this is for real! This is going on like every hour around here. Like—not just sporadically days apart—this is for real! And it's going on constantly" (Female, age 49).

Source: From "Victims of Crime and Labeling Theory: A Parallel Process?" by J.S. Kenney, 2002, Deviant Behavior, 23(3), pp. 235–266.

I also recall one particularly difficult instance when I interviewed a woman about the murder of a five-year-old girl by a pedophile young offender. She described in grim detail how the little girl died and the unspeakable things that had been done to her. The respondent and her family found this out in court through a video re-enactment by the offender without any warning.

Particularly disturbing in this case, the respondents also gave me a picture of the little girl to keep. Needless to say, I found it very difficult when I transcribed and reviewed these comments and saw the picture in the file. In situations such as this, I found that I had to take a break from work, sometimes for the rest of the day.

It was also difficult at times when I had to share such information with others I worked with. For instance, I had hired a student to assist with transcription. I was careful to consider her feelings when asking her to transcribe an interview. Yet, at times, needless to say, she did not find this easy material to deal with. Also, as this research was my Ph.D. dissertation, I shared these data with my thesis committee. Writing up the data was one thing, but having to relay it was quite another. I know that some of these data upset my supervisor: she told me so. I was constantly aware of the difficulties this presented for others who had to deal with them.

The sheer volume and complexity of qualitative data collected for this study required an intensive and organized approach to coding and analysis. Before data analysis began, all of the tape-recorded interviews and field notes, as well as the

Box 8.3: Unwelcome Surprises

" [The offender] made a video re-enactment for the police the day he confessed. First we hear about it! Boom! There we are, we're in the court, they put the video on, and we're watching as he goes through it. You could not imagine how horrible this tape was. We were watching this, and he showed how he picked her up, and how he carried her, and he was nonchalant, you know, hands in the pocket, not nervous. It showed how he, like he made this claim on the videotape that he heard [the deceased's brother] calling her, and he was molesting her, and she screamed, 'Mummy!' So he killed her! Just like that. She was dead when he assaulted her. She was on the ground, and he said on this videotape that he kicked her in the head once, and then he stood on her chest. Then, he showed them how he jumped on her. He took this tremendous leap in the air and jumped on her. We're like ... we're sitting there going like ... (respondent gestures, expressing shock and horror). Then it showed how he went back to the apartment, and he went up to the bathroom and he said, 'I had to take my shoe off.' He said, 'There was this thing in it. I think it was shit'—and he laughs on this videotape! So we just freaked. We just freaked. I ... we were just ... you know how you know that you're going to scream, and you're going to cry, and you're just completely out of control? And we'd never been warned" (Female, age 44).

Source: From *Coping with Grief: Survivors of Murder Victims*, by J.S. Kenney, 1998, unpublished doctoral dissertation, McMaster University, Hamilton, Ontario.

open-ended mail-back surveys and criminal injuries compensation files, were entered verbatim into separate files in WordPerfect. Paper copies were also made of these documents.

In time, I found that as analysis progressed, I gradually became more and more desensitized to the data when compared to the interview, transcription, and initial analysis stages. This was most likely due to the repeated exposure to the data day after day, thus rendering it less upsetting. Sometimes I still question whether that is a good thing.

PRESENTATION OF DATA

I was very concerned about how to present such sensitive and upsetting material. In giving my respondents a voice, which is the intention when undertaking grounded theory methodology, it is the responsibility of researchers to ensure that the respondents' meanings and perspectives are presented just as they were described. I have presented these data professionally in a number of contexts. This includes lectures at universities and academic conferences. All that I can offer on this account is that I try as sensitively as possible to prepare my audiences by informing them that the nature of the data is graphic and may be upsetting to hear. I always find that there is a level of discomfort among even professional audiences, yet there is also much interest in knowing how I was able to manage such sensitive research.

In addition I have provided summaries of my research to interested respondents and organizations that I worked with during the process. For the most part I have received favourable responses. Indeed, I have been warmly received by several of my respondents upon encountering them later at conferences.

In all of this I must again stress the importance of confidentiality, particularly in presenting the data in an anonymous fashion such that individuals cannot be identified. In my sample, many of the respondents knew or were aware of each other and their circumstances. Safeguards such as changing names and omitting identifiable features were integral to the overall favourable responses that I received.

CONCLUSION

For the most part I did not find the research particularly upsetting to do on the surface (with the notable exceptions above). Because I had experienced a murder in my own family more than a decade before, I had largely learned to deal with it before the time I began the research. It was not so unfamiliar that I was shocked by it. Indeed, near the end of my dissertation, the disturbing feelings that had given way to desensitization started to slip into feelings of tedium and a heartfelt desire to get the whole thing finished once and for all (a not uncommon feeling among students who spend years writing their thesis!). I often noted to friends and colleagues that I was "sick to death of death."

Nevertheless, I did fear at times that constantly reviewing such shocking and depressing material would get to me "beneath the surface." In this vein, I realized a great irony some months after completing my research. Much of the data in this study focused on active coping strategies utilized by the respondents. However, my own coping strategies in dealing with this material in some ways paralleled those of the participants. For instance, many respondents found that in order to deal with their grief they had to balance their time between focusing on their grief and other life activities that occupied their thoughts—to deal with it a bit at a time in "more easily digestible chunks." Upon reflection, this had proven to be a useful coping strategy for many of my own activities in relation to this material as well. Not only did writing about the emotionally upsetting materials enable me to work through my own upset in this regard (Francis, 2000), balancing this with other activities (e.g., exercise, socializing, reading about other things) become a useful strategy of emotion management (Hochschild, 1983).

Of course, this quickly became a useful insight in other ways, as finishing one's thesis is never really the end. Working in academia, I soon had to take this dissertation research and rework it into a series of publishable journal articles—a process that, several years later, is thankfully nearly complete. I have had to draw upon the coping practices noted above again and again to deal with the diverse feelings still evoked by this material. Moreover, now that I have two small children of my own, not only have I had to draw anew upon these coping skills in completing such endeavours, but I feel that this has deepened my insights. All the same, I question whether I would personally have difficulties conducting the same research today.

Clearly, working with sensitive and emotionally upsetting data raises many complex issues. In the end, it is ironic that those subjects that are so difficult to access and to research, the very subjects that many in society shy away from, may prove to be the most rewarding and personally enlightening in one's research career.

GLOSSARY

Emotion management: In the work of Arlie Hochschild (1983), this refers to the active work that people do to create a publicly acceptable facial and bodily display, as well as their efforts actually to feel the appropriate emotion for a given social context. Hochschild indicates that this is accomplished by altering our expression ("surface acting"), or by attempting, through various forms of self-deception, to actually change how we feel about an upsetting situation ("deep acting"). While applicable to both employment and private settings, such practices are invaluable to the process of conducting qualitative research in emotionally upsetting situations (e.g., in not becoming or appearing so upset oneself that one upsets key respondents or radically alters ongoing social processes).

Gatekeepers: In the qualitative analysis literature, this refers to individuals or organizations who act to guard the potential research setting, along with the individuals, groups, and processes therein, from the prying eyes of outsiders (Berg, 1995). Developing rapport and trust with such parties is often a must when conducting qualitative research on subcultures, particularly related to sensitive, private, or deviant topics around which there may be considerable misunderstanding, emotion, or stigma. In many cases, the endorsement of one's research by such agents makes it possible to access subjects, processes, behaviours, and settings that would be impossible otherwise.

Grief cycle: Inextricably linked to traditional gender roles, this involves recurrent patterns of thought, behaviour, and emotion management in relation to grief that results in the same painful experiences being repeated again and again. Typical of male and female homicide survivors who strongly adhered to traditional gender roles, individuals whose socialization, circumstances, reactions, and coping choices lead them into these "traps" invariably suffered enormously. The male grief cycle is dominated by guilt, repression of certain thoughts or feelings, exhaustion, explosions of anger or an inability to handle one's valued responsibilities, followed by further feelings of failure and guilt—which starts the "vicious cycle" all over again. For women, it involves continual focus on the crime, their loss, feelings of violation and upset over a considerable time period, such that feelings of despair begin to feed back on themselves and incapacitate the individual. In either case, these patterns could become cyclical and serve as a block to coping.

Homicide survivors: The most common term utilized by individuals or organized groups of individuals who have suffered the murder of a loved one ("co-victim" and "secondary victim" are sometimes also used). While an apparent oxymoron when applied to the direct victim, the idea is that those close to the direct (deceased) victim have been severely injured by the murder as well. However, rather than necessarily succumbing to all of the stigmatizing connotations of victimhood, they have taken this injury as a badge of honour and evidence that they are, at least potentially, capable, active agents.

Labelling: This refers to the social process whereby deviants are defined by the rest of society. In this process, stigmatizing terms or categories are invented or applied by individuals or groups, formally or informally, to individuals exhibiting various traits or behaviours. Arguably, this stabilizes and reinforces these self-same behaviours through fostering a deviant self-image and reaction by the labelled individual. Traditionally utilized in the sociology of deviance, I have argued that a parallel labelling process occurs for victims as well, with corresponding consequences for self-image and behaviour (Kenney, 2002b).

REFERENCES

Berg, B.L. (1995). *Qualitative research methods for the social sciences* (2nd ed.). Needham Heights, MA: Allyn & Bacon.

Chatzifotiou, S. (2000). Conducting qualitative research on wife abuse: Dealing with the issue of anxiety." *Sociological Research Online*, 5(2) August. Retrieved on November 12, 2004, from http://www.socresonline.org.uk

Denzin, N.K. (1989). *Interpretive interactionism*. Newbury Park, CA: Sage.

Francis, L.E. (2000). *The health benefits of narrative: Why and how?* Association Paper: American Sociological Association.

Gelles, R.J. (1978). "Methods for studying sensitive family topics." *American Journal of Orthopsychiatry*, 48(3), 408–424.

Hochschild, A.R. (1983). *The managed heart*. Berkeley: University of California Press.

Kenney, J.S. (1998). *Coping with grief: Survivors of murder victims*. Unpublished doctoral dissertation, McMaster University, Hamilton, Ontario.

Kenney, J.S. (2002a). Metaphors of loss: Murder, bereavement, gender, and presentation of the "victimized" self. *International Review of Victimology, 9*, 219–251.

Kenney, J.S. (2002b). Victims of crime and labeling theory: A parallel process? *Deviant Behavior, 23*(3), 235–266.

Kenney, J.S. (2003). Gender roles and grief cycles: Observations on models of grief and coping in homicide cases. *International Review of Victimology, 10*, 19–47.

Kinard, E.M. (1996). Conducting research on child maltreatment: Effects of researchers. *Violence and Victims, 11*(1), 65–69.

Lee, R.M. (1993). *Doing research on sensitive topics*. Newbury Park, CA: Sage.

Van den Hoonaard, W.C. (2000). *Research ethics review as a moral panic*. Paper presented at the 17th Annual Qualitative Analysis Conference, University of New Brunswick.

PART 1D

Writing about Social Life

C h a p t e r   9

The Question of "Whose Truth"?: The Privileging of Participant and Researcher Voices in Qualitative Research

Linda L. Snyder

INTRODUCTION: DUAL PERSPECTIVES

Qualitative research presents the perspectives or truths of the study participants and of the researcher. Sometimes a primary objective is to give voice to participants. This is frequently so when our findings illuminate an area where participants' experience is not well understood. In other research projects, the researcher's holistic appraisal is paramount. In program evaluations, for example, conflicting perceptions must be examined, tentative notions need to be tested against existing theory, and some study participants' practices must be criticized. The question of whose truth has important implications for the research process—particularly member checking and seeking participants' agreement with the conclusions.

Two perspectives are present in qualitative research—that of the researcher/self and that of the participant/other. In our analysis and reporting, we make decisions about the relative emphasis of each of these perspectives. These choices invoke questions related to the issues of representation and voice of the participant, and interpretation and place of the researcher (Altheide & Johnson, 1994; Porter, 2000).

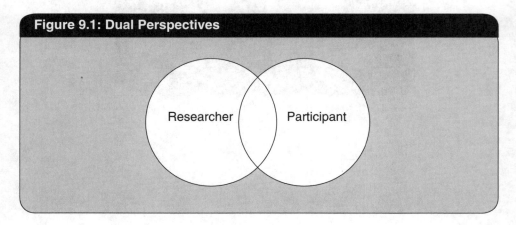

Figure 9.1: Dual Perspectives

Researcher   Participant

In recent years, these issues have been the subject of lively debate. There are varied positions on how best to represent accurately the studied phenomena. In addition, there are fundamental challenges about the very possibility of accurate representation, since all that we observe is inevitably refracted through our own perception (Snow & Morrill, 1993).

Geertz (1988) locates the challenge of representation within the demanding context of qualitative research that attempts to provide both "an intimate view and a cool assessment" (p. 10). He describes the dilemma regarding the place of the researcher in the text as one of developing a research signature that is neither so vivid as to obscure the field nor so subtle as to create "the deception that the research text speaks from the point of view of the participant" (Clandinin & Connelly, 1994, p. 424).

The distinction between the researcher and the participant perspectives became vividly apparent to me at the Qualitative Analysis Conference in 2000. I was struck by the contrasting approaches described by two presenters and how the approaches used by each researcher conveyed an impressive commitment to accurate representation and appeared, in each situation, to be the best means for achieving a high level of validity or truth value (Lincoln & Guba, 1985). Norma Jean Profitt (2000) described an emphasis on the participants' perspective in her exploration of the experiences of women survivors of abuse and their subsequent involvement in social action. Profitt's dedication to ensuring accurate representation included far more than normal **member checking**—she held second interviews with each participant and continued to consult with participants about her interpretation via telephone conversations throughout completion of the analysis and writing of her dissertation. A similarly inspiring, although dramatically different, research approach was recounted by Deirdre Smyth (2000). Smyth's research experience highlighted the importance of the researcher's perspective in her historical sociological study, which received a chagrined response from the biographied figure who disliked the honesty of the portrayal.

In my own multiple case study of women's employment initiatives, I utilized both approaches—emphasizing participants' perspectives by putting their voices forward to illustrate certain themes and stressing my own interpretations interwoven with voices from relevant literature to illustrate other themes (Snyder, 1999). Hence I was eager to explore this topic further to re-evaluate my own methodological, analytical, and authoring choices and in order to make more conscious decisions in future endeavours. The question regarding the two perspectives, it seems to me, is, whose truth?

TRUTH

Before we can address the question of "whose truth," some attention must be given to the meaning of truth within the constructivist **paradigm** in which qualitative research is situated. We acknowledge that the social world is an interpreted world (Altheide & Johnson, 1994). Clearly, there is no pretence of attempting to discover universal truths; the more humble and attainable objective is to explore normative truths in particular contexts (Gitlin, 2000). We recognize our restriction as human beings to a mind-mediated version of truth that can only be perceived and "re-presented" to others through our own particular lens (Alldred, 1998; Eisner, 1998). Therefore, as Altheide and Johnson note, our hope is "to provide an account that communicates with the reader the truth about the setting and situation, as the ethnographer has come to understand it" (p. 496). We cannot proclaim our findings with absolute certainty, but we can make answerable claims with good grounds (Eisner, 1998; Lincoln & Denzin, 1994).

Table 9.1: What Is Truth?

Research Paradigm	Social Constructivist / Interpretivist Paradigm	Positivist Paradigm
View of the social world	An interpreted world	An empirically knowable world
Nature of truth	Multiple truths	Universal truth
Attainable knowledge	Subjective, mind-mediated version of reality	Objective knowledge of reality
Applicability of research findings	Particular contexts	Can be generalized
Nature of assertions	Well-founded claims	Certainty
Trustworthiness criteria	Credibility	Internal validity

Lincoln and Guba (1985) developed criteria for establishing trustworthiness in the **constructivist paradigm**. The criterion of truth value, which the researchers in the positivist paradigm seek to meet through attention to internal validity, is addressed in the constructivist paradigm through means to enhance credibility. The now familiar techniques for qualitative researchers seeking to produce credible analysis include prolonged and persistent observation, triangulation, peer debriefing, negative case analysis, referential adequacy, and member checking (pp. 290–316).

In the last decade or so, work in the constructivist paradigm has become increasingly self-critical. As noted by Richardson (1994), in "the contemporary postmodernist context ... truth claims are less easily validated now; desires to speak 'for' others are suspect" (p. 523). Altheide and Johnson (1994), in putting forth a model for accountable ethnography that they call "analytic realism," stress that ethnographers must support their interpretations with a reflexive account of their research process, and "explicate *how* we claim to know *what* we know" [emphasis in original] (p. 496). A transformed ethnography has emerged that Hertz (1996) describes as "comprised of multiple layers, multiple truths, and multiple voices" (p. 3).

Thus, it is within this framework of a socially constructed reality, and a rigorous and reflexive constructivist research paradigm allowing for multiple truths, that the question of whose truth is explored. Consideration will first be given to emphasis on the participants' perspective, then the importance of the researcher's interpretation will be examined.

PARTICIPANTS' PERSPECTIVE: PRIVILEGING OFT-SILENCED VOICES

The current concern with privileging the voices of the research participants arises from criticism of the hierarchical and undemocratic nature of traditional ethnographic work (Atkinson & Hammersley, 1994). Feminists, in particular, found fault with knowledge built on a solely masculine interpretation (Fontana & Frey, 1994). What feminist as well as post-colonialist scholars identified was missing voices, silenced voices, and misunderstood voices (Lincoln & Denzin, 1994; Saukko, 2000). In response to the critique, the practice has emerged of giving voice to the powerless. Slim and Thompson (1995) describe the role reversal in the collection of oral testimony wherein "the interviewer sits at the feet of the people who are the obvious experts on their own life and experience" (p. 10). A continuum of levels of power transfer are evident in practices ranging from "recuperating silenced or misunderstood voices" (Saukko, 2000), through Freire-style pedagogy to "take back voice" (Lincoln & Denzin, 1994), to "using our own voices and experiences" (Gluck, 1984). The higher levels of power transfer are found in social change-oriented research and participative research described below.

An orientation towards social change is evident in the work of scholars promoting the creation of text that challenges "hierarchies of power and knowledge" (Standing, 1998, p. 201) and puts forward alternative voices as "resistance to marginalization" (Lincoln, 1995, p. 282). It is even more pronounced in Tierney's (1998) objective to not just give voice, but "to create the conditions in which individuals claim voice" (p. 56) and participate in the transformation of society (Mertens, 1999). Perhaps the strongest social change orientation is the research process Gitlin (2000) describes, in which the development of voice means, for participants, "attaining the right to tell their stories ... and have those stories make a difference" (p. 111).

In participative research, the power shift is located in the immediate relationship between the researcher and the researched and not necessarily in the social environment in which they are located. One type of participative research focuses on an interactive relationship in the process of interpreting the data, whereby "the researcher and the subject attempt to come to a mutual understanding based on their own strongly articulated positions" (Gitlin, 2000, p. 97). This type of long-term interaction to validate the worldviews of the participants (Jansen & Davis, 1998) is illustrated in the process that Profitt (2000) adopted.

An even more fully participative research process is represented in the practice of co-operative inquiry described by Heron (1996), in which shared decision making extends to all aspects of the research process:

> Co-operative inquiry ... does research *with* other people, who are invited to be full co-inquirers with the initiating researcher and become involved in operational

decision-making, and is committed to this kind of participative research design both politically and epistemologically. The co-inquirers are also fully involved in decisions about research content, that is, about the focus of the inquiry, what it is seeking to find out and achieve. (p. 10)

Looking beyond participative research to a total emphasis on participant perspective, one can imagine participant-controlled research with the research funds being provided to the studied group who would release monies to the researcher when they have agreed to the final text being published. What, then, of the value of the researcher's perspective?

RESEARCHER'S PERSPECTIVE: THE RESPONSIBILITY FOR INTERPRETATION

The importance of the researcher's perspective is underscored in the abundant writings by qualitative research scholars, which emphasize the researcher's final responsibility for the interpretation and analysis of the data (for example, see Strauss & Corbin, 1994; and Tutty, Rothery, & Grinnel, 1996). Dorothy Smith (1989), who is one of Canada's foremost pioneers in feminist research methodology, reminds us that "a moment comes after all the talk has been inscribed as text and become data when it must be worked up as sociology" (p. 35). Kleinman and Copp (1993) assert that the credibility of the research depends upon not accepting participants' stories at face value. Instead, the researcher must weigh the evidence from the "competing voices" that Song (1998) describes in her study of siblings and "put forth her own interpretation" (p. 12). Eisner (1998), as well, points to the centrality of the interpretive process, in which the researcher examines the multiple sources of data "to seek a confluence of evidence that breeds credibility" (p. 110). As Lincoln and Guba (1985) insist, "in the final analysis, the [research] team must use its own best judgment" (p. 378). In particular types of qualitative research, such as biography and investigative research, this position is most evident.

As mentioned earlier, Smyth (2000) described her experience in creating an historical sociology piece in which the central figure was displeased with the honesty of the portrayal. "In the final analysis," Smyth needed to maintain her own independent analytic stance in order to preserve the integrity of her work. She provided commentary from academic literature on the "perils of biography" (p. 9) that document the not unusual negative reaction of the subjects of biography "despite the fact that it might be an authorized, entirely ethical, and reasonable treatment [Origo in Davenport, 1965, p. 369]" (p. 16). In a chapter entitled "The Burdens of Biography," Schorer (1986) speaks of the conflicting stories, the faulty memories, and the imperfect documents "that must be checked against other documents and back again against that talk from personal witnesses that may or may not represent the truth" (pp. 80–81). Clearly this older art of biography has something to teach us about the process of reaching credible conclusions.

Even more poignant caution about placing too much emphasis on the participants' perspective comes from the area of investigative research. In contrast to the often romanticized view of the marginalized, Douglas (1976) emphasizes a conflictual view of life and the need, sometimes, to "wrench the truth" from those in the study setting (p. 176).

MULTIPLE VOICES AND MULTIPLE TRUTHS

Finding one's own position along the continuum between total emphasis on the participants' perspective and complete attention to the researcher's interpretation is one of the greatest challenges in qualitative research (Geertz, 1988). Much of the literature displays thinking in terms of two dichotomies, as Tierney (1995) has noted: "Either no thought has been given about how to involve those whom we study, or the argument is made that if our interviewees are not coparticipants in the research enterprise then the researcher is involved in an unethical undertaking" (p. 387).

Some scholars have cautioned that the extreme postmodern or poststructuralist procedural self-consciousness about participant perspective can be to the detriment of the empirical analysis and can lose itself in nihilistic self-doubt (Gubrium & Holstein, 1997; Heron, 1996).

In place of the dichotomous thinking, a more reasonable approach has been suggested with a pluralistic presentation of the multiple voices, including the inquirer's voice along with those of the other participants (Guba & Lincoln, 1994; Lincoln & Denzin, 1994). In the multi-voiced presentation the **emic** concepts emphasizing the participants' insider view and the **etic** concepts featuring the researchers' outsider view are illuminated and connected (Geertz, 1983). The openness to the alternative voices becomes a criterion for quality (Lincoln, 1995). This presentation of the participants' and researcher's perspectives allows the reader to choose to agree or disagree with the researcher's interpretations (Rogers, 2000). However, as Jansen and Davis (1998) remind us, ultimately the author decides which voices to include and which stories best illustrate the themes that emerged in the analysis.

The issue of which voices—whose truth—has received some considered attention in the literature, although its resolution is not likely in the near future. Snow and Morrill (1993) ask: "Are decisions on whose voices to privilege not contingent on the exigencies of the setting under study and the questions and issues pursued?" (p. 11). Gubrium and Holstein (1997) add that each approach "offers its own groundings, assumptions, topics, and analytic machinery [and each] is especially well-suited to examine and portray particular senses of everyday reality" (p. 100). But these decisions are more than matters of the questions pursued or methodology. These decisions, particularly given the responsibility for "changing those conditions that seek to silence and marginalize" (Tierney, 1993, p. 5) are political and ethical ones (Schwandt, 1997). Interestingly, as biographers have realized, some accurate portrayals of subjects may not be complimentary, and that in these situations a less than full disclosure to subjects may be most consistent with good ethics (Goode, 1996).

These thoughts ring true for me, as I reflect on the decisions I made regarding the level of participant involvement in my own research on women's employment initiatives in Canada and Chile. Certainly I was very careful in recording and transcribing all of the events; at times, asking a Chilean professor to ensure the correctness of my translations. I used the member-checking technique by preparing a preliminary report of the findings for each of the four case studies, which I circulated (in some cases, sequentially) to all of the participants in order to solicit their feedback on the accuracy of my understanding. I was persistent in seeking out this commentary, and I was pleased to receive some corrections and many endorsements through a variety of individual meetings, group meetings, telephone conversations, and return mailings—including one aerogram from Chile that a participant with limited schooling had asked her 10-year-old daughter to write.

Although I believe this was a sufficient level of attention to credibility in my study, it was not as in-depth nor as long term as the ongoing consultation with participants in which Profitt (2000) engaged. One of the differences between my level of participant involvement and Profitt's prolonged engagement relates to the purposes of the research. The greater attention to participant perspective may be more important in studies of women's own experiences than in studies where programs are the unit of analysis.

Let me provide some illustrations, however, from my research, where variations in the primacy of the participants' and researcher's voice occur in the same piece. The themes that emerged in my research that relate most closely to the women's experiences are the topics peppered with the participants' direct quotes in the final report. For example, the women described important features of the programs, such as the benefit to them of having instructors with the same characteristics:

> When I read about her, I became interested in working with her, because she combines business with family and that's what I wanted to do. They are good trainers because they are persons like us. They are very human … We don't elevate them … we are all equal.

As another example, the women's stories documented a sharp contrast between the Canadian and Chilean initiatives in the attention that the programs gave to the couple relationship. From a Canadian program instructor:

> Sometimes, I feel like a home wrecker. As the participants' self-esteem increases and they gain confidence in their ability to implement their business plans, the dynamics in the couple relationship change; many relationships have ended.

From a Chilean program participant:

> My husband was distinctly different before; this course helped our communication … When I tried to participate in decisions, he didn't give it much importance. But now—yes, since the course, my opinions carry more importance. I explain what I am doing, so that he understands too … I stood firm, saying I also need to do things—not just serve … In general, the program was very good. But for me, it was good for a mountain of things—the whole family.

In contrast, another theme concerned the potential for social mobilization within the initiatives—a theme that arose from my interests and interpretation, rather than from participant initiation of discourse on the topic. In the cross-comparison of the programs, the importance of leadership style and organizational structure emerged as important to the likelihood of social mobilization and political outcomes. Although the director of one of the initiatives has made a contribution of historical proportions in the founding and development of the program, I found it necessary to be critical of her leadership style in relation to the program participants' underdeveloped sense of political efficacy. This analysis had not come clear to me when I prepared the preliminary findings, and it seemed to me to be unnecessarily hurtful to share the critique with her when it developed later.

This theme, it seemed to me, was the result of my analysis of the empirical data and the relevant literature and not a matter requiring consultation and the development of "mutual understanding" with the participants.

Box 9.1: Criticism of the Director's Leadership Style

The ... director's contribution has been central to the establishment of the artisan workshop development program: her artistic skill and creativity; her teaching experience; her commitment to ensuring that the poor share in the enjoyment of basic sustenance, social interaction, and the beauty of art; as well as her determination to see the organizational supports for these goals in place. With the tremendous contribution she has made to this organization, it is not surprising that she is looked upon with a form of reverence. This charismatic style of leadership, however, raises some concern in terms of the organization's ability to deal with her eventual departure and the participants' limited sense of ownership or power as a result of their collective accomplishments.

The notion of charismatic leadership was introduced by Max Weber (1924/1947), who saw charismatic leaders as highly esteemed, gifted individuals who exude confidence, dominance, and a sense of purpose (Bass, 1990). Lassey and Sashkin (1983), writing about leadership and social change, note that while some degree of charisma may be essential, charisma must be complemented with other critical skills in order to be most effective. Musser (1987), similarly cautions that charismatic leadership can produce dependent followers rather than a model inspiring self-actualizing people.

A more recent leadership concept, that of transformational leadership ...

Source: From *Women's employment initiatives as a means of addressing poverty: A comparative study of Canadian and Chilean examples* (pp. 335–336), by L. Snyder, 1999, unpublished doctoral dissertation, Wilfrid Laurier University, Waterloo, Ontario.

One of the reasons for the distinct choices of participant voice or researcher voice in the examples from my own study is congruent with the explanation for the different levels of participant involvement in my study and in Profitt's—the particular question being explored. Again the themes related to the women's own experiences were best illuminated with their own words, and close consultation was necessary to ensure the accuracy of my understanding. In contrast, the theme related to the program (in this case, style of leadership) was not a focus of the participants' comments and called for my own analysis and interpretation. But in examining the decisions regarding "whose truth" within my own study, there seem to be other reasons as well.

Another determinant is whether the participant or the researcher has the greater level of expertise regarding a particular theme—which party identified the issue and where one is likely to find further enlightenment. It was the study participants who raised the issues regarding the importance of having instructors with similar characteristics and the impact of the programs on couple relationships. Hence I looked to the participants for a deeper understanding of these themes, probing their meanings and findings their words to be the clearest expression of the ideas. In contrast, the matter of leadership style emerged from an accumulation of observed actions and incidental comments with no indication of an examined awareness of the topic on the part of participants and no dramatically illustrative quotes. For greater understanding of leadership style, I looked to the academic literature and put forward my analysis as the researcher's interpretation.

The sensitivity or critical nature of the topic is another factor. In this circumstance the researcher must consider whether direct conversation with the participant(s) is likely to yield honest and illuminating responses or to present a risk of alienating participants or causing harm to participants' self-esteem or relationships. Related to this factor is the intended audience of the text. If the participants are the intended audience, as in a program evaluation, then any critical material is best shared and discussed with them before the text is published. On the other hand, if the audience is an academic one, the risk of potential harm may outweigh any likely benefits of sharing the uncomplimentary material.

An important consideration before deciding to leave a participant's voice unheard is the matter of power. The researcher bears a greater responsibility to put forward the voices of the powerless (Mertens, 1999). The omission of an opportunity for the program director in this example to engage in a discussion about leadership style is not an abrogation of this responsibility.

A final factor in the decision regarding whose voice is given pre-eminence is the relationship between the participants or setting and the researcher. Is an ongoing

Box 9.2: Participant Voices

Give primacy to the participants' voices when:
- the study participants' insider (emic) view is paramount
- the theme was raised and illuminated by participants
- the topic relates to participants' lived experience and unique reality
- the participants are members of a group that typically has been marginalized and silenced

relationship possible throughout the analysis and writing of the research? After completion of the particular study, is future collaboration likely? Had the matter of leadership style arisen in one of the Canadian case examples with which I have an ongoing relationship, perhaps some discussion of it could have been productive and any differing perspectives satisfactorily worked through. However, since the theme emerged from one of the Chilean case examples and only came clear to me after I had returned to Canada, the lack of feasibility of an ongoing relationship also contraindicated the pursuit of the participant's voice.

Box 9.3: Researcher Voice

Give primacy to the researcher's voice when:
- the researcher's outsider (etic) view is paramount
- the theme emerged from the researcher's observations and analysis
- the topic is sensitive or critical of participants and seeking their perspective may damage their self-esteem
- an ongoing collaborative relationship between researcher and participants is not feasible

---

CONCLUSION

I conclude that some qualitative analysis benefits immensely from engaging participants as fully as possible in the research process, particularly in the interpretation of the findings. However, other analysis must rely more on the independent interpretation of the researcher. Surprisingly perhaps, these variations can occur within one piece of research.

The fullest amplification of participants' voices is possible regarding themes that emerge from the participants' lived experience, especially where the insights are initially identified by participants and reveal considerable reflection on their part, or where there is an opportunity for the researcher to engage the participants in a thorough examination of the topic. Providing ample opportunity for negotiating mutual understanding with participants is also highly feasible when there is no sensitive or uncomplimentary data or when conditions promote the successful resolution of potential defensiveness or divergent views. The foregrounding of participants' voices is most important when the participants have been silenced or disempowered and the research holds some potential for influencing change. The resultant text expressed in a multitude of voices is a credible one.

The emphasis on the participants' perspective is less likely with themes that emerge from the researcher's general observations rather than being raised by participants in interviews. Involving the participants in productive discussions is more likely to be difficult when the findings may be critical of some aspect of the participants' actions and could potentially harm participants or relationships. Other challenges arise when the researcher cannot remain in the setting or in close communication with participants due to long distances and prohibitive costs.

However, when the researcher's voice is not augmented by those of participants, interpretations must be qualified as tentative and requiring further substantiation in other research findings.

The question of "whose truth" must then be answered: all truths, if at all possible—with the voices sometimes in harmony and sometimes discordant; with the participants' voices featured much of the time and with the researcher's voice carrying the melody at others; and with clarity about the reasons for the particular orchestration at all times.

GLOSSARY

Constructivist paradigm: A research paradigm based on the assumption that the social world has been socially constructed and that its meanings can be understood best through the study of qualitative data. It is frequently contrasted with the positivist research paradigm, which assumes an objective reality that can be known best through the analysis of quantitative data.

Emic: The insider perspective of the person experiencing a phenomenon.

Etic: The outsider perspective of one who doesn't have first-hand experience.

Member checking: A method for enhancing the accuracy of the researcher's understanding of study participants' comments and experience by seeking the participants' (members') feedback regarding the researcher's preliminary interpretations.

Paradigm: A framework for viewing the world that contains fundamental assumptions about reality as well as methods for dealing with it that are consistent with those core beliefs.

REFERENCES

Alldred, P. (1998). Ethnography and discourse analysis: Dilemmas in representing the voices of children. In J. Ribbens & R. Edwards (Eds.), *Feminist dilemmas in qualitative research* (pp. 147–170). London: Sage Publications.

Altheide, D., & Johnson, J. (1994). Criteria for assessing interpretive validity in qualitative research. In Y. Lincoln & N. Denzin (Eds.), *Handbook of qualitative research* (pp. 485–499). Thousand Oaks: Sage Publications.

Atkinson, P., & Hammersley, M. (1994). Ethnography and participant observation. In Y. Lincoln & N. Denzin (Eds.), *Handbook of qualitative research* (pp. 248–261). Thousand Oaks: Sage Publications.

Clandinin, D.J., & Connelly, F.M. (1994). Personal experience methods. In Y. Lincoln & N. Denzin (Eds.), *Handbook of qualitative research* (pp. 413–427). Thousand Oaks: Sage Publications.

Douglas, J.D. (1976). *Investigative social research*. Beverley Hills: Sage Publications.

Eisner, E. (1998). *The enlightened eye: Qualitative inquiry and the enhancement of educational practice*. Upper Saddle River, NJ: Merrill/Prentice-Hall.

Fontana, A., & Frey, J. (1994). Interviewing: The art of science. In Y. Lincoln & N. Denzin (Eds.), *Handbook of qualitative research* (pp. 361–376). Thousand Oaks: Sage Publications.

Geertz, C. (1983). *Local knowledge*. New York: Basic Books.

Geertz, C. (1988). *Works and lives: The anthropologist as author*. Stanford, CA: Stanford University Press.

Gitlin, A. (2000). Educative research, voice and school change. In B. Brizuela, J. Stewart, R. Carrillo, & J. Berger (Eds.), *Acts of inquiry in qualitative research* (pp. 95–118). Cambridge: Harvard Educational Review.

Gluck, S. (1984). What's so special about women? Women's oral history. In D. Dunaway & W. Baum (Eds.), *Oral history: An interdisciplinary anthology* (pp. 221–237). Nashville: American Association for State and Local History.

Goode, E. (1996). The ethics of deception in social research: A case study. *Qualitative Sociology, 19*(1), 11–33.

Guba, E., & Lincoln, Y. (1994). Competing paradigms in qualitative research. In Y. Lincoln & N. Denzin (Eds.), *Handbook of qualitative research* (pp. 105–117). Thousand Oaks: Sage Publications.

Gubrium, J., & Holstein, J. (1997). *The new language of qualitative method.* New York: Oxford University Press.

Heron, J. (1996). *Co-operative inquiry: Research into the human conditions.* London: Sage Publications.

Hertz, R. (1996) Introduction: Ethics, reflexivity, and voice. *Qualitative Sociology, 19*(1), 3–9.

Jansen, G., & Davis, D. (1998). Honouring voice and visibility: Sensitive-topic research and feminist interpretive inquiry. *Affilia: Journal of Women and Social Work, 13,* 289–311.

Kleinman, S., & Copp, M.A. (1993). *Emotions and fieldwork.* Newbury Park, CA: Sage Publications, Inc.

Lincoln, Y. (1995). Emerging criteria for quality in qualitative and interpretive research. *Qualitative Inquiry, 1,* 275–289.

Lincoln, Y., & Denzin, N. (1994). The fifth moment. In Y. Lincoln & N. Denzin (Eds.), *Handbook of qualitative research* (pp. 575–586). Thousand Oaks: Sage Publications.

Lincoln, Y., & Guba, E. (1985). *Naturalistic inquiry.* Newbury Park: Sage Publications.

Mertens, D. (1999). Inclusive evaluation: Implications of transformative theory for evaluation. *American Journal of Evaluation, 20*(1), 1–14.

Porter, E. (2000). Setting aside the identity furor: Staying her story-course of same-ness. *Qualitative Inquiry, 6*(2), 238–250.

Profitt, N.J. (2000). *Feminist research with survivors of women abuse: Lessons for the learning.* Paper presented at the 17th Qualitative Analysis Conference, Fredericton, New Brunswick.

Richardson, L. (1994). Writing: A method of inquiry. In Y. Lincoln & N. Denzin (Eds.), *Handbook of qualitative research* (pp. 516–529). Thousand Oaks: Sage Publications.

Rogers, A. (2000). Voice, play and a practice of ordinary courage in girls' and women's lives. In B. Brizuela, J. Stewart, R. Carrillo, & J. Berger (Eds.), *Acts of inquiry in qualitative research* (pp. 149–176). Cambridge: Harvard Educational Review.

Saukko, P. (2000). Between voice and discourse: Quilting interviews on anorexia. *Qualitative Inquiry, 6*(3), 299–317.

Schorer, M. (1986). The burdens of biography. In S. Oates (Ed.), *Biography as high adventure,* 77–92. Amherst: University of Massachusetts Press.

Schwandt, T. (1997). Textual gymnastics, ethics, and angst. In W. Tierney & Y. Lincoln (Eds.), *Reframing the narrative voice* (pp. 305–311). Albany: State University of New York Press.

Slim, H., & Thompson, P. (1995). *Listening for a change: Oral testimony and community development.* Philadelphia: New Society Publishers.

Smith, D. (1989). Sociological theory: Methods of writing patriarchy. In R. Wallace (Ed.), *Feminism and sociological theory* (pp. 34–64). London: Sage Publications.

Smyth, D. (2000). *"I feel anything but motherly toward you and your work": When historical sociology is understood as biography*. Paper presented at the 17th Qualitative Analysis Conference, Fredericton, New Brunswick.

Snow, D.A., & Morrill, C. (1993). Reflections on anthropology's ethnographic crisis of faith. *Contemporary Sociology, 22*(1), 8–11.

Snyder, L. (1999). *Women's employment initiatives as a means of addressing poverty: A comparative study of Canadian and Chilean examples.* Unpublished doctoral dissertation, Wilfrid Laurier University, Waterloo, Ontario.

Song, M. (1998). Hearing competing voices: Sibling research. In J. Ribbens & R. Edwards (Eds.), *Feminist dilemmas in qualitative research* (pp. 103–118). London: Sage Publications.

Standing, K. (1998). Writing the voices of the less powerful. In J. Ribbens & R. Edwards (Eds.), *Feminist dilemmas in qualitative research* (pp. 186–202). London: Sage Publications.

Strauss, A., & Corbin, J. (1994). Grounded theory methodology. In Y. Lincoln & N. Denzin (Eds.), *Handbook of qualitative research* (pp. 273–285). Thousand Oaks: Sage Publications.

Tierney, W. (1993). Developing archives of resistance: Speak, memory. In D. McLaughlin & W. Tierney (Eds.), *Naming silenced lives: Personal narratives and processes of educational change* (pp. 1–5). New York: Routledge.

Tierney, W. (1995). (Re)Presentation and voice. *Qualitative Inquiry, 1*(4), 379–390.

Tierney, W. (1998). Life history's history: Subjects foretold. *Qualitative Inquiry, 4*(1), 49–70.

Tutty, L., Rothery, M., & Grinnel, R. (1996). *Qualitative research for social workers.* Boston: Allyn & Bacon.

Chapter 10

Quote, Unquote:
From Transcript to Text
in Ethnographic Research

Katherine Bischoping

INTRODUCTION

A recovered black box from a crashed airplane, a loved one's last words: their listeners attend closely to each tone, syllable, inflection, convinced that in order to ascertain meaning, statements must be preserved as completely as possible. At other times, listeners may believe that the validity of statements is best honoured when they are honed artfully, that Neil Armstrong might as well have said "one small step for *a* man" during the first moonwalk.

Whether preservation or artful editing makes for better validity concerns ethnographers. The most avid preservationists are **conversation analysts**, such as Sacks (1992), who study how the smallest parts of speech can contribute to the social construction of reality. They seek continually to improve transcript fidelity by using instruments to measure voice amplitude and intonation (Labov & Fanshell, cited in Wengraf, 2001) and by distinguishing carefully among types of laughter such as "ho ho" and "eeyah," and between in- and out-breaths (denoted ".hhh" and "hhh")(Edwards & Lampert, 1993; Psathas & Anderson, 1990). Exemplary segments of these transcripts are then subjected to detailed analysis.

"I insisted on the quotation marks."

At the other extreme are ethnographers who shape informants' words into poetry. Using an example of an erroneous statement about the end of World War Two, Portelli (1998, p. 40) demonstrates that how readers understand a passage "depends to a large extent on the historian's decision to transcribe it, respectively, as linear prose, verse or epigraph." Richardson (1997) believes that when informants' voices take poetic form, readers are constantly reminded to question how they interpret texts and create knowledge (see also Denzin, 2001). Further, she suggests that the rhythms and cadences of poetry help keep readers embodied.

But what of the ordinary ethnographer, neither poet nor conversation analyst, shy about verse, and indifferent to distinctions between ".hhh" and "hhh"? Much is known about how she does and should design research, conduct interviews, and analyze data. Yet with few exceptions, her editing processes are ignored by methodologists. What is it that is left on the ethnographer's cutting room floor, and why?

In this chapter, I identify issues that arise as everyday ethnographers transform interview transcripts into manuscript quotes. I do so by reconsidering how, nine years ago, I edited transcripts of interviews, conducted for a dissertation on knowledge about the Holocaust, in order to prepare publications. The "Methods" sections of my articles are silent about editing, which seemed to me then to have the transparent goal of providing concise, vivid, and representative quotations. But the practice was murkier, involving obsessively counting numbers of quotations per respondent, worrying because some respondents' transcripts had no good soundbites, and agonizing about using a few dots to signify that I'd skipped anywhere from a word to several pages of a transcript. I've since learned that such experiences are common. I would argue that they are significant to ethnographers' work because they suggest that elusive, yet systematic, biases may enter research findings during editing.

Here I will use examples from six undergraduate respondents' transcripts to show how my editing decisions may have been influenced by differences between spoken and written language, the **conversational maxim** of quality, prevailing Western discourses about emotions, and my feelings towards respondents. In these quotes, my statements appear in parentheses.

INARTICULATE SPEECH AND POLISHED TEXT

Let's begin with the published quotation from Kathryn, who is recalling *The Diary of Anne Frank* film (see Box 10.1). This quotation, with its "like apprehensive feel" and other awkward phrasings, conveys that Kathryn has a youthful and somewhat inarticulate style of speaking. Yet the Kathryn of the transcript is far more garbled. A good deal of what I edited out are her flustered pronunciations, such as the "appre-, apprehension, a-, bluh" sequence (segments 7–10) that precedes "apprehensive," and repetitive speech (segments 15–18).

Are these edits appropriate? To some ethnographers, they would reflect the differences between ordinary spoken language, which is a **time-based medium**, and written language, which is time-independent. That is, spoken language is experienced by speaker and listener spontaneously, in the moment, and can be

Box 10.1: Kathryn Remembers *The Diary of Anne Frank* Film

Segment	Quotation	Omitted transcript segments
1.		I thought
2.		I thought it was done
3.		I thought it was done very well
4.		it gave you a really neat perspective on how people had uh-
5.		I mean you obviously
6.	I've always had this like	
7.		appre-
8.		apprehension
9.		a-
10.		bluh
11.	apprehensive feel when you saw that kind of situation	
12.	someone's gonna get you	
13.	so when you mention that	
14.	(mhm)	
15.	I felt that fear like all through watching that movie	
16.	I mean	
17.	…	it was like
18.		it was really
19.	it was really	
20.	it was opening to see the, her feelings about it	
21.	…	it was actually done rather
22.		(mhm)
23.	I was sad that she didn't make it through	
24.		[Kathryn laughs]

Source: From "Interpreting Social Influences on Holocaust Knowledge," by K. Bischoping, *Contemporary Jewry, 17,* p. 116.

corrected only as the moments pass, while written language appears in an already perfected form that readers can experience repeatedly (see Bellantoni & Woolman, 1999; Etter-Lewis, 1993). As a result, when we read novels, we can become convinced that a character is inarticulate just by the few glitches in a sentence such as, "We've had him on our books for nearly eleven years now, ever since he sort of quarrelled with Holton and Watson, and he's been um, very, very lucrative indeed" (Harrod-Eagles, 1994, p. 55). However, neither my interview respondents nor I ever achieved this level of eloquence.

McBeth (1993) calls the editing of ordinarily fragmented speech into orderly text a translation process, aimed at producing what the intended audience will consider both spontaneous and intelligible. Frisch (1990) would concur. Maintaining that "the integrity of a transcript is best protected, in documentary use, by an aggressive editorial approach" (p. 84), he suggests that use of unedited transcripts may "magnify precisely the class distance it is one of the promises of oral history to narrow" (p. 86). McBeth and Frisch would edit Kathryn's transcript heavily so that a journal audience, mostly holding graduate degrees, would appreciate and not dismiss her perspective.

Others, fascinated by inarticulacy, would hesitate. To DeVault (1999), inarticulacy indicates that hegemonic discourse prevents certain life experiences from coming to voice. Her perspective suggests that, before Kathryn's flustered speech is deleted, we consider its possible origins. Perhaps for Kathryn, as for many humanists struggling to represent the at once knowable and unknowable nature of the Holocaust, ordinary ways of speaking about it fail. In contrast, Schachter, Christenfeld, Ravina, and Bilous (1991) propose that speech disfluencies, such as "uh," mark that a speaker is filling time while choosing from an embarrassment of discursive riches. While DeVault and Schachter et al. offer contradictory interpretations of inarticulacy, both their works suggest that my quotations from Kathryn's transcript should have retained, and focused more on, her flusters.

MEANINGS IN REPETITION

A second caveat can be developed by considering Grice's conversational maxims, summarized by Levinson (1983). Among them is the principle that for speakers to co-operate while conversing, they should either obey the maxim of quantity— i.e., be just as informative as their turn requires, and no more so—or disobey it meaningfully, as in tautologies such as "war is war." Accordingly, we should inquire whether transcript repetitions, which flout the maxim of quantity, convey some deeper meaning.

For an example, examine the published quotation from Robert (Box 10.2), which I used to counter the view of some Holocaust researchers that many African-Americans are anti-Semitic. Robert's opening lines assert that Black and Jewish students' concerns differ. His use of "you know"—a phrase that DeVault (1999, p. 69) interprets as a request for understanding—and my "hmm" indicate familiarity with this assertion (segments 2–3). However, on balance, the quote illustrates how Robert feels affected by the Holocaust through his connections to a new circle of friends in university.

Box 10.2 doesn't show it, but somewhere in the editing process, my "mhm" in segment 3 became misprinted as "hmm" in the quotation. Though this change is minute, in the transcript I sound agreeable, whereas in the published quotation I am non-committal. The quotation also omits segment 8, in which Robert again reiterates his position, as well as segments 9 and 10, which contain another "you know"—"mhm" sequence. While Robert's segment 11—"Our concern was more of a slavery type of thing"—does appear in the quotation, segment 12's underscored contrast to Jewish students' concerns doesn't. Therefore, the quotation shifts Robert's emphasis towards a greater assertion of similarity between his and Jewish students' concerns.

Box 10.2: Robert Begins to Care about the Holocaust

Segment	Quotation	Omitted transcript segments
1.	I went to a school that was basically all Black	
2.	so you know	
3.	(mhm)	
4.	I didn't care 'cause	
5.	you know	
6.	no Jews were in the school	
7.	so I would imagine didn't nobody care	
8.	....	I mean 'cause all Blacks,
9.		you know
10.		(mhm)
11.	our concern was more of a slavery type of thing	
12.	...	instead of more based, dealing with the Holocaust itself
13.		[9 pages omitted]
14.		(How important or central would you say the Holocaust is to you?)
15.		um
16.		again
17.	It's more important to me now because	
18.	...	I know people who have people who it has actually affected
19.		so if they have those people, it affected them
20.		it has also affected those people that I know as well
21.		that's a little confusing:
22.	I know people who the Holocaust has had an effect on	
23.	so now it affects me	
24.	to give an example, it's like this AIDS thing	
25.	AIDS didn't mean much —	
26.	it meant something —	
27.	but until it affects someone that you know personally	
28.	is when you actually wake up	
29.	like when Magic Johnson announced it	
30.	a lot of the world woke up	
31.	because they felt that Magic Johnson is somewhat, you know, on a personal level	
32.	so, you know, it woke them up	
33.		so now I have those friends who have been affected by the Holocaust
34.		so now I'm waking up
35.		that was nicely put

Source: From "Method and Meaning in Holocaust-Knowledge Surveys," by K. Bischoping, 1998, *Holocaust and Genocide Studies, 12*, p. 464.

What more? In graduate school, I had heard that three ellipses were usually used to indicate that words or phrases had been omitted, while four ellipses denoted omission of larger segments of text. The quotation mixes up these conventions. In the second "...", after segment 12, I am collapsing nine single-spaced pages! In them, Robert tells me that he was dismayed to hear from friends about Hitler's concept of a perfect race, interested in attending events related to the Holocaust but reluctant to expose himself to a negative atmosphere, and curious about a children's book about the Holocaust, which I had brought as an interview prop. He also describes a hectic family life with little time for conversation. By the time we reach segment 14, when I ask Robert about the importance of the Holocaust, his response of "um again" (segments 15, 16) — omitted from the quotation — is probably meant to point out that I am flouting the maxim of quantity by repeating myself. Perhaps to rescue the conversation, Robert reframes my topic as something fresh: the relative importance of the Holocaust to him (segment 17), which has been growing (segments 22–34). Note that Robert doesn't quite state that the Holocaust is important to him, only that it is more important than it used to be. Therefore, while the quotation makes a nice case for the significance of the Holocaust to an African-American student, as I reread the transcript, I hear Robert's equivocations and observe how we jointly constructed the meaning of topics (Mishler, 1986).

IT FEELS VIVID

Other deletions from Robert's and Kathryn's transcripts also appear systematic. Kathryn's quotation omits transcript passages in which she judges the effectiveness of *The Diary of Anne Frank*, such as "I thought it was done very well"; "It gave you a really neat perspective on how people had uh" (see segments 1–4 and 19–20). Robert's quotation omits a first attempt to explain that the Holocaust affected him indirectly (segments 18–20) and his judgment that this explanation was "a little confusing" (segment 21). I quote Robert's Magic Johnson-AIDS analogy to friends and the Holocaust, but not his conclusion (segments 33–34) or his self-appraising "that was nicely put" (segment 35). Thus, Kathryn and Robert make fewer evaluations in the quotations than in the transcripts.

I think that I edited in this way largely because I hoped to engage readers by using vivid text. By removing Kathryn's assessment of the film and Robert's self-monitoring, I tailor their voices to evoke with greater immediacy their empathy for Anne Frank and Magic Johnson. These segments gain power through a Romantic formulation of emotions that still influences Western discourse about emotions (Lutz, 1988). In this formulation, emotion is "the seat of the true and glorified self" (Lutz, 1988, p. 56), counterposed to indifference, estrangement, and the distance of "that was nicely put." Because they are so feeling, Kathryn's and Robert's quoted words sound more authentic.

Though I did not realize it at the time, in editing for vividness I also stripped away much that was not story. Kathryn recalls *The Diary of Anne Frank* in a **narrative** (Riessman, 1993) with a definite beginning ("I've always had this like apprehensive feel"), middle ("I felt that fear like all through watching that movie"), and ending

("It was opening to see the, her feelings about it"). Robert's example about AIDS and Magic Johnson is a short story embedded as an example in the larger narrative of his increasing concern (see Etter-Lewis 1993, pp. 194–196). Narratives compel, as Mishler (1986, pp. 66–69) explains by citing interdisciplinary works about how narrative is a psychological deep structure or a primary means of understanding our lives.

Finally, my focus on emotions in these quotations also reflects my intellectual trajectory from undergraduate work in statistics to graduate work in sociology. When I conducted the interviews for my dissertation, I was surprised that I couldn't easily tell which respondents had scored low on a survey measure of Holocaust knowledge and which had scored high. To better understand respondents' diverse ways of knowing, I began to read about emotion work (Hochschild, 1975), empathy as a cognitive emotion (Jordan, 1984), and Western **emotion discourses** (Lutz, 1988). I began to propose that knowing the Holocaust emotionally mattered as much, or more, than knowing it cognitively. It seems likely to me that this new orientation imbued my editing, which celebrates emotion.

Or does it? Let's spin the wheel again. An alternate reading would be that, by emphasizing respondents' feelings while remaining scientifically silent about my own, I fall into an old convention wherein research subjects merely feel, while it is researchers who think. If so, I could be participating in a Western discourse on emotions contradictory to the Romantic formulation mentioned above, in which reason and rationality trump passionate irrationality (Lutz ,1988).

REVENGE OF THE NERD

Pratt makes a related point when she contrasts ethnographers' personal narratives about fieldwork, in which authority is "anchored to a large extent in subjective, sensuous experience" (1986, p. 32), to their formal ethnographies, in which they gain authority by claiming to be objective. Many ethnographers have taken up Pratt's call for a more complex, self-reflexive voice that examines authority explicitly. In this section, I provide an example of how my subjective experiences with Kathryn, Robert, and a new respondent named Jessica influenced how they appear in print.

In Bischoping (1996, p. 123), I quote Jessica to illustrate that a student with one Jewish parent could come to know little about the Holocaust: "I don't consider myself Jewish at all. (mhm) I'm not, I mean, my mom wasn't, didn't really consider herself that Jewish either. It was just the name of the religion. (mhm) I mean, we're just not religious. And uh, I don't know, that's just not what they emphasized (mhm) teaching me. You know, so. (okay) How was I to know anything about it?" Unlike Kathryn's and Robert's transcripts, Jessica's transcript received only a light edit, in which I deleted a prefatory "well, I mean, well." Because I preserved her repetitions and backtrackings, Jessica appears far less coherent to readers than Robert or Kathryn.

Jessica's apparent incoherence could parallel her inchoate relationship, or non-relationship, to Jewish identity. However, from a personal perspective, it does rather more. To tell the truth, I detested Jessica, who seemed to me the epitome of anti-intellectualism. She told me she hated all of high school history, couldn't remember whether a family friend who was a Holocaust survivor had been in a concentration camp, had no opinion of a Holocaust-denial advertisement appearing in the campus newspaper, and hated the Palestinian situation because her class had to spend a year on a computer simulation of the Middle East conflict. Worst of all, I became complicit in Jessica's chosen ignorance. I assured her that although the Holocaust happened to interest me particularly because it was my dissertation topic, she should just "be you" and not be affected by my interests. A key exchange read: "I'm sorry I don't know anything! [Laugh] (No, it's fine, I'm just trying to say like it's better if you answer how you really do think and try not to be influenced by this [topic of mine])." While this kept the interview going, years later I am still embarrassed to remember my complicity.

Box 10.3

In *Methods, Sex and Madness*, Julia O'Connell Davidson (1994) depicts a troubling interview she conducted on the topic of prostitution. The respondent regaled her with sexist, racist descriptions of his experiences with young prostitutes in Thailand: "He told me that he effectively haggles for human life, using safer sex as a bargaining counter by offering [the prostitutes] less money for sex with a condom" (p. 216). At the end of the interview, Davidson recounts, "he actually sat back, spread his legs and started masturbating through his trousers" (p. 217).

For Davidson, this encounter brought a serious ethical issue to light. She wondered whether it was wrong of her to have adopted, insofar as possible, a non-judgmental demeanour during the interview. On one hand, this did help her to obtain information that was otherwise unavailable; on the other, it might have suggested to her respondent that she endorsed his attitudes and behaviour. We can also ask whether Davidson's choice of an ambiguous pseudonym—Dick—was a not-so-subtle way of retaliating when it came time to edit and present her transcript. (Certainly undergraduate students at York University hooted at my awkward rhetorical question, "Do we care about Dick?") If so, was her treatment of Dick, like my less obvious treatment of Jessica, really ethical?

It is altogether likely that by preserving Jessica's incoherence, I was taking what revenge I could for my discomfort. Certainly I presented other respondents more sympathetically. I edited out Kathryn's laughter (segment 24) and her description of *The Diary of Anne Frank* as giving "a really neat perspective" (segment 4), probably because I thought they might make her sound callous whereas really she was nervous and likeable. Returning to Frisch's (1990) terms, my lack of editing could be said to magnify the distance between Jessica and her readers. Moreover, it does so unobtrusively, concealing my dislike in the semblance of diligent transcription.

VOICES UNHEARD

Of the 40 students whom I interviewed, 27 were quoted or had summaries of responses attributed to their pseudonyms in publications. I was preoccupied with the goal of representing respondents' voices equally and, as a former statistician, I operationalized this by trying to use equal numbers of quotes from each person. While writing the dissertation, I was astonished to read Linden's (1993) commentary on the editing methods she used in a manuscript called "Phenomenology of Surviving." Linden had interviewed 12 Holocaust survivors, but her manuscript quoted just one, variously identified as "Susan," "one survivor," "every survivor," and so forth (1993, p. 106). Linden became dissatisfied with this, not because it ignored other informants' voices, but because it provides her key informant with anonymity at the cost of fragmenting her life history. Linden's and my approaches to representation had very different priorities.

As Linden did, I am now revisiting the question of whose voices my articles omit. Some of the 13 missing are hard to remember even with transcripts in hand. But, using three unforgettable respondents as examples, I will discuss how speaking styles and interview rapport may have affected who made it into print.

Miles was a voluble individual who seemed not to know what he was saying until he had heard himself say it. While looking at a children's novel about the Holocaust, he said:

> Um. I. I don't know if I've mentioned it, this is hard to say because I haven't read this, but it's probably so fictionalized (mhm) that without reading this, I wouldn't just try to pull something off like this. I take something that, I noticed you had Anne Frank, that obviously because it is the actual diary of (uh huh)—I know I would trust that more, I wouldn't myself, read the whole thing, a lot of it so (uh huh). That would be something I'd, um, I thought that, I don't know how old the child would be, um. My friend who took the class, went through the Primo Levi stuff, and [can't hear] probably do that, that was really good (uh huh), interesting I think. So [can't hear] the Holocaust probably do something like that.

Text like this resisted my usual methods of cutting repetitions and inarticulacy; it would have required considerable reorganization to edit.

Miles's transcript also became a narrative in which, by shifting pronouns, he gradually divulged his sexual identity. "Some of my friends" became "one of my friends ... he had a Holocaust class," and then "my friend who took the class" and simply "my friend." I began to uh-huh when The Friend was mentioned, showing that I was keeping this individual in mind. I also validated their relationship by asking about his views. Soon after, when I asked to whom Miles thought the Holocaust was central, his answer included "well, I would say as, as a gay man (mhm) knowing that it would, it also affected them." After the interview, Miles told me about how he had just received a letter from his mother, pressuring him to see a priest. I felt myself moving from a neutral interviewer role to that of a confidante or big sister. None of this made it into print: it seemed too intimate an exchange to publicize, even with a pseudonym.

Jane is another unquoted respondent with whom I connected. I was relieved to meet someone whose parents had also been born in Europe before World War Two (hers in the Ukraine, mine in Germany) and who had similar views of how the Holocaust influenced her ethnic identity. Following other interviews I often felt that I was confusedly returning to my true self, after having taken on the patterns of another person's thoughts and said "mhm" to everything. With Jane, I crossed the line by concurring genuinely and even letting loose with my own opinions. An example is when we discussed religion: "I guess there's something that could have put this all in motion [laugh] but it certainly can't be this sort of Zeus-like character sitting up there at all. (Uh huh, uh huh, uh huh. [laugh] Ok. Well, this is very much like my thoughts.)" I conjecture that Jane remained unquoted because she was an outlier, too much like me to represent the population of respondents. I also worried that I had unduly influenced her by being, for a change, sincerely myself.

Then there's Jon, who sat tensely, gazing mainly at a paper clip with which he fidgeted. The atmosphere seemed oppressive and our untranscribed silences grew long. Jon indicated repeatedly that he and his family preferred to avoid discussing the Holocaust, which he referred to euphemistically as "such a negative thing." At the close of the session, when Jon hesitated about choosing a pseudonym, I suggested—as I would have to other respondents—that he might just pick some family member's name. He demurred, appalled, and I imagined that he took me to be ill-wishing his family (since in Jewish custom, a newborn child can be named after someone who has died). Although Jon's transcript had many passages relevant to my dissertation, the unspoken tension seemed to outweigh whatever had been said.

Box 10.4

Respondents' silences are speech acts offering listeners a multitude of interpretations. Some silences are empty, as George Eliot (1866, p. 270) quipped: "Speech is often barren; but silence also does not necessarily brood over a full nest." Other silences are fraught with meaning, such as unease, dissent, or even passion. Compare Avril Lavigne's (2002) lyrics for "Things I'll Never Say"—"I'm staring at my feet / My cheeks are turning red / I'm searching for the words inside my head"—with Sappho's (1993) narrator from the 6th century B.C. who, dumbstruck in the presence of her crush, describes how "subtle fire races inside my skin, my / eyes can't see a thing."

The way these two artists depict silence helps us to understand further Catherine Lutz's (1988) work on discourses about emotions in the West. Lutz argues that we see emotions as a natural, creative, raw material, separate from the social constructions of conscious thoughts. As a result, "thought and its offshoot, social speech, come to be seen as less authentic and less 'really real'" (p. 68). Accordingly, Sappho's and Lavigne's speechless lovers convince us that they feel more deeply than chatty ones could.

These three instances lead me to reconsider Linden's (1993) opposition to fracturing subjectivities and to preserving an anonymity that her research participants did not seek. I now see that my decisions not to quote certain respondents may have arisen from a similar reluctance to present fragments of their words, while more personally significant narratives of trust, connection, or unease remained in the shadows. However, unlike Linden, who believed that it would be most ethical to name her informants and openly acknowledge them, I wanted to shield the intimacies of my interviews from readers' analytic eyes.

CONCLUSION

Thus, the mess on my cutting room floor may have unexpected order, comprised of heaps of inarticulacies and repetitions, paragraphs of self-analysis, entire transcripts of complex accounts, and some clear spots where I abandoned editing altogether. In preparing publications from my dissertation interviews, I deleted what may be indicators of discursive opportunity or constraints (from Kathryn's transcript), conversational norms (from Robert's transcript), Western constructs of the relation of thought to emotion (from Kathryn's and Robert's transcripts), and subjectivities too complex to fragment and moments too intimate to reveal (as in Miles's, Jane's, and Jon's transcripts). Last but not least, I retained the option of taking covert vengeance (as on Jessica).

These conclusions are, of course, tentative. My memories of several other interviews that I conducted have faded altogether, and the six I describe are blurred in parts, and vivid—though potentially inaccurate—in others. I can't remember what Jane looked like, I'm surprised that Jon's transcript is so lengthy when the interview seemed so halting, and so forth. I find myself constructing plausible stories about distant decisions without being able to assess the reality. Nonetheless, my distance from the interviewing, editing, and writing process has its advantages. The analysis provided in this paper is one that I have set repeatedly as an assignment for graduate students, for whom it has proved challenging to achieve a distanced take on freshly completed editing decisions.

What hinders us, I think, is the solitary nature of most editing work. In order to find perspective on our work as it is ongoing, we need to open a space for exchanges about what it is that ordinary ethnographers, as opposed to conversation analysts and ethnodramatists, do. For example, after presenting a first version of this paper at a conference in 2001, I had several fascinating conversations about editing: a sociologist who had a separate career as a creative writer challenged the use of italics and sentences written in upper case (Rhoda Howard, personal communication, May 2001), a researcher advocating for developmentally disabled adults speculated that it had been discriminatory of him to edit out his informants' grammatical errors (Scott Anthony Thompson, personal communication, May 2001); and a video-maker documenting lost Canadian gay and lesbian history described, with regret, a wonderful quotation that was unusable because of a factual error in its middle (Nancy Nicol, personal communication, November 2001). These dialogues are as important for us to transcribe, analyze, and disseminate as our interviews.

Box 10.5

The greatest legacy of George W. ("Dubya") Bush, 43rd president of the United States, may be his unwitting contribution to poetry. Hundreds of websites feature "Make the pie higher!" This poem, credited to political satirist Richard Thompson (cited in Mikkelson & Mikkelson, 2003), is comprised of ludicrous lines such as "Knock down the tollbooth!" purportedly uttered by Bush at his best. Internet debates rage about the fairness and accuracy of such quotations. For example, on one Bush quotation website, bonedog444@hotmail.com (n.d.) railed, "How would you like it if someone was standing next to you with a pad and paper writing down everyting [sic] you said? You say something dumb and BAM some democrat will publish it." Meanwhile, on another site, Barbara and David Mikkelson (2003) attempted to check whether the lines in the poem were truly Bush's words, or simply urban legend. The Mikkelsons' criteria for accuracy were that the lines had to be from quotations appearing in major newspapers, accompanied by information about the date and place that Bush uttered them, and printed within a few days of that date. Their conclusion: almost all of the poem is genuine Dubya.

Ethnographers interested in questions of how to produce and edit transcripts can frame these debates about George Bush's malapropisms differently. How does what we know about the contrasts between spoken and written speech influence our reading of quoted absurdities? How do the Mikkelsons' standards for accuracy in the print media compare with those of conversation analysts? How do political perspectives enter this public debate about editing methods? And how do they enter sociologists' debates about methods in general?

GLOSSARY

Conversation analyst: An ethnographer who focuses on how even the smallest parts of speech contribute to the social construction of reality.

Conversational maxim: Principles of co-operative conversation that we must either follow or break in ways that themselves convey meaning.

Emotion discourse: A set of taken-for-granted assumptions that constrain how we think and talk about emotions.

Narrative: Information organized as a story, which means that it will resonate more powerfully than if it were organized in other ways.

Time-based medium: A means of communication, such as speech, that is experienced in the transient moment (as opposed to time-independent media, such as texts, that can be experienced repeatedly).

REFERENCES

Bellantoni, J., & Woolman, M. (1999). *Type in motion: Innovations in digital graphics*. New York: Rizzoli International.

Bischoping, K. (1996). Interpreting social influences on Holocaust knowledge. *Contemporary Jewry, 17*, 106–135.

Bischoping, K. (1998). Method and meaning in Holocaust-knowledge surveys. *Holocaust and Genocide Studies, 12,* 454–474.

bonedog444@hotmail.com. (n.d.). Untitled. Retrieved January 5, 2004, from www.columbiacentral.com/dubya/hatemail.htm

Davidson, J.O., & Layder, D. (1994). *Methods, sex and madness.* New York: Routledge.

Denzin, N.K. (2001). The reflexive interview and a performative social science. *Qualitative Research, 1,* 23–46.

DeVault, M. (1999). *Liberating method: Feminism and social research.* Philadelphia: Temple University Press.

Edwards, J. A., & Lampert, M.D. (Eds.). (1993). *Talking data: Transcription and coding in discourse research.* Hillsdale, NJ: Erlbaum.

Eliot, G. (1995). *Felix Holt, the radical.* New York: Penguin. (Original work published 1866.)

Etter-Lewis, G. (1993). *My soul is my own: Oral narratives of African American women in the professions.* New York: Routledge.

Frisch, M. (1990). *A shared authority: Essays on the craft and meaning of oral history.* Albany, NY: SUNY Press.

Harrod-Eagles, C. (1994). *Dead end.* London, England: Warner Futura.

Hochschild, A. (1975). The sociology of feeling and emotion: Selected possibilities. In M. Millman & R.M. Kanter (Eds.), *Another voice: Feminist perspectives on social life and social sciences* (pp. 280–307). New York: Anchor.

Jordan, J.V. (1984). *Empathy and self boundaries.* Wellesley, MA: Wellesley College Press, Stone Centre for Developmental Services and Studies, Work in Progress No. 16.

Lavigne, A. (2002). Things I'll never say. On *Let go* (CD recording). New York: Arista.

Levinson, S. (1983). *Pragmatics.* New York: Cambridge University Press.

Linden, R. (1993). *Making stories, making lives: Feminist reflections on the Holocaust.* Columbus: Ohio State University Press.

Lutz, C. (1988). *Unnatural emotions: Unnatural sentiments on a Micronesian atoll and their challenge to Western theory.* Chicago: University of Chicago Press.

McBeth, S. (1993). Myths of objectivity and the collaborative process. In C. Brettell (Ed.), *When they read what we write: The politics of ethnography* (pp. 145–162). Westport, CT: Bergin & Garvey.

Mikkelson, B., & Mikkelson, D. (2003). *Make the pie higher!* Retrieved January 7, 2004, from www.snopes.com/politics/bush/piehigher.asp

Mishler, E.G. (1986). *Research interviewing: Context and narrative.* Cambridge, MA: Harvard University Press.

Portelli, A.(1998). Oral history as genre. In M. Chamberlain & P. Thompson (Eds.), *Narrative and genre* (pp. 23–45). New York: Routledge.

Pratt, M.L. (1986). Fieldwork in common places. In J. Clifford & G.E. Marcus (Eds.), *Writing culture: The poetics and politics of ethnography* (pp. 27–50). Berkeley: University of California Press.

Psathas, G., & Anderson, T. (1990). The "practices" of transcription in conversation analysis. *Semiotica, 78,* 75–99.

Richardson, L. (1997). *Fields of play: Constructing an academic life.* New Brunswick, NJ: Rutgers University Press.

Riessman, C.K. (1993). *Narrative analysis.* Newbury Park, CA: Sage.

Sacks, H. (1992). *Lectures on conversation* (G. Jefferson, Ed.). Oxford, England: Blackwell.

Sappho. (1993). Like the gods ... *Sappho: A garland: The poems and fragments of Sappho* (J. Powell, Trans.). New York: Farrar, Straus & Giroux. (Original work published 6th century B.C.)

Schachter, S., Christenfeld, N., Ravina, B., & Bilous, F. (1991). Speech disfluency and the structure of knowledge. *Journal of Personality and Social Psychology, 60,* 362–367.

Wengraf, T. (2001). *Qualitative research interviewing.* Thousand Oaks, CA: Sage.

Critical Thinking Questions

1. The case can be made that researchers have an ethical obligation to protect participants' privacy and to avoid deceiving and harming them. Should this commitment be absolute, that is, in all circumstances, or might it be weighed against the value of the knowledge to be gained? Who decides? Are there instances, in your view, where matters of confidentiality and anonymity should, if necessary, be waived?

2. Suppose you were asked to research how homeless people organize their daily lives in order to survive. You are invited to rely upon any methodological approach that would lead to better understanding of their predicaments and challenges. Make the case for how research relying upon participant observation, extending over a six-month period, would provide kinds of information that survey research would fail to deliver.

3. Research Ethics Boards typically expect that the research protocol will include a signed consent form by the research participants in which the latter acknowledge and approve their participation in the study. Can you think of instances, or kinds of studies, in which the insistence of a signed consent form may actually heighten suspicions and jeopardize a researcher's ability to carry out the study?

4. If, as is often claimed, the presence of a researcher in a setting raises the likelihood that people in it will fashion their behaviour to create a favourable impression, thereby altering their routines while she or he is present among them, might this be sufficient reason to argue in favour of covert research? Can you identify problems that are created for the researcher when engaging in covert, or secret, research?

5. If, as is maintained, research settings are unique, thereby precluding a fixed set of rules for data gathering and data analysis, is it reasonable to be suspicious of research findings based on field research? In other words, should conclusions derived from data gathered by field research methods be treated seriously and with confidence? Indeed, might a case be put forward that studies based on field research methods are likely to provide a more credible analysis of a research

problem than conclusions derived from the use of alternative methods, such as survey research or controlled experiments?

RELEVANT WEBSITES

1. <www.sas.upenn.edu/anthro/CPIA/methods.html>
   A good practical guide to doing ethnographic research.
2. <http://sun.soci.niu.edu/~sssi/papers/ethics.html>
   Papers dealing with ethical issues involved in ethnographic research.
3. <www.goshen.edu/soan96p.htm>
   Internet resources for Participatory Action Research (PAR).
4. <www.aces.uiuc.edu/%7EPPA/KeyInform.htm>
   Useful tips for conducting key informant interviews.
5. <www.ualberta.ca/~iiqm/>
   A Canadian-based site for the International Institute for Qualitative Methodology, a group that promotes qualitative research, often hosting conferences and workshops.
6. <www.qualitativeresearch.uga.edu/QualPage/>
   Resources for qualitative research.

PART 2

ETHNOGRAPHY IN PROCESS: CASE STUDIES OF EVERYDAY LIFE

While the papers in Part 1 look at the process of doing ethnographic research, the papers in this part of the book present the findings of studies that have been done within an ethnographic tradition. The topics they cover are broad and they make contributions to many of sociology's sub-fields. Rather than organizing the papers according to their links to these sub-fields, however, we have chosen to organize them in terms that are more consistent with symbolic interactionism's focus on process. Each section concerns itself with a social activity or generic social process, that is, with "doing."

CONSTRUCTING PERSPECTIVES

A group of workers is assigned a task that no one else wants and that the workers themselves feel ambivalent about, yet they find tremendous satisfaction and rewarding (Chiappetta-Swanson). Family members are forced to care for a loved one in hospital because the staff are not doing so, yet express satisfaction with the hospital services they are receiving (Sinding). HIV-positive women have the option of using medications that have the potential to benefit them, yet turn to complementary therapies (Pawluch, Cain, & Gillett). Female university students watch a film clip in which a woman is being verbally attacked by her male partner, yet do not see emotional abuse (Newman, Poulin, Brazier, & Cashmore). A group spends its time "hacking" computers, yet does not see itself in any way as deviant (Kleinknecht). How do we make sense of these situations? The clue in each instance lies in understanding the perspective of those involved.

At the heart of the "ethnographic quest," as Prus calls it in Chapter 1, is a desire on the researcher's part to capture the point of view of social actors, to see the world as they see it, and to uncover the meanings that provide the context for their actions. This quest is premised on the view that human beings do not passively respond to the world "as it is." For symbolic interactionists, the world is not imbued with intrinsic meaning. Meaning is constructed by social actors as they continuously, and in conjunction with others, try to make sense of their environment. William

Thomas, an early symbolic interactionist, is famous for formulating the concept of the "definition of the situation." "Preliminary to any self-determined act of behaviour," he wrote (1937, p. 42), "there is always a stage of examination and deliberation which we may call the definition of the situation." These definitions of the situation inform and shape our actions. We act not on the basis of what is real, but on the basis of what we assume to be real. In another famous quote, William Thomas and Dorothy Thomas wrote that if people "define situations as real, they are real in their consequences" (1928, p. 572).

In order to understand why people do what they do, then, we need to know the interpretive frameworks that underlie their actions. These frameworks cannot be studied from a distance. As Herbert Blumer (1969, p. 188) argued, to try to catch the interpretive process by remaining aloof as objective observers and refusing to take the role of the acting unit is to risk the worse kind of bias or subjectivism. Blumer (1969, p. 86) insisted that no one can "catch the process merely by inferring its nature from the overt action which is its product. To catch the process, the student must take the role of the acting unit whose behaviour he is studying." Researchers need to empathize and identify with the groups they are studying. They need to put themselves in the position of social actors and gain a deeper understanding of how they "define, construct, and act toward the 'realities' that constitute their everyday worlds" (Sandstrom, Martin, & Fine, 2003, p. 14).

Each of the papers in this section considers the actor's perspective. Catherine Chiappetta-Swanson's paper deals with the difficult subject of nurses who provide care for women undergoing genetic terminations (GTs) or abortions because prenatal testing has shown that there are problems with their fetuses. Using the concept of "dirty work," one of the richest ideas to have come out of symbolic interactionism, Swanson explains the burdens of this work from the nurses' perspective. With institutions ambivalent about the services they provide and many health care professionals reluctant to have anything to do with this work, GT nurses are left to fend largely for themselves. They feel their isolation keenly. Yet they also take advantage of it to provide the kind of special care that they feel these patients need and to develop routines that help them to overcome institutional obstacles. As a consequence, the nurses acquire a perspective that allows them to define work that is seen as "dirty" by most others as the source of great professional reward and pride.

Christine Sinding's paper describes a sobering trend in health care in Canada. Those who are sick and dying are increasingly reliant on the informal care provided by family and friends. While this has always been true of care at home, it is becoming increasingly true of care in hospitals and other health care settings. Family and friends are picking up the slack for overworked professionals who are finding it difficult to respond in a timely way to the needs of their patients. They do what health care professionals are too busy to do. They also play a critical role in actually securing care from health care professionals. While these informal caregivers have reason to complain, Sinding shows that they work hard to avoid being critical of health care workers. Instead, they understand the pressures that formal caregivers are under and sympathize with their situation.

Sinding uses the experiences and perspectives of these caregivers to reflect on the state of our health care system. She asks what happens to those who do not have informal caregivers in their lives. She also suggests that we should not take at face value evaluation surveys that show satisfaction with health care received within the health care system. Looking beyond the simple "yes" responses that consumers of health care often provide in such surveys, there is a story about what these consumers are really saying about the quality of health care provided by our system.

Dorothy Pawluch, Roy Cain, and James Gillett focus on the perspectives of women who are living with HIV/AIDS and using complementary therapies as a way of managing their health. Their interviews with HIV-positive women showed that women bring unique concerns to their decisions to use such therapies, concerns that are different from the factors that affect men's decisions. First, women often have care-giving responsibilities that lead them to seek out treatments and therapies that have fewer debilitating side effects and are less likely to disrupt their lives. Second, women have reproductive concerns. Women in the study who had become pregnant after their diagnosis or who hoped to become pregnant in the future date saw complementary therapies as more natural, benign, and compatible with pregnancy than the treatments recommended by their doctors. For those who opted for birth control or a hysterectomy following diagnosis, complementary therapies were seen as more natural and safer substitutes for hormone replacement therapy. Third, many women expressed a sense of betrayal by traditional Western medicine. They felt that their unique needs and responses as women with HIV had been neglected. This prompted them to look elsewhere for care. Pawluch and her co-authors conclude that social characteristics, including gender, are an important factor in the perspectives that social actors develop.

The context for the paper by Kristin Newman, Carmen Poulin, Bette Brazier, and Andrea Cashmore is the increasing attention being paid to family violence and abuse of various types. Newman and her co-authors showed a group of university students (six women) a film clip depicting a conflict between a man and a woman involved in a dating relationship. They were interested in the students' perspectives on the film and in how the women interpreted the actions of the protagonists. Put in more symbolic interactionist terms, the authors wanted to see what meanings the young women attached to what was going on in the film clip and where they made attributions of deviance (abuse), if they did so at all. Their findings suggest that while there may be a heightened sensitivity to emotional abuse within relationships, the six young women who viewed the film clip were reluctant to label what they saw as abuse. To the extent that they saw anyone as culpable for the conflict, it was the female, rather than the male protagonist. They rationalized and made excuses for the male character, while constructing the female character as either naive or a "tease." These interpretations lead the authors to question how far views have really changed when it comes to the roles that we expect men and women to play in relationships, whose job it is to "keep the peace," and what sorts of behaviours are acceptable when and if conflict erupts.

Steven Kleinknecht's paper on hackers provides an inside look at the hacker subculture. While the media perspective on hackers and other members of the "computer underground" tends to be negative, Kleinknecht's insider perspective, based on 15 semi-structured interviews with self-defined hackers and participant observation research with a group of hackers, enables us to better appreciate how this social world is defined by hackers themselves. We become familiar with the views shared by members of this community, the patterns of activities that distinguish them from outsiders, and their common language. Unlike the public's image of hackers as persons associated with criminal computer activities, those in Kleinknecht's study regard themselves as enjoying a passion for expressing their ingenuity, developing pieces of technology and solving technological problems. They resist outsiders' definitions of them as deviants, and enjoy testing and extending their technical skills and expertise for its own sake.

CONSTRUCTING IDENTITIES

The point has been made that, in responding and working out our lines of action, we define objects, events, and people around us. Another key premise of symbolic interactionism is that we are able to define ourselves. As human beings we have the capacity to become objects to ourselves, to stand outside of ourselves and see ourselves as we think others see us. It is this capacity to be self-reflexive that gives us a sense of self. Self and identity—how we answer questions related to who we are, how we present ourselves in the world and deal with how others define us—have been enduring themes in symbolic interactionism and the focus of many ethnographic studies.

Writing about identity in a book aptly titled *Mirrors and Masks: The Search for Identity*, Anselm Strauss (1959, p. 9) acknowledges the elusiveness of the concept, but uses interesting imagery to capture the significance of identity in our lives:

> [W]hatever else it might be, identity is connected with the fateful appraisals made of oneself—by oneself and by others. Everyone presents himself to the others and to himself, and sees himself in the mirrors of their judgments. The masks he then and thereafter presents to the world and its citizens are fashioned upon his anticipations of their judgments. The others present themselves too; they wear their own brands of mask and they get appraised in turn. It is all a little like the experience of the small boy first seeing himself (at rest and posing) in the multiple mirrors at the barber shop or in the tailor's triple mirrors.

Strauss's discussion also captures the fact that much of what we do is bound up with identity. Identity is an ongoing concern. We all engage in efforts to manage both how we see ourselves and how others see us. These efforts may be described as "identity work" (Gubrium & Holstein, 2001). Identity work becomes especially visible in cases where we are dealing with a potentially "spoiled" identity. Erving Goffman (1963) defined a spoiled identity as one that carries with it a mark of disgrace that leads others to see us as untrustworthy, incompetent, or tainted in some way. At these moments in our lives, identity work becomes critical. All of the papers in this section deal in one way or another with such moments.

Florence Kellner used interviews to examine how attitudes about cigarette smoking relate to the self-construction and self-presentation of young female university students. She found that among non-smokers an anti-smoking discourse prevailed that emphasized the differences between those who smoke and those who do not. Abstinent women considered themselves to be wise, attractive, and independent. Women who smoke, on the other hand, were seen as being unattractive, although some students felt that men who smoke could be appealing. Notably, views about the immorality of smoking were especially strong when it came to women and their relationships with children, with women who smoke being seen as unfit mothers and even abusive.

Among the smokers, positive attributes such as creativity and tolerance were attributed to women who smoke. However, these women too drew the line where children were concerned. They expressed their intention to stop smoking before they had children and to refrain from smoking if there were children in the household. The women who smoked also agreed with non-smokers that smoking reflected differently on women than men. They felt that smoking was considered more shameful for women and that non-smoking men were particularly repelled by women who smoked. This had implications in terms of how they presented themselves. On the other hand, women who smoked also considered their smoking to be a reaction to the pressure to conform to various feminine ideals. They linked their smoking to resistance and enhanced feelings of power and control in some situations. Kellner concludes by noting that the women in her study, like most women, were attempting to conform to ideal standards of health and beauty, and that how they saw themselves was a major preoccupation, whether they smoked or not.

Karen March's paper offers another example of attempts to achieve an idealized identity. March looks at perceptions of motherhood through the lens of adoption. She argues that the "culture of womanhood" is organized around motherhood and that women are affected by this "motherhood ideal" whether they give birth or not. Using participant-observation and in-depth interviewing, March reports her findings for adult adopted women, birth mothers, and adoptive mothers.

March found that adult adopted women feel that the secrecy associated with adoption, and the lack of information about their biological backgrounds, impedes their ability to be good mothers. Their desire to adhere to the motherhood ideal transforms itself into "searching" behaviour and a desire for a birth reunion in numbers disproportionate to adopted adult males. In the case of birth mothers, March found that the social censure accompanying the decision to place a child for adoption leads to reservations about future mothering activities. The decision to search for an adopted child, according to March, provides an opportunity for the birth mother to validate her sense of self-worth. Contact through a birth reunion gives birth mothers an opportunity to conform to the "motherhood" ideal by enacting the role of a mother who still loves and is concerned about the child she has placed for adoption. The role of adoptive mother, however, has different requirements according to March. The motherhood ideal translates itself in the adoptive mother in openness and honesty with her children. This means acknowledging the differences between her motherhood identity as a primary caregiver and the biological motherhood offered by birth mothers. The motherhood ideal is attained when the adoptive mother helps her children to search and supports them through contact. As March concludes, all three groups of women have internalized a romanticized image of the "ideal" mother and each group, in its own way, seeks to achieve this role identity for themselves.

Leanne Joanisse considers how our identities are tied to what we look like. She studied a group of women who had undergone bariatric surgery in an effort to lose weight. In some cases the surgery was successful; in other cases, it was not. Beginning with an insightful discussion about how closely tied our sense of self is to the appearance of our bodies, Joanisse contrasts how these women constructed themselves before and after surgery. She also contrasts those for whom the surgery was successful with those for whom it failed. She found that the surgery produced a more positive sense of self in almost all of the women, whether it was successful or not. The self-loathing that characterized their lives prior to surgery was reduced.

There was a difference, however, between the two groups of women—those for whom the surgery had been successful and those for whom it had not—in *how* they achieved a more positive self. Those who had been successful in losing weight dealt with the contradiction between what their bodies looked like and who they really were by trying to eliminate the gap between the two and bringing their "deviant" bodies into line. Those for whom the surgery failed achieved a more positive self by rejecting the notion that our bodies reflect who we really are. The first strategy involved subscribing to societal appearance norms; the second involved challenging them. Joanisse concludes with a call for more research into the connections between body and self.

William Shaffir and Stephen Kleinknecht take up the interesting question of what happens to individuals when the careers around which they have constructed their identities disappear. They look at the case of politicians who, defeated at the polls, find themselves facing a difficult period of adjustment. Despite the public's perception that politicians are highly paid, enjoy access to lucrative appointments following their political career, and enjoy considerable free time when not in the legislature, this study paints a different picture, pointing to the range of sacrifices that are typically required of those who enter political life. Shaffir and Kleinknecht show that after a defeat at the polls, politicians spend a good deal of time accounting for their failure despite claims that they, personally, were undeserving of the loss. They examine the rhetoric ex-politicians adopt to cope with their unexpected loss. More specifically, we learn how in an exercise to preserve a more positive sense of self politicians deflect responsibility for the defeat, attributing it instead to events and circumstances they present as being beyond their control.

Finally, Jacqueline Low's study deals with attempts to neutralize a deviant label. Low's study is based on qualitative interviews with a group of individuals who use alternative or complementary therapies as a way of dealing with Parkinson's disease. Long relegated to the status of marginal or fringe health care, alternative therapies have become extremely popular over the past two decades. As Low points out, the percentages of people who use these therapies in one form or another is high. Yet, perhaps as a legacy of their past status, some people view the therapies as suspect and those who use them as gullible, superstitious, or disturbed. The users of these therapies are well aware of the stigma attached to them and, as Low shows, have developed ways to counter others' negative views. They are careful about who they tell. They also distance themselves from certain therapies and therapists, drawing a line essentially between those they are prepared to try and those they avoid. There is an interesting paradox in this strategy that is worth thinking about: while its objective is to protect the image or identity of the particular individuals who use alternative therapies, it reinforces the idea that some users really are "cranks" and some therapies really are "quackery."

DOING AND RELATING

The ethnographies in this final section focus on people doing things together. They present case studies of individuals interacting with each other to get a job done (Greenberg, Knight, MacNeill, & Donnelly), achieve goals (Puddephatt), create communities (Cain), and maintain relationships (Gouliquer & Poulin).

Josh Greenberg, Graham Knight, Peter Donnelly, and Margaret MacNeil analyze how news production unfolds at a local television station in its coverage of the 2000 Sydney Olympic Games. Interest groups within the organization developed competing definitions of how the work and activities should proceed. Greenberg et al. maintain that their respective definitions need to be situated within a body of structural and legal constraints in order to fully appreciate how this news organization managed to coordinate its activities to reach the targeted objectives. Despite hierarchical differences and power differentials among the staff, interest groups within the organization were able to manoeuvre tactically and strategically to negotiate an order that, in some measure, at least, reflected their definition of what was both appropriate and acceptable.

Antony Puddephatt introduces us to the chess world. Drawing on open-ended interviews with 21 amateur chess players, as well as his personal experiences playing the game, Puddephatt offers an inside look at how players go about developing proficiency—including practising skills and gathering knowledge—and marshalling resources towards this end. He attends to features of career advancement within the chess world, but also considers how these features are more generic and extend to other relevant social careers.

Roy Cain examines gay choristers in predominantly heterosexual choirs. Of particular interest, for Cain, are the varying side benefits offered by such participation, in addition to fulfilling a love for singing. The choirs they sang in helped some gay respondents to identify as gay and integrate into gay social worlds. Cain argues that such involvements by gay men enable us, but also gay men themselves, to better appreciate the intersections of gay and non-gay social worlds and how such mixed settings connect to matters of gay identity.

In the final paper, Lynne Gouliquer and Carmen Poulin approach their research on gay servicewomen from a feminist standpoint, using ethnography as a methodology to uncover and explain the institutional "relations of ruling" that give meaning and direction to the everyday experiences of women. The authors seek to understand how lesbians in a military milieu make sense of their everyday experiences and cope with the contradictions in their lives. This approach directs the authors to start with the stories of gay servicewomen and their partners, and their social experiences of an institutional reality—the Canadian military. Gouliquer and Poulin discuss the effects of the military's organizational processes, such as postings and attached-postings, on lesbians' long-term relationships. They document how the military lifestyle impacts on lesbians' ability to create social networks, come out when they are ready to do so, pursue career goals, establish equity in their relationships, share time together, and maintain communication. Gouliquer and Poulin also address how these gay servicewomen and their partners maintain their long-term relationships in the face of contradictory norms.

REFERENCES

Blumer, H. (1969). *Symbolic interactionism: Perspective and method.* Englewood Cliffs, NJ: Prentice-Hall.

Goffman, E. (1963). *Stigma: The management of a spoiled identity.* Englewood Cliffs, NJ: Prentice-Hall.

Gubrium, J.F., & Holstein, J.A. (Eds.). (2001). *Institutional selves: Troubled identities in a postmodern world.* New York: Oxford University Press.

Prus, R. (1996.) *Symbolic interaction and ethnographic research: Intersubjectivity and the study of human lived experience.* Albany, NY: State University of New York Press.

Sandstrom, K.L., Martin, D.D., & Fine, G.A. (2003). *Symbols, selves and social reality.* Los Angeles, CA: Roxbury.

Strauss, A.L. (1959). *Mirrors and masks: The search for identity.* Chicago: The Free Press of Glencoe.

Thomas, W.I. (1937). *The unadjusted girl.* Boston: Little Brown.

Thomas, W.I., & Thomas, D. (1928). *The child in America.* New York: Alfred A. Knopf.

PART 2A

CONSTRUCTING PERSPECTIVES

Chapter 11

The Process of Caring: Nurses and Genetic Termination

Catherine Chiappetta-Swanson

INTRODUCTION

This paper presents the experiences of 41 female registered nurses from four Canadian hospitals, who manage the **genetic termination** (GT) procedure (abortion) for women who end a wanted pregnancy due to fetal anomaly. GTs are the result of **prenatal diagnostic technology** that was implemented in the 1960s, established to identify pregnancies considered to be at high risk for fetal abnormality such as Down's syndrome, spina bifida, and Tay Sachs disease. More and more, the technology is becoming accepted by the medical profession and the public as routine prenatal practice. Medical tests, which include ultrasonography, amniocentesis, maternal serum screening, and chorionic villi sampling, are performed on women at the end of the first trimester of pregnancy. Results are typically not available until well into the second trimester. The GT procedure is overseen in hospitals by registered nurses.

GT nursing is intense. It is one-to-one care across a range of extremely sensitive procedures, which are emotionally and morally charged for both patient and nurse. Typically, GT nurses are responsible for admitting patients, assessing patients' emotional status and level of understanding of the procedure, and preparing for **labour induction**—which in some cases patients are unaware they will undergo. The nurses also manage the delivery of the baby, assess patients for physical complications, and decide whether a physician should be called in.

The nurses' work does not stop when the delivery is over. GT nurses aid parents in making decisions about burial and memorial services for their baby and prepare them and their families for the grieving process. Since the grieving process includes seeing and holding the baby, GT nurses prepare the baby for viewing, and the parents for seeing a baby, which although fully formed is under two pounds and sometimes bears visible physical abnormalities. The nurses assess the emotional impact of the viewing on the parents. Since it is not uncommon for parents to have difficulty giving up their baby, the nurses must often also decide how best to guide them through the process.

GT nurses have a greater scope of responsibility than many other nurses, and they feel that their work is made even more difficult by a lack of institutional

> **Box 11.1: How a Genetic Termination Is Done**
>
> Once a patient has been admitted to hospital, the nurse records necessary information and has the patient sign a medical consent form. Vital signs are taken and an IV (a small catheter inserted into a vein in the arm) is started so the patient can receive fluids and pain medication. Patients are taken to a treatment room where a doctor and a nurse induce labour. Babies in utero typically stop breathing during the labour process as they are not mature enough to tolerate this process (SATFA, 1995). Once delivery begins, it happens quickly. The nurse guides the delivery of the baby, and assesses for any complications such as a breech delivery, haemorrhaging, or the mother going into shock. After delivery, the nurse covers the baby with a sterile pad, and cuts and clamps the umbilical cord.

support. They follow patients and their families from the beginning to the end of their hospital experience, either entirely on their own or with minimal involvement of doctors and other hospital staff. They typically receive little training and have few procedures or explicit guidelines to follow. There is also a shroud of secrecy that surrounds GTs, necessitated in part by the concern for the security and privacy of both patients and nurses. In almost every sense they work in isolation. Their experience working with GT patients is ignored, and their calls for change in how the procedure is handled generally go unheeded. They feel unacknowledged, unsupported, and silenced in their work. Ironically, however, they find this work professionally fulfilling and personally rewarding.

In this chapter my objective is to explain this paradox. The chapter is divided into two parts. The first part deals with the difficulties that these nurses experience. I use the concept of **dirty work**—a concept coined by sociologist E.C. Hughes—in this part of the analysis. The second part deals with the ways in which GT nurses respond to their working conditions so that they are able to experience their work as fulfilling. They re-define their work as an essential element of **nurses' caring function.** I begin with a brief description of how the study was done.

METHODOLOGY

The research is based on in-depth interviews with 41 female registered nurses from four Canadian hospitals who manage the genetic termination procedure for women who end a wanted pregnancy due to fetal anomaly. Thirty-five of these nurses were working as clinical care nurses, three were nursing directors and three were clinical nurse specialists whose role was to professionally support clinical nurses. All worked on the units where GTs were managed. Three nurses had assisted with the GT procedure but had not taken on the role of primary nurse, that is, the nurse responsible for managing the procedure. This group had been nursing between four and 25 years. Their ages ranged from late twenties to late fifties.

Hospital protocol required that permission to speak with nurses be obtained from each hospital's ethics committee. Upon receiving ethics approval, I approached the vice-president of nursing and the nursing director of each hospital and asked for their approval. During this communication we established how best to proceed with the interviews. The nursing directors arranged for me to meet with their clinical nurses and present my research proposal to them. It was through these meetings that most nurses learned of the study.

The interview location was chosen by each nurse. In most cases the nurse was working a 12-hour shift and was given permission by the nurse manager to take time out for the interview. Thirty-nine of the interviews took place at the hospitals on the ward, in the nursing director's office, clinical nurse specialist's office, nurses' lounge, or in a vacant hospital room. In some cases we met in the room where the GTs were managed. Two interviews were done outside of the hospital. The majority of interviews were tape-recorded.

The interviews lasted from 45 minutes to one and a half hours. The interviews were semi-structured, open-ended, and based on the following question: "Could you tell me what the experience of caring for women who end pregnancies for fetal anomaly is like for you?" The interview then followed the nurse's lead. An interview guide was used to focus the discussion through the process of managing genetic termination. The intention was to explore the impact of a number of issues based on the nurses' own meanings and experiences.

GT NURSING AS DIRTY WORK

GTs are seen at their best as tragically unfortunate and at their worst as immoral and unconscionable. These terminations are viewed by many as figuratively unclean not only because they violate social taboos against abortion but also because they deal with death and destruction. In a hospital where nurses are subordinate to physicians and administrators, GT nurses are expected to do the dirty work for others "whose respectability keeps them above such tasks" (Hughes, 1971).

Box 11.2: The Sociological Concept of Dirty Work

Sociologist Everett Hughes (1971) coined the term *dirty work* to describe work that is viewed in one way or another as tainted, unpleasant, or undesirable. It is work that most people would prefer not to do. The concept of dirty work draws attention to outsiders' views of the work in question and the difficulties this raises for those who do it. Hughes focused on types of work that have low status within an occupation or profession, such as hospital workers who "perform the lowly tasks without being recognized among the miracle workers" (1971, p. 307). He also argued that a profession itself can become connected in a negative way with work that is not considered respectable in the larger society; for example, medicine's negative connection to abortionists.

Source: From *Social Organization of Medical Work*, (p. 246), by A. Strauss, S. Fagerhaugh, B. Suczek, & C. Wiener, 1985, Chicago: University of Chicago Press.

Managing GTs is difficult and emotionally charged work. Yet, instead of acknowledging this and providing nurses with assistance and a supportive environment, hospitals have organized GTs in a way that suggests they attach a low priority and a moral ambivalence to them. As a result, nurses face a working situation fraught with uncertainties, tension, dilemmas, and frustrations. They experience the work as dirty work. In fact it is not uncommon for the nurses to use this term to describe features of their work. The nurses' complaints centred around four themes: (1) GTs as a surgical/gynaecological procedure; (2) lack of professional backup; (3) lack of adequate procedures, protocols, and policies; and (4) lack of support.

GTs as a Surgical/Gynaecological Procedure
In all of the sites studied, the GT procedure took place in surgical/gynaecological wards rather than in labour and delivery (L&D) wards. Surgical/gynaecological wards, although busier than L&D wards, were seen by administrators as better suited to the demands of the GT procedure. There is a greater degree of predictability to their schedules and routines, making it easier to provide the constancy of care that GTs require. On L&D wards there would also be the issue of the emotional impact of undergoing a GT in such close proximity to women giving birth to healthy babies.

Many GT nurses, though, questioned whether they had the necessary skills and expertise to manage the termination procedure. They were not trained to do pelvic examinations as a way of assessing the progression of labour. As Donna, a GT nurse explained: "We are expected to treat this like we would any other surgical procedure, and it's not. We are not labour and delivery nurses, we are surgical nurses. We are fortunate that we have had a few midwives join our team. We can't physically examine them as they do in L&D, so we can't give them a progress report. We also don't know ourselves when delivery will happen."

Nor are the nurses able to give spinal epidurals—a technique available to L&D nurses to control labour pain. The only thing GT nurses can do to offer relief to the birthing mother is to administer oral pain control medication such as Demerol or morphine. The problem with this is that while it may offer partial relief, it also makes the patient groggy, thus prolonging labour and emotional pain. Epidurals allow mothers to be more alert during the delivery, making it easier to push the baby out. The frustration and sense of powerlessness this creates for the nurses is captured by Sarah: "Analgesics can often slow things down. The waiting is an issue. All you can tell patients is 'yes, it will happen, but I don't know when.'"

Some GT nurses are also skeptical about the argument advanced by administrators that it is better emotionally for women to undergo GTs on this ward so they need not witness other women giving birth to healthy babies. Nurses wonder whether by shielding women from other mothers they are diminishing their experience of the birth as a real birth. Elaine wondered: "I'm of two schools of thought. Do we shield them from all babies, or do we recognize the loss and hope that women [on the L&D ward] would be more empathetic because they can appreciate their loss?

I can appreciate that it would be difficult to hear other babies crying. Maybe other babies would help the healing begin."

The nurses feel strongly that decisions about where the procedure is provided should be made on the basis of the patient's best interest rather than being driven by institutional concerns.

Exacerbating the whole situation is the lack of information that patients often have when they enter hospital. Many women arrive unprepared for the procedure. Nurses believe that the doctors and counsellors who deal with these women prior to their entering hospital prefer to avoid the difficult and unpleasant discussions involved in explaining what the GT procedure actually entails. It is a task they say that other health care workers prefer to leave to GT nurses. Audrey explained: "Patients' expectations are high. They expect to be on the maternity ward and have an epidural. Most of the time they are not. Patients are often surprised to discover that the birth will be managed by a nurse rather than a doctor." As Alice's experience with patients shows, "when patients are told [by the nurses] that they will be staying in the room to deliver and not going to L&D, some are alarmed. Also, when they realize that there won't be a doc present."

As a result, patients become distracted and even more emotional, further complicating the nurses' role. On top of the difficult demands already being made of them, GT nurses find themselves having to break the news and pick up the emotional pieces.

Lack of Professional Backup

Another source of frustration for GT nurses is that they are left to manage GTs more or less on their own. The normal division of labour that characterizes patient care in hospitals tends to disappear in GT cases. Doctors, genetic counsellors, social workers, and chaplains rarely show any initiative in involving themselves in GT cases. Even when GT nurses call on some of their colleagues, the response comes slowly if at all. Carrie described a strategy used to resist involvement: "The genetics department won't come to see the patient if they have not counselled her before the termination. Sometimes a patient will just arrive on the ward having come from her doctor's office. In this case the nurses must do everything."

GT nurses are particularly incensed by the almost complete absence of doctors at GTs. As they see it, the technical aspects of performing a GT fall under the purview of medicine and should be managed by doctors. This would leave them free to perform what they see as their primary function—attending to the emotional needs of their patients. As Melanie put it: "We are not doctors. We are nurses. We should not be expected to do a doctor's job."

Doctors oversee the induction procedure, but typically are not present during labour and delivery, nor do they participate in the aftercare, including the cutting of the umbilical cord, the delivery of the placenta, or assessment for complications such as haemorrhaging or shock. The release of the patient technically requires a final examination by a doctor. However, doctors may or may not show up when called by the nurses. This means that nurses are left to muddle through tricky clinical decisions they were not trained to make. Corey provided an account where a patient was left waiting by a doctor:

> Some docs are disrespectful. When you call, they don't come. The time and emotional energy needed to wait for the doc is difficult. You phone the doc, they say, "I want to see her before she goes," I ask, "When will you come?" They say, "I'll be there when I get there," Well, I can't make her stay, this isn't a happy place for her right now. Sometimes I will take the heat from the doctor, but the patient will go.

While they are eager for more physician involvement, nurses feel strongly that this will be beneficial only if it is accompanied by a major change in attitude and greater sensitivity to the patient's needs. As Jeanette pointed out: "If a doc comes for a delivery he or she only delivers the baby and placenta, then leaves right away, often not even talking to the patient! We need the docs involved. We need to see them more often, talking with patients, not at them. And the docs need to support the nurses more—we are not doctors."

Lack of Procedures, Protocols, and Policies

In the hospital, an institution notorious for its rigid adherence to procedure, there is remarkably little standardization when it comes to doing GTs. A particularly revealing and heart-wrenching example of the degree to which nurses are left to figure things out as they go along involves the birth of a live baby. It is not uncommon for some babies to survive the trauma of birth, even at this early stage of gestation. Approximately half of the nurses in this study had experienced this situation at least once. Babies born live cannot survive long due to prematurity. They may continue to breathe between five and 20 minutes after birth. Their birth creates a host of difficulties, not the least of which is how to care for them. Lorraine recalled her first experience: "I was shocked! I didn't know what to do, so I called the doctor and asked him what to do. He simply said, "Drop it into the saline solution." There was no way I was going to do that. These babies are human beings that deserve to be treated with dignity and caring. I washed and dressed the baby, wrapped him in a blanket and carried him around the ward with me until he stopped breathing. Then I took him to his parents."

While it is easy to focus on the insensitivity of the doctor's response, the more telling point is how little thought had been given by the hospital to developing standard care programs that anticipated this situation and assisted staff—nurses and doctors—in dealing with it.

In terms of physical set-up of the ward for GTs, little regard seems to have been given to the space and equipment that nurses need to do this work. There is only one patient room on the ward for GTs. In most cases it is located in an "out-of-the-way" section of the ward for reasons of security and to offer both patient and nurse some degree of privacy. While labour and delivery takes place in this room, aftercare, bathing, wrapping, and preparation of the baby for viewing by parents, and afterwards, the preparation of the baby's remains for testing or release, is done in the ward's dirty utility room: a small, multi-purpose space containing a utility basin, a refrigerator, and medical and cleaning supplies.

The GT nurses find these arrangements completely unsatisfactory. They claim it is not a suitable space for washing, dressing, and bundling a baby. Nor are they given the supplies they need, for example, a baby bassinet, baby bath, soap, or the baby blankets and bonnets to dress the babies for presentation to parents.

Also of concern is the lack of suitable containers necessary for nurses to safely transport the body to the morgue. Daria explains the difficulty she encountered in having to place the body into a jar of saline solution. "The fetal container is like a peanut butter jar. Where is the dignity? Because of the shape of the container you have to drop the fetus in—it's like a plop!"

Nurses also recount "accidents" that commonly occur as they are transporting the body to the morgue. Donna described this: "Oh, the peanut butter jar! The problem is we used to have a 24-hour urine bottle that was great. Then they changed it to this small-neck jar that was useless. Then we got this plastic Tupperware jar—a spill waiting to happen. I had one that flooded the elevator. I had it double bagged, I was walking it down to pathology myself. It [the jar] was wrapped in two green garbage bags and wrapped in a blue sterile pad. I was walking on eggshells and it still flooded pathology."

Jean explained her experience: "I was walking to the elevator to go to the morgue. In front of the nursing station I dropped the container, which was in a green plastic bag. It shattered all over the floor. Thank goodness it was late at night so there weren't a lot of patients and visitors around. All of us just rushed around to clean it up."

Lack of Support

Finally, there is the issue of how little acknowledgement and emotional support there is for GT nurses. Given the unease and ambivalence about GTs, there are few people inside or outside the hospital that nurses can talk to about their work. Given the stigma surrounding GTs, nurses feel that they cannot utilize hospital support programs. None of these nurses had ever consulted a hospital social worker.

This isolation is heightened by the security concerns about GTs. All four hospitals have experienced difficulties with pro-life groups. Hospitals also stress the need to maintain a low profile for GTs. Although they do not expressly forbid staff from talking about GTs, there is an expectation that, both for security reasons and in order to maintain patient privacy, there should be little discussion. Linda, a nursing director, argued: "Security measures are very important for nurses and patients. The idea of abortion draws out radical groups, there can be violence, there is a risk involved. Society still goes back to the old way of thinking of abortion as a birth control method. We keep a low profile on this procedure."

Their security comes with a price; GTs are shrouded in a veil of secrecy. This means that nurses get little support and recognition for their work and its unique problems.

GT NURSING AS "REAL NURSING"

Despite the overwhelming difficulties attached to GTs, nurses talk about experiencing personal satisfaction, gratification, and professional challenge in this work. They see GT nursing as a way to put into practice the core values of their profession—patient-centred care. Powerless to escape the dirty work aspects of their job, nurses have redirected their attention to the meaningful and rewarding aspects of their work. They devote themselves to attending to their patients' physical and emotional needs, finding ways to work around the institutional constraints and barriers.

Caring for Patients Physically

Nurses view physical patient care as an important part of the GT procedure. Without the use of epidurals, they have learned to make effective use of the techniques they do have such as analgesics like Demerol or morphine. Nurses get a prescription from the doctor, enough to last through the labour and delivery.

Two hospitals recently introduced patient-controlled analgesics (PCA) in the form of a pain medication pump, as a result of the nurses' persistence. Patients press a button to release a pre-set amount of medication when they need pain relief. The nurses agreed that it is an improvement, although it is still inadequate. The nurses recognized that the pain pump also serves to give patients a measure of control over their situation. Those nurses who did not have access to pain pumps developed other ways to help patients control the pain. They have sought out the advice of L&D nurses and have learned that massage, breathing techniques, and walking can be helpful. The nurses often enlisted the assistance of patients' partners and family to assist in this care.

The most critical part of GTs is the actual delivery. Almost all of the nurses had stories to tell about difficult, complicated, and messy deliveries. Among the most dramatic was the following situation, described by Cynthia: "One patient got up to go to the bathroom and she started bleeding all over the place. She was going to deliver in the toilet. That was the icing on the cake for me that day. Here I was on my hands and knees, we were running around like chickens with our heads cut off. I called the doc, who said it would take half an hour to get there. It was an emergency! She needed a D&C. I called the OR and told them to get ready. We were trying to manage her so she wouldn't go into shock. Her boyfriend was acting like a bodyguard. We asked him to wait outside the room. Every time we went out the door, he was asking a lot of questions. It was hard."

Not surprisingly, once the baby is on its way nurses move into a state of high alert. They ready themselves for any eventuality and concentrate on getting the patient through the delivery safely. Daria explained it well: "At the point of delivery you're very detached—it's very clinical. You want to make sure the fetus passes and you get the clamps on and hopefully it passes in one piece. I am trying to be supportive to the patient, I'll say, 'You're doing a good job, but this is what we have to focus on right now [getting the baby out].'"

Caring for Patients Emotionally

The nurses seek to provide reassurance and unconditional support for their patients. For example, patients often are very confused and unsure of their decision. Nurses try not to rush them, answer their questions, and invite them to express their fears while reassuring them they have made the best decision. Whether nurses approved or not was seen by them as less important than their ability to set aside their own views in the best interest of their patients. Debbie summed up the sentiments of many nurses: "I have no judgment of the patient whatsoever. It's something I have worked on, the moral stuff. It's not my job to judge. Oh yes, they pick up on your attitude. This day is not about me."

Supportive care means empathetic care—relating to and crying with patients. Unlike most health care professionals who are governed by norms of professional detachment and affective neutrality, GT nurses see it as acceptable, even desirable, to share in their patients' suffering. Sarah recalled an emotional situation: "At delivery they often let out a deep-pitted cry or scream. That last push when the baby comes out. It's a deep-pit scream that comes from deep in their stomach. I don't know what to say to them at this time. Sometimes I cry with them."

A factor that may contribute to this professional attachment is the closeness of the relationship that nurses build with patients. They work hard to establish a bond of trust.

Lorraine said: "Every family is so different. Certain patients, it's like you are part of their family. There are families that seem to latch on, they look for you, and they seek you out. I tend to feel the loss more with them. It wouldn't be uncommon for me to cry. I don't apologize for that. It's how I feel. I say to them, 'I feel this way because you are feeling this way.'"

This emotional attachment represents for many what nursing is all about—total commitment and devotion to one's patient. Sue, a nursing director claimed: "What personifies nursing is when she takes the fetus, cleans it up and presents it to mom and puts her arm around her, and there are tears in the nurse's eyes."

CONCLUSION

In looking at the various ways GT nurses experience their work as dirty work and the strategies they create to cope, it is clear their problems are in many ways a function of how hospitals have structured the procedure and the negative institutional attitudes towards GTs. Though hospitals have introduced GTs as part of an effort to be responsive to women's health care needs, their approach suggests a moral ambivalence about GTs. Yet, as bleak as the conditions may be, GT nurses have responded in a way that makes their work not only manageable but gratifying. First, rather than dwelling on the dirty work aspects of the job, the nurses redefine GT nursing as a unique opportunity to practise nursing as they believe it should be practised. Second, the nurses have developed routines that allow them to get the job done safely, effectively, and efficiently despite the lack of support. Nurses successfully manage GTs without the presence of a doctor.

Looking more broadly at the nurses' experiences, there is an interesting paradox concerning the caring function. Nurses become focused on caring for patients and on seeing them through the procedure by trying to minimize their physical and emotional pain. Yet in caring so intensively for their patients, the nurses are also caring for themselves. It is the quality of care they provide that transforms their job from dirty work to nursing as it should be practised. Both patients and nurses derive benefits that are critical in sustaining the nurses' commitment to this difficult work.

Another interesting paradox concerns the relative isolation of the nurses. They complain about being set apart both figuratively and literally from the rest of the hospital and about not being able to talk to others about their work. Yet, what many nurses did not appreciate is that their isolation has given them the latitude to redefine their tasks in a way that they find professionally rewarding and to develop routines that support these redefinitions. Knowing, for example, that a physician will not be present for a delivery puts nurses in the position of making clinical and ethical decisions based on their own professional sense of what is best for their patients.

Finally, this study contributes to our understanding of dirty work and how workers adapt to such work. It shows that workers' powerlessness does not extend as far as their capacity to define the work—if not the conditions under which it is done—on their own terms. Workers always have the power to redefine their tasks and themselves in more positive and valued ways. Most GT nurses welcomed the additional responsibility and the opportunity to exercise independent professional judgment. GT nursing provides them with many opportunities to do so.

GLOSSARY

Dirty work: Genetic terminations can be viewed in a sense as dirty work because it is work that is deemed undesirable and immoral by some. Although labour and delivery is very messy work, so too is the delivery of a live, healthy baby. Yet in normal deliveries, the work brings a high degree of prestige to physicians. Genetic termination can be viewed as figuratively unclean because it violates social taboos against abortion and society's negative views of working with the dead. GTs are organized to allow higher status doctors to pass off the task of dealing with emotionally distraught patients and a messy abortion procedure and to avoid being identified with a morally controversial procedure.

Genetic termination: A genetic termination is a second trimester abortion procedure occurring between the 17th and 24th week of pregnancy that results from prenatal diagnostic testing that has positively identified a fetal abnormality. There are no cures for the more than 400 detectable medical abnormalities. Parents either continue the pregnancy and knowingly give birth to a baby with an abnormality or terminate the pregnancy. The most commonly used procedure in Canada is labour induction and delivery of a stillborn. This procedure, which can take between one and three days, is managed in hospital by registered nurses.

Labour induction: The most commonly used procedure for inducing labour and delivery is prostaglandin induction. It is a two-stage procedure. The drug prostaglandin initiates uterine contractions in order to bring on labour. The drug is first administered in the form of a vaginal suppository or by injection into the amniotic sac through the mother's stomach muscle. The second part of the procedure is the insertion of laminara. These are small, tapered sticks of seaweed inserted into the woman's cervical opening to slowly expand the cervix in preparation for the delivery. Laminara help to reduce delivery time and serves to decrease incidence of cervical injury. There is often pain and cramping associated with the procedure as the body is not prepared for delivery and must be forced. The procedure takes between 20 and 30 minutes.

Nurses' caring function: Nursing is considered to be among the most noble of professions. As sociologist Daniel Chambliss (1996) highlights: "Care is the key term in nursing's definition of itself and it defines what nurses believe their job to be. Many nurses say that 'care' is what distinguishes nursing from medicine: nurses care, doctors cure" (p. 80). Caring as an historically created experience was premised on the expectation that nurses would act out of a gendered obligation to care, thus taking on caring more as an identity than as work. Consequently, much like others who perform what is considered to be women's work in North American society, nurses contend with a dichotomy between their duty to care for others and their right to control their own activities within their own work. It would be a mistake though to view nurses' work as being essentially one of exploitation. Chambliss (1996) has noted that an appeal of nursing as a profession is the intensity that the job demands: "People don't become nurses to avoid seeing suffering or to have a quiet day'" (p. 18). Nursing is meaningful work.

Prenatal diagnostic technology: The prenatal diagnosis of a genetic condition is a two-step process. The first involves gathering information or genetic material to make a diagnosis. This may require an ultrasound, amniocentesis (the most common and invasive procedure), a blood test such as for a maternal serum alpha-fetoprotein test (AFP), or a biopsy as in the case of chorionic villus sampling (CVS). The second step involves laboratory analysis and interpretation of information to reach a diagnosis.

REFERENCES

Bernal, E. (1995). The nurse as patient advocate. In F. Baylis, J. Downie, B. Freedman, & B. Hoffmaster (Eds.), *Health care ethics in Canada* (pp. 179–190). Toronto: Harcourt Brace and Company Canada Ltd.

Bosk, C. (1992). *All God's mistakes: Genetic counselling in a paediatric hospital.* Chicago: University of Chicago Press.

Chambliss, D. (1996). *Beyond caring: Hospitals, nurses and the social organization of ethics.* Chicago: University of Chicago Press.

Davis, A., & Aroskar, M. (1992). *Ethical dilemmas and nursing practice.* New York: Appleton-Century-Crofts.

Glaser, B., & Strauss, A. (1967). *Discovery of grounded theory: Strategies for qualitative research.* Chicago: Aldine Publishing Company.

Hughes, E.C. (1971). *The sociological eye: Selected papers.* Chicago: Aldine Publishing Company.

Leininger, M.M. (1990). *Ethical and moral dimensions of care.* Detroit: Wayne State University Press.

SATFA. (1995). *A handbook for parents when an abnormality is diagnosed in their baby: Support after termination for abnormality.* London: The Good News Press.

Strauss, A., Fagerhaugh, S., Suczek, B., & Wiener, C. (1985). *Social organization of medical work.* Chicago: University of Chicago Press.

Chapter 12

Perceptions of Oncology Professionals' Work: Implications for Informal Carers, Implications for Health Systems

Christina Sinding

INTRODUCTION

While incidence and mortality rates for most cancer sites are relatively stable, population growth and changing patterns of age distribution have resulted in a steady increase in the numbers of people dying of cancer (National Cancer Institute of Canada, 2003). The majority of deaths in Canada occur in hospitals (Government of Canada, 2000). Yet, as is true generally in the Western world, most dying takes place at home (Rhodes & Shaw, 1999), and most care for people who are dying is provided as **informal care** by family members and friends.

Trends supporting informally provided **palliative care** reflect shifts in the wider economic and political context of health care provision. Since the mid-1970s, public discourse and government policy have organized a relatively residual role for the state in the care of people who are disabled, elderly, or ill. In keeping with principles of **neo-liberalism**, the market has assumed greater importance in the allocation and distribution of care. And, central to the point of this chapter, informal social networks have a much more critical (and even celebrated) role.

The study described here explored people's accounts of caring for a relative or friend who died of breast cancer. In its initial stages the study focused on informal carers' accounts of interactions with the health professionals involved in supporting their dying relative or friend. I intended to explore how the experience of caring for someone who is dying is made more difficult, and how it is eased, by meanings drawn from these interactions.

Over the course of my research I became increasingly curious about how the people I interviewed talked about **oncology** professionals' work. I came to see that the conditions of professionals' work mattered to family members and friends of ill people in ways I hadn't anticipated.

My objectives in this chapter are to show how perceptions about health professionals' work and working conditions can shape the actions of informal caregivers, and affect their reports of difficult health care experiences. In the research reported here, strain and overwork among health professionals lent health policy and politics—macro sociological forces—immediate meaning and relevance to family members and friends of ill people. The social processes that unfolded from carers' awareness of strain among health professionals contain implications for quality and equity in care.

METHODS

Respondents who cared for someone who had died within the past three years and who had engaged in interactions with formal service providers were recruited for this study with the assistance of oncology nurses, staff at hospices and Community Care Access Centres (provincial government agencies that assess service eligibility and oversee its provision), and through informal social networks.

Thirteen people took part in the study, among them seven spouses (five husbands, one lesbian partner, and one wife), two sisters, three friends, and one daughter. The age of the respondents ranged from 41 to 73, and of the person who died, from 46 to 77; more than half of the respondents were between 50 and 58. All were born in Canada and responded to a question about ethnicity with either "White" or British heritage.

Two interviews were conducted with each of 12 study participants, and one carer responded by letter to a series of questions drawn from the interview guide. Initial interviews, which lasted between one and two–and–a–half hours, encouraged the respondent to "tell the story" of caring for the person who had died. Prompt questions focused on times when respondents found themselves doing more for the other person; on shifts in the relationship between the carer and the ill person; and on moments of strain and reward or ease in caring. Second interviews clarified respondents' earlier comments and further explored their responses to and assessments of interactions with health professionals. The interviews were conducted in respondents' homes or in rooms in nearby cancer treatment centres or service agencies. Accounts gathered over the course of the study were analyzed with reference to grounded theory methods (Charmaz, 1990; Strauss & Corbin, 1990).

ANALYSIS

In this study, respondents often commented on the difficult working conditions faced by health professionals in hospitals and cancer centres. In a typical comment, one respondent said, "They've got so much to do and there's so few of them." It became clear that this kind of awareness of strain among professionals affected informal carers—it affected what they did, and it affected how they assessed health care.

Perceptions of Health Professionals' Working Conditions: Effects on Informal Carers' Actions

In her narrative about caring for her partner, Ellen described arriving at the hospital at seven o'clock each morning to provide practical care: helping Jill on the commode, getting basins so she could brush her teeth and wash her face. Ellen did not suggest that Jill would not have had these basic needs met had Ellen not been there, just that she would have had to wait. In this regard Ellen describes watching as the other women in Jill's hospital room rang for a nurse, and then waited:

> In the morning they're just so busy doing things, the nurses … One woman sat on the edge of the bed and she'd just wait. She'd just sit waiting for someone to come and I really believe it's because they don't have the staff … If they had to go to the bathroom—and these are cancer patients, these are people that maybe they can't hold it, you know, that sort of … I mean Jill wouldn't have been able to wait.

Obviously the perception that health professionals were overworked was not the only reason family members and friend provided the care that they did. Ellen herself saw her decision to ensure that Jill did not wait partly in the category of "catering" to Jill's "whims," "mothering her to pieces." Yet as is clear from this quote, Ellen also judged nurses as unable to respond to patients' needs in a timely way, and this was one of the prompts for her actions.

In a few instances participants in this study described working directly with health professionals to provide specific kinds of routine care. Ruth, for example, would often assist the nurses to turn her friend Kay in bed. Sometimes she moved to help simply because she was there and not busy; in this way, her assistance was, as she says, "automatic." Yet it was also clear to Ruth that prompt nursing care for her friend sometimes relied on her own willingness and capacity to help:

> I'd say, "It's time for her to be turned, she needs to be turned." And they said, "Well, we're just in the middle of something, unless you want to help me, it's going to be like 20 minutes," or whatever, and I said, "Okay, I'll help you."

Here, the allocation of caring work is made explicit, with Ruth agreeing to stand in for a busy health professional.

Like Ellen and Ruth, other carers in this study sometimes responded to conditions of health professionals' work by providing care themselves, or working with professional staff. Yet also very significant were family members and friends' accounts of working to *secure* care from health professionals. Strategies used to do this included trading services and progress chasing.

In several instances participants in the study spoke of "helping" health professionals. As mentioned, assisting a nurse or physician was one of the ways that informal carers ensured that the ill person's care needs were met in a timely way. Yet other valued outcomes were apparent. Diane, for instance, perceived that the assistance she offered nurses was something they appreciated, and thus was a kind of inducement to their services:

> The nurse would come in and say, "Oh, good, you're here." I think they were more prepared to give her some extra time, maybe in the middle of the night if nobody was there, because they knew that during the day I'd be there (Diane).

Dan also described caring for his wife throughout the night at the hospital. "It helped them—understaffed and overworked and everything else," he said. He then went on to link the nurses' appreciation for his help to subsequent interactions with them. Trying to sort through documentation about his wife's medication after she was transferred between hospitals, he phoned one of the nurses whom he had "helped." He described his pleasure that she remembered his first name, and commented on how she dealt with his request: "It was almost like having personal service or whatever, but she immediately went and got what we needed." Informal carers' "services" to nurses, especially important in relation to their difficult working conditions, were seen to facilitate future goodwill and responsiveness to future care needs.

"Progress chasing" was a term used by a study participant, Martin, to describe his relationship to the health professionals involved in his wife's care. As he put it, "Progress chasing is, you know, we got this to do next, okay, well, is it happening?" Progress chasing includes the actions of monitoring the ill person's condition, tracking care schedules, and tracking down health professionals to address discomfort or to provide routine care. Sometimes family members and friends described their "progress chasing" in quite offhand ways. In other instances, participants outlined very active and conscious attempts to understand symptoms and care routines. The attention an informal carer devoted to monitoring the ill person and her care was sometimes explicitly connected to an awareness of nurses' working conditions:

> I have notes of every day … everything. How many pills she's taken, when did she have a bowel movement, colour of her skin, temperature, everything. Because they [nurses] can't. They got 110 patients (Martin).

Progress chasing was a responsibility that every person who took part in this study, in different ways, took on. Yet it was clear in respondents' accounts that the activities associated with progress chasing could easily lead to them being perceived as demanding, or needlessly anxious about the patient. "The only thing I didn't want to do is bug them if they were busy," said Ruth, reflecting the sentiments of several respondents. Yet informal carers, at the ill person's bedside, are acutely aware of care needs and the cost to the ill person of those needs going unmet. Ruth's friend, after a surgery, needed help getting to the commode:

> And so you're trying to help her out of bed and all that other stuff, and that's when you're supposed to get a nurse. And they would get a little exasperated at that because she was constantly thinking that she had to get up. But she also didn't want to pee the bed. You know, it was very … that dignity being robbed from her, that independence. [pause] That was—oh man, that was trying.

In comments like these, respondents captured one of the central contradictions of informal carers' roles. Informal carers feel compelled to "chase" health professionals because care needs would go unmet if they do not, and informal carers are at pains not to bother health professionals because care might be withheld or compromised if nurses or physicians become irritated. When health professionals are "run off their feet," both the requirement and the risks of progress chasing are heightened.

> ### Box 12.1: Burdens and Benefits of Informal Care
>
> Many feminist scholars document the costs—social, emotional, and economic—of being responsible for the care of disabled, elderly, and ill relatives. Hooyman and Gonyea (1995), for instance, review literature that points to carers' restricted time, friendships, and community engagement; their worry, loneliness, depression, and anger; their foregone earnings and missed career opportunities, and expenditures on private services and equipment.
>
> Yet while strain cannot be disputed, research on caring has tended to obscure the positive meanings carers derive from their caring work (Opie, 1992). Both sociological and nursing accounts of end-of-life care giving have highlighted the rewards relatives or friends report (Seale, 1990), the opportunity this particular care-giving situation represents, and the sense of pride it generates (Grbich, 2001).
>
> My own research (Sinding, 2003) alerts us to the coexistence of a subjective sense of reward and almost unbearable strain. Informal care can, it seems, be provided at tremendous personal cost, receive entirely unsatisfactory health and social service support, and still be described as deeply meaningful. Particularly in the current policy context, we must guard against the tendency to equate a rewarding care situation with an adequately supported one.

The possibility that care needs will go unmet is higher; so, too, is the possibility that health professionals will perceive informal carers' efforts to secure their attention and labour as demands.

Perceptions of Health Professionals' Working Conditions: Effects on Informal Carers' Reports of Difficult Experiences

My curiosity about how respondents spoke about difficult care experiences emerged from two puzzles—one presented by Dan, the other by Martin. In an early interview, Dan told me about a conversation he and his wife Linda had had after the oncologist told them there was no further treatment available for Linda. He said:

> Dan: "Linda was mad. She felt that [the oncologist] had let her down. I don't think he let her down. I think, again ... She herself said many times throughout the three years, it's a crapshoot. And ... what will be will be. But on the other hand I can see where she sort of felt ... why her?"
>
> CS: "Is that your sense as well, I mean is that ... your feeling, that it was a crapshoot?"

In my question here, I had been trying to encourage Dan to focus on his own experience, to shift us away from his perceptions of what his wife felt or thought. I had not in my own mind questioned his conviction that the physician had delivered the best possible care for his wife.

In responding to my question, though, Dan started to cry. He went on to describe interactions with the oncologist in which he had come to believe his wife would benefit from an experimental treatment, and yet it was never offered to her. He took me through the steps of it—where he had heard about the trial, presenting it to the oncologist, the oncologist indicating that his wife would qualify, his raising the subject of this experimental treatment on two more occasions, and nothing ever coming of it. So in our conversation, Dan approached the possibility that it was not, in fact, a crapshoot: that his wife might not have had to die when she did, and that a physician may have been culpable in this. And yet at the end of this section of talk, Dan said, "You know, that's not—that's not a commentary on the care."

Another man who took part in my study, Martin, took his wife to the emergency ward when she was unable to stop vomiting during the days following surgery to her spine. Martin's wife spent over 24 hours on a gurney in the emergency ward as the nurses tried to find a bed on a ward for her.

> She was in so much pain … You can't have anybody on a gurney with a back surgery issue for that many hours and expect them to live … It was hard, it was a very, very difficult time. That was horrendous. That was just brutal.

"Dissatisfied" was not the kind of language or response I expected from someone who had endured those hours—I expected something far more vehemently critical. But what did Martin do after that incident? He wrote letter of thanks to the nurses: "I wrote them a letter that was, I'm sure they still have it on the wall, I mean I tried to write them the most incredible letter to say, thank you."

Box 12.2: Palliative Care in Canada

- Canadians who are dying receive significantly different treatment in various institutions across the country.
- Rural residents have considerably less access to palliative care than the residents of large urban areas.
- Most of the costs and other burdens of home care are assumed by the family.
- Integrated, interdisciplinary palliative care teams often include nurses with specialized palliative care skills, a family physician, a physician specialized in palliative care, a social worker, a spiritual counsellor, and a pharmacist. Only five percent of dying Canadians receive integrated and interdisciplinary palliative care, and the number of institutional palliative care beds has been cut as a result of health care restructuring.

Source: From *Quality End-of-Life Care: The Right of Every Canadian*, www.parl.gc.ca/36/2/parlbus/ commbus/senate/com-e/update/rep-e/repfinjuneoo-e.htm, by the Government of Canada, 2000, Ottawa: Subcommittee to update "Of Life and Death" of the Standing Senate Committee on Social Affairs, Science and Technology.

It was as a result of these two puzzles—two instances in which accounts of care seemed mismatched with evaluations of care—that I started to identify in a systematic way in the interview transcripts what I called "nascent complaints" or "almost complaints." Almost complaints, as I defined them, were stories that had the makings of a complaint (stories where there was suffering or loss, and a health professional or the health system was implicated) but that were not ultimately framed as complaints. As I reviewed the transcripts, I came to see the many ways these "almost complaints" were disarmed—derailed, or reformulated, or transformed to praise—as study participants' stories unfolded.

The question that captured me was, of course, why—why did family members and friends of ill people, in the face of suffering in which health professionals are implicated—why did they *not* express dissatisfaction with care? Especially, why, in these situations, did they sometimes wind up commending, praising, the care? It became clear as I examined the transcripts that the conditions of oncology professionals' work also played a part in this process of complaints being disarmed.

A few different aspects of the conditions of professionals' work featured in the disarming of "nascent complaints." The first related to health professionals'

Box 12.3: Metaphorically Speaking …

Coffey and Atkinson (1996) contend that metaphors can be fruitfully employed as part of the process of qualitative data analysis. I worked for a while with the idea that respondents' "almost complaints" about health professionals and health services were "palliated" in the course of talk. The metaphor had the obvious appeal of being linked to the substantive area I was exploring. It also usefully evoked two key aspects of what I saw happening with expressions of dissatisfaction: in talk, the source of pain in the complaint was both eased and covered up. Yet as I proceeded, the metaphor of "disarming" seemed to connote more thoroughly the range of what happened to expressions of dissatisfaction in the course of respondents' talk.

Disarming can involve mollifying or placating, and indeed, in many instances respondents' judgments about health professionals' actions were eased as actions were assessed in relation to conditions of health professionals' work. In a few accounts, the suspicions an ill person had about care were pacified by the caregiver, as he or she contextualized health professionals' decisions and actions; to pacify suspicions is another meaning of disarm (Bisset, 2000). To disarm is also to deprive of the power to injure (Bisset, 2000), and it was apparent in respondents' talk that expressions of dissatisfaction have the power to injure both the speaker and, at least theoretically, the health professional implicated in his or her account.

Finally, one of the narrower meanings of disarm is to deactivate an alarm system. As complaints are disarmed, inadequacies of care and attention go unrecorded, and the call to collective action that might be provided by carers' experiences remains unformed.

resources: their knowledge resources, and their emotional and psychological resources. Conditions of overwork were also cited.

Dan was the study participant who had understood a clinical trial would be available for his wife, but it never came about, and yet he went on to say, "That's not a commentary on the care." How did he get there? In talking further about the lost possibility of that trial, Dan said,

> I think this thing [the disease] snuck up on him [the oncologist] as fast as it snuck up on her. I mean there was no indication ... I mean yes, he was doing her levels and everything else, and ... so he'd look at her blood levels, but it [snaps fingers] hit like that. And then it was too late.

Here Dan suggests that health professionals' capacities to monitor and predict the illness's course are inadequate in the face of this disease. Yes, he was checking her blood levels—yes, he did have a certain kind of knowledge that might have offered some capacity to predict the path of the disease—but the oncologist's resources were not sufficient; the movement of the disease, and when it would move, cannot be fully known. The complaint is thus disarmed—taken out of action, in a way, by the swiftness and ultimate unpredictability of the cancer adversary, and the inadequacy of health professionals' resources against it.

Also relevant to the disarming of nascent complaints were respondents' assessments of health professionals' emotional and psychological resources in the face of death and dying. One woman described how the oncologist managing her friend's care frequently failed to acknowledge her in the waiting room; the respondent also wondered if, at times, the oncologist deliberately made himself unavailable for the ill woman's appointments. "I'm sure that was distressing for her," Cathy noted. Yet, as Cathy also said,

> I think maybe he was young and maybe he was just afraid you know ... You know, if you're dealing with death and dying all the time, wouldn't you be like this? Well, wouldn't you be evasive? Well, wouldn't you want to just sort of keep walking?

Another respondent commented on care from nurses:

> When they're abrupt, it just takes you back a bit. But then you think, that isn't, to them, I mean they're not being rude. They're just being mechanical. You know, they're not ... and there must be for them a point ... I mean this is a palliative care unit. They can't invest something in every person that comes in there. Because they couldn't (Ruth).

In these two passages, what might have been complaint talk—about a physician's avoidance of a patient, and about nurses' brusque manner and depersonalized approach to care—is disarmed by the assertions about the psychological limits to engagement with dying people.

Box 12.4: Deaths in Canada

- Over 220,000 Canadians die each year.
- Seventy-five percent of all deaths occur in people over 65 years of age.
- Seventy-five percent of the deaths take place in hospitals and long-term care facilities.

Source: From *Quality End-of-Life Care: The Right of Every Canadian*, www.parl.gc.ca/36/2/parlbus/ commbus/senate/com-e/update/rep-e/repfinjuneoo-e.htm, by the Government of Canada, 2000, Ottawa: Subcommittee to update "Of Life and Death" of the Standing Senate Committee on Social Affairs, Science and Technology

As noted earlier, the theme of health professionals as "busy," the awareness on the part of family members and friends that nurses and physicians have "so much to do and so few of them, also featured in the disarming of respondents' complaints. Jill spoke during our interview of travelling with her partner to the cancer centre for a regularly scheduled meeting with the oncologist. When they arrived, the nurse told them the oncologist was not available, and that another oncologist would see them:

> I was really annoyed about that, and I said, "You could at least call us and tell us that he is not here and let us make the decision whether we need to come and see another doctor." And a lot of times it's not easy for the patient to come … And to come and not have your doctor there is just not acceptable to me in my mind. And I think that the least that they could do is give you a phone call and say, "Dr. So-and-So isn't here, the other doctor is here," you know.
>
> The other side of that, in all fairness to the people at [hospital], at the cancer clinic is, it's packed. The cancer clinic is packed, and it's just … in the six years that I've been going to that cancer clinic it's gotten more and more and more. It's unbelievable to me. And so I guess really it's not feasible for them to call everybody on the day and say, "Well, your doctor's not here," which I mean, they'd probably be there all day, but I wish that there was something that they could do.

In this excerpt, we can follow the course of Ellen's "almost complaint." Early in the account the patient and carer occupy positions of **entitlement** in relation to health professionals: if the oncologist was not there, *at least* the nurse could call and let them know. Information about the unavailability of their regular physician is their right, and it is a health professional's minimal duty to ensure that right.

And yet, as Ellen says, the cancer clinic is packed. Set in relation to conditions of overwork among health professionals, earlier assertions of entitlement are eroded. Initially claiming her right to a particular action on the part of health professionals, by the end of this passage Ellen is wishing for an undefined "something they could do." The energy of her account dissipates, and her complaint is disarmed.

In this context, we can also return to Martin and his thank-you letter. His wife spent hours on a gurney in the emergency ward; he describes the experience as "brutal." And yet he writes a thank-you letter. His explanation for the letter: "Because the nurses did everything they possibly could."

In Martin's account, the experience he and his wife had—an experience that could easily form the basis for an expression of considerable dissatisfaction—is situated in talk in relation to current conditions in the health system. In this process, something that might reasonably be expected from health professionals, the timely securing of a bed for an acutely ill patient, is located beyond the bounds of their effort and will. It may well have been, of course, that not a single bed was available in the entire hospital. The point here is that it is quite possible to talk about this differently. Martin might have railed about his wife's (and his) suffering, and blamed health professionals. Quite the opposite happens: in an "unbelievable" situation, the nurses also are described as "unbelievable," their attempts to provide care exalted in the face of the conditions of their work.

IMPLICATIONS FOR QUALITY AND EQUITY IN CARE

The importance in this study of informal carers' roles in ensuring health care for ill relatives and friends begs the question of what happens when ill people do not have relatives and friends with them. As Graham (1991) points out, the giving of care in the informal sector reflects the obligations of carers rather than the statutory rights of dependants. People with limited or fractured social networks are denied access to informal care.

In the context of the current study, to be denied access to informal care is not only to be denied access to the labour and support of relatives and friends: it is also to have access to the attention and empathy of health professionals compromised. In this study informal caregivers took responsibility not only for providing care, but also for securing care from health professionals. As is clear, securing care from professionals is a complex dance requiring subtlety and skill.

In Canada, universality and accessibility are key principles of health care. Yet insofar as the findings of this study speak to general processes, the level and timing of health care in Canada is (perhaps increasingly) contingent on informal carers and on ill people themselves. It is, thus, unequally distributed among the population—accruing more readily to people with informal carers, and unequally distributed by the capacities and resources of informal carers themselves.

One of the reasons that informal carers' views about health care are sought is to understand what is working, and what is not, and to make change where it is needed. Yet we can see in this study that in assessing the care their ill relative or friend received, informal carers often took health professionals' working conditions into account. When family members or friends of ill people saw health professionals doing the best they could in difficult circumstances, they sometimes swallowed their concerns and important quality of care information was lost.

It might seem that a solution to this problem would be to develop more sophisticated ways of gathering informal carers' comments about health care. Yet this move, while welcome, would miss a central point of this study. Evaluation research generally fails to capture or examine what lay people take into account when they express satisfaction or dissatisfaction with care. In some instances, however, it is precisely that which is "taken into account"—like health professionals' working conditions—that calls for change.

GLOSSARY

Entitlement: Entitlement is commonly defined as a right to benefits, especially those specified by law. Under the *Canada Health Act*, for instance, insured residents of Canadian provinces and territories are entitled to reasonable access to insured health services, unimpeded by charges (user charges or extra-billing) or other means (age, health status, and so on). Entitlement also involves the acknowledgement, in our eyes and the eyes of others, that we deserve these benefits.

Informal care: Informal care is unpaid care provided by relatives and friends of people with a long-term need for help and support (people who might otherwise require institutional care) (Graham, 1991). Informal care "effectively elides the twin ideas of 'labour' and 'love'" (Ungerson, 1987, p. 11); it is both work and the expression of a relationship. The sense of being responsible for the cared-for person is a core feature of care giving (Twigg & Atkin, 1994).

Neo-liberalism: Neo-liberalism is a belief system that supports the dominance of economic markets and the market model. It holds that markets (rather than governments) are the best and most efficient allocators of resources (including the resource of health care) (Coburn, 2000).

Oncology: The field of medicine concerned with the diagnosis, treatment, and study of cancer.

Palliative care: Palliative care "is aimed at relief of suffering and improving the quality of life for persons who are living with or dying from advanced illness or are bereaved" (Canadian Hospice Palliative Care Association).

REFERENCES

Bisset, A. (Ed.). (2000). Disarm. *The Canadian Oxford dictionary*. Don Mills, Canada: Oxford University Press.

Canadian Hospice Palliative Care Association. *What is palliative care?* Retrieved February 12, 2004, from www.chpca.net

Charmaz, K. (1990). "Discovering" chronic illness: Using grounded theory. *Social Science and Medicine, 30*(11), 1161–1172.

Coburn, D. (2000). Income inequality, social cohesion and the health status of populations: The role of neo-liberalism. *Social Science and Medicine, 51*(1), 135–146.

Coffey, A., & Atkinson, P. (1996). Meanings and metaphors. In *Making sense of qualitative data* (pp. 83–107). Thousand Oaks, CA: Sage.

Government of Canada. (2000). *Quality end-of-life care: The right of every Canadian*. Ottawa: Subcommittee to update "Of Life and Death" of the Standing Senate Committee on Social Affairs, Science and Technology.

Graham, H. (1991). The informal sector of welfare: A crisis in caring? *Social Science and Medicine, 32*(4), 507–515.

Grbich, C. (2001). The emotions and coping strategies of caregivers of family members with a terminal cancer. *Journal of Palliative Care, 17*(1), 30–36.

Hooyman, N., & Gonyea, J. (1995). *Feminist perspectives on family care*. Thousand Oaks, CA: Sage.

National Cancer Institute of Canada. (2003). *Canadian cancer statistics 2003*. Toronto: National Cancer Institute of Canada.

Opie, A. (1992). Qualitative research, appropriation of the "other" and empowerment. *Feminist Review, 40*(Spring), 52–69.

Rhodes, P., & Shaw, S. (1999). Informal care and terminal illness. *Health and Social Care in the Community, 7*(1), 39–50.

Seale, C. (1990). Caring for people who die: The experience of family and friends. *Ageing and Society, 10*, 413–428.

Sinding, C. (2003). "Because you know there's an end to it": Caring for a relative or friend with advanced breast cancer. *Palliative and Supportive Care, 1*(2), 153–163.

Strauss, A., & Corbin, J. (1990). *Basics of qualitative research: Grounded theory procedures and techniques*. Newbury Park, CA: Sage.

Twigg, J., & Atkin, K. (1994). *Carers perceived: Policy and practice in informal care*. Buckingham: Open University Press.

Ungerson, C. (1987). *Policy is personal: Sex, gender and informal care*. London: Tavistock.

Chapter 13

Gendered Experiences of HIV and Complementary Therapy Use

Dorothy Pawluch, Roy Cain, and James Gillett

INTRODUCTION

In this chapter we discuss the experiences of women who are living with **HIV/AIDS** and who use **complementary therapies** as part of their health care strategy. Our data are drawn from a larger qualitative study of complementary therapy use among people living with HIV/AIDS. The larger study was concerned with why people turn to complementary therapies, what they classify as complementary, how they think about them, and how they make decisions about their use. While there were many themes that cut across gender lines in respondents' answers (Gillett, Pawluch, & Cain, 2001; Pawluch, Cain, & Gillett, 2000), there were aspects of the interviews with women that set them apart. Our chapter focuses on three themes that underline the **gendered** nature of complementary therapy use among those living with HIV/AIDS: (1) the role that women's care-giving responsibilities play in their selection of health care strategies, (2) the unique reproductive concerns of women, and (3) the sense of marginalization that many women feel in their dealings with Western medicine. First, however, we discuss briefly the literature that provides a context for this paper, our methods, and the findings of our larger study.

BACKGROUND

The past two decades have seen a significant rise in the popularity of complementary approaches to health in Western industrialized countries. A Canadian poll showed that one in five Canadians used some form of alternative therapy in the first six months of 1990 (Northcott, 1994). A more recent survey showed that 73% of respondents had used at least one complementary therapy in their lives, and 50% had used at least one in the previous 12 months (Ramsay, Walker, & Alexander, 1999). In the United States, a 1990 survey found that 34% of Americans used one or more "unconventional" therapies (Eisenberg et al., 1993). A follow-up survey (Eisenberg et al., 1998) found that by 1997, the proportion had increased to 39%. The growth in the use of complementary therapies in various countries of the European Community, including France, Belgium, Germany, Denmark, Finland, and the Netherlands, has been described as "massive" (Lewith & Aldridge, 1991, p. 7), and in the UK and Australia, as "exponential" (Cant & Sharma, 1996, p. 579; Saks, 1994).

There is evidence to suggest that the number of people with HIV/AIDS turning to complementary forms of health care is also significant. A recent Ontario study (Furler, Einarson, Walmsley, Millson, & Bendayan, 2003) found that 77% of 104 HIV-positive participants interviewed were current users of complementary therapies. When vitamins and minerals were included as a complementary therapy, the percentage rose to 89. In a study of people with HIV/AIDS in Toronto, 78% had used some form of complementary therapy (Canadian AIDS Society, 1995). These percentages are consistent with studies done in the United States (Barton, Davies, Schroeder, Arthur, & Gazzard,1994).

The popularity of complementary therapies among people with HIV/AIDS is rooted at least partly in the fact that, until the mid-1990s, Western medicine had little to offer in the way of effective treatments. AZT, an anti-HIV drug developed in the late 1980s, had powerful and toxic side effects, and questionable efficacy. Faced with such limited and unattractive choices, many people with HIV/AIDS sought other treatment options. In 1996, a class of drugs called protease inhibitors became available. Taken in combination with other drugs, protease inhibitors have proven effective in reducing the probability of opportunistic infections and improving the prognosis for those who are HIV-positive. Most, though certainly not all, HIV-positive people in Canada opt to take these drugs. These new combination therapies are not a panacea. They too can have serious side effects and do not work for everyone. Despite the availability of these more effective treatments, complementary therapies remain popular.

While the initial flurry of scholarly interest in complementary therapies focused on documenting their growing popularity, questions are increasingly being asked about how to understand this development. There is agreement that we need to know more about the experiences of those using complementary therapies—the meanings they attach to them, why they find them appealing, and what they hope to get from them. There is growing recognition as well that these meanings are connected in integral ways with individuals' social characteristics and circumstances. By looking specifically at the experiences of women with HIV, we hoped to glean insight into the role that gender plays in the experience and use of complementary therapies.

METHODS

The larger study from which the data for this paper were derived was conducted in 1997–1998. We sought to interview a diverse range of individuals living with HIV. We targeted not only women but individuals from a broad range of racial, cultural, and ethnic backgrounds and individuals who were injection drug users. We made contact with the women who ultimately agreed to be interviewed through a variety of means, using both general and more targeted strategies. Our general strategy involved approaching various health clinics and AIDS service organizations in South Central Ontario, including the Hamilton AIDS Network, the AIDS Committee of Toronto, the Community AIDS Treatment Information Exchange, the Toronto Person with AIDS Foundation, Black Coalition for AIDS Prevention, and Two Spirited People (an organization that provides services to the Aboriginal community). Each organization allowed us to put up posters and/or brought the study to the attention of its members or clients. The targeted strategy involved approaching an organization called Voices of Positive Women (VPW), a community-based group started in Toronto in 1991 to provide support and services to women living with HIV/AIDS. VPW allowed us to distribute information about the study to its membership and women who came into their offices. Besides interviewing those women who contacted us after seeing our posters, we relied on **snowball sampling**; that is, some of the women we interviewed put us in touch with others.

In all, 10 out of the 46 interviews we conducted were with women. Five of the women were White and described themselves as either Anglo-Saxon, French-Canadian, or Eastern European. Five of the women were women of colour, describing themselves as Aboriginal, Caribbean, African, or South Asian. The group ranged in age from 21 to 50 years, with most (six respondents) in their thirties. Though most of the women had worked prior to their diagnoses at occupations that included clerical work, social service work (outreach work or counselling), graphic design, and dance, most were not working when we interviewed them and were living on either disability insurance or social assistance. The average income was $12,000. At the time of the interviews, all of our respondents were largely asymptomatic, though most (eight) had experienced episodes of serious acute illness related to their HIV infection. Most of the respondents (seven) were mothers. Four women had children living with them. One woman had children who were grown and living on their own. Two women had children who were in the care of ex-partners or other family members. One respondent was pregnant.

Box 13.1: DID YOU KNOW?

- In Canada, as of June 2003, a total of 1,555 cases of HIV/AIDS have been reported among women 15 years of age or older.
- These women represent about 9% of all cases of HIV/AIDS reported in Canada as of June 2003.

Source: <www.hc-sc.gc.ca/pphb-dgspsp/hast-vsmt/public_e.html>

All of the interviews were conducted in the homes of respondents and were audio-taped. The interviews were semi-structured. We identified key issues we wanted to address. We used a list of these issues to guide ourselves, but for the most part we let respondents determine the course the interview took and allowed ourselves to probe into comments that seemed significant. Participants received a $25 subject fee.

In both the collection and analysis of the data, we used a **grounded theory** approach (Glaser & Strauss, 1967). After each interview we met to discuss both the substance of the interviews as well as the process. It was at these meetings that certain analytical themes began to emerge. As they did, we incorporated them into the list of issues to address in subsequent interviews. The analysis of the transcribed data allowed us to refine and develop our initial categories.

CARE-GIVING ROLES

What stood out most remarkably in the interviews was the significance that the women attached to their care-giving functions. As partners and/or mothers, they had people in their lives towards whom they felt a strong sense of responsibility, despite their health problems. It was in part this sense of responsibility that led them to seek out medical care as soon as they were diagnosed. If there were treatments that would help them to maintain their health and prolong their lives, they were eager to take advantage of them. All of the women talked about how faithfully they complied, at least initially, with their doctors' recommendations. However, debilitating side effects and a compromised ability to function eventually had them reconsidering their options. While they continued to be committed to their health, they sought out therapies that would either reduce the severity of the side effects or more usually take the place of the drugs they were taking. A paramount consideration was finding something that would allow them to function as caregivers. One woman described the day she decided to stop taking AZT:

> The AZT made me really sick. My daughter was dragging the CD player into my bedroom, and making sandwiches and cutting off the crusts and staying there cuddled up to me, trying to keep me warm. I still get choked up when I think about it, how she said to me, "It's going to be okay, Mom." I said, "You should be outside playing with your friends," and she said, "It's okay, Mommy. I'll stay with you." And, you know, trying to look after me. Trying to mother me, when she was six, seven years old. I thought at that point, I've got to get my act together. She needs me. Stop believing all these assholes, and I flushed [all my medications] down the toilet.

Another woman who had, for a time, taken protease inhibitors, recounted a similarly emotional experience:

> [While I was on the protease] I passed out. My son was home and kept asking if I was dead. I could hear him, but I couldn't answer him. He was shaking me and I could hear him. I was conscious of hearing him. But I couldn't lift myself up or answer. It was like I was in this deep sleep ... Thank God my partner was home because he took care of him. And I stopped taking the protease. I thought, this is too much, and I stopped.

The women did not all have the same expectations for the therapies they were using. Some women believed that the therapies would keep the levels of HIV in their blood in check, the infection from progressing, and symptoms at bay. In other words, they expected the complementary therapies to result in the same outcomes as the medications they had been taking, though in more benign ways.

Others, while they were hopeful that the complementary therapies would keep them alive, felt that in rejecting drug treatments they might be sacrificing their long-term health. These women conceived of the decision as a trade-off: Drugs might give them a better chance at long-term survival, but at a cost to their quality of life, particularly in relation to their children, that they were not prepared to pay. The decision to turn to complementary therapies represented a decision to prioritize quality over years of life.

> I believe in quality of life. I don't care how short it is. I just want to have a good quality of life. I want to be able to go outside and play ball with my son. I don't want him to see me lie down on the couch every day, sick, sick, sick. You know what I mean? I would rather live three years and live three nice healthy years than live six years and I'm sick all those six years. That's how I see it.

The same sentiment was expressed by this respondent:

> I just thought, why am I trying to take all these medications, trying to live longer? It's going to make me live a little bit longer, but I'm going to feel crappy taking them. I'm going to have all these side effects and everything else. So I just stopped. And the doctors always recommend me to take something like, "You should take this cocktail now." And all my friends are doing it. A friend of ours started it and then it stopped working. And now he has to try something else. I just don't want to go through that. I just want to live my life how it is. Have fun and enjoy my life. My children. Not worry about how long it's going to be. Just have a good life … I could spend a lot of time taking medications and going back and forth to the doctors and making sure my T-cells haven't dropped a little bit and panicking about it every time they go down two or twenty points. No, I won't.

Finally, there were women who talked about the benefits of complementary therapies not in terms of improved quality of life, but in terms of stress reduction. They felt that the stress of living with HIV, more than the side effects of medications, compromised their ability to function as caregivers. For these women, complementary therapies, particularly massage-based therapies and meditation, offered momentary relief from the anxieties they sometimes felt would overwhelm them. The following quote from a woman whose partner was also HIV-positive offers a glimpse into the ever-present undercurrent of despair that some respondents worked hard to keep at bay.

> I worry a lot. I worry about the kids, and I worry about dying once in a while, and I worry about John dying or who's going to die first. And all these thoughts are just in my head, and where are the kids gonna go, and you have to make sure everything's planned, and you just have to get out and stop thinking like that. I

just gotta make sure I have a plan, and then try and relax myself. That's where I
find it helps me.

The literature (Broun, 1996, p. 155) shows how important it is for women
diagnosed with HIV/AIDS to continue to function normally. They are especially
reluctant to give up their role as family caretaker and nurturer. The literature
also suggests that because of their responsibilities, women will ignore their own
health needs and are thus receiving "suboptimal" HIV care (Shappiro, Morton, &
McCaffrey, 1999; Valdiserri, Holtgrave, & West, 1999).

Our findings show that women are not ignoring their needs. They may not
be seeking out medical care, that is, traditional bio-Western care. However, they
do make decisions about how to manage their HIV. Our study also shows why
complementary therapies may be particularly appealing to them. The significance
they attached to their care-giving roles heightened their need to find strategies that
did not debilitate them. Complementary therapies appealed to them because they
felt they were deriving the benefits of the therapies without the incapacitating side
effects so often connected to conventional Western therapies.

REPRODUCTIVE CONCERNS

The majority of HIV-infected women in North America are between 25 and 44
years of age, that is, in the middle of their child-bearing years. Since there is a risk
of passing the infection on to their children, doctors typically advise HIV-positive
women not to become pregnant and, if they do, to terminate their pregnancies (Berer,
1993, p. 89). While many follow this advice, significant numbers do not. Among the
explanations for this reaction is the possibility that these women are assessing risk
differently and emphasizing the chances of non-infection for their children rather
than the chances of infection. Another possibility is that they see child-bearing as
life-affirming, a way to leave something of themselves behind (Bedimo, Bessinger,
& Kissinger, 1998).

We found a range of views on reproduction among our respondents. Some had
opted for hysterectomies or were practising birth control. Some had conceived
children after their diagnosis and against the advice of their doctors. Some were
leaving the possibility of pregnancy open as an option. One respondent was pregnant
at the time of the interview. Wherever they stood on the question, complementary
therapies figured in their decisions in one way or another.

A respondent who opted for a hysterectomy shortly after her diagnosis saw
complementary therapies as a more natural and safer substitute for the estrogen
replacement therapy that was recommended after the procedure. In part, she argued,
having discovered complementary therapies, she felt more inclined to use these
therapies for all her health needs. Beyond this, however, she was concerned that
because she was HIV-positive, the estrogen replacement therapy would adversely
affect her and perhaps speed up the progression of the infection. She had looked
for, but was unable to find, any information on the subject—a point we discuss in
our next section. In the absence of such information, she decided to take the lesser
risk.

Among those women who thought that they might want to become pregnant at some point, complementary therapies were seen as a way of doing something to deal with their HIV without jeopardizing their ability to have children. They worried about the powerful toxic effects of Western medicine. Complementary therapies were seen as more natural, more benign, and therefore more compatible with pregnancy. They did not want to fill their bodies with medications that might interfere with their ability to have children or with the possibility of eventually bearing a healthy child.

The one pregnant respondent in the study faced a dilemma in her choice of therapies. Prior to becoming pregnant she had tried, and stopped, using AZT because of its debilitating side effects. Instead, she turned to vitamins and herbs that her Jamaican grandmother suggested. Though her doctors urged her to reconsider, she continued to resist medical treatment. The pressure increased significantly, however, after she became pregnant. Told repeatedly that without medication she would be putting her child at great risk, she relented.

> I'm pregnant, so I'm taking the AZT... But as soon as I finish the baby, I'll finish with AZT ... I thought I would never go on it. But like I said to my boyfriend, when you have another life, when it's not you alone to think about, you'll do anything. Whatever your doctor tells you that is good. Because you think, it's not just me. With me, it's me. I have to take the consequences for what I do for myself. So when I decided I don't want the drugs, that was me. But now I have to think of my baby ... I'm taking everything they give me, because I don't want this baby to be positive.

Complementary therapies, however, continued to be part of her daily regimen. She felt that the vitamins and herbs were working alongside the AZT. She also credited these therapies with mitigating the worst of AZT's side effects, which were much less severe for her this time.

Box 13.2: WANT TO KNOW MORE?

Visit:

<www.thebody.com/women.shtm>

An informative website about women and HIV, featuring personal profiles, health facts, interviews, and more.

<www.aidslaw.ca/Maincontent/issues/cts/cam/toc/htm >

A site operated by the Canadian HIV/AIDS Legal Network, featuring a comprehensive report on the legal, ethical, and policy issues involved in the use of complementary therapies by those living with HIV/AIDS.

<www.hc-sc.gc.ca/english/women/facts_issues/facts_aids.htm>

A site operated by Health Canada's Women's Health Bureau, featuring current information about HIV among women in Canada.

THE EXPERIENCE OF GENDER BIAS

A third theme that emerged was the sense of betrayal that many women felt in relation to Western medicine. Respondents felt that their unique needs and responses as *women* with HIV had been neglected. Disease processes and treatment reactions in men, they pointed out, are often generalized to women without any solid basis for doing so. Men's experiences with HIV are prioritized over those of women. Little is known about how HIV affects women. They felt continually frustrated in their efforts to find information relevant to their particular health care needs as women.

Critics have been pointing to the gender bias in AIDS research for years. While pregnant women have received some attention, women more generally continue to be under-represented in research programs and clinical trials (Schneider & Stoller, 1995, p. 8). As Nechas and Foley (1994, p. 91) have put it: "Like heart disease, AIDS has been studied primarily in men, and research findings simply extrapolated to women. Just as the hearts of men and women are different, so too are many of their other organs. Virtually nothing is known about the risk factors and unique manifestations of the disease in women."

The respondents in our study show how this neglect is experienced in personal terms:

> It's not the same for women as it is for men. Our chemistry is different, but there's no information. I had myself sterilized because I didn't know about all the problems with HPV (human papilloma virus) and the effects of hormones in HIV ... Women either haven't been studied, or only slightly studied, or a small percentage of women have been studied. There's no real solid information out there about women ... For me, as a woman, there's not a lot of statistics out there. So, statistics don't really matter. The statistics that are out there are for gay males, and they don't apply to me. So I kind of have to write my own book in terms of where I'm going and what I'm doing and how to treat myself.

The idea of needing to "write their own book" was common among our respondents. Many felt that they could not afford to let others, particularly doctors, make decisions for them. They valued their doctors' opinions, but felt determined to take charge of their own health. In doing so, they were prepared to consider the full range of options open to them, including complementary therapies. If Western medicine had so little to offer to them as women, they were prepared to look elsewhere.

CONCLUSION

Those who have criticized the gender bias in research on AIDS have targeted not only the basic and medical sciences, but social sciences as well (Jenkins & Coons, 1996, p. 71). Schneider (1991, p. 148) has called for more research on the experiences of women with HIV/AIDS—"research that takes special care to deal with the particular subjectivities of these persons, to see the problem of AIDS from their point of view." In focusing on the experiences of the women in our study we hope to contribute towards a better understanding of the lives of women with HIV/AIDS.

Our analysis suggests a number of conclusions. Though there is much in women's experiences with HIV/AIDS that they share with anyone living with HIV/AIDS, there are certain concerns that set them apart. They are often mothers and partners with families to care for. They worry about whether they will be able to continue to meet their families' needs and about what will happen to their families when they are gone. In the face of a diagnosis of HIV/AIDS they have complicated decisions to make about their fertility. In exploring their options many discover that there is a dearth of basic information and feel that they are making their decisions "in the dark."

All of these factors affect how women manage their HIV and the health care decisions they make, including, for some, the decision to turn to complementary therapies. In various ways complementary therapies are seen as congruent with their ultimate goals. Some women use complementary therapies to minimize the side effects of Western therapies so that they can continue to look after their families. Some use them in place of Western therapies for this same reason. Some want nothing more from the therapies than momentary relief from their burdens—something that will make it just a little easier for them to get from day to day. Some value the therapies because they are seen as less likely to jeopardize their ability to bear healthy children. Most women see complementary therapies as a benign way to "do something" about their infection without taking a major risk and as presenting them with relatively safe options in a situation where science and Western medicine have few sure answers to offer.

In relation to the research on complementary therapy use, our research underlines the need to look beyond simple explanations for the growing popularity of complementary therapies. To attribute the dramatic growth to any single factor would be a mistake. We need instead to consider more closely the range of meanings that individuals ascribe to these therapies and how they fit them into their ways of coping with health problems. In doing so, however, we need to pay attention to these individuals' social characteristics—including gender. An understanding of why people use complementary therapies has to include not only some understanding of the meanings these therapies have for their users, but an understanding of who these users are and the social contexts in which they live.

GLOSSARY

AIDS: The most severe manifestation of infection with the Human Immunodeficiency Virus (HIV), diagnosed when a person tests positive for HIV and exhibits one or more of 27 "opportunistic infections" or cancers associated with AIDS and/or tests at 200 or fewer T-cells.

Complementary therapies: Approaches that are generally found outside the bounds of conventional, mainstream Western medicine—acupuncture, massage, naturopathy, herbal medicine, and therapeutic touch, to name just a few.

Gendered: Reflecting the experiences of one sex more than the other.

Grounded theory: A way of arriving at generalizations about social phenomena based on what one sees rather than generating propositions that are then empirically tested.

HIV: A virus that leads to gradual deterioration of the human immune system.

Snowball sampling: A technique for recruiting respondents that involves asking interviewees to suggest the names of others who might be willing to participate in a study.

REFERENCES

Barton, S., Davies, S., Schroeder, K., Arthur, G., & Gazzard, B. (1994). Complementary therapies used by people with HIV infection. *AIDS, 8*(4), 561.

Bedimo, A.L., Bessinger, R., & Kissinger, P. (1998). Reproductive choices among HIV-positive women. *Social Science and Medicine, 46*(2), 171–179.

Berer, M. (1993). *Women with HIV/AIDS: An international resource book.* London: Pandora.

Broun, S.N. (1996). Clinical and psychosocial issues of women with HIV/AIDS. In A. O'Leary & L.S. Jemmott (Eds.), *Women and AIDS: Coping and caring* (pp. 151–166). New York: Plenum Press.

Canadian AIDS Society. (1995). *The complementary therapies project: HIV treatment project report.* Ottawa, ON: Canadian AIDS Society.

Cant, S., & Sharma, U. (1996). Demarcation and transformation within homeopathic knowledge: A strategy of professionalization. *Social Science and Medicine, 42*(4), 579–588.

Eisenberg, D.M., Davis, R.B., Ettner, S.L., Appel, S., Wilkey, S., Van Rompay, M., et al. (1998). Trends in alternative medicine use in the United States, 1990–1997: Results of a follow-up national survey. *Journal of the American Medical Association, 280*, 1569–1575.

Eisenberg, D.M., Kessler, R., Foster, C., Norlock, R., Calkins, D., & Delbanco, T. (1993). Unconventional medicine in the United States. *New England Journal of Medicine, 328*, 246–252.

Furler M., Einarson, T., Walmsley, S., Millson, M., & Bendayan, R. (2003). Use of complementary and alternative medicine by HIV-infected outpatients in Ontario, Canada. *AIDS Patient Care STDS, 17*(4), 155–168.

Gillett, J., Pawluch, D., & Cain, R. (2001). Diverse perspectives on complementary therapy use among people living with HIV/AIDS. *AIDS and Public Policy Journal, 16*(1–2), 18–27.

Glaser, B., & Strauss, A. (1967). *The discovery of grounded theory.* Chicago: Aldine.

Jenkins, S.R., & Coons, H.L. (1996). Psychosocial stress and adaptation processes for women coping with HIV/AIDS. In A. O'Leary & L.S. Jemmott (Eds.), *Women and AIDS: Coping and caring* (pp. 33–86). New York: Plenum Press.

Lewith, G., & Aldridge, D. (1991). *Complementary medicine in the European Community.* Essex: C.W. Daniel.

Nechas, E., & Foley, D. (1994). *Unequal treatment: What you don't know about how women are mistreated by the medical community.* New York: Simon and Shuster.

Northcott, H.C. (1994). Alternative health care in Canada. In B.S. Bolaria & H.D. Dickinson (Eds.), *Health, illness and health care in Canada* (pp. 487–503, 2nd ed.). Toronto: Harcourt Brace and Company.

Pawluch, D., Cain, R., & Gillett, J. (2000). Lay constructions of HIV and complementary therapy use. *Social Science and Medicine, 51*, 251–264.

Ramsay, C., Walker, M., & Alexander, J. (1999). *Alternative medicine in Canada: Use and public attitudes.* Vancouver, BC: The Fraser Institute.

Saks, M. (1994). The alternatives to medicine. In J. Gabe, K. Kelleher, & G. Williams (Eds.), *Challenging medicine* (pp. 84–103). London: Routledge.

Schneider, B.E. (1991). Women, children and AIDS: Research suggestions. In R. Ulack & W.F. Skinner (Eds.), *AIDS and the social sciences: Common threads* (pp. 134–148). Lexington: University of Kentucky Press.

Schneider, B.E., & Stoller, N.E. (Eds.). (1995). *Women resisting AIDS: Feminist strategies of empowerment*. Philadelphia: Temple University Press.

Shapiro, M.F., Morton, S.C., McCaffrey, D.F., et al. (1999). Variations in the care of HIV infected adults in the United States. *JAMA, 281,* 2305–2315.

Valdiserri, R.O., Holtgrave, D.R., & West, G.R. (1999). Promoting early HIV diagnosis and entry into care. *AIDS, 13,* 2317–2330.

Chapter 14

Conflict and Abuse in Dating Relationships: Young Adult Women in University React to a Film Clip

Kristin L. Newman, Carmen Poulin,
Bette L. Brazier, and Andrea L. Cashmore

INTRODUCTION

Young heterosexual women attending university are at an age where they begin to establish themselves in long-term intimate relationships with men (Hyde, 1996). Over the last several decades, the women's movement has raised awareness about the prevalence and negative consequences of violence against women within interpersonal relationships. Due to the increased knowledge of violence and its negative consequences, it is easy to assume that young women today are better equipped to discriminate between abusive and non-abusive behaviours within intimate relationships. However, violence against women perpetrated by their intimate male partners remains prevalent among university women (Dekeseredy & MacLeod, 1997).

DeKeseredy and MacLeod (1997) argue that mass media are partially responsible for the perpetuation of violence against women. Indeed, mass media are criticized for portraying violence against women as either justifiable or erotic (e.g., Deer & Deer, 1991; Giroux, 2000; Kellner, 1998; Meyers, 1994). Research consistently demonstrates that mass media increase the perceived social acceptability of violence against women (Krafka & Linz, 1997; Linz, Donnerstein, & Penrod, 1988). Since studies show that, before graduating from high school, the typical North American adolescent will have spent more time watching television and films than studying (Belcher, 1998; Taylor, 1995), young women's ability to discriminate between abusive and non-abusive behaviours within intimate relationships may be negatively influenced by their exposure to mass media that normalize this violence.

Emotional abuse, a form of violence often targeted at young women in dating relationships (MacLeod, 1987), has been defined as "an ongoing process in which one individual systematically diminishes and destroys the inner self of another" (Loring, 1994, p. 1), with the goal of maintaining or obtaining control (Loring, 1994; O'Leary, 1999). This may be accomplished either overtly (e.g., name-calling, verbal threats) or covertly (e.g., withholding of validation, inattention to feelings). Whatever forms it takes, emotional abuse is detrimental to a person's psychological well-being (Marshall, 1999; Orava, McLeod, & Sharpe, 1996). In fact, although

Box 14.1

Research on the portrayal of women in television drama reveals that women appear less often than do men (Signorielli, 1989). When female characters do appear, they are typically younger and more attractive than male characters, and are more likely to be portrayed as a romantic partner or as a mother. In contrast, male characters are more likely to have prestigious occupations such as those of doctors or lawyers.

it is generally assumed that physical harm has greater detrimental effects than emotional harm (O'Leary, 1999), research on battered women indicates that over the long term, emotional abuse may be more damaging than physical abuse (Loring, 1994; MacLeod, 1987; Marshall, 1999; O'Leary, 1999). Furthermore, perpetrators of emotional abuse will often engage in other forms of relationship violence, such as physical and sexual assault. Therefore, emotional abuse may be a precursor to other forms of interpersonal violence (Hogben & Waterman, 2000; Neufeld, McNamara, & Ertl, 1999).

Box 14.2

Many people consider jealousy a sign of love (Gagne & Lavoie, 1993; Puente & Cohen, 2003). However, a growing body of research reveals that jealous feelings are related to emotionally abusive behaviours such as domination and control, as well as other types of relationship violence.

According to a Canadian national survey, 86.2% of university women have experienced emotional abuse within a dating relationship (DeKeseredy, Schwartz, & Tait, 1993).

The purpose of the present study was to explore how young university women reacted to a film clip depicting a woman and a man having an argument. The clip, from the film *Reality Bites* (DeVito & Samberg [producers], & Stiller [director], 1994), tells the story of friends and roommates, Lelaina and Troy. When coming home late one night, Troy sees Lelaina kissing a man in the back of his car, parked in the driveway of Lelaina and Troy's shared apartment. Troy enters the apartment and waits in the dark for Lelaina. Lelaina enters the apartment quietly so as not to wake her roommate. Troy turns on the light, startling Lelaina. He asks her how she could justify having sex with such a "yuppie" on the first date. Lelaina defends herself by saying that Troy has had sex with a lot of undesirable women on the first date. She then states that if Troy has a problem, he should be "man" enough to tell her. Troy responds by walking up to Lelaina, gently cupping her head in his hands, and telling her that he loves her. Lelaina looks touched and surprised. Troy laughs and then asks her if that is what she expected him to say. Lelaina looks hurt, tells him to "go to hell," and walks out of the room.

There was no overt physical abuse in the film clip. However, the nature of the encounter was such that it raised the possibility of an interpretation involving emotional abuse. We were curious to see how young university women perceived the encounter and what sorts of issues they considered in deciding where to draw the line between emotionally abusive and non-abusive relationships. In their reactions to the film clip, we hoped to glean insight into their more general understandings of conflict and violence in heterosexual relationships.

METHOD

The principle researcher (Kristin Newman) showed the film clip to eight women in their late teens and early twenties, enrolled in an introduction to psychology course at the University of New Brunswick. Seven of the participants were Canadians of European descent and one was a second-generation Canadian from Central America. Six of the women were in their first year of university, and two were in their second year.

Following the presentation of the film clip, Kristin Newman led a focus group discussion exploring the participants' thoughts on: the film clip in general, whether the film clip represented typical heterosexual conflicts, the probable consequences of the characters' actions, and whether the interaction was abusive. Bette Brazier remained in the background to take notes, but asked for clarification on a few occasions. Having a focus group discussion was beneficial, since, as Fontana and Frey (2000, p. 641) suggest, "the multivocality of the participants limits the control of the researcher over the research process." Therefore, the focus group discussion provided an opportunity for themes to emerge that were unanticipated by the researchers.

In the week following the focus group, Kristin Newman conducted individual interviews with each woman who had participated in the focus group discussion. This represented an opportunity to explore each participant's interpretation of the film clip outside of a group context. In these interviews, the participants were asked to reflect on the same issues that had been discussed in the focus group discussion. In this context, free of group pressure, they could also comment on whether or not they agreed with what was said during the group discussion.

The focus group discussion lasted approximately one and a half hours, while the average time for individual interviews was 30 minutes. Both group and individual interviews were audio-recorded and then transcribed. The data were analyzed thematically with the help of a qualitative software program (Nvivo, version 1.2.142). Recurrent themes were identified and analyzed for **schemata**; that is, key ideas and concepts (Bem, 1993).

RESULTS

Group versus Individual Interviews

A comparison of the group and individual interview data revealed a change in the candour with which participants spoke: Individuals avoided expressing controversial ideas in the group and hedged statements to avoid standing out. It was in the individual interviews that a wider range of thoughts and opinions emerged. For example, Jacquie was silent during the focus group discussion when other participants spoke negatively of feminists, but felt comfortable identifying herself as a feminist in the individual interview: "I made a point anytime I said anything [in the group] not to say the word 'feminist.' At one point, Sonia said, 'I don't want to say FEMINIST!' [negative connotation]. I thought, 'Okay, I know there are negative feelings towards that word and that's fine, but I am [a feminist].'"

Similarly, Liz disclosed her desire for a traditional life only in the individual interview: "I want to tell you my plans. I want to be a housewife when I grow up. I want to stay home and cook … like that would make me happy." The disclosure of personal experiences within heterosexual relationships was also more common in the individual interviews. This may be due to participants feeling uncomfortable sharing personal stories in a new group setting. Alternatively, they may have had more time to process the issues discussed in the group and then to recognize links with their own experience. Finally, they may have felt more comfortable speaking with Kristin Newman about personal topics given the previous group encounter.

Schemata

Five dominant schemata were identified: "unsophisticated girls," "unruly women," "typical men," "traditional love relationship," and "abuse as physical violence." Each will be discussed using relevant themes and quotes from the group discussion and individual interviews.

Unsophisticated Girls

A common reaction among the participants was that Lelaina was naïve, submissive, and emotional. Although participants considered these characteristics to be normative for women, they saw them as signs of weakness and showed an impatience for them. Referring to women she knew who exhibited these traits, Lisa explained: "You always see the women, like somebody will say something, and they will get that look where you know that they're going to start bawling their eyes out if you don't start saying something really nice, really quickly."

What bothered Lisa the most about women who respond in this way was that they reinforce a view of women as emotionally unstable: "It's just the social thing where women are more or less generally viewed as less, quote unquote, emotionally stable."

According to some of the participants, women frequently become emotional and give up control in relationships in order to avoid conflict with male partners. Sonia argued: "It's usually more that the woman backs down, and kind of … goes and licks her wounds and … cries and does more of that." The majority of participants felt that, instead of backing down, women should be more assertive. For example, when asked to advise Lelaina, Carrie said: "Stand up for yourself. Get into it more and don't let him push you around." At the same time, however, the participants felt that Lelaina had played a part in generating the conflict with Troy. Though she had no commitment to Troy, they assumed that she had not made this sufficiently clear to him and therefore should have considered his feelings before becoming intimate with another man. Erin demonstrates this view while thinking aloud as Lelaina: "Well, it seemed like a good idea at the time and then all of a sudden, 'Well maybe I shouldn't have done that. I should have known how that was going to feel [for Troy].'"

What emerged from the discussion, then, was a view of some women as "unsophisticated girls." They involve themselves in relationships and behave in ways that are inconsiderate, if not irresponsible, and then react emotionally when this culminates in conflict. Sonia put it this way: "I'd hate to say that women always get in over their heads, but it seems to be more often than not, what they do."

Unruly Women

The participants also considered that Lelaina's character may not have been naïve and unsophisticated, but was perhaps acting in provocative and unruly ways. Wendy speculated: "Maybe she did it just to get a reaction from him, ya know? Just to see, does he really love me? ... to see if he did get jealous." As the participants discussed Lelaina's motivations, another view of women emerged. According to some of the participants, some women are manipulative and will do anything to get what they want without considering other people's feelings. Sonia illustrated this view with examples from her personal experience: "I see so many of my friends and just so many of the girls I know that really hurt a guy, because they're being manipulative ... I don't like girls who play games with guys." From this perspective, Lelaina is seen as precipitating Troy's angry reaction. Her actions, and in particular her dating behaviour, are considered manipulative, making her culpable.

As participants talked in more general terms about the "unruly woman" schema, the discussion turned to feminists as a subcategory within this group. In other words, they suggested that among those women who treat men cavalierly and manipulatively are feminists who distrust men. When men respond in anger to this treatment, they are accused of emotional abuse. Some participants felt that accusations of emotional abuse are being made in unwarranted and illegitimate contexts by women they characterize as "feminists." Erin commented: "Some women have taken this little FEMINIST thing so far that you tell them that you don't like their shirt and it doesn't matter if you're a guy or a girl or a monkey, they're abused by that."

Typical Men

If, from the participants' perspective, women can be either naïve and unsophisticated, or unruly and manipulative, men were seen as often being proud and constantly needing to assert their masculinity. The participants believed this to be a result of a social climate that denigrates vulnerability in men. Furthermore, they believed that the repression of sensitivity leads to pent-up anger and frustration, which, when unleashed, results in violence, usually directed at women. For example, Lisa and Sonia had this exchange:

Lisa: "The men will just kind of—"
Sonia: "Repress it—"
Lisa: "*Yeah!* Until they finally snap and do something really bad."

Sonia added: "They just lash out at the first thing that comes to mind ... and it usually is a female."

The participants also focused on the limited range of emotions men are allowed to express. They saw it as socially acceptable for men to express anger, but not sadness. Lisa explains: "I suppose it's one of those old boy school rules! Men don't show emotion. It's almost like it's a social not-to-do. Men are supposed to be the top ones. Always cool, calm exterior. Yes they can get angry, but they are not allowed to cry."

Furthermore, they described men as experiencing difficulties relating on an emotional level. Wendy and Sonia expressed this thought:

Wendy: "Most men just don't know how to relate, how to show emotion and feeling."
Sonia: "I think that at one point or another, women do get fed up with men not being able to express their feeling and emotions."

The participants viewed men as victims of their insecurities and vulnerabilities. While perhaps not ready to excuse men's behaviour, when they do become angry, they were inclined to understand the impulses that might contribute to these responses. Trisha commented on the strong emotions that Troy was grappling with in the film clip: "I think it was just like the way he felt he needed to react. Not that he had a right to do it. It was just ... he was so upset about it, that's the way he felt." Similarly, Sonia has sympathy for Troy, suggesting that he became angry "probably, because he was hurt himself."

Traditional Love Relationship

The participants shared similar dating experiences and ways of thinking about relationships with men. They all identified a power differential, with men generally having more control in the relationship. Jacquie commented: "I think a lot of times when men and women interact, men take the dominant [role]. When it is the issue of someone having control in the relationship, it's typically the male."

Women were thought to have greater responsibility for the emotional work in the relationship, and were seen as needing to back down and compromise to keep the peace. Wendy explained: "I'm not sure why, but it seems to me that the woman takes [emotional] responsibility for the relationship, if things aren't going right." A related theme in the discussion was the idea that men have an inflated sense of entitlement in relationships, in contrast to women who expect less. Participants viewed these differences as salient aspects of relationships, especially in times of conflict. For example, they believed that Troy would have felt confident and secure after his confrontation with Lelaina:

Erin: "I don't think he probably felt any remorse."
Jacquie: "I think he probably felt he had every right to say everything he said to her. He probably went to bed and didn't bat an eye!"

Their views of Lelaina's reactions were different. For example, they imagined that Lelaina might have questioned her feelings of anger and behaviour during the conflict:

Lisa: "Well, maybe she kind of regrets ... kind of feels bad about her actions."
Liz: "She'd regret doing that because then Troy wouldn't have come at her like that [in an attacking way] and said all of those things [that hurt her]."

The participants agreed that these power differentials often lead to negative patterns of interaction, where women are compromising their own needs for the sake of the relationship. This pattern of interaction, they suggested, emerges gradually, and because of its subtlety, is difficult to identify. Men gradually attempt to control the thoughts and behaviours of their female partners. This can have a destructive effect on women's self-esteem. Furthermore, women typically remain blind to the patterns that are emerging and make excuses for men's controlling behaviours, before recognizing them as negative. The following quotes from the group discussion illustrate their understanding of these patterns:

Lisa: "According to her friends, Anita [friend of Lisa] was in an emotionally abusive relationship. She was completely oblivious to it, but everybody else saw it. We saw her self-esteem go from up to just boom! Right down, while she was with him for two years. We're just like, 'You gotta get out of it or at least let us knock some sense into him.'"
Wendy: "But when you're in it—you don't realize that you are in it. Because you feel that the other person loves you and you make excuses like, 'Oh well, they're having a bad day' or 'I can see where it's coming from.' And when you're in it, you don't know [how bad it really is]."
Jacquie: "Everyone else can see but you."
Sonia: "Yep, love is blind."

Abuse as Physical Violence

On the question of whether the encounter between Lelaina and Troy constitutes abuse, participants spoke in ways that suggested they associated the word *abuse* with physical violence. For example, when asked directly whether the interaction in the film clip was abusive, Wendy and Lisa pointed out that Troy was not physically violent:

Wendy: "It wasn't like he hit her. It wasn't like he screamed at her. It wasn't all that bad."
Lisa: "It's not like he whacked her up against the wall and shook some sense into [her]."

Sonia and Trisha insisted that the scene depicted in the film clip was normal and not even emotionally abusive:

> Sonia: "I think that it's just an argument that got carried away. We've all had those with our parents and with our friends."
> Trisha: "I didn't really find what he did as abuse. I thought it was hurtful, but I didn't really—myself I wouldn't really classify it as abuse."

In the absence of physical violence, the participants tended to see no abuse at all. Furthermore, their conception of abuse was associated with violence sufficiently serious to be legally actionable. When asked if she thought the scene was abusive, Sonia immediately associated the word abuse with the law: "I wouldn't go ahead and press charges."

Although participants conceded the existence of emotional abuse, they had difficulty clearly defining it. Emotional abuse was a concept that made sense to them in the abstract, but that created problems for them in terms of how it manifested itself in action. Trisha defined emotional abuse in a way that she recognized matched Troy's behaviour, but like the others, she was reluctant to label Troy's behaviour as abuse: "I think it [emotional abuse] can be used to make people feel less than they are, but that's kind of what he [Troy] did in a way." Trisha recognized the inconsistency between her characterization of Troy's behaviour as "hurtful, but not abusive" and her definition of emotional abuse, but was unable to reconcile the two. In sum, the participants felt ambivalent about where the line was between emotional abuse and a disagreement between partners.

DISCUSSION

Overall, the participants in this study exhibited reactions that indicate a tendency to criticize or condemn women for their behaviours in heterosexual relationships while either justifying or romanticizing the behaviour of men. Men were seen as capable of extreme insensitivity and aggression, but these qualities were often attributed to societal pressures that constrain and frustrate them. In some cases, they were attributed to the provocation of women. In addition, there was a tendency to romanticize the jealousy and dominating behaviours of men. Men's aggression was sometimes seen as an expression of love, a way of showing that they care. According to this schema, men are rarely accountable for their aggression; instead, external factors such as women and/or socialization processes are to blame.

Women were seen as either unsophisticated girls or unruly women. These schemata reflect popular good girl/bad girl stereotypes, which have traditionally served to control women (Bell, 1987; Lerner, 1986). These representations are oppressive because they dictate limited and contradictory options for women in terms of how to behave in relationships with men, and create circumstances where being a woman leads inescapably to negative consequences. Frye (1983, p. 2) calls this circumstance a double bind, "situations in which options are reduced to a very few and all of them expose one to penalty, censure or deprivation." Furthermore,

> **Box 14.3**
>
> Invite a group of female and male friends to watch a popular film or television drama depicting heterosexual relationships. Ask them how the women and men are portrayed. Is there gender-role stereotyping? Ask them if they see any emotional abuse occurring. Record what they say. Observe the dynamics of the discussion. For example, who is talking the most? Who is interrupting whom? Who is arguing from what position?
>
> In a discussion with a group of friends, come up with television programs or films that portray women as independent, intelligent, and assertive. Do these programs or films also portray these women in a sexual manner? If so, what impact do you think this has on the portrayal of a strong female character?

these schemata leave no cognitive room for positive representations of women in heterosexual dating relationships. This is illustrated in the participants' discussion of women's sexuality. Women are seen either as naïve, sexually inexperienced, and essentially unavailable, or as sexually promiscuous and manipulative. Whichever role they play, the roles problematize relationships in ways that are seen as provoking the ire of their male partners. A consequence of these dual and opposing representations of women is that, to maintain relationships with men, women must walk a tightrope between good girl/bad girl representations.

Evidence suggests that the acrobatics women do to maintain relationships with men serve to keep them in abusive and unfulfilling relationships (Way, 1995; Woods, 1999). For example, identification with the traditional female role is linked with negative life decisions and circumstances such as the inability to initiate condom use with a male partner (Gavey & McPhillips, 1999), and an increased acceptance of violence within dating relationships, what is termed **dating violence** (Price, Byers, & Dating Violence Research Team, 1999).

The participants in this study had difficulty clearly identifying and defining emotional abuse. This is not surprising given that even those who study emotional abuse have not arrived at a consensus as to what emotional abuse entails (DeKeseredy, 2000). What is more telling is that, while they agreed that relationships can be emotionally abusive, the majority of participants did not see abuse in the conflict between the characters in the film clip. They considered the conflict to be a normal part of relationships with men. The participants' understanding of the word *abuse* appears to be tied closely to physical violence. This makes it difficult to imagine any non-physical interaction that might have elicited an "abuse" label from them.

This study reveals that despite a feminist movement that has been challenging traditional views of male-female relationships for several decades, traditional views continue to shape young women's views of heterosexual relationships. While an increase in gender role flexibility may be present in some contexts, there are limits to the progress that has been made. Traditional **gender roles** remain important influences on young women in dating relationships with men (Bem, 1993).

The results speak to the importance of promoting a schema of heterosexual dating relationships where young women's needs and wants have a place. This alternative representation could provide the cognitive material needed for the development of more positive schemata of young women so that their behaviours are not so restricted by good girl/bad girl stereotypes. This, in turn, could offer women the possibility of behaving in ways that are more healthy and positive in their relationships with men. Given the power of the mass media to influence people's thinking, and since young adults are so often exposed to it, mass media may be an ideal forum for promoting these alternative conceptualizations of egalitarian heterosexual dating relationships.

GLOSSARY

Dating violence: Behaviour, whether emotional, sexual, or physical, intended to hurt a partner in a dating relationship (Health Canada, 1995).

Feminist: "A person who favours political, economic, and social equality of women and men, and therefore favours the legal and social changes necessary to achieve that equality" (Hyde, 1996, p. 4).

Gender roles: The personality traits and behaviour that are typically associated with either men or women (Bem, 1993; Hyde, 1996). For example, women are generally believed to be gentle, sensitive to others' feelings, and to enjoy art and literature, whereas men are generally believed to be aggressive, independent, and to enjoy math, science, and watching and participating in team sports.

Schema (plural: schemata): An idea or concept used to understand the world or a set of cognitive associations related to a particular situation (Bem, 1993). This script serves to simplify the processing of complex sensory and perceptual information and allows us to "fill in the blanks" where information may not be provided.

REFERENCES

Belcher, S. (1998). Watching TV doesn't help children watch their weight. *Bayview News* (spring). Retrieved February 12, 2002, from http://www.jhbmc.jhu.edu/OPA/baynews/sp1998/weight.html

Bell, L. (1987). *Good girls/bad girls: Sex trade workers and feminists face to face.* Toronto, ON: Women's Press.

Bem, S.L. (1993). *The lenses of gender: Transforming the debate on sexual inequality.* London: Yale University Press.

Deer, H.A., & Deer, I. (1991). Women as outsiders in the movies and television. *The aching hearth: Family violence in life and literature.* New York: Plenum Press.

DeKeseredy, W.S. (2000). Current controversies on defining nonlethal violence against women in intimate heterosexual relationships. *Violence against Women, 6,* 728–746.

DeKeseredy, W., & MacLeod, L. (1997). *Woman abuse: A sociological story.* Toronto, ON: Harcourt Brace.

DeKeseredy, W.S., Schwartz, M.D., & Tait, K. (1993). Sexual assault and stranger aggression on a Canadian university campus. *Sex Roles, 28,* 263–277.

DeVito, D., & Samberg, M. (producers), & Stiller, B. (director). (1994). *Reality Bites* [motion picture]. (Available from Universal Home Video, Inc., 70 Universal City Plaza, Universal City, CA, 91608.)

Fontana, A., & Frey, J.H. (2000). The interview: From structured questions to negotiated text. In N.K. Denzin & Y.S. Lincoln (Eds.), *Handbook of qualitative research* (pp. 645–672, 2nd ed.). London: Sage Publications, Inc.

Frye, M. (1983). *The politics of reality: Essays in feminist theory.* Freedom, CA: Crossing Press.

Gagne, M.-H., & Lavoie, F. (1993). Young people's views on the causes of violence in adolescents' romantic relationships. *Canada's Mental Health, 41,* 11–15.

Gavey, N., & McPhillips, K. (1999). Subject to romance: Heterosexual passivity as an obstacle to women initiating condom use. *Psychology of Women Quarterly, 23,* 349–367.

Giroux, H.A. (2000, October). *Private satisfactions and public disorders: Fight Club, patriarchy, and the politics of masculine violence.* Paper presented at the meeting of the Performative Sites: Intersecting Art, Technology, and the Body. Retrieved May 6, 2001, from www. gseis.ucla. edu/courses/ed253a/FightClub

Health Canada. (1995). *Dating violence: Information from the National Clearinghouse on Family Violence.* (Catalogue no. H72-22/5-1995E)

Hogben, M., & Waterman, C.K. (2000). Patterns of conflict resolution within relationships and coercive sexual behaviour of men and women. *Sex Roles, 43,* 341–357.

Hyde, J.S. (1996). *Half of the human experience: The psychology of women.* Toronto, ON: D.C. Heath and Company.

Kellner, D. (1998). Hollywood film and society. In J. Hill & P.C. Gibson (Eds.), *The Oxford guide to film studies* (pp. 354–362). New York: Oxford University Press.

Krafka, C., & Linz, D. (1997). Women's reactions to sexually aggressive mass media depictions. *Violence against Women, 3,* 149–182.

Lerner, G. (1986). *The creation of patriarchy.* New York: Oxford University Press.

Linz, D.G., Donnerstein, E., & Penrod, S. (1988). Effects of long-term exposure to violent and sexually degrading depictions of women. *Journal of Personality and Social Psychology, 55,* 758–768.

Loring, M.T. (1994). *Emotional abuse.* New York: Lexington Books.

MacLeod, L. (1987). *Battered but not beaten ... Preventing wife battering in Canada.* Ottawa, ON: Canadian Advisory Council on the Status of Women.

Marshall, L.L. (1999). Effects of men's subtle and overt psychological abuse on low-income women. *Violence and Victims, 14,* 69–88.

Meyers, M. (1994). News of battering. *Journal of Communication, 44,* 47–64.

Neufeld, J., McNamara, J.R., & Ertl, M. (1999). Incidence and prevalence of dating partner abuse and its relationship to dating practices. *Journal of Interpersonal Violence, 14,* 124–137.

O'Leary, D. (1999). Psychological abuse: A variable deserving critical attention in domestic violence. *Violence and Victims, 14,* 3–23.

Orava, T.A., McLeod, P.J., & Sharpe, D. (1996). Perceptions of control, depressive symptomatology, and self-esteem of women in transition from abusive relationships. *Journal of Family Violence, 11,* 167–186.

Price, L.E., & Byers, S.E., & the Dating Violence Research Team. (1999). The attitudes towards dating violence scales: Development and initial validation. *Journal of Family Violence, 14,* 351–375.

Puente, S., & Cohen, D. (2003). Jealousy and the meaning (or nonmeaning) of violence. *Personality and Social Psychology Bulletin, 29,* 449–460.

Signorielli, N. (1989). Television and conceptions about sex roles: Maintaining conventionality and the status quo. *Sex Roles, 21,* 341–360.

Taylor, L.E. (1995). Home brutal home. *Canada & the World Backgrounder, 60,* 24–27.

Way, N. (1995). "Can't you see the courage, the strength that I have?": Listening to urban adolescent girls speak about their relationships. *Psychology of Women Quarterly, 19,* 107–128.

Woods, S.J. (1999). Normative beliefs regarding the maintenance of intimate relationships among abused and nonabused women. *Journal of Interpersonal Violence, 14,* 479–491.

Chapter 15

Ethnographic Insights into the Hacker Subculture

Steven Kleinknecht

INTRODUCTION

What is a hacker? As Taylor (2001) points out, over the course of the last 40 years the word *hacker* has become a highly contested term. In recent years the media has solidified the notion of hacker to mean someone who gains "unauthorized access to, and subsequent use of, other people's [computer] systems" (Taylor, 2001, p. 284). However, "hacker" has not always been synonymous with **deviant behaviour**, at least not of the criminal sort. The term was first coined at the Massachusetts Institute of Technology (MIT) in the 1960s to denote the highly skilled but largely playful activity of academic computer programmers searching for the most elegant and concise programming solution to any given problem (Levy, 1984). Three generations of hackers later, and the term is almost exclusively used to depict people who engage in the illicit use of computers.

Working from the symbolic interactionist perspective (Blumer, 1969; Mead, 1934; Prus, 1996), this chapter does not take any definition of hacker for granted. Rather, using an ethnographic approach to gain "intimate familiarity" (Blumer, 1969) with the life-world of hackers, this study seeks to acquire an inside look at the hacker

---

Box 15.1: Fear of the Unknown

Taylor (2001) argues that the current deviant labelling of hackers has a great deal to do with cultural lag. He contends that the computer revolution has resulted in a period of social and technological transition. With this transition comes feelings of vulnerability and social unease surrounding the new technology, which, when combined with the information/generation gap, has ultimately led to a fear of the unknown and mysterious world of the hacker.

Source: From "The Social Construction of Hackers as Deviants," 283–292, by P.A. Taylor, 2001, in *Readings in Deviant Behaviour,* edited by A. Thio and T.C. Calhoun, 2nd ed., Toronto: Allyn and Bacon.

---

subculture. In order to gain insight into the experiences of hackers, it was necessary to determine the various methods of communication they use and discover where this group tends to congregate. As one might expect, being a fairly geographically disparate group, and given the highly technical (and sometimes illegal or covert) nature of their activities, hackers use the Internet as their predominant medium of choice through which they not only communicate with one another, but also gather as a virtual community.

Box 15.2: Definitional Shift: From Computer Virtuoso to Computer Criminal

Within popular discourse, the term *hacker* has undergone what social constructionists refer to as a definitional shift. In the late 1950s through to the mid-1970s hackers were largely defined in non-deviant terms as being technological wizards. More recently, however, the term *hacker* has acquired a deviant connotation and has become synonymous with being an electronic vandal or a computer criminal.

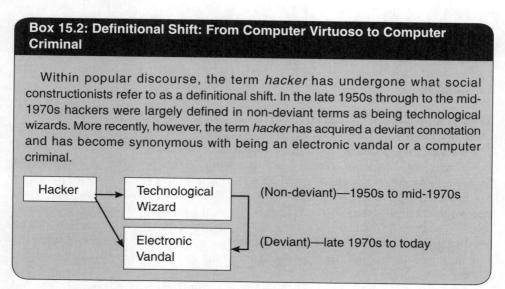

While "traditional" ethnographic ventures have grounded their inquiries into human behaviour as it occurs in the "real world," the Internet has opened up new avenues of communication and has allowed for the formation of virtual communities. Therefore, in order to fully appreciate the experiences of hackers, it is not only necessary to meet with them on a face-to-face basis, it is also essential to delve into their communities as they exist in the virtual realm.

In terms of interacting with hackers on a face-to-face basis, I met with a small group of hackers (approximately five to eight members) during their monthly meetings. I will refer to this group as *the Crew*. While not much time had been spent with this group when the paper was first written, the time I had spent with them provided for some preliminary insights into how hackers interact with one another and the types of things they discuss when they meet in person. In addition to these "offline" interactions, I had also been carrying on correspondence with members of the group over the Internet. Otherwise, this study has been informed through online conversations and interviews with other hackers, by examining postings in hacker newsgroups and bulletin boards, and by reading literature propagated by hackers via the World Wide Web.

The notion of *subculture* is the central concept upon which the hacker community will be discussed. Prus (1997) defines a subculture as "a set of interactionally linked people characterized by some sense of distinctiveness (outsider and insider definitions) within the broader community" (p. 41). He indicates that, "subcultures typically develop around some form of activity, but imply reflectivity, interaction and continuity over time" (1997, p. 41). Drawing and abstracting from Prus's (1997) writing, some of the main features characterizing a subculture can be said to include: (a) an **ideology** or perspective shared by members of the community; (b) common patterns of activity that distinguish those within the subculture from outsiders; (c) a unique language or **argot** that is particular to the subculture; (d) symbolic objects or artefacts that hold unique meaning to those within the subculture; (e) community norms or rules of behaviour; and (f) a self-image/identity that is closely linked to the subculture's ideology. The ensuing discussion will focus on examining the hacker subculture in terms of the first three characteristics (i.e., ideology, activities, and language).

THE HACKER SUBCULTURE: HACKERS, CRACKERS, WAREZ D00DZ, ET AL.

The hacker subculture is very much what Prus (1997) has termed a *transnational subculture*. Transnational subculture is used to define a group that is connected by some focal activity over a broad geographical region (Prus, 1997). Therefore, the focal activity of hackers is hacking and its related activities, and the broad geographical region they cover, via the Internet, is the world. The Crew represents what Prus (1997) has termed a *local subculture*, or simply, in the current case, a smaller group of hackers. Although operating somewhat autonomously from the transnational subculture, this smaller group very much identifies with the larger hacker community.

This section aims to describe the hacker subculture by first examining and delineating insider and outsider definitions of the term *hacker* and then discussing the aspects of the hacker ideology, common patterns of behaviour, and the subculture's argot.

Towards a Definition of *Hacker*: Hacker as a Contested Term

As I set out on this project, I began to correspond with a researcher from Israel who was in the process of writing her dissertation on the hacker subculture. She described to me the difficulty that one faces when coming up with a definition of *hacker*: "About defining hackers—this is a problem, since there isn't any consensus about the definition. There are a number of different names given to the phenomenon and there are differences between elite hackers and lamers, script kiddies, etc." (e-mail correspondence). As is illustrated by this statement and the following comments made by a hacker, a number of different people within the *information underground* have adopted the term *hacker* as a label to describe their activities: "'Hacker' can mean anything from AT&T Switch Ninja to Linux Perl Scripter. It just implies a certain grade of above-average skill and enthusiasm, and unorthodox technique ..." (e-mail correspondence).

Hacker is quite a difficult term to situate, as it is highly dependent upon group definitions. The term not only varies in meaning between the different groups of hackers, but insider and outsider definitions also tend to be divergent. By way of the formal labelling process, law enforcement, through the media, has perpetuated the notion of hackers as criminal deviants. As Huss (1998) argues, "the prototypical computer crime story presents a hacker who is a maladjusted, teenage, computer genius who is a thrill seeker that breaks into a military computer system and brings humanity to the brink of World War III" (p. 1). Although popular culture's version of the hacker is largely associated with criminal computer activities, there are a number of "true" or "old-school" hackers who represent the original essence of the term—i.e., a computer virtuoso.

Box 15.3: The "Outsider" Perspective

A hacker is defined by the RCMP as any individual who, via a modem or some other computer-related communication device, can break a computer's code or password and enter the system ... These criminals include everyone from petty computer vandals to the top echelons of organized crime. Once inside, hackers can do everything from steal data and sabotage information to simply browse around.

Source: From "Casting a Net of Security," by D. Churchill, September, 12, 2000, *The Hamilton Spectator*, p. R08.

The word *cracker* was introduced in the early 1980s by hackers to distinguish themselves from those who were using their computer expertise for illegal purposes (Raymond, 2003). In the traditional sense (i.e., as used by old-school hackers), the term *hacker* is used to describe a person who has exceptional technological knowledge of, and an extremely keen interest in, learning the ins and outs of computers and electronics (especially software programming). A cracker, however, can be defined as a person who may or may not have as much computer knowledge as a hacker, but ultimately uses his or her knowledge in an attempt to break computer security. There are a number of different types of crackers, each characterized by varying levels of computer proficiency and substantive computer interests. Some examples include script kiddies, phreaks, cyber punks, lamers, leechers, and warez d00dz.

While the hacker subculture can be divided into its smaller subsets, there does appear to be some common features of the culture as a whole that distinguish it from those outside the community. What follows is an attempt to describe the subculture by discussing it in terms of its shared characteristics, and also by making indications where the subculture diverges in terms of true hacker versus cracker characteristics.

The Hacker Spirit

A major characteristic distinguishing a particular subculture from the broader community is its ideology or group perspective (Prus, 1997). An ideology represents a unique way of understanding the world, which tends to justify what the subculture is all about. Within the hacker subculture, this ideology is commonly referred to as the "hacker spirit" or "hacker ethic."

The essence of the hacker spirit involves a passion for using creative ingenuity to develop new pieces of technology, such as computer programs and electronic devices, and solving technological problems. Another central tenet of the hacker spirit is the belief in sharing knowledge and information to help solve problems: "To behave like a hacker, you have to believe that the thinking time of other hackers is precious—so much so that it's almost a moral duty for you to share information, solve problems and then give the solutions away just so other hackers can solve new problems instead of having to perpetually re-address old ones" (Raymond, 2001).

Eric Steven Raymond has been writing about the hacker subculture for the past 20 years and is somewhat of an icon among hackers, especially old-school hackers. He points out that an essential component of the hacker attitude or spirit is a tendency to be suspicious of those people who hold power in our society (Raymond, 2001). As he indicates, the reason for this is because authority figures tend to abuse their power and ultimately stifle creative development:

> Hackers are naturally anti-authoritarian. Anyone who can give you orders can stop you from solving whatever problem you're being fascinated by—and, given the way authoritarian minds work, will generally find some appallingly stupid reason to do so. So the authoritarian attitude has to be fought wherever you find it, lest it smother you and other hackers. Authoritarians thrive on censorship and secrecy. And they distrust voluntary cooperation and information-sharing—they only like "cooperation" that they control. So to behave like a hacker, you have to develop an instinctive hostility to censorship, secrecy, and the use of force or deception to compel responsible adults. And you have to be willing to act on that belief" (Raymond, 2001).

Hackers' anti-authoritarian attitude carries itself over into a general distrust of authority as it is assumed that outsiders do not truly understand the hacker mindset. During one of my meetings with the Crew, a Bell Canada telephone technician was supposed to show up but never did. This was somewhat of a relief for members of the group as they suspected that he might be attending only in order to "sabotage" the meeting. One of the attendees jokingly commented, "If the guy did show up, he might only stay long enough to point us out to the police" (field notes). Additionally, as I have been meeting with people online to discuss their experiences with the hacker subculture, I have found that they are somewhat suspicious of my intent and true identity. They are apparently worried that I may be an undercover police officer or someone who will turn them in to the authorities. The following is an excerpt from an interview I conducted with a hacker from the United Kingdom:

> Steve: "Do you have any questions before we start?"
> Max: "Nope."
> Steve: "All right."
> Max: "Oh, wait."

Box 15.4: The Conscience of a Hacker by The Mentor

When asking hackers about their ideology, a number of them cited a widely disseminated document on the Internet going by titles such as, "The Conscience of a Hacker," "The Hacker's Manifesto," and "The Mentor's Last Words." Although some hackers see "The Hacker's Manifesto" as being somewhat cliché or overzealous, a significant number suggest that the text epitomizes the hacker spirit. Here is an excerpt:

[D]id you, in your three-piece psychology and 1950s technobrain, ever take a look behind the eyes of the hacker? Did you ever wonder what made him tick, what forces shaped him, what may have moulded him? I am a hacker, enter my world ... Mine is a world that begins with school ... I'm smarter than most of the other kids, this crap they teach us bores me ... Damn underachiever. They're all alike ...

I made a discovery today. I found a computer. ... [A] door opened to a world ... rushing through the phone line like heroin through an addict's veins, an electronic pulse is sent out, a refuge from the day-to-day incompetencies is sought ... a board is found. "This is it ... this is where I belong ..." I know everyone here ... even if I've never met them ... Damn kid. Tying up the phone line again. They're all alike ...

You bet your ass we're all alike ... We explore ... We seek after knowledge ... and you call us criminals. ... You build atomic bombs, you wage wars, you murder, cheat, and lie to us and try to make us believe it's for our own good, yet we're the criminals. Yes, I am a criminal. My crime is that of curiosity. My crime is that of judging people by what they say and think, not what they look like. My crime is that of outsmarting you, something that you will never forgive me for. I am a hacker, and this is my manifesto. You may stop this individual, but you can't stop us all ... after all, we're all alike.

Source: From "The Conscience of a Hacker," by The Mentor, 1986, *Phrack, 1*(7), Phile 3. Retrieved on December 3, 2004 from www.phrack.org/show.php?p=7&a=3

Steve: "Yup?"

Max: "Are you a law enforcement officer or in anyway affiliated with law enforcement? I have to ask that!"

Sometimes this anti-authoritarian perspective remains at the level of mere suspicion. However, it is also quite common for hackers (especially crackers) to openly express hostility towards big business (especially Microsoft), government, and law enforcement. Take for example this hacker's comment: "I'm not interested in hurting people. I would prefer to blow up billboards" (field notes).

While hackers' creative attitude and their beliefs in freedom of information and anti-authoritarianism are very much part of their ideology, the extremes to which members will actually act upon their belief varies. True hackers prefer to rebel against corporations by developing open source software (i.e., software that is free and open to the public to contribute to its development) in an attempt to produce computer programs, such as Linux, to rival Microsoft and its dominant Windows operating system. Crackers on the other hand tend to resort to criminal measures such as stealing program code from Microsoft, defacing government web pages, and spreading viruses through the popular Microsoft Outlook e-mail system (e.g., the "I LOVE YOU!" virus).

As will be shown in the following sections, subcultural activities and the hacker language are closely tied to the subculture's ideology.

Distinguishing Activities of the Hacker Subculture

Hackers tend to have their own set of activities, which are more or less distinct to the subculture. Some of these activities include: zealous computer programming (especially open source software); sharing information about subcultural events, activities, computer security, and tricks of the trade; attending hacker conventions; creating new technological gadgets; and cracking computer security.

As a result of the subculture's belief in freedom of information and developing software, the shared development of open source software has become a central activity of the hacker community. One hacker comments, "[C]heck out open source software and its philosophy, which identifies absolutely with the 'hacker spirit.' I've never met a hacker who isn't all for open source software." Raymond (2001) indicates that the development and sharing of open source software is probably the key ingredient to achieving a good reputation within the hacker community: "The first [thing you can do to gain respect within hacker culture] is to write programs that other hackers think are fun or useful, and give the program sources to the whole hacker culture to use." Hackers pride themselves on their exceptional programming skill. And as Raymond (2001) indicates, although the proper hacker attitude is important, it is no substitute for competency in programming.

A significant amount of verbal warfare on the Internet—known as *flaming*—is generated as hackers insult one another's capability. True hackers dismiss this type of behaviour as immature and unproductive. However, crackers regularly engage in *flaming*, criticizing each other's "hax0r skillzors" (hacker skills), denouncing incompetent crackers as "script kiddies" and thus not having what it takes to be an "1337 hax0r" (elite hacker). Therefore, it is not only programming competency but also the discussions and arguments that centre on the varying levels of computer aptitude that define the hacker subculture.

Hacker activity predominantly revolves around the use of the Internet. Hackers meet (in the virtual sense of the term) in online forums such as chat rooms and newsgroups to discuss their latest exploits. Via the Internet hackers disseminate various types of information, including: manuals on such things as hacking techniques, instructions on how to make certain electronic devices, security measures to protect your computer from crackers, codes that will allow a person to use software for free, and phone numbers of various people, companies, and government agencies (e.g., the FBI) for the purposes of prank calls and breaking into computer systems; general information regarding such things as upcoming conferences and hacker meetings, personal information on the individual or group that hosts the web page, and various anti-authoritarian slogans; links to other hacker websites and resources on the Internet; downloads such as open source software, "cracked" computer programs and games, and e-zines (i.e., electronic magazines); and news headlines and stories related to the latest advances in computer technology, developments in the "information underground," and legal issues surrounding hacking and cracking. While many people outside of the hacker community use the Internet to disseminate information, it is the hackers' focus on learning and sharing information about computer technology and the hacker subculture in general that tends to set them apart.

There are also a number of computer conferences and conventions held each year, which hackers make an effort to attend. Some of these conferences are arranged by hackers for hackers; others are computer security conferences organized by corporations and governments. I was told that if I want to get a good close look at the hacker subculture I should make a point of attending some of their conferences. For instance, one informant suggested, "If this project will be going on for awhile you'll definitely want to attend some hacker conventions. HOPE and DefCon are by far the largest regular conventions, with HOPE occurring every three to four years and DefCon happening annually and attracting, generally, any hacker who has the means to get there" (e-mail correspondence). He went on to tell me that the conferences are more about networking with other hackers and having fun than anything else.

While hacking is generally associated with computers, a number of hackers are also very involved in building electronic gadgets, which are often quite eccentric and sometimes have somewhat of a sci-fi or futuristic slant to them:

> Steve: "What types of hacking activities are you involved in?"
> Max: "Well my latest projects are focusing on EMI (electromagnetic interference) and their effect on computers and electronics (range/power is a big factor). I am also developing an electromagnetic gun for accelerating slugs. There are many already in existence, but I thought I would put one together myself" (interview).

Like Max, the Crew was also quite keen on creating new devices, especially by employing used parts from broken electronic equipment. The following is an excerpt from my field notes after attending one of their meetings: "They didn't really talk much about computer hacking, but more about electronic circuitry (e.g., how to make a tesla coil, a gauss gun, using transformers from old electronics to create new electronical devices) ... One thing that did seem to be clear was that they were discussing imaginative/creative uses for the items they were looking at" (field notes). Raymond (2001) indicates that this type of activity is very much in keeping with the hacker perspective as it involves the creative development and problem-solving elements that characterize the hacker spirit.

The activity that is most often associated with hackers is the breaching of computer security. As mentioned earlier, true hackers refer to this as "cracking." However, crackers use the terms "hacking" and "cracking" interchangeably. For the sake of avoiding confusion I will use "cracking." Cracking actually entails two separate forms of activity, both of which are illegal. The first involves using a modem and a cracking program or the proper passwords to break into someone else's computer. Once the computer's security is breached, the cracker is able to browse the computer's contents, collect and delete information, place a computer virus in the system, and possibly even seize control of the computer. The second form of cracking involves breaking the copyright protection on a software program or game so that it can be copied without actually purchasing the software. The software, once "cracked" is referred to as pirated software. The pirated software is then usually disseminated over the Internet through "warez" sites—i.e., Internet locations for distributing "warez," a synonym for pirated software. Most pirated software can be downloaded for free from these sites. However, some sites are "ratio sites" requiring the person who wants the pirated software to upload some of his or her own pirated software onto the site first.

While many forms of cracking can be quite destructive and costly, the majority involve reasonably harmless acts of curiosity or mischief. A couple of informants described some of their high-school pranks that they pulled on teachers and other students: "Martin talked about his and Terry's high-school computer teacher. He described that their teacher was a 'boob' and how Terry would hack into the teacher's computer while in class and take control of it ... The two laughed as they recounted their high-school hacking stories" (field notes). Another interviewee described the following high-school "hacking" antic: "We all had to do a long-ass project, and all the students saved their work to the hard drive. So right before they would show it before the class, I would open it up and fuck it all up, like delete some facts and get rid of a picture or two. It was funny. The guy next to me couldn't stop laughing 'cause it was funny. I deleted everything and put 'I didn't do it.' So this girl went up and started to read her project ... And that girl that read 'I didn't do it' started to cry. So me and the dude next to me were laughing" (interview). This type of behaviour requires very little knowledge of computers, and within the hacker subculture it is often viewed as immature by both true hackers and crackers alike (Raymond, 2003). Raymond (2003) points out that this behaviour is typical of "script kiddies"—i.e., individuals, usually young adolescents, who use others' computer programs or scripts to exploit a computer's security—and should not be considered true hacker behaviour.

Hacker Argot: Jargon and Techspeak

Hackers not only pride themselves for being technologically creative, but also take delight in employing creative linguistics. The various jargon and "techspeak" of the hacker subculture are what make up its distinctive language or argot. As I observed after one of my meetings with the Crew, if you are an outsider to the hacker subculture or are unfamiliar with science fiction and technical terminology, it is very difficult to penetrate their conversations and understand what they are discussing: "When it came to a lot of the electronic stuff, for the most part, I had really no clue what they were looking at and what they were talking about when they discussed its uses. When I asked them to explain it to me, they ended up using words that I didn't understand" (field notes). Even before meeting with the Crew I was skeptical of an outsider's ability to comprehend their discussions. During one of my meetings with them, I shared my skepticism with Jerry, one of the members of the group, but he assured me that understanding the hacker language just takes time and that it is a learning process that all newcomers go through: "I told Jerry that all I really could do was observe because a lot of the stuff was just going right over my head. He said that after a couple of months of listening you get to know the lingo—the hacker language as he referred to it" (field notes). As when entering into most unfamiliar groups, newcomers encounter new symbols and redefinitions of objects and activities. Part of the involvement process for new group members, then, will necessarily revolve around their ability to develop communicative fluency within the group.

There are some significant differences between jargon and techspeak. Techspeak is the formal technical language of hackers. It is not so much unique to hackers; rather, it is typically used by people in programming, computer science, electronics, and related fields of study and employment (Raymond, 2003). Raymond (2003) indicates that techspeak involves standard computer terms (e.g., Operating System, megabytes, Interrupt Requests, ports), which appear in textbooks, technical dictionaries, and other technology-oriented manuals.

Jargon on the other hand is the slang of the hacker language. While the various terms that make up the hacker jargon may eventually become part of techspeak (i.e., become formalized in dictionaries and manuals), they usually remain at the level of informal usage. Hacker jargon has an extensive history dating back to the early days of the culture at the MIT labs (Raymond, 2003). In fact, hacker jargon appears to be one of the most developed traditions of the subculture. Take for example the 450-plus–page *Jargon File*. The *Jargon File* is somewhat of a dictionary of the hacker language, defining not only the *established* jargon of the subculture, but also describing jargon construction procedures and the reasoning behind these techniques.

Like any language, not all the terms are frequently employed by the subculture. Some groups extensively use hacker jargon, while others mix in the odd term with techspeak and the English language. One of the most common styles of hacker jargon is the substitution of numbers for letters or groups of letters, commonly referred to as "l3375p34k" (elitespeak) within the subculture. Sometimes a number is used to represent the sound of a group of letters:

> Cory: "Then there's l8er … or m8 is mate. 8 sounds like ate I guess. L-ate-r. l-8-r"
> (interview).

Other times numbers are substituted for the letters that they resemble:

Steve: "I've been seeing a lot of writing in this style: 'AAS ICAN AT LEaST ADMIT ... lame i 4lso underst4mnd,' what's the significance of it? Why the numbers and seemingly random caps?"

Max: "Well, the numbers are meant to look like letters. It was a thing in the 1980s that people would do. If you look at my handle '14rry-ph33r' it means 'Larry-fear' (3 = E and 4 = a and l or i = 1). I dunno about the random caps, that's just lameness?!" (interview).

As Max indicates, the use of capital letters is usually seen by hackers as being "lame." Lame is used frequently in the subculture as a derogatory put-down. The term "lamer" is reserved for those people in the hacker subculture with very little hacking skill who feed off other people's work to crack computers (Raymond, 2003). Additionally, Raymond (2003) indicates that writing in capital letters is used by lamers (e.g., script kiddies, warez d00dz) to make it look like they are yelling.

Raymond (2003) argues that the frequent substitution of numbers for words (e.g., warez = wares), abbreviated wording (e.g., u r supa c00l! = You are super cool!, brb = be right back, np = no problem), and misspelled words (e.g., phreaks = phone + freak), are typically used only by the underclass of the hacker subculture (e.g., script kiddies, wannabees, warez d00dz, warez kiddies, leechers). He contends that the closest that a true hacker will get to such usage is the switching of the dollar sign for "s" in the names of companies whose services are felt to be overly expensive (e.g., Compu$erve, Micro$oft). The intentional misspelling of words, blatant grammatical errors, and other forms of wordplay may also be related to the counterculture/anti-authoritarian attitude of hackers. Such misuse expresses unconcealed disrespect for the conventions of proper English and shows contempt towards those who are seen as pushing society to conform.

As can be observed from the previous hacker quotes, a great deal of the creativity in their language can be appreciated only through observation of their written text. For example, the pronunciation of words such as "d00d," "warez," and "ph33r" are the same as their English language counterparts: dude, wares, and fear. Therefore, hearing the word "Microsoft" does not convey the same meaning as it does when observed by the reader as "Micro$oft." This seems fitting as probably the majority of hacker-to-hacker communication takes place via the Internet in textual format.

While this section has only touched on some of the unique aspects of the hacker language, it does show how the language sets the subculture apart from larger society.

CONCLUSION

Until more recently it would have been difficult to characterize hackers as existing as a transnational subculture. While much of their activity still occurs in isolation, there has been a growing amount of information sharing occurring as the Internet and its related technologies have opened up the lines of communication and made it more feasible for the once disparate group to form a virtual community. The current statement has attempted to describe this community by taking an ethnographic approach to examine the subculture's ideology, activities, and language.

A closer look at how hackers define themselves through their ideology, subcultural activities, and unique language reveals that insider perspectives are often very much at odds with media portrayals of the community. Given that the media tends to focus on the sensational, highlighting the criminal exploits of crackers (over the more mundane field of lawful hacking, as practised by elite computer programmers) is very much in keeping with their agenda. However, this biased attention on the criminal realm of hackers also tends to stigmatize other hackers who do not use their knowledge for malicious purposes. Eric Steven Raymond is an example of a hacker who has tried to help true hackers shed the criminal stereotype. On his web page he argues that the basic difference between (true) hackers and crackers is this: "Hackers build things, crackers break them" (Raymond, 2001). For the same purpose, he also advertises the slogan "Don't worry! I'm a hacker, not a cracker!"

The hacker subculture is diverse and quite complex. Without exploring how hackers actually accomplish their activities by engaging them about their perspectives and examining their behaviour, any outsider definition of the community is bound to be quite limited. Although this paper represents only a preliminary inquiry into the hacker subculture, it has paved the road for a more informed understanding of the hacker subculture as it is practised by those within the hacker community.

GLOSSARY

Argot: A specialized language used by a particular group.

Definitional shift: A change in the meaning associated with a word over a period of time.

Deviant behaviour: Unlike objectivists, who define deviant behaviour as a violation of some absolute norm, interactionists take a more relativistic or subjectivist approach. Recognizing that deviance is defined differently across cultures, contexts, and time periods, interactionists define deviant behaviour as any behaviour that is socially defined as deviant.

Ideology: The way in which a group views and makes sense out of the world that serves to justify the existence of the group and its accompanying values and beliefs.

Subculture: As defined by Prus (1997), a subculture is a set of interactionally linked people characterized by some sense of distinctiveness (outsider and insider definitions) within the broader community (p. 41).

REFERENCES

Blumer, H. (1969). *Symbolic interactionism*. Berkeley, CA: University of California Press.

Churchill, D. (2000, September 13). Casting a net of security. *The Hamilton Spectator*, p. R08.

Huss, S.T. (1998). *Hackers: Practices, motivations, and identity*. Unpublished master's thesis, University of Tennessee, Knoxville.

Levy, S. (1984). *Hackers: Heroes of the computer revolution*. New York: Bantam Doubleday Dell.

Mead, G. (1934). *Mind, self and society* (C.W. Morris, Ed.). Chicago: University of Chicago Press.

Prus, R. (1996). *Symbolic interaction and ethnographic research: Intersubjectivity and the study of human lived experience*. Albany, NY: State University of New York Press.

Prus, R. (1997). *Subcultural mosaics and intersubjective realities: An ethnographic research agenda for pragmatizing the social sciences*. Albany, NY: State University of New York Press.

Raymond, E.S. (2001). *How to become a hacker*. From www.catb.org/~esr/faqs/hacker-howto.html, retrieved December 3, 2004.

Raymond, E.S. (Ed.). (2003). *The on-line hacker jargon file, version 4.2.2*. From www.catb.org/jargon/, retrieved December 3, 2004.

Taylor, P.A. (2001). The social construction of hackers as deviants. In A. Thio & T.C. Calhoun (Eds.), *Readings in deviant behaviour* (pp. 283–292, 2nd ed.) Toronto: Allyn and Bacon.

The Mentor. (1986). The conscience of a hacker. *Phrack, 1*(7), File 3. From www.phrack.org/show.php?p=7&a=3, retrieved December 3, 2004.

PART 2B

CONSTRUCTING IDENTITIES

Chapter 16

Smoking and Self: Tobacco Use Effects on Young Women's Constructions of Self and Others

Florence June Kellner

"When the language of verbs becomes a language of nouns, either through formal certification procedures or general social recognition, the labelling process occurs, and produces additional elements of social identity." (Rosenberg, 1979, pp. 10–11)

INTRODUCTION

This chapter is about young women's relationship to tobacco use. Through an examination of this relationship, it attempts to elucidate their experience in the process of coming of age. Common observation and survey data (Bondy, Cohen, & Rehm, 1999; Poulin, 1997) indicate that the majority of young women—and women of any age—don't smoke. This study suggests, however, that tobacco use is highly salient for those who use it and for those who do not. Some attitudes towards tobacco are reminiscent of the Women's Christian Temperance Union's ideas about alcohol in their degree of emotionality around the subject (Cook, 1995; Gusfield, 1963). The study of alcohol use is established enough in academic disciplines that its examination extends to many areas of non-problem use, including analyses of ritual and customs in cross-cultural contexts, history, and literature. Almost all investigation of tobacco use takes place with a social and/or health problem orientation. While not denying the negative health effects of tobacco use, this analysis employs attitudes about cigarette smoking to uncover dimensions of **self-construction** among young women.

METHODS

Interview data were originally collected for a study of women and tobacco use (Frederick, 1995), sponsored by Health Canada and the Ontario Tobacco Research Unit. Thirty women students in an Ontario university were interviewed during March 1995. The research instrument was a semi-structured interview schedule. Topics covered concerned respondents' tobacco use or abstinence; smoking or abstinence behaviours and attitudes of the respondents' families, friends, and partners; and meanings of smoking and abstinence for **self-concepts** and views of others. The interviews lasted about an hour and a half and were tape recorded and transcribed verbatim. This analysis employs the transcriptions of the interviews.

The sample was achieved through a variety of efforts: a request for respondents on a university Internet newsgroup; visits to undergraduate courses and tutorial groups requesting volunteers; and asking respondents for referrals to other potential respondents. In other words, this was a "convenience" sample. The sampling objective was to capture equal numbers of respondents who had never smoked regularly; who had quit smoking, and who were current smokers. We assumed that a range of smoking statuses would ensure a range of attitudes and meanings concerning tobacco use.

The final sample consisted of nine current smokers, who had cigarettes daily, or almost daily; two "social" or occasional smokers, who smoked only when they had alcohol with others; six former smokers; and 13 non-smokers. To preserve space, former smokers are not discussed in this chapter. There were fairly equal numbers in the four undergraduate years, and there was one student in the Master of Arts program. The age range was from 18 to 30, with a median and modal age of 21. The backgrounds of the respondents, as indicated by parents' occupations, were mainly middle class and professional and semi-professional.

CONSTRUCTING AND PRESENTING THE SELF

The analysis concentrates upon self-construction and **self-presentation**. Constructing a self refers to attending to a self-concept and manipulating it in order to maintain and achieve a favourable image of the self. The self-concept employed here is that of Morris Rosenberg (1979, p. 7): *"the totality of the individual's thoughts and feelings having reference to himself as an object"* [emphasis in the original]. Self-presentation involves a conscious effort to achieve a desired response from others. Desired responses from others—and frequently, but not always, as we shall see, favourable responses from others—are solicited in attempts to maintain and enhance the self-concept. This is the lesson of the symbolic interaction perspective in sociology and is a crucial aspect of all social life.

While self-construction and self-presentation are analytically separate, they are intertwined when activated. Insofar as self-construction is dependent upon input from the social environment, the presentation of self represents an effort to control that input. The subjects of the study are deeply concerned with self-construction and conception. They are in life's third decade, and, in this society, among the more privileged. This time is a prelude to perceived future certainties: crucial decisions about careers, spouses, and children are pressing for some resolution. The success of many of these decisions is very largely influenced by the opinions of others regarding capability, morality, and attractiveness. The analysis shows ways in which smoking and abstinence have become overwhelmingly salient symbols that inform views of others and views of selves.

NON-SMOKERS

People who do not smoke represent a majority of the population and a plurality in this sample. While the representativeness of the sample may be questioned, it is probably the case that the tobacco attitudes of these respondents are fairly accurate reflections of the attitudes of the women students in the university society of which they are a part. There was considerable repetition and agreement between different respondents' views on tobacco, indicating the interviews elicited reliable (and probably valid) content.

Views of Smoking and Smokers

When respondents were asked why they abstained from tobacco use, the immediate response for most of them concerned health effects of smoking. Some could not smoke because of respiratory conditions. Some could not abide smoke in their environments. The expense—especially for students with limited finances—also provided a rationale to avoid tobacco.

As well as short-term discomfort and illness, such as nose, throat, and eye irritation and asthma attacks, long-term consequences were also mentioned: cancer, other lung disease, cardiovascular disease, and premature aging. The role of tobacco use in decreasing current well-being was described: tobacco use decreases energy and is antithetical to a good health regime. Moreover, respondents described other "bad habits" such as junk food consumption and drinking too much coffee and exercising too little. They did not wish to add smoking to what they thought to be an excess of bad habits. As a point of interest, alcohol was not mentioned as a problem.

Of the 13 non-smokers, three had been in treatment for eating disorders. While the three had definite clinical symptoms, such as dangerous weight loss and/or bingeing and purging, their views on out-of-control behaviour are not discontinuous with those of other respondents in this sample, nor with descriptions of women with eating disorders (Caskey, 1985). The following quotation by a respondent who was treated for an eating disorder is typical of most of the respondents in the entire smoking and non-smoking sample: "I think I've tried just what everybody else has tried. You know, dieting, excessive exercise. I think that's what everyone else has tried. Sometimes shopping. I don't think it would get out of hand. They've gotten out of hand in the past. But from now on, no, it never will."

Respondents communicated far more emotion when they talked about aesthetic/cathectic considerations of smoking. This global statement is typical of the anti-smoking attitudes among the respondents: "I think it's disgusting. I hate it! I'm the type of person that if someone's smoking and, like, its in my—it's coming onto my plate I'll, like, turn around and say something or—because I really—I really dislike it a lot."

More specifically, the smell of tobacco was the most frequently mentioned negative aspect of smoking and those who smoke. The smell of tobacco is in the houses of smokers as well as in their hair and clothing. Some said it was especially unattractive for women to smoke: "I always have this dirty picture of a woman with yellow hands and teeth."

Typical of non-smokers is the claim that they would not be in a relationship with a person who smoked cigarettes because of the smell and because they said it is revolting to be close to or to kiss a person who uses tobacco. On the other hand, some of the women admitted to a mystique about men who smoke: "[T]here's a certain aesthetic quality to the practice of smoking cigarettes that I do find appealing ... first thing I noticed physically when he (a former boyfriend) lit up this cigarette and taking out of his pocket this really flashy gold, very simple, though, it was like a brass lighter, old style, and flipping off the lid and lighting it and, like this enormous flame, you know ..."

A constant concern of non-smokers was the acquisition of attributes of smokers if a lot of time were spent in their company. The cleaning of the self after contact with smokers is reminiscent of purification rituals. Showers and the cleaning of clothing and staying out in fresh air often follow extended contact with cigarette smoke in people's houses and typically at parties or in bars.

Antipathy towards tobacco use and users was expressed with vehemence in discussions of morality issues. Responsibility to the self is lacking in smokers, because they willingly pollute their insides and introduce substances that have no business in the body. There is also the fact of environmental pollution. Views about the immorality of smoking are especially strong when it comes to women and children. There was frequent mention of smoking while pregnant and of harm to very young children. The following quotation illustrates the identification of women's smoking with unfit motherhood.

> Interviewer: "What about when you see a woman smoking—does the fact that she's smoking make you think differently about her?"
>
> Respondent: "Stupid! Stupid, stupid, stupid! Well, I mean, I do think it's stupid. It—you know, honestly, it tends to look worse to me for a woman to smoke just because of all—you know, we don't get enough money for research as it is. Why should we smoke and make it worse? If they're pregnant and smoking, I get really pissed off."
>
> Interviewer: "What if a woman is just with children and she's smoking?"
>
> Respondent: "I still get pissed off. I mean, the kids—if she's smoking and she's got little kids, it tends to give you the idea she was smoking all through her pregnancy and that's just very, very immature and irresponsible and you're wasting a whole lot of money. Just from hanging around the convenience store, you see a lot of mothers, young mothers, coming in with their kids and buying cigarettes when you know they're not making much money. If any. So, it's such a waste."

Other respondents equated smoking in the home with child abuse, and one even mentioned animal abuse if pets were forced to live with smokers. It is not only children, but everyone around the smoker who suffers, according to most of the comments on the subject.

The Self

Respondents were asked whether the fact that they don't smoke defines who they are. They indicated that non-smokers were good role models to those around them.

Not smoking identified these women to be wise and rational, for given the health effects of tobacco use, it is not smart to smoke.

The abstinent woman is also a more attractive woman. Skin is better and so are hands and teeth. Breath is fresh and the non-smoker is usually free of the smell of tobacco. "Cleanliness is next to godliness." (I don't know the original source of this quotation. When I was a child in a New Jersey school at mid-century, book covers were given out in our classes along with our texts. The covers had a picture of a girl with braids and folded hands and a halo. "Cleanliness is next to godliness," was the caption below the picture.) Smoking is dirty, and the non-smoker is "a better person; a cleaner person" and "a healthy person; not dirty inside."

Another positive attribute is that of character strength or independence. The non-smoker is immune from influences that would seduce her to smoke. She does not have to fit into the crowd or to be comfortable while socializing or drinking. She does not need to affect a "cool" image; she is not a slave; she is not weak. Character strength is associated with social responsibility, as this quotation illustrates:

> It [not smoking] is part of—it's part of a number of decisions that I've made in an effort to be conscious of my own personal health and the health of my environment. I'd say the environment is more important. I'm going to die anyway, whether I smoke or not. But the environment—and you know, it's not just even in terms of this—the thrown-out cigarette butts, the, you know, the lighter fluid, disposable lighter industry that's adding to our—our garbage disposal problem that's generated because of the need to smoke. And it's not just a matter of the pollutants that are put into our air by the cigarettes themselves, by the manufacturing process that the cigarettes require. It's also a matter of all that land that is being used to grow tobacco that we smoke and put into the air. If we could use that land to grow grain and to feed a lot more people.

It is the conflation of rationality with aesthetic views and with notions of right and wrong that produce a powerful anti-smoking discourse.

Tobacco Abstinence and Social Relations

Remarks during the interviews made it clear that smoking and abstinence issues surfaced often in the day-to-day social lives of these young women. Whether or not a woman was tolerant of smoking in her presence, the subject of tobacco use in family, friendship, and love-relationship contexts are ongoing negotiations. Observations of some of the respondents who found themselves to be in a minority in some milieus indicated that abstinence had some cachet.

> I find that when I was dating the smoker ... and hanging out with all his group who were all smokers ... I was usually the only non-smoker and the only non-drinker in the room. And so, I was, like, you know, on a pedestal ... And I noticed that when people who would smoke would light up around me and offer to me ... and I'd say "no," immediately comes this flurry of justifications on their part

... "I don't smoke very much," or well, "I quit for a long time and I just started," or "I'm going to quit soon."

The comment also indicates the cultural status of the situation of tobacco use. Even in situations where smokers are in a majority, the accounts—explanations, excuses, justifications—come from those who smoke. Lyman and Scott (1970) wrote that accounts are identity negotiations: that those who offer accounts are deferring to those to whom the account is offered. The purpose of the account is to attain or maintain a positive view of the self from the other. Given the cultural position of smokers, abstinent people may choose to express tolerance, benevolence, aggression, or claim victimization. Having the choice to accept an account and confer approval is having considerable power in social circumstances.

Friendship and family situations were reported to be the most frequent areas for negotiation. All of the non-smokers could maintain smoke-free territory, for the most part. Their living spaces—either the house/apartment or their room in a house were places where people were not allowed to smoke. Nevertheless, there remained considerable strain in relationships between the abstinent women and others who were close to them and who smoked. When there was smoking in the homes of parents or step-parents, visiting was often difficult and unpleasant. When boyfriends smoked, the issue became a consistent source of arguments.

SMOKERS

The 11 young women who smoked cigarettes represented a range of commitment to the habit—from those who had no intention to stop smoking in the near future to those who were actively attempting to quit or cut down at the time of the interview. None of the respondents intended to smoke the rest of their lives. All intended to stop before they had children and to stay abstinent with children in the household. All those who smoked had done so for over a year. Most had started smoking during high school, and a few had started during the first year of university.

Similar to the abstinent women, smoking was a bigger issue than they would have wanted it to be. Unlike the non-smokers, and to no surprise, they reported positive aspects of smoking and positive attributes of smokers. Theirs was an uncomfortable situation, for they also shared much of this culture's anti-smoking ideas, which produced considerable self consciousness, guilt, and discomfort.

Smoking and Smokers

When asked to comment on the positive aspects of smoking, respondents were likely to mention immediate internal effects. Smoking also involves some satisfying activities such as handling the package, the matches, lighting, and the act of inhaling and exhaling. The ritual, combined with pleasurable physical sensations, were rewarding aspects of the smoking process.

While smoking for all of the respondents began as social acts, many of the rewards were solitary and individual in nature. The young women were students, and smoking was associated with contemplation, with creativity, and with productivity.

Box 16.1: Girls Match Boys for Smoking

United Nations—In a disturbing downside to the goal of sexual equality, a new Canadian-backed study finds that almost as many young teenage girls in the Americas and Europe now smoke cigarettes as boys that age. But far fewer girls than boys smoke in areas where gender equality is less pronounced, according to the survey, which questioned more than one million teenagers aged 13 to 15.

[The study] concludes girls are just as likely to adopt bad habits as boys when they are given equal freedom to choose ... Previous estimates of adolescent smoking were based on adult trends which show only one woman smoking for every four men, globally ...

The survey found in Europe, 33.9 percent of boys smoke regularly, compared with 29 percent of girls. In the United States, the figures are 17.7 percent for boys and 17.8 percent for girls. In Canada, Statistics Canada says 23 percent of boys aged 15–19 smoke, compared with 21 percent of girls. Here, where advertising is heavily controlled, observers say the trigger is the girls' desire to be "one of the boys."

Source: From "Girls Match Boys for Smoking: Gender Equality Gives Them That Freedom," by S. Edwards, August 8, 2003, *The Vancouver Sun*, p. A12.

Respondents reported increases in smoking while writing essays and during examination periods. Smoking was also employed to alleviate stress, and for that, it was found to be invaluable. "I don't really—I don't really deal with stress, really. I just sleep or smoke ... usually the only thing I'm really, really, really, really [sic] stressed out about is school. So, I mean, I'll smoke double the amount that I do when I'm writing an essay or when I'm studying—for sure."

Negative individual effects were health effects. Accounts of health effects were presented with considerable embarrassment and with self-deprecation relevant to the irrationality of pursuing the habit. Smoking was seen to be associated holistically with a lifestyle that is not healthy. Conversely, quitting smoking would involve changes in eating and an increase in exercise.

Smokers were considered to have some positive personality characteristics: they are more tolerant and easygoing and less "anal." However, imputed negative attributes of smoking and smokers were more numerous than the positive ones, and negative aspects of smoking were far more elaborated on than were the good things about smoking. By far, the smell of tobacco smoke in rooms and on persons was the most frequently mentioned negative aspect of smoking. The smell was experienced as so unpleasant that, even though respondents smoked, they dedicated considerable effort to avoiding the odour. "Oh, smell—the smell bothers me. That's the worst part ... In my house, the windows are open, fans going—don't smoke in the bedroom where your clothes are so at least you have clean clothes to put on."

Other descriptions involved wedging wet towels in the space between the bottom of a door and the floor in order not to let the smell enter the room; leaving clothing that has been worn throughout a smoky evening outside the bedroom so that it will not contaminate that space; and wrapping hair in a towel while smoking to contain its smell.

As well as regarding the smell of tobacco as unpleasant in itself, it threatens to identify a person as a smoker. Avoiding the stigma—or negative sanctions, in cases of parents or non-smoking partners—was a constant concern. If parents smoked, it was easier to hide one's own smoking, as the smell of tobacco is not usually apparent to someone who smokes regularly. If they did not smoke, it was likely they would detect their daughter's tobacco use if she did not take care to hide it. "Well, I never smoke around the house. If they [parents] are not home, I'll go outside and smoke. My sister smokes in the bathroom, and I think she's crazy. In that way, like, before I come home, I always wash my hands and my neck and my face so I don't smell, and I put perfume on ..."

Respondents observed that a negative characteristic of some smokers—although never of the speaker—is a lack of consideration for non-smokers: smoking often takes place in situations where it clearly bothers others. Also, smokers are seen to suffer general disdain and are made to feel self-conscious about their habit. Often, respondents who smoked did not want to be identified with others who smoked. "[E]ven when you have to leave the building to smoke, and people walk by and see you smoking and it's minus 30 ... you think: What an idiot! Why are they standing outside freezing to have a cigarette? You know what I mean? And that's probably the most discriminatory thing, I think. And you can feel it. I mean, like, I felt stupid going between classes outside in the cold to have a cigarette."

For the most part, smokers both knew and accepted the imputation of negative attributes. This acceptance suggests the dominance of an anti-smoking stance in the culture. Respondents also indicated that smoking was more shameful for women than for men. By and large, smoking tended to look worse for women, and they thought that non-smoking men were particularly repelled by smoking women.

Smoking and Self

For those who smoked, the task of self-presentation and the urge for a positive self-appraisal had some understandable dilemmas. They were all too aware of the persuasiveness of the negative view of smoking, and, for the most part, they agreed with this view. The deviance literature—especially that based upon symbolic interaction—emphasizes the idea that the deviant and the conformist are members of the same culture and share the same ideas about truth, beauty, and morality (e.g., Becker, 1963; Clinard & Meier 1995; Goffman, 1963; Rubington & Weinberg 1987; Stebbins 1988). Therefore, explaining smoking to one's self, as well as to others (in this case, the interviewer), involves an exercise in aligning personal histories and present circumstances in order to set forth a "presenting self" that is at least coherent, if not also attractive and interesting (Rosenberg 1979, pp. 45–51).

Almost all of the respondents intended to stop smoking sometime, if not very soon. Current smoking was explained and justified with reference to the respondents' deliberate efforts at self-construction. To most of those who smoked, regular tobacco use began as statements about independence, rebellion, and "growing up." Initially, smoking worked to counter authority, but later, the statements made about tobacco use became entangled with more sophisticated, complex aspects of self-construction and self-presentation. "In a weird kind of way and for me, smoking was like an anti-establishment kind of stance. The girlfriend I started smoking with was a rebel, and she introduced me to a whole world I would have never been exposed to." For this respondent, as was the case for some of the others, smoking was associated with other high-risk activities that took place in high school: experimentation with illicit drugs and having sexual relations.

Respondents reacted against parents, the school, and the church regarding conformity to various feminine ideals that the respondents found to be unacceptable.

> [B]y being dependent on something like the cigarette ... you may be—or you may think you would be less dependent on something else. And as a woman and as somebody that's always rebelled against putting me into a certain place because I am a woman, I've always been very, very scared of being dependent upon people, and my big thing with my father was not to be dependent upon him. And as soon as I could, to break away from that. And he's a very dominant person. Very overbearing in many ways. And maybe my smoking was a stance against that. Of my individuality. Of my right to do that if I wanted to.

Continuing to be introspective, this respondent mentioned that guilt seemed to be an aspect of her personality development and her view of herself; that smoking "keeps me grounded; keeps me marginal."

The idea of making one's own statement through smoking was also expressed in terms of taking control of situations. This is especially the case for women, for whom situation control was thought to be more difficult than it is for men. Sometimes, if women can manage to offend others through smoking, it enhances the sense of control—of being able to behave in such a such a way as to have an effect on a situation.

Smoking was also mentioned to be useful in control over eating. In this case, eating was part of self-presentation. "I don't want to be, like, mowed down on this huge meal when I'm going out with this guy. When he first meets me, I want to, you know, do the girl thing: eat nothing and first smoke, you know. Or I can control myself—have a coffee and a cigarette instead of dessert afterward ..."

There was concern that smoking made more than one statement to the world, and, furthermore, that the smoker was not in complete control of the kind of statement she was making. "[T]here's totally two different images. There's that powerful woman image and then there's that idiot. That idiot-girl-smoking-what's-she-doing? image. And I think I kind of change them around, depending on what moment I'm in."

Because smoking communicated not only power and control, but also stupidity and weakness, most respondents would refrain from smoking in front of some authority figures, such as their university professors. As well, they would not reveal their smoking habit to people who might have some influence upon their careers.

And last year, I volunteered in a school, an elementary school ... I don't even know who the smokers are in that school, right? So I—I would go the whole day without smoking because I didn't want them to think of—this little loser is in university, comes here, smokes, and she's so dumb. And I think that's the image I'm most worried about.

When I was doing that apprenticeship and I was going around with a reporter and a cameraman ... and I did not have a cigarette, because I didn't know if they were going: "Oh, my god; she's a smoker!" So I—like I went to grab some lunch in a diner, and I had, like, two cigarettes to tide me through the day. I usually don't smoke around people I don't know.

Smoking may enhance feelings of power and control in some situations. The interviews here suggest that, as far as ego is concerned, such communications have the desired consequences in situations where people are well known. Thus, parents, peers, and partners are appropriate recipients of smoking statements. In situations where the opinion of others may matter, but these people are not well known, the safest impression-management strategy is not to smoke.

Smoking, as is true of eating and other sumptuary behaviours, occupies an unstable position in its contributions to the presentation of self. While smoking might express power and control, it threatens to indicate the opposite. Respondents remarked about being out of control—or worse: *appearing* to be out of control. It is degrading to display a dependency upon tobacco. Just the act of smoking may suggest dependency, but smoking in situations that may be inappropriate, or in which smokers are in a minority, may communicate dependency with certainty. Dependence upon tobacco for most (9 of 11) of the respondents who smoked was an attribute they admitted to, did not wish to display, and worked hard to conceal.

CONCLUSION

Young, educated women in prosperous North America would seem to have little to worry about. This analysis of university students suggests that self-construction and self-presentation are of considerable concern. Most are in the third decade of life: a time when people in this stratum in this country are least subject to familial control. After childhood and before career and family is a time of maximum freedom and probably maximum temptation.

There is the time/space to become involved with active self-construction: expectations of the future may dominate behaviour in the present. There are cultural imperatives to prepare for success in the future. The primary role is the student role, and success in studies increases chances for economic and social well-being. Outside of this role, there are additional, constant pressures to measure up in other ways: to look good; to be and to appear physically healthy; to stay "in control" and present the self as a person "in control." The importance of these sorts of self-presentation demands should not be overlooked, for not only are they pervasive, they are also pernicious. Aside from considerable psychic costs involved in attempts and (perceived or "real") failures to control the self, evidence of control or lack of it operates in ways that produce painful social divisions. Findings from this study reveal the antipathy that smoking and non-smoking issues generate within families and among friends.

It is clear that smoking is not "just" smoking. To the militant non-smoker, cigarette use indicates a spoiled identity, in Goffman's sense of the term (1963). Smoking generates suspicion of other questionable qualities: irresponsibility, sloppiness, immorality. By contrast, the non-smoker may have opposite, "good" qualities. The findings illustrate the importance of invidious comparisons in the construction of self, as well as in the manufacture of a respectable self (Adams, 1997; Erikson, 1966). This is not to say that non-smokers were in any way able to relax. As was the case for the entire sample, with a very few exceptions, control of eating and fear of weight gain were issues that seemed to be more important than smoking. In the construction of self, the game is zero-sum: ego profits when there is something wrong with alter. Whatever else may be wrong with the non-smoker, at least she does not smoke.

Further investigation and analysis of smoking and non-smoking as social phenomena should consider smoking and non-smoking in the context of the **health movement**. Examination of what smoking and non-smoking mean in the present climate entails a consideration of the effects of the restrictive aspects of the health movement. The health movement entails the medicalization of more and more areas of life. A consequence of the movement is that some of us are "sick" mentally, physically, spiritually, and socially, and even more of us are "at risk" for becoming sick (Goldstein, 1999). Cigarette smoking, along with other at-risk practices, indicates that there is considerable social cost involved in deliberately assuming an "at-risk role."

There is an anomic aspect to the health movement because it sets forth practices, goals, and standards that are impossible to realize. Reactions to anomie vary, as sociologists know very well. Most of us, like the women in this study, attempt to conform to ideal standards of health (and therefore beauty and godliness), all the while suspecting/expecting certain failure. But not only are we punishing ourselves for our misdeeds, as the smokers do, we punish others for their failures as well. In social and physical spaces, such as in universities, that may provide some shelter from the tyranny of economic and racial differences that separate and stratify people—in areas where we believe in and even practise gender equality—we can still embrace the tyranny of the health movement, whose demands can never be satisfied, and whose capacity for marginalizing seems to be infinite.

GLOSSARY

Health movement: A set of ideas and corresponding activities about physical, mental, and sometimes spiritual well-being and risks to that well-being.

Self/Self-concept: All of an individual's thoughts and feelings having reference to that individual as an object. This is a dynamic phenomenon, as these thoughts and feelings are subject to change as a result of (primarily) ongoing social interaction.

Self-construction: Manipulation of the self-concept in order to maintain a favourable self-image. For example, non-smokers may focus upon the fact that they don't use tobacco and feel good about themselves for that reason.

Self-presentation: A set of activities designed to manipulate others' perceptions of the actor.

REFERENCES

Adams, M. Louise. (1997). *The trouble with normal: Postwar youth and the making of heterosexuality.* Toronto: University of Toronto Press.

Becker, H.S. (1963). *Outsiders.* New York: Free Press.

Bondy, S., Cohen, J., & Jurgen, R. (1999). Past trends in tobacco use and some thought on future trends. In R. Ferrence, J. Slade, R. Room, & M. Pope (Eds.), *Nicotine and public health.* Washington: American Public Health Association, Inc.

Caskey, N. (1985). Interpreting anorexia nervosa. In S.R. Suleiman (Ed.), *The female body in Western culture: Contemporary perspectives* (pp. 175–189). Cambridge, MA: Harvard University Press.

Clinard, M.B., & Meier, R.F. (1995). *Sociology of deviant behavior* (9th ed.). Fort Worth, TX: Harcourt Brace College Publishers.

Cook, S.A. (1995). *Through sunshine and shadow: The Women's Christian Temperance Union, evangelicalism, and reform in Ontario, 1874–1930.* Montreal and Kingston: McGill-Queen's University Press.

Erikson, K.T. (1966). *Wayward puritans: A study in the sociology of deviance.* New York: John Wiley & Sons, Inc.

Frederick, J. (1995). *Cigarette smoking and young women's presentation of self.* Unpublished document. Ottawa: Sociology and Anthropology, Carleton University.

Goffman, E. (1963). *Stigma: Notes on the management of spoiled identity.* Englewood Cliffs, NJ: Prentice-Hall, Inc.

Goldstein, M.S. (1999). The origins of the health movement. In K. Charmaz & D. A. Paternitim (Eds.), *Health, illness, and healing: Society, social context, and self* (pp. 31–41). Los Angeles: Roxbury.

Gusfield, J. (1963). *Symbolic crusade: Status politics and the American temperance movement.* Urbana: University of Illinois Press.

Lyman, S.M., & Scott, M.B. (1970). Accounts. In S.M. Lyman & M.B. Scott (Eds.), *A sociology of the absurd* (pp. 111–143). New York: Appleton-Century-Crofts.

Poulin, C. (1997). Tobacco. In P. MacNeil & I. Webster (Eds.), *Canada's alcohol and other drugs survey 1994: A discussion of the findings* (pp. 43–51). Ottawa: Health Canada.

Rosenberg, M. (1979). *Conceiving the self.* New York: Basic Books, Inc.

Rubington, E., & Weinberg, M.S. (1987). *Deviance: The interactionist perspective* (5th ed.). New York: Macmillan.

Stebbins, R.A. (1988). *Deviance: Tolerable differences.* Toronto: McGraw-Hill Ryerson.

Chapter 17

Perceptions of Motherhood through the Lens of Adoption

Karen March

INTRODUCTION

In Western society, the **social institution** of motherhood presents an ideal image of mothers as self-sacrificing madonnas who deny self unconditionally for the good of their children. Like all stereotypes, the motherhood ideal is an exaggerated one offering little opportunity for flexibility, modification, or deviation from the norm. Given the individuality of women and the distinctiveness of their particular life circumstances, most mothers fail to meet this ideal.

The normative values and customary rules supporting the motherhood ideal are communicated through family gender roles and peer group interaction. Specifically, female children internalize it during the process of female gender socialization as they interact with, and relate to, their own mothers (Chodorow, 1978). Young women of child-bearing age integrate it further into their identity structure when they encounter a larger social world with its messages about their importance for reproducing the next generation (McMahon, 1995; Solinger, 2001). Women may gain a sense of value and moral worth as mothers because their society instills motherhood with these qualities, but their personal assessment of self as mothers emerges through the process of social interaction with others whom they view as either validating or discounting their motherhood claims.

Females are affected by the motherhood ideal whether or not they give birth. The "culture of women" is centralized around motherhood and "the anticipation of the **role** of mothering, more than anything else, seems to distinguish girls from boys" (Fox, 1997, p. 144). Adult women gain status and social position through motherhood. They also gain a sense of personal failure from not achieving motherhood, or for not meeting the stereotypical standards inherent in the motherhood ideal (Miall, 1987). The influence of both significant and generalized others persists throughout women's lives to maintain the standards of ideal motherhood set before them.

In this chapter, I examine how one particular population of women perceived others' evaluation of their identity as mothers and how that perception affected their sense of self as having achieved the motherhood ideal. Over the past 18 years of conducting research on **adoption** (March, 1995, 1997, 2000), I have met numerous

> **Box 17.1: Looking-Glass Self**
>
> Central to the theoretical understanding of how women experience motherhood is Cooley's concept of "looking-glass self." According to Cooley (1967, p. 217), "a self of this sort seems to have three principle elements: the imagination of our appearance to the other person, the imagination of his judgment of that appearance, and some sort of self-feelings, such as pride or mortification. The thing that moves us to pride or shame is not the mere mechanical reflection of ourselves, but an imputed sentiment, the imagined effect of this reflection upon another's mind."

adoptive mothers, birth mothers, and female adoptees who reproached themselves for not being "good enough" mothers. These women had taken the motherhood ideal, measured themselves against that ideal, and found themselves to be lacking. In face of this sense of personal failure, they came to define secrecy in adoption as a structural impediment affecting their ability to mother. This definition of the situation led them to view adoption reunion as a way of gaining access to more socially acceptable mothering characteristics. Their description of this self-reflection process demonstrates how both social location and personal interaction may affect a woman's ability to establish and maintain a positive sense of self in a society where the social institution of motherhood is severely delineated and the motherhood ideal is paramount.

METHODOLOGY

The data for this chapter emerged mainly from a larger study conducted on adoptee-birth mother contact (March, 1995). As part of that study, I engaged in 15 months of participant-observation with two self-help search groups in Ontario, Canada. I also conducted in-depth interviews with 60 reunited adoptees. Recently, I renewed my attendance at support group meetings and interviewed 36 birth mothers about their adoption and contact experiences.

Although adoptions are more open today than in the past, all of my research informants experienced closed adoptions. Under a closed adoption system, birth

> **Box 17.2: Adoption Council of Canada**
>
> Based in Ottawa, Ontario, the Adoption Council of Canada (ACC) is the umbrella organization for adoption in this country. The ACC promotes public awareness of adoption, the recruitment, matching, and placement of children with families, and an open record adoption system. ACC lists self-help search group contact addresses as well as references to research studies on search and contact results. Information on the ACC, its services, adoption research, and adoption in Canada can be gained by telephoning 11-888-542-ADOPT (1-888-542-3678) or by consulting their website at <www.adoption.ca>.

and adoption records are sealed and kept in care of the courts. Adopted children are denied contact with their biological families, adoptive parents receive limited information on their child's birth family history, and birth parents relinquish all rights to the child. The lack of open communication among **adoption triad** members has created a social phenomenon by which one triad member (usually the adoptee) searches for and establishes contact with the other (usually the birth mother). This social phenomenon is called adoption reunion (March, 1997).

My research participants represent all age groups ranging from 18 to 85. The majority is Anglo-Saxon, but this racial distribution is typical of members of the adoption triad in both Canada and the United States (Pacheco & Eme, 1993; Sachdev, 1992). I cannot establish the participants' social class status directly, but their attire, speech, and discussion of current life circumstances indicates most are middle class. For example, many adoptees and birth mothers reported professional occupations and post-secondary educational achievements, as did adoptive parents.

This research study is based on a grounded theory approach. Researchers who take this approach employ a constant comparative technique "whereby the analyst jointly collects, codes, and analyses his data and decides what data to collect next and where to find them in order to develop his theory as it emerges" (Glaser & Strauss, 1967, p. 45). Constant comparison requires examining many population groups and social situations looking for similarities and dissimilarities of data that may lead to new theoretical categorizations or the further development of theoretical properties. Often, researchers return to previously collected data or seek out new forms of data when new theoretical themes emerge or old theoretical themes are drawn into question.

Participant-observation and in-depth interviews support a grounded theory approach because the researcher becomes a member of the group and slowly develops a sympathetic understanding of the group's frame of reference. To do so requires an open attitude of acceptance towards group rules and group members' behaviour. It also requires a flexible disposition whereby any social situation or personal conversation becomes a moment for data collection or theoretical insight. In consequence, I have met numerous adoptees, birth parents, and adoptive parents in many different social settings under a variety of circumstances. A noticeable number have told me information not given to other group members and discussed topics of interest not related directly to search and contact. It was while I was examining such accounts that I discovered a pattern of relationship between a woman's position in the adoption triad and her perception of self as a mother. That relationship forms the basis for the data analysis appearing in the sections below.

To give voice and clarity to the motherhood issues connected with each woman's adoption triad position (i.e., as an adoptee, a birth mother, or an adoptive mother), the data are presented in three sections: (1) the overrepresentation of female searchers, (2) placement reconciliation, and (3) raising non-biological children. For reasons of confidentiality, I use pseudonyms and have removed any potentially identifying material in the data presentation.

DATA ANALYSIS

The Overrepresentation of Female Searchers

The adoption search literature reveals a predominance of female adoptees as searchers with approximately three times as many women seeking birth family contact as men (March, 1995). Explanations of this overrepresentation focus on the central role women play in conception, pregnancy, and childbirth. Motherhood raises women's consciousness of the significance of biological bonds, genealogical background, and genetic inheritance for the development of self. Unlike their male counterparts, participation in these life-change events is believed to make female adoptees view access to biological background information as more important than the risk involved in contacting unknown biological relatives (Pacheco & Eme, 1993; Sachdev, 1992).

Most of the female adoptees I met began their search stories with discussions of how pregnancy and childbirth affected their desire for birth family contact. Significantly, the majority of these accounts included descriptions of social circumstances in which others had used the women's adoptive status to discredit their motherhood. For example, Anne reported, "I have a son who went deaf when he was seven. Now, my mother-in-law said it wasn't from her side of the family so it must be my fault. I accepted it. It must come from me because I can't prove it doesn't." Linda noted, "One of my children has long fingers and my husband's family would say, 'Oh, he has long fingers just like Auntie.' I would think, 'I have long fingers too. Give me some credit.' But, it was as if I had nothing to offer because I was adopted." Similarly, Susan said, "My youngest has a speech impediment. He had to go to Sick Kids and get all of these tests. They ask for your background history and obviously I don't have any. So, they wrote across his sheet in big red letters, 'Mother Adopted.' It really bothered me. I felt like my kid was being labelled because of me."

Pregnancy and childbirth may embody the initial stages in the transformation of woman to mother, but motherhood makes women accountable for their children's outcome, committing them to a lifelong role as primary caregivers and nurturers of the future generation (Bergum, 1997; McMahon, 1995). For these women, search stemmed from a process of self-reflection involving their idealized image of what a good mother should be. Thus, rather than being initiated by a specific life crisis event, such as pregnancy or childbirth, the majority reported making their search decision over a period of time as one discreditable mothering event built upon the next. To quote Diane:

> It got so I would avoid things ... birthday parties and baby showers. Sometimes even weddings. Family things like that. People start talking about their children and their relatives. Everyone around you can relate their children and themselves to other members of their family. They say, "He acts like Uncle Joe," things like that. I can't do that with myself or my children. Our heritage was taken away from us for good reasons. But, when you take that away from a person, you are taking

away a lot that you really don't know about. Events like that reminded me. I tried not to go. Finally, I decided to find out. Not, just for me, I had lived with this all of my life, but for my children and their future.

Quotes such as the ones presented above indicate an association between secrecy in adoption and satisfactory performance of the motherhood role. These women reported a pattern of social interaction in which their lack of biological background information hampered their ability to establish a positive image of self as mothers. Although they saw this information lack as the product of a legal barrier inherent in the social institution of adoption, they had internalized others' response to this missing information as a personal flaw affecting their children's outcome and, hence, their ability to mother effectively. Birth family contact offered them a way of resolving that flaw.

Reconciling Placement

Until recently, a single pregnant woman was viewed as "getting herself into trouble" and social service providers directed their efforts towards helping her "overcome her mistake" (Solinger, 2001, p. 70). In particular, young, pregnant White women were sent to maternity homes where they delivered their babies in secret, placed them for adoption, and returned home to continue on with their lives as if the event had not happened (March, 1997; Solinger, 2001). Follow-up studies of birth mothers indicate that this type of experience hampers a woman's ability to grieve for her loss and produces "prolonged feelings of unworthiness, diminished self-esteem and depression" (Deykin, Campbell, & Patti, 1984, p. 279).

The birth mothers I met also grieved for the loss of their placed children and perceived contact as a way of resolving the emotional pain they had suffered from

Box 17.3: Canadian Council of Natural Mothers

The Canadian Council of Natural Mothers (CCNM; <http://nebula.on.ca/canbmothers>) was created in February 2000. Affiliated with Parent Finders, Canada, the CCNM operates as a volunteer organization and lobbies actively for adoption reform, in particular, an open record system by which all members of the adoption triad may gain and maintain contact. CCNM provides a listserv in order that adopted persons and natural mothers may discuss their placement, search, and contact concerns. Recently, as noted on their web page, CCNM revoked the title of "birth mother." This action was taken in response to its members' view that, rather than being a term of their own making, the title of "birth mother" had been applied to them by social workers and legal professionals. The membership believes that the term *birth mother* carries the same symbolic meaning as other disreputable labels used to describe them (e.g., "fallen woman" or "unwed mother") and socially stigmatizes their role in the adoption process.

years of "not knowing." However, secrecy in adoption also meant "not telling," and the majority had hidden their birth mother status from others. In consequence, rather than symbolizing an act of sacrifice committed by a caring mother, their placement became viewed as an escape from social censure. From this perspective, all future mothering experiences were suspect. For example, almost one-third of the interviewed birth mothers reported not having other children because they "couldn't trust [themselves] to take care of another child after what [they] had done." Others described future pregnancy or childbirth difficulties as "punishment from God for what I had done. I didn't deserve to be a mother." Many observed, "I was always so careful with my other children. It was like I was afraid that something might happen to them. Almost hovering, you might say. I wanted to make sure I took good care of them. I think I worried that I might not be able to. Because of what had happened."

This perception was supported by significant others who tended to question the women's mothering abilities. Thus, Kathryn replied, "I married the birth father and we had a son. My father-in-law sent his wife to stay with me when I got out of the hospital to watch how I took care of the baby. He asked her, 'Is she a good mother?' I felt like he didn't trust me to love or take care of my son because of what had happened to my daughter. As if none of this was his own son's fault. Only mine. That still haunts me. I always feel like I'm being watched by him in case I do something wrong to his grandson."

In contrast, Nancy observed, "I went to a meeting and I told this politician I was a birth mother. He said, 'Well, you seem to have overcome your past quite nicely. Do you have other children? Are they okay?' It was like I might not take care of other children because of this mistake in the past."

These birth mothers had taken the message of "making a mistake" and internalized it as a personal character flaw affecting their identity as mothers. Secrecy in adoption reinforced this perception because it denied them access to the knowledge they needed to legitimate the mothering sacrifice they had made. Contact offered them a way of validating self by providing them with knowledge that their child was safe and secure with a loving adoptive family. More important, contact gave them the opportunity of enacting the role of a mother who still loved and demonstrated concern for the child she had lost. To quote Edith:

> Meeting her let me explain what had happened. Like, she has never said to me, "You weren't there when I needed you," but she could. As birth mothers, we all have this guilt feeling. Because we weren't there. And, I can understand if the adoptee feels that way. But, then, you have to understand our feelings too. Most of us would have loved to have been there. But, as the social workers put it, "It's for the best of the child that you do this." But, is it really? Mostly, I just wanted to meet her and tell her that I didn't want to do it. I had to do it. To show her I do love her. That I always loved her and will love her until I die.

Raising Non-biological Children

Considerable material exists on the primacy of the blood bond in the formation of family and the cultural conception of adoption as "second best." Studies on adoption outcome support this view by focusing on the distinction between biological and adoptive families and the importance of the **biological kinship group** for healthy identity formation (March & Miall, 2000). This focus reinforces the image of adoptees as "potentially damaged individuals" and strengthens the public's belief in adoption "as an inferior means of family formation" (Wegar, 1997, p. 74). In consequence, adoptive motherhood is devalued and the adoptive mother-child bond discredited (Miall, 1987).

The adoptive mothers I met managed these public perceptions by acknowledging the social distinction between their own and other family structures. As Janet noted, "When we adopted, we were told that families that tended to recognize the difference between the fact that their children were adopted and other people's were more likely to adjust to the adoptive situation more favourably. We took this advice and applied it to our situation. I tried to be open with both of my children. I tried to answer all of their questions as fully as possible and deal with their feelings about their adoption as they arose. So, when my daughter told me she wanted to find her birth mother, I told her I would help her."

Janet's open attitude towards her children's adoptive status and their questions about adoption reinforced her ideal image of self as a good mother—a woman who puts her children's needs before her own. Specifically, her actions fulfilled the role requirements expected of a woman who adopts, that is, accepting the differences between her motherhood identity as primary caregiver and the biological motherhood offered by birth mothers. Being an adoptive mother entailed helping her children with search and supporting any contact concerns they might encounter. In fact, participation in these events represented an extension of her care-giving activities and an opportunity to deepen her mother-child bonds. Good mothers nurture their children through all of life's contingencies.

For these adoptive mothers, part of acknowledging their status as "caregiver" meant acceptance of the birth mother's status as "life giver" and, hence, a person who had something of value to offer her adopted children. Given their perception of this mothering distinction, these mothers viewed contact as part of the task involved in raising an adopted child. To quote Donna:

> I didn't see reunion as a rejection of me because we have always had such a good relationship. We have been able to talk about almost anything. So, when he asked me about this, I knew he needed to try. I felt more fear in him being hurt than anything else. When they met, I was really excited for him. I wanted to be there so much. He didn't want me to. I understood. It was personal. But, I would have loved to have been at that first meeting to share that with him. Just as I have shared all the other parts of his life: his first step, his first day of school, his graduation. Everything.

Bergum (1997, p. 65) notes that, "when one explores adoption from the point of view of experience, one must consider the experience of both the birth mothers and the adopting mothers at the same time … for one cannot exist without the other." Although these mothers had experienced closed adoptions, they were very aware of the birth mother's existence. Increased incidents of reunion and the current publicity surrounding contact had also made them aware of the possibility of this event occurring for their children. Some may have found it difficult, but the majority came to see removal of secrecy as a way of validating their own motherhood. Thus, Rosemary claimed,

> I had to say to myself, "Well, if she goes searching am I going to feel insecure? Am I going to feel that she's looking for something better?" Once I came to the point that I could say that if she does I will be pleased for her, then, I wasn't afraid. Like, you can't replace your mother. You have been with that mother all of your life. She's the person who was there all the time, during the important things. So, I have kept all of her school pictures just so that if she does find her mother she can have a look. Because, I don't know how they feel, but that's what I would be interested in if I was a birth mother. Seeing how they grew up and who raised them.

CONCLUSION

In this chapter, I have shown how female members of the adoption triad may experience social sanctions from others who question their motherhood. Because the women I met had internalized aspects of closed adoption as personal character traits affecting their ability to mother effectively, they experienced difficulty achieving their ideal image of self as good mothers. In their desire to gain more positive assessments of self, they had to mediate the legal constraints and cultural perceptions of that social institution. Female adoptees sought access to their biological families, the birth mothers sought forgiveness for their placement, and the adoptive mothers sought to remove the status uncertainty produced by the existence of a phantom birth mother with primordial rights.

All three types of mothers repeated similar themes in their account of their need for reunion. These themes replicate the vocabulary used to support the motherhood ideal as it currently exists in the Western world. Whether an adoptee, birth mother, or adoptive mother, the women I met referred repeatedly to ideas about love, devotion, caring, self-sacrifice, bonding, responsibility, accountability, and best interests of the child in their accounts. In this way, they demonstrated their internalization of the romanticized image of good motherhood and their quest to achieve this identity for self.

All three types of mothers were influenced also by their own adoption triad position and the characteristics attached to that social location. They presented contrasting accounts of the social constraints placed on their mothering by secrecy in adoption and alternate strategies for mediating those constraints. As such, they stood as individual women facing the demands of a social environment that failed to support their need for contact and criticized their motherhood. Only by understanding the impact of the perceptions of others on self can we help them be "real mothers, as true to themselves and their children as they can be" (Bergum, 1997, p. 130).

GLOSSARY

Adoption: This is the transfer of a child from his or her birth parents to other parents who take social and legal responsibility for raising him/her. Many cultures engage in traditional adoption whereby children are placed with other kin and maintain knowledge of their birth parents' identity and their biological family background. In contrast, the Canadian adoption system uses formal legal procedures and generally involves third-party, non-kin family members. Although there is a recent trend towards the open transmission of information between members of the adoption triad, this practice is voluntary and dependent upon the agreement arranged between the adoptive and biological parents.

Adoption triad: This term encapsulates adoptive parents, biological parents, and adoptive children as a single entity and emphasizes the strong interconnection existing among all three parties involved in the adoption process.

Biological kinship group: A network of persons related by birth. Membership within a biological kinship group tends to include specific role designations (e.g., mother, son, cousin) accompanied by particular social rights and responsibilities (e.g., inheritance of property or provision of emotional support).

Social institution: An intangible structure constructed on the basis of social values, normative expectations, social roles, and rules of behaviour that help society function. For example, the social institution of family produces, cares for, protects, and socializes children to become functional adult members of their society.

Social role: The part a person is expected to play in accordance with the status he or she holds within a society. For example, women who hold the social status of mother are expected to act in particular ways and perform certain activities with their children. In doing so, they are enacting a social role.

REFERENCES

Bergum, V. (1997). *A child on her mind: The experience of becoming a mother*. Westport, CT: Bergin & Garvey.

Chodorow, N. (1978). *The reproduction of mothering: Psychoanalysis and the sociology of gender*. Berkeley: University of California Press.

Cooley, C.H. (1967). Looking-glass self. In J.G. Manis & B.N. Meltzer (Eds.), *Symbolic interaction: A reader in social psychology* (pp. 217–219). Boston: Allyn and Bacon. (Original work published 1902.)

Deykin, E.Y., Campbell, L., & Patti, P. (1984). The post-adoption experience of surrendering parents. *American Journal of Orthopsychiatry, 54*, 271–280.

Fox, B. (1997). Reproducing difference: Changes in the lives of partners becoming parents. In M. Luxton (Ed.), *Feminism and families: Critical policies and changing practices* (pp. 142–161). Halifax, NS: Fernwood Publishing.

Glaser, B.G., & Strauss, A. (1967). *The discovery of grounded theory*. Chicago: Aldine.

March, K. (1995). *The stranger who bore me: Adoptee-birth mother relationships*. Toronto: University of Toronto Press.

March, K. (1997). The dilemma of adoption reunion: Establishing open communication between adoptees and their birth mothers. *Family Relations, 46*, 99–105.

March, K. (2000). Who do I look like? Gaining a sense of self-authenticity through the physical reflections of others. *Symbolic Interaction, 23*, 359–373.

March, K., & Miall, C. (2000). Adoption as family form. *Family Relations, 49*, 359–362.

McMahon, M. (1995). *Engendering motherhood: Identity self-transformation in women's lives*. New York: The Guilford Press.

Miall, C. (1987). The stigma of adoptive parent status: Perceptions of community attitudes toward adoption and the experience of informal sanctioning. *Family Relations, 36*, 34–39.

Pacheco, F., & Eme, R. (1993). An outcome study of the reunion between adoptees and biological parents. *Child Welfare, 72*, 53–64.

Sachdev, P. (1992). Adoption reunion and after: A study of the search process and experience of adoptees. *Child Welfare, 71*, 53–68.

Solinger, R. (2001). *Beggars and choosers: How the politics of choice shapes adoption, abortion, and welfare in the United States*. New York: Hill and Wang.

Wegar, K. (1997). *Adoption, identity, and kinship: The debate over sealed birth records*. New Haven: Yale University Press.

Chapter 18

"This Is Who I Really Am": Obese Women's Conceptions of Self following Weight Loss Surgery

Leanne Joanisse

INTRODUCTION

Weight loss surgery, known as bariatric surgery in the medical profession, is becoming an increasingly popular method for the treatment of morbid obesity. An individual is considered morbidly obese if she or he weighs more than 100 pounds above ideal weight. Morbid obesity is associated with numerous, significant health problems, including high blood pressure, coronary heart disease, Type 2 diabetes, various cancers, osteoarthritis, musculoskeletal problems, and premature death (Balsiger, Murr, Poggio, & Sarr, 2000).

This chapter examines women's lived experiences of weight loss surgery and their changing sense of **embodiment** and self as they make the transition from

---

Box 18.1: Facts about Bariatric Surgery

Bariatric surgery is an umbrella term for over two dozen different types of surgical procedures designed to induce weight loss by reducing the size of the stomach (Sjöström, 2002). The two most popular bariatric surgical procedures performed in the United States and Canada are the **vertical banded gastroplasty** (VBG) and the **Roux-en-Y gastric bypass** (RNY). In the VBG, a small pouch is created at the top of the stomach, using several rows of gastric staples. The pouch holds between 1 to 2 ounces of food and induces weight loss by decreasing food intake (Balsiger et al., 2000).

In the RNY, a small stomach pouch is also created; next, a Y-shaped section of the small intestine is attached to the pouch to allow food to bypass most of the small intestine where calorie and nutrient absorption take place (Balsiger et al., 2000). This operation induces weight loss by combining stomach restriction and decreased intestinal absorption.

Weight loss surgery is an extremely gendered surgical procedure, with women representing 87% of the patient population (Mason, Renquist, & Jiang, 1992).

---

pre-surgery to post-surgery. These experiences offer a fascinating opportunity to not just note surface change but also to understand how changes in embodiment impact the self and identity.

The self is the cornerstone of symbolic interactionist theory (Blumer, 1969; Cooley, 1902; Mead, 1934). According to the symbolic interactionist perspective, the self is not present at birth but is socially created; that is, our sense of self develops through social interactions. Cooley (1902) coined the term *looking-glass self* to describe how the self is formed through interaction with others who reflect back to us an image of ourselves. In other words, we learn who we are from others and our imagination of the way we appear to them. Goffman (1959, 1963) further pointed the significance of the body in social interactions and its centrality to the formation of the self. Goffman emphasizes that, in virtually every social situation, individuals are evaluated and interacted with on the basis of their bodies. The reactions that an individual receives from others, which are mediated by that individual's embodiment, are crucial factors in the development of the self. As Gimlin (2002, p. 3) observes, "The body is fundamental to the self because it serves to indicate who an individual is internally, what habits the person has, and even what social value the individual merits."

Obesity, especially obesity in women, is viewed negatively in Canada, the United States, and other Western societies. The empirical literature shows that obesity impacts virtually all aspects of a person's life. Obese people are victimized by children, parents and other family members, strangers, and prospective and current romantic partners (Allon, 1982; Breseman, Lennon, & Schulz, 1999; Millman, 1980; Puhl & Brownell, 2001; Rothblum, 1992). Obesity is also correlated with inequities in wages and promotions (Breseman et al., 1999). Not surprisingly, obese people—particularly White obese women, tend to have lower self-esteem than their non-obese counterparts (Averett & Korenman, 1999; Crandall & Biernat, 1990; Quinn & Crocker, 1998). Negative **body image** is also common in obese individuals (Friedman & Brownell, 1995). Myers & Rosen (1999) found a positive correlation between the number of stigmatizing situations and the presence of mental health symptoms, negative body image, and lower self-esteem in their obese respondents. These studies clearly indicate that **stigma** and negative consequences are attached to individuals, especially women, when they do not conform to the dominant appearance norms.

LIMITATIONS OF PREVIOUS STUDIES

Weight loss surgery has been researched almost exclusively from a medical perspective. This literature abounds with studies in which surgeons analyze the medical outcome of bariatric surgical procedures, but they do not discuss, in any depth, the emotional and social implications of the surgery for their patients. Moreover, current research in the medical literature on patients' experience of bariatric surgery overwhelmingly employs research techniques consistent with quantitative methods such as questionnaires or structured interviews. The emphasis is typically on the amount of weight lost and its correlation with subsequent improvements in the physical and mental health of the patient, as well as the occurrence of side effects.

While these research strategies are particularly useful for hypothesis testing, one of the strengths of qualitative research is that it allows a rich exploration of issues that may have been previously overlooked (Taylor & Bogdan, 1998). Since very little research exists that attempts to understand the personal experience of weight loss surgery from the point of view of the patient and its impact on self and identity, qualitative research methods are useful in a study of this topic. A further strength of a qualitative approach is the possibility it offers of gathering rich, detailed data that are not limited by preconceived concepts and categories (Taylor & Bogdan, 1998).

METHODOLOGY

Maynard (1994) suggests that feelings and perceptions about the body are best explored with research strategies that are relatively open-ended. Therefore, in studying the lived experiences of women who undergo weight loss surgery, I chose an in-depth, semi-structured interview format. The participants consisted of 30 weight loss surgery patients recruited using techniques ranging from personal contacts, snowballing, online advertisements on surgical support group sites, and a size acceptance organization's website, as well as physician referrals. Fifteen respondents lived in Canada at the time of the interview while the others lived in the United States. The time elapsed since surgery ranged from five months to 28 years (mean 7.9). Four of the sample members were "re-ops"; that is, they underwent more than one bariatric procedure before they achieved permanent weight loss. Their ages ranged from 22 to 61 years (mean 43.4). All were White. All were heterosexual. The respondents' preoperative weights ranged from 238 pounds to 500 pounds (mean 337). Their postoperative weights ranged from 136 pounds to 600 pounds (mean 254). Twenty sample members considered their surgery a success, while 10 thought the procedure was a failure. Consequently, the sample is divided into two clusters: surgical successes and surgical failures. It should be noted, however, that most women who have undergone multiple procedures have experienced both failure and success, and that most of the surgical failures were successful at least for a time. Another point, which bears emphasizing, is that of the 20 surgical successes, only three had weights in a normative range at the time of the interview. Of the remaining 17, 14 were obese by clinical standards, while three were morbidly obese.

The interviews, which took place in a variety of venues, lasted approximately one and a half hours. With the consent of the participants, the interviews were tape recorded and then transcribed verbatim. Five of the interviews were conducted in French and then translated into English. The data were analyzed using principles of analytic induction for the discovery of grounded theory (Strauss & Corbin, 1990). To protect their anonymity, all participants were asked to choose pseudonyms.

FINDINGS

Not surprisingly, the research findings are characterized by a "before and after" theme. The surgical successes, in particular, were more likely to depict their pre-surgical lives as having been filled with unhappiness and despair and to describe the post-surgical phase as one of liberation and happiness. The surgical failures, who largely experienced postoperative complications, were more likely to describe the immediate postoperative phase as being an extremely negative time in their lives. However, they too spoke of having become liberated and transformed—but through self-acceptance rather than surgical modification. These findings are explored in further detail in the following sections.

Before the Surgery: A Context of Suffering

Both surgical clusters describe their lives prior to their surgery as having been dominated by their weight. Consistent with the findings in the literature, they experienced stigmatization and discrimination from multiple sources. They were routinely harassed and victimized by strangers, family members, medical professionals, and, in some cases, spouses. As Elaine observed, "People are not kind to the overweight. I had people come up to me in the grocery store and chastise me for what I was buying. People didn't see it as discrimination; they saw it as being kind by telling me I was fat." Numerous respondents reported they also experienced employment discrimination. Their access to public spaces such as seating on buses, restaurants, movie theatres, and stadiums was greatly restricted. They complained of lack of choice in clothing for large women. Two-thirds of the sample reported obesity-related diseases such as high blood pressure, Type 2 diabetes, shortness of breath, limited mobility, and clinical depression.

Respondents also reported acute feelings of disembodiment and estrangement from the self prior to their surgery. When asked, "How did you feel about your body before you had your surgery?" they almost uniformly answered that they hated the pre-surgical body, describing it using pejorative adjectives such as "ugly," "gross," "disgusting," "repulsive." So great was their loathing of their bodies that they often refused to even look at them. They habitually avoided mirrors, especially when they were undressing. Moreover, they hated themselves for "allowing" their bodies to become objects of scorn and hatred.

The surgical successes, in particular, viewed their pre-surgical bodies as a prison. Their morbidly obese bodies trapped them by restricting their mobility and by masking what they considered to be their "true" selves. As Gimlin (2002) notes, the body is assumed to be the manifestation of the self. According to this logic, a deviant body signifies a deeply flawed self.

Thus, fat women carry multiple burdens: They carry the literal burden of their physical weight. They also carry the burden of society's disapproval and contempt as well as their own burden of shame and self-hatred. As Millman (1980, p. 220) points out, fat women are burdened with an additional self: "Like Cinderella or the Frog Prince, the fat person lives with a double identity. Her present self-in-the-world may be fat, ugly, despised, or disregarded, but inside, carefully nourished, is a private future self that is beautiful, powerful, lovely." Similarly, the belief in the presence of a fat person's secret, better self is vividly illustrated in the aphorism "Trapped inside every fat person is a thin person trying to get out."

The respondents described lives of suffering beyond endurance. They viewed their quality of life as greatly compromised by their morbid obesity. They had tried to lose weight using conventional measures such as dieting regimens and pills, but were never able to maintain significant, permanent weight loss. Weight loss surgery was a radical solution to a seemingly intractable problem.

The women expressed varying motivations for undergoing the surgery, although the desire to improve their health status and to regain mobility were the reasons most often cited. The participants who had young children expressed a fear of not living long enough to see them grow up. Five women cited a concern with appearance as the primary motivating factor driving their decision to have the surgery. Three women sought acceptance from their parents or spouses, and one woman had the surgery in the hopes of reviving a flagging marriage.

Transformation and Liberation: The Case of the Surgical Successes

For most respondents the initial postoperative period was a chrysalis period in their lives. Their bodies, so long hated and rejected, now became objects of wonder. They kept careful track of weight loss. Shopping for clothes, once an onerous project, became a pleasure not only because they could wear smaller sizes but because they had a wider choice of attractive clothing. Many respondents took great delight in the fact that significant others in their lives did not recognize them:

> Elaine: "So many people didn't recognize me. I went down to see my best friend—I was going to be the maid of honour at her wedding. I lived with her in college, she has known me for over 10 years now—she walked past me three times at the airport and did not recognize me."
>
> Barbara: "I didn't come home right away ... I spent six weeks in [city where I was operated] and I went to [another city] ... and spent two weeks with my sons. At that point, I had lost 42 pounds ... My son Robert was going to pick me up at the airport ... I waited a long time, but he wasn't there ... Then, someone came up behind me and just put his arms around me and said, 'Mom, I can't believe you! I didn't recognize you!'"

Moreover, for the first time in many years, most of the women experienced the freedom of unrestricted mobility and increased access to public spaces. Fitting into seats and manoeuvring in crowded restaurants was no longer problematic. Various respondents described the difference this made in their lives:

> Jennifer: "I loved it when I started losing the weight ... I found I was able to do more. My husband and I can go out now on our bikes. It's just a night and day difference ... I could never go out and ride a bike before; I had never ridden a bike in my adult life. I can go out on a bike and see things I hadn't seen before."
>
> Isabella: "I can walk. I can go anywhere. I can do anything. I can swim in public. I snorkelled last fall and swam with dolphins. Last year, we went on a cruise to Alaska. I flew in a helicopter, which I could never have done before. I can get on an airplane and fit into any seat. I can get in and out of any car. I mean,

it's a whole new world. Yesterday … we went grocery shopping. I didn't have to get one of those carts they have. I just walked through the store and it was like nothing. I mean, I'm like a normal person. I feel *normal*" (emphasis in original).

Another outcome of the surgery discussed by respondents was their reduced conspicuousness. Most respondents claimed to be experiencing less public harassment, attributing this to the fact that they now "look normal" and are accepted as such by other "normals" (Goffman, 1963):

> Isabella: "No one stares at me. No one makes remarks. I can go anywhere and there's no kids pointing at me. There's no people staring at me—nothing like that anymore. I look normal; I feel normal."
> Casey: "When I walk around in public, I don't know if people are looking at me, but I feel okay about them looking at me—men, in particular. I hold my head up more and I look people in the eye instead of not really meeting people's gaze because of what I might see in their faces … I feel more accepted, I guess, because I am more of a normal size than I used to be."

These women's accounts illustrate that successful weight loss surgery can be a truly liberating experience for those who felt entrapped in their morbidly obese bodies. A massive weight loss freed them from the prison of immobility, public opprobrium, and self-hatred. Their bodies, so long an impediment to normal functioning, had now been converted to bodies that allowed them to realize a normal lifestyle.

For the surgical successes, weight loss was usually accompanied by a dramatic improvement in their physical and mental health. The seven women who had diabetes or pre-diabetes prior to their surgery attained normal blood sugar levels. A wheelchair-bound respondent was able to walk. Young mothers who once feared a premature death were no longer consumed with their mortality and the possibility of leaving their young children behind.

There were also positive changes in mood and attitude. Respondents experienced a remarkable surge in self-confidence and a corresponding increase in self-esteem. Numerous women reported having become more assertive. This, in turn, prompted them to become more outgoing and adopt a more positive attitude towards life:

> Jennifer: "My outlook has also changed: I'm more optimistic now. I can see more things. I can accomplish more things."
> Trudy: "I feel wonderful, both physically and mentally. There have been, in the time that I was off the year and a half from work [before the surgery], during that time I isolated myself. I wouldn't even talk to people on the phone. I had just … I didn't do anything. Now I want to do everything. I want to garden because I can. I want to walk to the mall because I can. Things I couldn't do before, I can now."

These dramatic changes in body and attitude had a profound, positive impact on the women's professional lives. Numerous participants felt their weight loss enhanced their employability; not only did they look better, they had a newfound self-confidence:

> Filomena: "I'm much happier, I have more confidence. I feel that more opportunities have opened up for me at work because of my weight loss. It's changed my life in every way."
>
> Cynthia: "After I lost weight, I got the confidence and I said, I want a better job. I went to Toronto and I found a kick-ass job, working with [high-profile employer]. It's just a big boost."

Similarly, Doris and Nicole felt sufficiently confident to return to school for secretarial diplomas, an achievement they maintained they would never have accomplished without first losing weight.

The women in the surgical success category noted that the surgery induced positive changes in their construction of self by reconnecting them to their bodies. They felt no connection to, nor did they grieve the loss of, their pre-surgical bodies, which they regarded as a source of anguish. Their pre-surgical bodies had betrayed them by resisting their best efforts to bring them under control. They also caused a fracture in these women's sense of identity, as they felt the pre-surgical body was not congruent with their sense of self. This incongruence was articulated in the frequently expressed conviction that their body misrepresented their authentic self ("This isn't who I really am").

However, virtually all surgical successes described their post-surgical body as representing the "real" them, or authentic self. Consistent with Millman's (1980) suggestion, they maintained this self was not a surgically constructed self but a self that had always existed; it was the self they had long nurtured but that had been buried under layers of fat. The following quotes reflect the double identity that respondents were burdened with prior to their surgery and the alignment between body and self after surgery:

> Julie: "I feel I'm closer now to how I really am. The person I really am is coming through. I like myself. I like how I feel and how I fit in the world. I'm still the same person I was, though, before my surgery. I haven't changed in that way. I'm still the same person in how I treat people, in how I view people. How I view myself is what changed."
>
> Cynthia: "I'm still the same person on the inside, but I feel a lot better about myself. This is me, someone who is vibrant, who has a lot of energy, who loves herself, and who loves her family and friends. I think that was the real me before the surgery, but it was hindered by my lack of self-esteem. It was hidden because I wasn't as outgoing, as outspoken before my surgery."

As the physical body changed and acquired more normative proportions, respondents felt they had the freedom to reveal—or in some cases, reclaim—their authentic self. A more normative body reflected a normative self. The women positioned the post-surgical body as the true indicator of selfhood. A consequence of the realignment between the body and the self, then, is that these women achieved an embodied self. The loss of weight enabled them to shed both the physical burden of the restrictions it imposed and the psychological burden of a false self. Weight loss surgery offered a way of establishing a state that Davis (1995, p. 161) calls "feeling at home in one's body."

Renegotiating the Relationship between Body and Self: The Case of the Surgical Failures

All 10 women in the surgical failure cluster had procedures that are now acknowledged by bariatric surgeons as ineffectual—either because they fail to induce permanent weight loss in the long term or are associated with such severe complications that these ultimately compromise the patient's quality of life to a greater extent than morbid obesity. Of these 10, five suffered intolerable effects such as intractable vomiting and chronic diarrhea. Three women had their procedures reversed because of complications associated with the surgery. While the other five women in this cluster did not experience side effects, their surgery did not result in permanent weight loss. Over time, virtually every woman in this group saw her weight revert to its pre-surgical level—and in some cases, greatly surpass it.

Seven women in the surgical failure cluster—who, in varying degrees, have been influenced by the size acceptance movement (Gimlin, 2002; Millman, 1980)—were adamant that further weight loss surgery was not an option for them. They maintained that they were not tempted by refinements in bariatric surgical techniques that increase the chances of a successful procedure because they were skeptical that bariatric surgery can be safe or effective in the long term. These women were very critical of weight loss surgery, with two respondents referring to the surgery as "self-mutilation." Another woman expressed contempt for the methods employed by bariatric surgeons to recruit patients: "They sell the surgery. They sell the dream. It's just like selling a used car or a cheeseburger or anything else. It's marketing." Only two women in the surgical failure group admitted to seriously considering further bariatric surgery, but doubted they would go ahead with it because of their fear of side effects.

A rejection of the possibility of further surgery did not always lead to the abandonment of weight loss as a goal. Two respondents in the surgical failure group were pursuing other weight loss options. However, the remaining eight women in this cluster had foresworn diets, pills, and other weight loss measures. They explained that since the ultimate solution to morbid obesity had failed, they felt they had no other option but to accept the fact they would be fat for the rest of their lives. Much like the surgical successes, who described their post-surgical bodies as "this is who I really am," all of the women in the surgical failure group had come to a similar conclusion: Their fat bodies were their "real" bodies, the bodies they were meant to have. They no longer thought of themselves as future thin women. This conclusion was reached with varying degrees of equanimity. For example,

Box 18.2: The Size Acceptance Movement

The size acceptance movement is diffuse and consists of "a loose collective of organizations, groups, and individuals connected through interpersonal relationships and more formal communications channels" (Sobal, 2003, p. 171).The largest, and most prominent, size acceptance organization in the United States is the National Association to Advance Fat Acceptance (NAAFA), founded in 1969 (NAAFA, 1995). NAAFA claims approximately 5,000 members, including 100 in Canada (Nemeth, 1994; Sobal, 2003, p. 172).

NAAFA is dedicated to eliminating size discrimination in employment, education, and public transportation. Full access to adequate medical care is another major concern. NAAFA promotes self-acceptance among its members and advises against weight loss pursuits, citing the high failure rates associated with these (NAAFA, 1995). NAAFA is very critical of weight loss surgery, claiming that it is inherently unsafe and, in the long term, unsuccessful (NAAFA, 1995).

For more information about NAAFA and its goals, see <www.naafa.org>.

some respondents, particularly the three oldest sample members, expressed more resignation and despair. These women were profoundly disembodied. One woman explained her determination to lose weight as a by-product of having been raised in Hollywood "where size is everything." Another woman was verbally abused about her weight by her mother throughout her life, while a third woman admitted to a lifelong abhorrence of her body. As she put it, "I don't like it. I never have liked it and I never will."

However, the other seven women in the surgical failure cluster positively identified as fat women. They had renegotiated the relationship between body and self by arguing that the two are independent entities. That is, they maintained that the body is merely a casing for, and not reflective of, self:

Wanda: "This is some body. It is what God gave me and this is what I have made it. It only houses what is inside me. It gives my heart and lungs a place to live. My spirit lives there and I think I'm a very nice person. I'm a loving person and if someone cannot see me through the fat, then that's their loss."

Marcia: "I still wish I were thinner because life would be easier, but as far as it being any kind of reflection on what kind of character I might have or what kind of worth I might have to society or to the world in general, fatness isn't an issue."

Gisèle: "You know, when it comes down to it, you can't judge someone's character by their weight. You should judge them by what they say or do, but not by their appearance ... So I'm fat, so what? This doesn't mean I'm a bad person."

These women challenge the pervasive inference that the body is a physical manifestation of the self (Gimlin, 2002). Their bodies may be considered deviant by society, but their selves are not deviant by association. Thus, they constructed the body as irrelevant to self. Severing the devalued body from the self allowed them to reclaim their bodies and construct a more normative, or at least non-deviant, identity by neutralizing the characterological stigma of fat (Goffman, 1963). Having come to terms with their fatness, they were also no longer burdened by two dichotomous selves, the double identity described by Millman (1980). They had only one self. They rejected the notion that this was an inherently flawed self on the grounds that the body is not indicative of the character of the person residing in it. Similar to the experience of the surgical successes, they were no longer plagued by a lack of alignment between body and self.

These women's renegotiated sense of self and the equilibrium they felt indicates that altering the body is not the only means by which fat women may find contentment. Altering one's sense of self and accepting one's fat body are also effective. The women who were able to alter their identity were also able to attain a certain degree of success in resolving their weight issues and reducing the significance of weight in their lives. It would be a mistake to characterize these women as weight management failures simply because their bariatric surgery did not result in the expected outcome. Success in the context of weight management should not be restricted simply to changes in the body but should include positive changes in self and identity.

CONCLUSION

This qualitative study of women's experiences of weight loss surgery confirms that non-normative bodies can have a profound impact on an individual's self and identity (Millman, 1980). Yet, this research has also yielded interesting findings about the relationship between the body and the self it allegedly represents. The women in the surgical success group reported that they were "new" people—both in terms of body and self. While they did not feel they had changed fundamentally since their surgery, they thought the surgery removed the layers of fat to reveal the "real" body and its corresponding "real" self. In other words, weight loss surgery enabled them to achieve an embodied self. Identity change for these women was achieved by bringing body and self together in a consonant relationship where one reflected the other.

The seven women in the surgical failure group who accepted the permanence of their fatness also experienced an identity change, but the change in this case was brought about by separating body and self into two distinct entities. Whereas the surgical successes position their bodies as a reflection of their selfhood, these women constructed positive identities independent of their non-normative bodies. They refused to see the fat body as reflective of a flawed self. They constructed the body as a mere casing for the self, not a mirror of that self. The self of a fat woman, they believed, cannot be inferred from her body.

This research suggests that we need to pay more attention to the ways in which the body is implicated in how individuals see themselves and construct their identities. At the very least we need to know more about the circumstances under which individuals embrace their bodies or disconnect from them as a reflection of self.

GLOSSARY

Body image: A person's perceptions, thoughts, and feelings about his or her body.

Embodiment: The lived experience of the body; sociologists of the body argue that one's sense of embodiment is the basis of individuality.

Roux-en-Y gastric bypass surgery: A surgical procedure for extreme obesity. This operation involves the creation of a small stomach pouch by stapling and the attachment of a Y-shaped section of the small intestine to the pouch. Weight loss is induced through a combination of restricted food intake and caloric malabsorption.

Stigma: A characteristic that makes a person devalued, spoiled, or flawed in the eyes of others. A stigma can be a deviant behaviour, physical characteristic, group membership, or moral failing.

Vertical banded gastroplasty (popularly known as "stomach stapling"): A surgical treatment for extreme obesity that involves the construction of a small pouch in the stomach by stapling, thereby limiting the amount of food the stomach can hold. Weight loss is induced through limited caloric intake.

REFERENCES

Allon, N. (1982). The stigma of overweight in everyday life. In B.B. Wolman (Ed.), *Psychological aspects of obesity: A handbook* (pp. 130–174). New York: VanNostrand Reinhold.

Averett, S., & Korenman, S. (1999). Black-white differences in social and economic consequences of obesity. *International Journal of Obesity, 23,* 166–173.

Balsiger, B.R., Murr, M.M., Poggio, J.L., & Sarr, M.G. (2000). Bariatric surgery: Surgery for weight control in patients with morbid obesity. *Medical Clinics of North America, 84*(2), 477–489.

Blumer, H. (1969). *Symbolic interactionism: Perspective and method.* Englewood Cliffs, NJ: University of California Press.

Breseman, B.C., Lennon, S.J., & Schultz, T.L. (1999). Obesity and powerlessness. In K.K.P. Johnson & S.J. Lennon (Eds.), *Appearance and power* (pp. 173–197). New York: Berg.

Cooley, C.H. (1902). *Human nature and social order.* New York: Scribner.

Crandall, C.S., & Biernat, M. (1990). The ideology of anti-fat attitudes. *Journal of Applied Social Psychology, 20*(3), 227–243.

Davis, K. (1995). *Reshaping the female body.* London: Routledge.

Friedman, M.A., & Brownell, K.D. (1995). Psychological correlates of obesity: Moving to the next research generation. *Psychological Bulletin, 117*(1), 3–20.

Gimlin, D.L. (2002). *Body work: Beauty and self-image in American culture.* Los Angeles, CA: University of California Press.

Goffman, E. (1959). *Presentation of self in everyday life.* New York: Anchor Doubleday.

Goffman, E. (1963). *Stigma: Notes on the management of spoiled identity.* Englewood Cliffs, NJ: Prentice Hall.

Mason, E.E., Renquist, K., & Jiang, D. (1992). Perioperative risks and safety of surgery for severe obesity. *American Journal of Clinical Nutrition, 55,* 573S–576S.

Maynard, M. (1994). Methods, practice and epistemology: The debate about feminism and research. In M. Maynard & J. Purvis (Eds.), *Researching women's lives from a feminist perspective* (pp. 10–26). London: Taylor and Francis.

Mead, G.H. (1934). *Mind, self, and society*. Chicago, IL: University of Chicago Press.

Millman, M. (1980). *Such a pretty face*. New York: Norton.

Myers, A., & Rosen, J.C. (1999). Obesity stigmatization and coping: Relation to mental health symptoms, body image, and self-esteem. *International Journal of Obesity, 23*, 221–230.

NAAFA. 1995. *Size acceptance and self-acceptance: The NAAFA workbook* (2nd ed.). Sacramento, CA: NAAFA.

Nemeth, M. (1994, May 2). Body obsession. *MacLeans*, 45–49.

Puhl, R., & Brownell, K.D. (2001). Bias, discrimination, and obesity. *Obesity Research, 9*, 788–805.

Quinn, D.M., & Crocker, J. (1998). Vulnerability to the affective consequences of the stigma of overweight. In J.K. Swim & C. Stangor (Eds.), *Prejudice: The target's perspective* (pp. 125–143). San Diego, CA: Academic Press.

Rothblum, E. (1992). The stigma of women's weight: Fact and fiction. *Journal of Psychology, 124*, 5–24.

Sjöström, L. (2000). Surgical intervention as a strategy for treatment of obesity. *Endocrine, 13*(2), 213–230.

Sobal, J. (2003). The size acceptance movement. In D.R. Loseke & J. Best (Eds.), *Social Problems: Constructionist readings* (pp. 169–174). New York: Aldine de Gruyter.

Strauss, A.L., & Corbin, J. (1990). *Basics of qualitative research*. Newbury Park, CA: Sage.

Taylor, S.J., & Bogdan, R. (1998). *Introduction to qualitative research methods: A guidebook and resource* (3rd ed.). New York: John Wiley & Sons.

Chapter 19

Coping with Electoral Defeat:
A Study of Involuntary Role Exit

William Shaffir and Steven Kleinknecht

INTRODUCTION

> Your observation about defeated politicians is correct. Some can't talk about it, and
> others need to talk about it, and I would put myself in both categories. For a long
> time, I couldn't talk about it because of how devastating it was to me personally,
> my own ego and sense of identity, and its effect on the family, and my desire to
> get back in. Then I accepted reluctantly that it was not going to happen, but I
> constantly revisited what went wrong with what happened. And I would say that
> it's only been in the last three or four years ... that I can talk about it a little more
> dispassionately and detached. (New Democratic Party)

Losing an election can have a tremendous impact on the politician's ego and sense
of self. Many hours are devoted to working for the public, and in the process the
politician ends up making a number of sacrifices, not the least of which involves
family. As 60- to 80- hour workweeks are common, the individual's identity becomes
reflexively linked to his or her work.

   Although there are substantial sacrifices made during the political career, the vast
majority of ex-politicians interviewed indicated that, if given the opportunity, they
would return to political life. David Docherty's data substantiate this observation.
His survey on former Members of Parliament contains some excellent data on the
challenges facing the latter when they try re-entering the non-political world. See his
article, "To Run or Not to Run: A Survey of Former Parliamentarians," 2001,*Canadian
Parliamentary Review*, 24(1), 16–23. Steve Paikin's *The Life* (2001) offers some excellent
insights into the seductive qualities of political life. His focus, however, is not centred
on how politicians respond to electoral defeat.

   While becoming involved in politics can take many years, the departure from
political life is often swift and without remorse. The suddenness of defeat and
loss of public attention has an abrupt and direct impact on the politician's identity.
Political ideals of caring and making a difference are inexorably sidelined and the
now ex-politician is forced to deal with his or her new reality and compulsory

---

Box 19.1: Past Rivals Join Forces to Get Over Defeats

Bob Rae and David Peterson really didn't get along, especially after Mr. Rae defeated Mr. Peterson in the 1990 election. But time heals, at least some of the wounds, and when the two former Ontario premiers were reunited at a Sudbury fundraiser a couple of years ago, they got to reminiscing over a coffee urn.

Each discovered the other had been devastated by his election defeat ... As the former premiers longingly eyed the butter tarts, both discovered they had dealt with the defeat in the same way: They ate, gaining 20 pounds in weeks.

Most of us cannot comprehend how it feels to lose an election. Despite four years of earnest work in the legislature and constituency, and weeks of 18-hour days campaigning, you are told in the presence of your family, friends, and supporters that the voters have decided your services are no longer required. It's a terrible way to be fired.

And often, defeated politicians quickly and painfully discover that their public life has harmed, not helped, their careers. A recurring theme among defeated backbenchers is that they're having trouble finding jobs, that they gave up four or more peak earning years, their company pensions, their old career, only to discover the taint of having been a politician—a defeated one at that—makes employers wary about taking them on.

This is why a group of former Ontario MPPs is hoping to create an association of retired members ... aimed at exploiting talents of former parliamentarians, while providing recently defeated politicians with advice and support.

Source: From "Past rivals join forces to get over defeats," by J. Ibbitson, November 19, 1999, *The Globe and Mail*, p. A7.

---

identity change. In the process, the individual develops coping strategies to come to terms with the loss and the **stigma** of political defeat.

Sociological research enjoys a rich tradition detailing how persons assume social identities and become transformed in the process (Becker, Geer, Hughes, & Strauss, 1961; Kleinman, 1984; Olesen & Whittaker, 1968). Less well attended to are generic processes of disengagement or disinvolvement from previous identities that have been central to the person's life (Prus, 1997; Shaffir, 1997). Typically, we are less informed about the dynamics surrounding career terminations than about processes of entry and commitment-generating activities to sustain and reinforce involvements. Considerably more studies focus on how individuals become prostitutes, politicians, or priests than how individuals' ties with such occupations are severed and the related rationalizations accompanying the change. To be sure, there are some notable exceptions (Ebaugh, 1988; Vaughan, 1986). Charting the process of subcultural involvements, Prus (1997) observes that whereas disengagement may, in some instances, be distinct from involvement and continuity, the intertwining, including eventual re-involvement, may be very close in others, and suggests that research should attend to the interlinkages and the fluidity of the sequences. Conceptualized as a process, disengagement typically involves a transformation—a distancing from a previous situation and identity, the construction of a new self, and attending to changing responses from those familiar with the individual in his or her previous status.

The study of politicians compelled to exit public office owing to political defeat at the polls offers a substantive instance of disengagement, and has yet to be the focus of sociological investigation. This involuntary disengagement may be fruitfully conceptualized along the dimensions of **status passage** outlined by Glaser and Straus (1971). Perhaps the singular component of this passage requiring underscoring is its public nature: It occurs in full view of the electorate, and even with the most sophisticated tactics at one's disposal, it cannot be disguised or concealed, thereby making it difficult to manage. Undoubtedly, parallels exist between politicians' experiences and other discreditations and degradations occurring in public, such as religious excommunication proceedings, divorces of public figures, professional athletes and coaches who are fired or retired, or high-profile businesspersons who are dismissed.

This chapter examines several means of coping adopted by defeated parliamentarians to manage their unexpected loss. We consider how they deflect responsibility for the defeat towards circumstances and events that were, they attest,

---

Box 19.2

Becoming an ex-politician can be conceptualized as a status passage. In addition to the more usual dimensions of status passage identified in the literature, Barney Glaser and Anselm Strauss (1971) indicate additional properties that can be absent or present in some degree in some types of status passage, and that may be relevant to ex-politicians: (1) its desirability and reversibility, (2) whether it is experienced alone or collectively, (3) whether it is undertaken voluntarily, (4) the degree of control that the individual has over various aspects of the passage, (5) the clarity of the signs of the passage and whether these may be disguised by various parties, and (6) the passage's centrality to the person. In a personal communication, Robert Prus emphasizes the generic nature of the exiting process and highlights numbers of examples where this occurs in everyday life that we have incorporated into the conclusion. Comparable research on the retirement process of high-performance and elite-level athletes (Sinclair, 1990; Werthner-Bales, 1985) provides a good example of the types of generic issues that individuals encounter, interpret, and attempt to resolve during and after the exiting process. Having been a nation's "media darlings" during times of great achievement, the choice or lack thereof to retire is one that becomes particularly difficult as athletes discontinue the activities that once defined their public identities. The process becomes all the more problematic when they feel powerless in the decision to sustain their athletic careers.

beyond their control. However, the data also indicate that, overwhelmed by the enormity of the loss—their ego having been publicly assaulted and bruised—not an inconsiderable number analogize the feelings experienced to death. We begin by examining this aspect of the defeat, and then turn to some commonly employed **techniques of neutralization**.

The data for this chapter derive mainly from a series of some 60 informal interviews conducted between 1999 and 2003 with former provincial and federal Members of Parliament in Canada. Reflecting the gender composition of the legislatures, the vast majority of conversations were with males, and in all cases attempts were made to meet with spouses and also children. Respondents represented the Conservative, Liberal, and New Democratic parties. The conversations were tape recorded, transcribed in their entirety, and occurred in a variety of venues including offices, hotel lobbies, homes, coffee shops, and restaurants.

THE TRAUMA OF DEFEAT, THE IMAGERY OF DEATH

Defeated politicians recall numerous instances where family-related activities were sacrificed to the demands of political office; for example, missed ballet recitals and hockey games, or family trips and vacations that could not be planned in advance or were suddenly postponed or even cancelled. For some, political life contributes to the dissolution of their marriage. From their perspective, the adverse effect on family is connected to the enormously long hours required for their work, much of which removes them from the family setting for lengthy periods.

Political life, however, is also exhilarating. Immersed within its subculture, politicians readily believe that they are effecting positive change. As they are socialized into this social world, they also become convinced that they are becoming better at doing their work. As uncertainty and confusion are replaced with confidence and determination, the label of politician becomes a **master status** (Hughes, 1945). Having committed themselves so completely to their political career, its termination—typically unexpected, sudden, and enacted publicly—is nothing less than shocking and, for many, utterly devastating. It is within this context that defeat at the polls is experienced as death.

Resonating with the vast majority of those interviewed, the metaphor of death best captures the profound disappointment they experience following defeat. "It's like the phases of death. You have loss, anger, sadness, and then you come to accept it," says a defeated Liberal. This individual offers a more graphic description: "It's as sudden as death. The only thing you don't go through is that you don't have to walk into a funeral home and peek into the box and say, 'Well, he was a nice guy'"(Liberal).

The analogy to death is meant to focus on the enormous regret occasioned by the loss. Political resurrection is not entirely uncommon, but its immediacy precludes any realistic long-term perspective imagining an eventual return to the political arena. Instead, the loss is viewed as the snuffing out of a promising political career with its projected achievements and successes. Quite often, the trauma of the experience is magnified owing to the all-possessing nature of political life: "...

because you invest so much of your life into this. You become preoccupied. You live and breathe this thing. It's part of your being. So when it's taken away, and you feel prematurely, of course there's disappointment. Intellectually I understand I shouldn't take it personally. Intellectually I think I can be objective, but it's hard not to [take it personally]" (Progressive Conservative).

Although some defeated members claim to have anticipated their defeat, particularly during the campaign's latter stages, it, nonetheless, constitutes a severe blow to their ego both because it occurs in public and they believe they deserved better. They are surprised and unprepared for its impact. Defeat represents rejection at its extreme: "You didn't get fired by one person, you got fired by 6,000," remarks a defeated NDP member. Embarrassed and upset by the defeat, it is not unusual for them to withdraw, as revealed in the following:

> I can imagine that some people were devastated and didn't want to go out, didn't want to go to a funeral, didn't want to go to a wedding, didn't want to go to a baptism, didn't want to go to a confirmation, didn't want to go to church. Didn't want to do a lot of things (Liberal).
>
> I thought I had come through it fairly well. When I woke up one day about a year and a half later, I realized that I had not responded to a single telephone call from Manitoba in those 18 months. I couldn't do it (New Democratic Party).
>
> [P]eople crawl into shells. They don't want to peak their head out because they think the public has turned them down. And that destroys their self-esteem (New Democratic Party).

It is not surprising, therefore, that in reflecting upon the defeat, defeated parliamentarians refer to periods of grieving and mourning that, in some cases, endured for periods of several months and even longer. As the Clerk of a provincial legislature remarks: "It's a loss so there's a grieving process and some people handle that better than others. People grieve in various ways and that's a reaction people have to being defeated." And a former provincial parliamentarian admits: "Ya, it's like a death. For some people there's a long mourning period." Referring to a colleague's defeat one year earlier, he adds: "I don't think that he's over it."

The mourning is not confined to the defeated politician alone, but may extend to family members and staff who also experience the accompanying disappointment and sadness:

> There was mourning, definitely. I mourned, my husband did. The next morning he woke up early to go and pick up the signs and he said that he was crying the whole time. He was very angry, angrier than I that the electorate wasn't loyal. It was very sad (Liberal).
>
> Many feel a sense of real disappointment, but Jenny (a work associate) said it very many times: "It's just like a death." Jenny and I worked extremely well together and that's why she felt this sense of loss (Liberal).

Staff and volunteers do not emerge unscathed from the defeat. Their loss is not easily ignored and the defeated member may feel some measure of responsibility for their new-found predicament. "There's a funny thing that happened the day of the election. I felt really bad for my people, not for me," a defeated Liberal member reminisces. Another defeated parliamentarian, a Progressive Conservative, observes: "I think of the concentrated time you put in and you also have a number of other people spending this kind of time for you too. And you have to feel a little bit responsible for what happened, not just for yourself but for the others who are involved." Along this line, another reflects: "I felt I owed a lot to the people who had volunteered to work for me as volunteers ... I had won every time ... So, for me, it was a taste of failure that I hadn't been used to. For a number of months, I felt really guilty about having let people down" (Liberal).

The imagery of death rings true for yet another reason. The defeat generates a series of sympathetic telephone calls and visits from family members, friends, and constituents offering words of solace and comfort. The spouse of a defeated Progressive Conservative member observes: "After the election, there's a period where we're still around for a little bit. The phone would ring, people would be leaving messages: 'Sorry about this.' People would be leaving e-mail messages: 'Sorry about this.' I remember taking one phone call, it was our minister and he wanted to offer his condolences. Like people wouldn't know what to say to us, or me. You're on the street, and people wouldn't know what to say. I'd say: 'It's okay, we're fine, we're okay with it.' I had to reassure them that we were okay with it. If anything, it was the others that weren't."

Intending to comfort, they are, instead, reminders of the bitter loss: "The last thing I wanted," recalls a defeated Liberal, "was for people to drop by and tell me what kind of great guy I was, and how they couldn't believe it happened."

Hoping to be on the winning side of the electoral contest, defeat, then, is a blow to their self-esteem. Attempting not to personalize the loss, the task before them is more challenging than expected. The defeat occurs in public for all to witness. Much like the stigmatized deviant who is suddenly shut out from social circles, the individual is no longer embraced and accorded special status but experiences rejection and isolation instead: "One of the things that struck me, but I expected it, I was half-ready for this, is that you just stop getting phone calls. You stop getting invitations to go places, people stop wanting to meet with you. [S]uddenly you're past tense. You don't exist anymore ... but that could be devastating, it really could. It's almost as though you were a social reject. It's the story of winners and losers. If you win, you're fine; if you lose, you lose. And then I could see somebody say: 'Well, why should I pay special attention to him. He's just another bloke like I am ...'"(Liberal).

As incapacitating as the defeat may be, the defeated member must make sense of it. Feelings of grief and rejection are not experienced to the exclusion of other emotions and thoughts helping to make the loss more understandable and palatable. In time, and with the assistance of others, a series of explanations for the loss— rationalizations—are embraced, serving to reduce the individual's culpability.

THE DISAVOWAL OF RESPONSIBILITY

To cope with their loss, defeated politicians develop a **vocabulary of motives** (Mills, 1940)—rationalizations and accounts (Scott & Lyman, 1968) to explain their situation. In particular, they engage in claiming a denial of responsibility that, according to Sykes and Matza (1957), is a type of rationalization that people use to redirect responsibility for the outcome of an event, which may have been influenced by one's actions, onto some external force beyond their influence. In the process the individual attempts to save face and deflect feelings of guilt or shame.

We now turn to the types of accounts employed by the defeated politicians to assuage their bruised egos. In short, they rely upon a variety of rationalizations that, whether recognized or not, serve to deflect responsibility for the outcome. Presented as justifications for the defeat, they situate the outcome of the election as being outside of their control.

The Party and the Leader

Attempting to come to terms with their loss, defeated politicians point to a number of external factors, not the least of which is their political party. Some rationalize that it was simply because they were affiliated with a particular party that led to their defeat. In terms of party dynamics, they may also blame their loss on their leader, the organization of the party, unpopular political decisions, or the calling of an election at an inopportune time. In this way, when the entire party is "swept" during an election, it supports the sentiment that the defeat was the result of the party platform or leadership issues rather than anything the politician could control or be responsible for. In the process, they distance themselves from responsibility for the loss and attempt to shield themselves from the negative repercussions accompanying the political defeat. For example:

> I think my government at the time caused its own defeat. Okay. So when we had the election and I lost, I was sort of a little more upset with my government than I was with anybody else, including myself (New Democratic Party).
>
> I expected to lose because people were angry with the NDP, they weren't angry with me personally. But hey, like you live and die with the party in this system. It's a parliamentary system ... (New Democratic Party).

In looking at party dynamics to explain their defeat, some politicians argue that the party did not have a sufficiently sound infrastructure in place to support its members. For instance, some maintain that proper educational mechanisms for maintaining constituency organizations were unavailable. In comparing their party to other parties during the election campaign, the competition, in their view, was better organized, thereby disadvantaging them in their quest for victory. For example:

> Some of the blame goes to the Liberal party of Manitoba because during the two-year period they did not educate us, as MLAs, as to how we can build

a constituency organization that would sustain itself ... Take a look at the Conservatives in our area. They have a constituency and one phone call and everybody's there. The NDP is the same ... (Liberal).

Tied to the issue of party organization is a belief that the party leader can either make or break one's own political campaign. Therefore, in an attempt to distance oneself from the defeat, these politicians also look to place some of the blame on the leader of their party. Cues from the public often supply the defeated member with the necessary ammunition to redirect the blame for the loss in this manner:

To be honest with you, I blame the loss only on one person, and that was our leader ... Number one, people were telling me on the street that Shirley was no longer the leader they thought she was. Number two, she doesn't have the ability to lead. Number three, Phil, we like you, we admire you, you got a lot of chutzpah, but not your leader. Not your leader (Liberal).

So what was more disturbing is that when you got the negative stuff, none of it was directed at me. It was all because I was part of Ericson's team. So while that contributed immensely to me winning in 1995, it dragged me down in 1999 (Progressive Conservative).

The Policy
Decisions that directly impact on the public, such as taxation, public spending, and legislation, can have a tremendous influence on how the party is seen as a whole. If these decisions do not sit well with the public, the belief is that there is nothing any one politician can do to overcome these impediments to re-election. Remarks a defeated politician: "What happens here, it's the death of a thousand paper cuts; it's the toll highway, it's the nursing home, hospitals, it's the policing" (Liberal). As the following example indicates, defeated members tend to identify unpopular decisions and policies as significant components contributing to their defeat: "I knew we were going down. I mean the timing was bad. We put in a really nasty budget, you know, raising taxes and all that. Normally in a four-year mandate, you do your bad stuff in the early part. So we had done the bad stuff and we're running on the bad stuff, right. Aside from that, we had raised rates in the auto insurance and people were just going nuts about that" (New Democratic Party).

Timing of the Election
In the eyes of politicians, the timing of an election is a crucial factor affecting their chances for re-election. In order to understand their defeat, some ex-politicians rationalize that the government chose a poor time to call an election; for example, the economic climate was not conducive to winning the election, or that key elements of the electorate, for one reason or another, were simply unavailable to support the candidate.

Politicians rationalize that there are situational factors such as recessions and public service crises that create a political atmosphere that is not conducive to re-election. In the following example, a defeated member situates these unanticipated developments in the "bad luck" category: "We had some very bad luck. I lost by 100 votes, which is 50 votes really. Here's what happened the week before the election. Ten thousand people without a doctor in St. John. Major crisis ... X-ray technicians are on strike. 'Tom, if you can't do something about this I'm not going to vote for you.' This is two or three days ahead [of the election]. Then a strike on the day of the election" (Liberal).

The next example illustrates how the timing for the election can hamper a member's chances to win. The individual in question develops a detailed rationalization, which outlines how his regular supporters were not around when the election was called: "You have to remember that a lot of our people in our area are seniors. They go to the beaches. They don't stay around. Only the younger people stay. And those are the younger people who voted and they voted ... for the Conservatives. So I got my butt kicked. Had my senior population stayed, I probably would have given a good run for the money or I might have even won. But that wasn't to be" (Liberal).

By developing a rationalization that situates blame on a variety of seemingly external factors, the defeated politician is offered a more convincing justification as to why he or she was unsuccessful. At the same time, it allows for face saving to deal with negative feelings experienced as the result of the defeat.

The Media
There is a strong consensus among defeated politicians that negative publicity can have an extremely detrimental impact on one's chances for re-election. Note the following observations:

> So no matter how good you are, it doesn't matter. It matters what they're saying on the front page and the editorial page, and they haven't changed their tune one iota over the last three years (Liberal).
>
> I think the media really turned negatively towards us as we started going for that re-election. They didn't want to hear what we had to say, distorted my words, and took them out of context. It was as if they created the stories in advance and were waiting for you to say something to reinforce their story that was already there (New Democratic Party).

Whether the coverage is directed towards the party as a whole or focused on a particular politician, the outcome in terms of one's chances for re-election are significantly impaired. More often than not, the ex-politician believes that the media provides inaccurate or biased coverage of issues that frame the politician or the party in a negative light. For example, ex-politicians may reason that a particular newspaper publisher had a vendetta against the party or that the paper was simply trying to bolster sales by writing a provocative smear campaign involving the politician or the party. Based on this type of reasoning they are able to formulate a further rationalization that situates blame for political defeat on the media.

In the following example, a former east coast MPP argues that his chances for re-election were hindered by erroneous media coverage of a particular project the party had completed: "But I felt the year leading into the election, the media had turned on us. The Moncton paper was vicious, and unjustifiably vicious. One of them was the park we built ... wonderful deal, worked out well, [but] the paper crucified us there" (Liberal).

As some politicians indicate, one can use the harshness and extent of negative media attention to judge how they might fare in an upcoming election. By being able to judge one's chances for re-election through the media, the ex-politician is provided with the opportunity to brace himself or herself for possible defeat.

Personal Health Issues

In discussing one's personal health and the impact it had on attempts to secure re-election, rationalizations take on a somewhat different focus. Rather than placing the blame on a factor far beyond the individual, some defeated members rationalize the defeat in terms of a very personal factor—their own well-being. While placing the responsibility for defeat more directly on oneself, by attributing the loss to issues relating to personal health, the ex-politician is able to displace blame onto an illness, something that they, given the nature of the illness or their job, could not control. For example: "For a number of months, I felt really guilty about having let people down. If only I hadn't been sick. I don't think there's any doubt that had I not been ill, I would have been able to get out. What are we talking about? A couple of hundred votes. It doesn't take much effort to swing a couple of hundred votes if you can get out there" (Progressive Conservative).

By rationalizing defeat as the result of personal health, defeated politicians are able to also frame their defeat in a positive light. As the following example illustrates, political defeat is sometimes viewed as the best medicine for the stress-induced illnesses that become associated with a career in politics. Very powerful personal examples are also offered as possible benefits of having lost an election due to health concerns: "Another term like that in government would have killed me. It truly would have, I worked that hard and I was just wasted so the defeat, when it came about, was a good thing because I was able to become my wife's number one caregiver. She passed away on December 24 of the same year, having been diagnosed with lung cancer. She wasn't well in September and then October came the diagnosis and December came the death" (Progressive Conservative).

CONCLUSION

This chapter has examined how politicians deploy deflection rhetoric to claim that circumstances beyond their control resulted in an undesired outcome—their defeat at the electoral polls. Face-saving efforts allow for the preservation of a credible self-image. Despite the rhetoric, the loss is deeply felt and an imagery of death is used to describe its impact. Data from the larger project indicate the defeat is not infrequently accompanied by a stigma that attaches to former parliamentarians and impacts on their efforts to secure gainful employment.

Box 19.3

Most of us in today's world are exes in one way or another. We have exited a marriage, a career, a religious group, a meaningful voluntary organization, an institutional way of life, or perhaps a stigmatized role such as alcoholic or drug user. For some types of role exit society has coined a term to denote exiters: divorce, retiree, recovered alcoholic, widow, alumnus. This is usually the case for exits that are common and have been occurring for a long time. Exits that have been around long enough to have been named are usually institutionalized in that they carry with them certain expectations, privileges, and status. In addition to these institutionalized exits, however, there are numerous exits that are simply referred to with the prefix, "ex": ex-doctor, ex-executive, ex-nun, ex-convict, ex-cult member, ex-athlete. The one thing all exes have in common is that they once identified with a social role which they no longer have ... The process of disengagement from a role that is central to one's self-identity and the reestablishment of an identity in a new role that takes into account one's ex-role constitutes the process I call role exit. While at first glance there may seem to be little in common between ex-nuns and transsexuals, ex-doctors and ex-convicts, or divorced people and ex-air traffic controllers, they have all experienced role exit.

Source: From *Becoming an EX: The Process of Role Exit* (p. 1), by H.R. Fuchs Ebaugh, 1988, Chicago: University of Chicago Press.

Feelings of anger, diminished self-esteem, and depression are not unique to defeated politicians. Whenever people's primary identity is severed from their sense of self, they are likely to experience a transition period wrought with external attributions of blame and feelings of self-deprecation. The experience is likely to be more traumatizing for those that involuntarily relinquish their former identity. For students, this may involve failing out of school; for workers, being fired from the job; for professional athletes, being injured or not making the team; for a bride or groom to be, being left at the alter. Indeed, the situations are limited only by the number of significant roles with which we identify.

Researchers should examine not only processes of identity construction, as commonly found in the discipline, but also processes of "un-becoming," or separating from an established identity. Ex-politicians, suddenly severed from their cherished status, serve as a case in point.

GLOSSARY

Master status: A status that is so central to an individual's identity that it overshadows all other statuses he or she may have.

Status passage: The transition of one's social position as he or she enters into and exits out of different substantive involvements (e.g., politics, sports, academia) and becomes identified with these areas.

Stigma: A discrediting social attribute that affects an individual or group's identity.

Techniques of neutralization: Ways of justifying a behaviour and counteracting feelings of guilt associated with the behaviour. Sykes and Matza (1957) identified five techniques, including denying responsibility, denying that injury has occurred, blaming the victim, and condemning those who condemn the behaviour.

Vocabulary of motives: Rationalizations and accounts to explain or justify one's situation or actions.

REFERENCES

Becker, H.S., Geer, B., Hughes, E.C., & Strauss, A.L. (1961). *Boys in white: Student culture in medical school*. Chicago: University of Chicago Press.

Docherty, D. (2001). To run or not to run: A survey of former parliamentarians. *Canadian Parliamentary Review, 24*(1), 16–23.

Ebaugh, H.R.F. (1988). *Becoming an ex: The process of role exit*. Chicago: University of Chicago Press.

Glaser, B.G., & Strauss, A.L. (1971). *Status passage*. Chicago: Aldine Atherton.

Hertz, R. (1997). *Reflexivity and voice*. Thousand Oaks, CA: Sage.

Hughes, E. (1945). Dilemmas and contradictions of status. *American Journal of Sociology, 50*, 353–359.

Ibbitson, J. (1999, November 19). Past rivals join forces to get over defeats. *The Globe and Mail*, p. A7.

Kleinman, S. (1984). *Equals before God: Seminarians as humanistic professionals*. Chicago: University of Chicago Press.

Mills, C.W. (1940). Situated actions and vocabularies of motives. *American Sociological Review, 5*, 904–913.

Olesen, V.L., & Whittaker, E.W. (1968). *The silent dialogue: A study in the social psychology of professional socialization*. San Francisco: Jossey Bass.

Paikin, S. (2001). *The life: The seductive call of politics*. Toronto: Penguin.

Prus, R. (1997). *Subcultural mosaics and intersubjective realities: An ethnographic research agenda for pragmatizing the social sciences*. Albany, NY: SUNY Press.

Richardson, L. (1990). *Writing: Reaching diverse audiences*. Thousand Oaks, CA: Sage.

Richardson, L. (1994). Writing: A method of inquiry. In N. Denzin & Y. Lincoln (Eds.), *Handbook of qualitative research* (pp. 923–949). Thousand Oaks, CA: Sage.

Scott, M., & Lyman, S. (1968). Accounts. *American Sociological Review, 33*, 46–62.

Shaffir, W. (1997). Disaffiliation: The experiences of Haredi Jews. In W. Shaffir & M. Bar-Lev (Eds.), *Leaving religion and religious life* (pp. 205–228). Greenwich, CT: JAI Press.

Sinclair, D.A. (1990). *The dynamics of transition from high performance sport*. Unpublished doctoral dissertation, University of Ottawa, Ottawa, Ontario.

Sykes, G.M., & Matza, D. (1957). Techniques of neutralization: A theory of delinquency. *American Sociological Review, 22*(December), 664–670.

Vaughan, D. (1986). *Uncoupling: Turning points in intimate relationships*. New York: Oxford.

Werthner-Bales, P.C. (1985). *Retirement experiences of Canada's successful elite amateur athletes: An exploratory study*. Unpublished master's thesis, University of Ottawa, Ottawa, Ontario.

ACKNOWLEDGEMENTS

This project was supported by a generous grant from the Social Sciences and Humanities Research Council of Canada.

Chapter 20

Avoiding the *Other*:
A Technique of Stigma Management among People Who Use Alternative Therapies[1]

Jacqueline Low

INTRODUCTION

Participation in alternative and/or complementary therapies continues to be a popular form of health-seeking behaviour in Canada. Even 10 years ago a sizeable number of Canadians used these types of health care (see Box 20.1), and today, upwards of 73% of Canadians include them among their health care strategies (Ramsey, Walker, & Alexander, 1999).

However, despite the widespread use of these therapies in the West (Eisenberg et al., 1998; Fulder, 1996; Health Canada, 2001), people who use them are often

---

Box 20.1: One in Five Canadians Using Alternative Therapies

A recent study by the *Canadian Health Monitor* revealed that 20% of Canadians had used some form of alternative health therapy in the 6 months before they were surveyed, compared with 25% who used services provided by conventional medical practitioners. The most popular alternative therapy was chiropractic services—approximately 9% of Canadians had visited a chiropractor in the 6 months preceding the survey—and another 6% had sought advice at a health food store. No other alternative therapy was used by more than 1% of the population. Use of alternative health care services was lowest in Atlantic provinces (13%), and usage in other areas ranged from 19% to 22%.

The survey found that 55% of respondents used alternative services in response to a specific health condition, while the remainder used them as part of the overall management of their health. It appears that Canadians are using alternative services in conjunction with conventional ones because people with a family doctor and those who had had a medical checkup in the past year were more likely to use alternative therapies.

Source: From "One in Five Canadians Using Alternative Therapies, Study Finds," 1991, *Canadian Medical Association Journal, 144*, p. 469.

---

labelled deviant. This raises the question of how people cope with the stigma they incur through their use of alternative/complementary forms of health care. The findings I present in addressing this issue emerged out of a qualitative study of the experiences of individuals with Parkinson's disease, living in the United Kingdom (UK), who participate in alternative/complementary forms of health care (Low, 2001).[2] Notwithstanding the continued popularity of alternative/complementary therapies, and their greater acceptance in the UK relative to North America, almost all of the people who spoke with me described instances of stigmatization they had experienced through their use of these therapies. One method of managing stigma used by these informants was to distance themselves from what they define as the *other* in accounting for their participation in alternative/complementary health care. By conceiving of some types of alternative/complementary therapies as *other*, and therefore deviant, they are able to normalize their health-seeking behaviour.

METHODOLOGY

I collected data for this study via semi-structured interviews with 14 informants I recruited through the Leicestershire Branch of the UK Parkinson's Disease Society (see Table 20.1). Informant demographic characteristics are reflective of not only the membership of the Parkinson's Disease Society, but also, with the exception of age, reflective of what we know about the general patterns of usership of alternative/

Table 20.1: Informant Demographic Characteristics

Characteristic	No.
Sex	
Male	7
Female	7
Age	
40–49	2
50–59	6
60–70	6
Class	
Working	1
Middle	11
Upper-Middle	1
N/A	1
Ethnic Category	
White	12
Asian	1
Afro-Caribbean	1

complementary therapies in Europe and North America (Eisenberg et al., 1998; Fulder, 1996; Ramsey et al., 1999). That this age distribution reflects a higher rate of usership of alternative/complementary therapies among older age groups than that found in the general population in the UK is partly explained by the popularity of alternative/complementary therapies as a means of coping with chronic illnesses and disability (Fulder, 1996; Sharma, 1992). I analyzed the data collected in this research by means of the grounded theory technique of comparative coding, whereby emergent concepts guide the focus of research (Corbin & Strauss, 1990). The theoretical perspective that informs my analysis is symbolic interactionism, where emphasis is on the meaning people give to significant symbols and how those meanings guide their actions (Blumer, 1969).

ALTERNATIVE/COMPLEMENTARY THERAPY USE AS DEVIANT BEHAVIOUR

The language used in the literature to describe alternative/complementary therapies has been and remains largely derogatory. For example, consistently and over time, alternative therapies have been styled unconventional, non-conventional, unorthodox (Dunfield, 1991); unscientific, unproven (Feigen & Tiver, 1986); "fuzzy stuff" (Monson, 1995, p. 170); or "deviant forms of health service" (Cassee, 1970, p. 391). One extreme example concerns Leech's (1999, p. 1) pronouncement that alternative therapies are "snake oil [that] belongs in the last century, not this or the next." Even when authors attempt neutrality through the use of such terms as *complementary therapy* and/or *medicine*, they still imply a slur against alternative/complementary approaches when they refer to **allopathy** as conventional or orthodox medicine. For example, while she uses the term *alternative medicine*, Monson (1995, p. 168) refers to allopathic health care as "proper orthodox medicine," implying that alternative therapies are unorthodox and improper. That allopathy is assumed by many to be legitimate, normative health care, and that alternative therapies are not, is something of which the people who took part in this research are well aware. For example, in telling me about her decision to continue using alternative/complementary therapies in the face of her consultant's disapproval, Billie said:

> The only thing, you always have that fear that if you try something and you get into deep water, who is going to get you out of it? And if you go and say to your specialist: 'I've done such and such a thing' does he turn round and say: 'Well you've only got you to blame.'

However, there is more to the deviant identity acquired through the use of these therapies than merely the "courtesy stigma" derived from participation in marginalized forms of health care (Goffman, 1963, p. 30; Saks, 1995). People who use alternative/complementary approaches to healing are seen as deviant in their own right. Their designation as deviant is less surprising in dated examples from the literature. For instance, over 40 years ago, Cobb (1958, p. 283) asserted that "there are four categories of patients who seek nonmedical treatment. There are the miracle seekers, the uninformed, the restless ones, and the straw graspers." Yet, the labelling of alternative/complementary therapy use as deviant behaviour has continued over time. For example, Northcott (1994, p. 498) restates Cobb's depiction of the user of alternative therapies in suggesting that these people may be "uneducated, ignorant, superstitious, gullible; hypochondriacs with psychosomatic problems ... motivated by fear [or] grasping at straws." Further, eight years after, Murray and Shepherd (1993, p. 987) cite Furnham and Smith's (1988) contention that people who use alternative therapies are to be found among the chronically disturbed, citing the "relatively high frequency of psycho-social problems and affective disorders" diagnosed among the users of alternative therapies. Finally, while Moore, Phipps, and Marcer (1985, p. 28) assert that the people they studied are not "cranks," the implication is that they are not cranks because they haven't "lost faith in conventional medicine," not because there is nothing deviant about being a user of alternative/complementary therapies.

Despite the continued popularity of these therapies, as well as Sharma's (1993, p. 15) pronouncement that "it will not be long before the term 'alternative'—with its connotations of ... deviant activity will no longer be appropriate," and the fact that alternative/complementary therapy use in the UK has a longer history of acceptance relative to that in North America, almost all of the people who participated in this study have been labelled deviant for their use of these types of health care. These informants all had anecdotes to tell about how friends, family, and health care professionals had reacted negatively to disclosures of their participation in alternative/complementary therapies. Verity put it this way: "[They're] very skeptical. I know sometimes when I'm trying to explain to people what [my therapist] does, I think the shutters come down and they're thinking clap trap." Megan's husband's reaction was also one of skepticism and characterizes the users of alternative/complementary health care as dupes vulnerable to exploitation by charlatans. In Megan's words: "my partner's the biggest cynic. The out and out skeptic ... He believes that a lot of people are making a lot of money out of people exploring things like I was."

Many medical professionals hold similar beliefs, seeing the users of alternative/ complementary therapies as "easily misled by false claims for unproven remedies" (Yates et al., 1993, p. 214). For instance, some of the people who spoke with me told me of instances where their physicians attempted to dissuade them from using alternative/complementary therapies by calling into question the efficacy of these forms of health care. For example, Ian said: "Well it seemed like 'this is the health service; this is the proprietary medicines that we deal with. This is herbal medicine, we've never been to that land at all,' and they don't really want to know, almost. The only thing he did say, last time I went, was that: 'No, it won't be any help, you save yourself so much money.' He didn't say: 'Look, there's been tests on it, and it's not been proven.' He just dismissed it."

Others characterized the reactions of their health care professionals as polite or abrupt expressions of disinterest. For instance, Oscar described his consultant's reaction to his use of Chinese wand in the following way: "Well, politeness really more than anything else." Eva said: "I mentioned having alternative [therapies], to the Parkinson nurse, but she didn't seem too impressed." Likewise, David said: "Both the local doctor and at the hospital as well, the neurologist there [said:] 'Hum,' just that, they said: 'Hum.'" In fact, only two informants reported active support and approval from their doctors concerning their use of alternative/complementary therapies. For example, Tracey said:

> He's in full agreement with them. He said: 'Anything that helps, it certainly won't do any harm.' It's the same with herbal remedies and sleeplessness. He said: 'You try them, if they don't do any good, they won't do you any harm.' He's got no objections to my trying them out. And he knows about **Reiki** and he's all for it. He knows I go to yoga, and he's in complete agreement with that. I think he thinks yoga certainly works. He's not very familiar with reiki at all, he's heard of it, but that's about it. So, yes, I mean I think he's both, he's supportive and he's aware of the benefits that you can get from them. *He's very good actually*, he's receptive to all sorts of things, all sorts of therapies [emphasis mine].

However, that Tracey praises her doctor for being good about alternative/complementary therapies suggests that physician approval of these forms of health care remains the exception rather than the rule. Finally, it should be noted that the instance and frequency of the labelling of these informants as deviant is shaped by the particular social context in which the interaction takes place. For instance, in describing his use of massage and *Ayurvedic* medicine, Raj, who is Asian, said: "I think it's alternative because these people [in the UK] don't believe in it."

MANAGING THE STIGMA OF ALTERNATIVE/COMPLEMENTARY THERAPY USE

Most of the people who spoke with me live with the "discreditable" identities they acquire through their use of alternative/complementary forms of health care, deviant identities that they then must manage (Goffman, 1963, p. 4). According to Goffman (1963), the difference between discredited and discreditable identities is that the latter identity depends on the degree to which individuals are able to reduce stigma by controlling disclosure of their deviant identities. In Goffman's (p. 42) classic phrasing, "to display or not to display; to tell or not to tell; to let on or not to let on; to lie or not to lie; and in each case, to whom, how, when, and where." For this reason, people who use alternative/complementary health care often make efforts to conceal their use of these therapies from others, especially doctors (Ramsay et al., 1999). Likewise, several of the people who participated in this research do not discuss their use of alternative/complimentary therapies with their physicians. According to Verity: "I'd never really consulted my consultants with any of this because you don't really want to have anything to do with them, having them look at you sideways." Other informants expressed concern regarding disclosure of their use of these therapies to their friends and family. Referring to her use of **kinesiology**, Verity said: "How am I going to explain all this to [my husband] when I get home?"

Managing Stigma via Avoiding the Other
In addition to coping with stigma through the ubiquitous method of managing disclosure, most of these informants managed the stigma associated with their participation in alternative/complementary therapies through conceiving of an *other* that they are then able to avoid. In other words, these people define certain therapies, certain practitioners, or certain therapeutic environments as other and therefore deviant. In doing so they are engaged in normalizing their own use of alternative/complementary therapies and thus reducing the stigma they experience as users of these forms of health care. The *others* conceived of by these informants can be grouped into three categories: The *non-medical other*, the *unprofessional other*, and the *dangerous other* (see Figure 20.1).

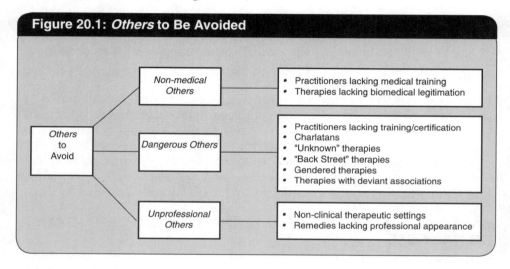

Figure 20.1: *Others* to Be Avoided

Others to Avoid

Non-medical Others
- Practitioners lacking medical training
- Therapies lacking biomedical legitimation

Dangerous Others
- Practitioners lacking training/certification
- Charlatans
- "Unknown" therapies
- "Back Street" therapies
- Gendered therapies
- Therapies with deviant associations

Unprofessional Others
- Non-clinical therapeutic settings
- Remedies lacking professional appearance

The Non-medical Other
For these informants, *non-medical others* to be avoided are simply those therapies, practitioners, or therapeutic settings they define as lacking medical legitimation. For example, Mary told me she avoids any therapy that has not received a medical seal of approval. In her words: "[My doctor] said: 'Well, I don't tell you you can't take it, but they've not been tested' and that decided me. I said: 'Oh, I won't do anything without the doctors, take any tablets or anything without the doctor saying about them, would I?' I'd have to be absolutely sure that's it's been tested, that's the main thing."

Likewise, Tracey avoided the non-medical other by using a medically trained acupuncturist. She told me: "My GP recommended that I try acupuncture, and the GP I was with then actually had a doctor who performed acupuncture, who was trained to do it." Elizabeth also sought medical approval in selecting her alternative therapist. In her words: "Well, I think a nurse knows what to look for, because there was one place she said: 'I wouldn't touch that with a barge pole.' Because it was dirty and disorganized and just like a room in somebody's house." Similarly, in explaining his initial discomfort with using Chinese wand, Oscar said: "It seemed to be something which had not been put forward by any of the authorities on this disease and it was something that just happened to be around." Finally, Billie felt uncomfortable during a Reiki treatment because her practitioner was not a medical professional. She said: "I didn't like being touched. It just felt peculiar that she wasn't a doctor who you tend to submit to."

These informants' use of the non-medical other in their designation of therapies to be avoided is reflective of this study's UK context. For instance, the process of co-option of alternative/complementary therapies is more advanced in Britain than it is in Canada and parallel systems of alternative/complementary health care exist in the UK whereby the user often has a choice between a medically trained and a non-medically trained practitioner.

The Unprofessional Other

For some of the people who spoke with me, the other to avoid in their use of alternative/complementary therapies is the *unprofessional other*. For instance, in designating aromatherapy as a fringe, and therefore suspect, therapy, David told me: "It's very, very unprofessional. You just have a feeling about it." Informants invoking the unprofessional other did so by making reference, in Goffman's (1959) dramaturgical sense, to the props and setting of the therapeutic performance. For David, it was the packaging of his aloe vera tablets that distinguished his therapy from the unprofessional other. He put it this way: "It seems to have a reasonable amount of professionalism in the packaging. It doesn't look as if it's a sort of cheap, made-in-the-back-room product." Raj and Tom focused on equipment in establishing the legitimacy of the therapeutic environment in distinguishing their therapies from the unprofessional other. For example, Raj told me: "She's got a kind of clinic in her room, which is all equipped with these special tables. She's got all that and I feel quite comfortable there." And Tom said: "He'd got the proper benches and all the equipment." For Steve, not only is appropriate equipment important, but his notion of professionalism also includes a business-like atmosphere and appearance. In his words:

> [The massage therapy] was in a fairly new block of offices ... and there was a receptionist when you went in, a nice comfortable chair to sit on. She sat at a nice desk with a telephone on it and all her notes and things like that, and it was more professional, like a business office I would think. You know your first impression when you go into a place, whether it's a business or whether it's a doctor or whatever, first impressions count and my first impression [of the acupuncturist's office] was this is a bit scruffy. I just looked around and I thought: 'This place could do with decorating you know.' So it wasn't very professional at all.

Finally, two of the informants who managed stigma through conceiving of an unprofessional other said that avoiding this other includes selecting a therapeutic setting that is clinical and/or sterile. According to Elizabeth: "It wasn't the cleanest house. Her treatment room is off the kitchen and you have to walk through the kitchen and it's piled high with dirty dishes. But she herself was okay and was very nice as a person. But the few people that I recommended to go, I said to them: 'Don't be put off by the appearances of the house' and in fact, I said: 'If you can, find another aromatherapist.'"

The Dangerous Other

The third and most popular category of other employed by the people who took part in this research is the *dangerous other*. Most often the dangerous other concerned therapies practised by therapists who are uncertified or who lack some kind of training. According to Billie: "Well, it's nice to know that they have had some training. If you go into somebody's house and they haven't any training, well, you let yourself into all sorts of things." Likewise, Raj said: "Well, I think [certificates] help, it does give you some assurance that she's not sort of just off the road somewhere." Similarly, Tracey avoided the dangerous other by seeking out therapists who had had training:

> She has all sorts of certificates on the wall indicating that she's passed various examinations, I suppose, in reflexology. And she'd also got a degree in ... I think it was something like human biology ... which indicated that she was fairly well qualified and she had various letters after her name. And I did get a list of people ... who were approved practitioners ... and her name was on it.

For some of these informants, avoiding the dangerous other was particularly important in cases of therapies that are invasive, such as acupuncture, and alternative/complementary remedies that are ingested, such as herbal and homeopathic preparations. In Tom's words: "I phoned somebody up and said: 'Could you send us a list of acupuncturists that are genuine.' She said: 'Yes' and 'This chap, he's on the register.' I thought I'd better check up first, I didn't want to go to someone that didn't know what they were talking about, just stuck pins in you."

Also within the category of the *dangerous other* are those therapies informants know little about, or those they see as esoteric. For example, avoiding the dangerous other means avoiding the "unknown." According to Megan: "There's a bit of unknown ... But beyond the ordinary sort of massage or something, I hadn't really started doing anything, particularly acupuncture. It's not exactly run of the mill. But it wasn't, I've heard of alternative/complimentary medicines, the names of which I was only just sort of starting to hear of. So it wasn't as if [acupuncture] was completely new, nobody had ever known about it, or hadn't had it done."

Additional dangerous others to be avoided are therapies based on spiritual or metaphysical philosophies. For instance, in telling me about kinesiology, Verity said: "There's nothing witchcraft about it." Later on in the interview when the discussion turned to how she determined that the practitioner she was seeing was safe, Verity began to laugh and point at candles I had on my coffee table. She went on to say: "I was going to say: 'No candles.' She was very down to earth and very, very knowledgeable. She certainly knew her subject. I'm sure if I went to, if I'd gone to the house and the curtains had been drawn and there had been candles and incense, I would have thought: 'Oh oh, this is not for me,' you know. But it was a perfectly normal house and she'd got this box full of crystals and various things."

In speaking about the dangerous other, several informants made reference to therapies they classed as "back street." For instance, David said: "I don't particularly feel inclined to try them. I'm just skeptical on aromatherapy. I used to work for a pharmaceutical company in Loughborough and you tend to go there for pills and potions more than some fringe therapies. They're still the back street." Other informants avoided the dangerous other by not consorting with those practitioners they believe are charlatans. According to Verity: "She said: 'I don't want to see you again for five months,' she said, 'unless you need to see me' because she said, 'the work we've done today ... won't come to fruition until about then.' And I thought well this woman is definitely no charlatan or she would have been having me back straight away."

A variety of social contexts such as social class, ethnic category, and health status are reflected in informants' constructions of dangerous others (see Box 20.2).

Box 20.2: Social Contexts and the *Dangerous Other*

For Elizabeth, who is White and middle class, defining something as "back street" involves her perceptions of ethnic and class status differences. For instance, one therapy she perceived to be a dangerous other involved a Chinese practitioner and a therapeutic setting in a low-income area that is home to a large Asian population. In her words:

> I did feel there that I'd gone to a bit of back street clinic really. She was Chinese and said she was a doctor but, I mean she wore a white overall and spent a long time listening to my pulse, studying my tongue. It was a dark and dingy room, you know. It had got all these bottles and all these potions. It was near East Park Road as well, the area, I thought: "Am I doing the right thing?"

Megan's association of charlatanism with the dangerous other was heightened by her status as a person living with mobility impairment. She said:

> I'm sure there are. In every other profession there are, so I don't see why there wouldn't be. Which is why it's important to check it out. So there's an element, there's always the potential for exploitation if you were involved with a charlatan, because you're very vulnerable.

For Tracey, avoiding the dangerous other meant avoiding practitioners who proselytize. For instance, in discussing her yoga instructor, Tracey told me: "But she did say: 'Keep an open mind about them until you've tried them because they don't agree with everyone.' She was very fair about it, she didn't try and push them on to you." Raj's dangerous other are those therapists whom he sees as being vulnerable to confusion with people engaged in what he feels are disreputable practices. In his words: "Well because she wasn't advertising in the newspaper columns to start with. I think in the local newspaper you've got a lot of these ads for these massage clinics and all this. When I phoned her it was nothing more than a brothel really." Finally, Oscar's dangerous other is based on gender role stereotypes. Specifically, Oscar avoids his dangerous other by eschewing those therapies he characterizes as effeminate. In the following exchange between Oscar and his wife, Oscar makes plain his belief that, in contrast to most alternative complementary therapies, Chinese wand is masculine.

> I mean with Chinese wand for a man of 70, Oscar's happy to do that. He'll do the eight strands of brocade because we finish off with it, 'it's nice.' But if I said to him, 'We'll do the eight strands of brocade every day,' it's not terribly masculine. He does it, but because it is more like Tai Chi. Chinese wand you feel is quite masculine, is that right? (Wife).
>
> That's right, yes; it's like having a golf club in your hand really (Oscar).

DISCUSSION

All but one of the people who took part in this study cope with the stigma they acquire through the use of alternative/complementary forms of health care therapies by defining an *other*, which they then avoid. The particular characteristics of the *others* invoked by these people varied from informant to informant. For example, candles and incense form part of Verity's dangerous other while gender roles are at issue for Oscar. However, it is not the presence or absence of candles that makes an alternative therapeutic setting normal for Verity; rather, it is the meaning she gives to candles and incense as props she associates with the other. What is common to each informant is the process of conceiving of an other, rather than the shape that the other takes, and it is this "generic social process" that is of theoretical import (Prus, 1997, p. xii).

Each of the categories of other invoked by these informants reflect processes in contemporary social life. For example, the category of *non-medical other* reflects the medicalization of life (Illich, 1975) and the continued co-option of alternative therapies by the medical profession. For example, in Billie's reluctance to be touched by her Reiki therapist, we see "the retention of absolute control by the medical profession over certain technical procedures," such as invading the body (Clarke, 1996, p. 238), and Tracey's selection of a medically trained acupuncturist illustrates the appropriation of alternative/complementary healing techniques by the medical profession. Both these processes reflect the continued dominance of biomedicine in all matters related to health and healing (Freidson, 1970).

The categories of *non-professional other* and *dangerous other* indicate the continued supremacy of the expert in matters of health and health care and suggests that in contrast to arguments that assert that **alternative therapy** use is symptomatic of a postmodern society, characterized by a distrust, and rejection, of professionals and experts (Lyotard, 1990), many people who use these therapies remain desirous of expertise and professionalism where their health care is concerned. Finally, the category of the dangerous other not only illustrates the continued marginal status of alternative/complementary therapies (Saks, 1995) but also reflects the "courtesy stigma" these forms of health care derive from their continued association with other practices labelled deviant, such as charlatanism and witchcraft (Goffman, 1963, p. 30).

CONCLUSION

In closing, regardless of the particular category of *other* invoked by these informants, by defining an other these informants create two categories of alternative/complementary therapies, one that contains legitimate health care strategies and another comprised of those therapies that are deviant. By avoiding those therapies and practitioners designated as other, these people are able to normalize their use of alternative/complementary therapies and thereby reduce the stigma they perceive they incur through their participation in alternative/complementary forms of health care. Moreover, there is a further practical significance to these informants' efforts at stigma management. Specifically, these people all told me of particular therapies they believe they derived a benefit from in coping with the symptoms of Parkinson's disease. To the extent that the stigma attached to alternative/complementary forms of health care presents a barrier to their use of these therapies (Low, 2001), imagining an other to avoid enables them to overcome it, thereby allowing them access to alternative/complementary therapies they believe are of benefit to them.

GLOSSARY

Allopathy: Another word for biomedicine or Western medicine.

Alternative therapy: Defined as health care "neither taught widely in medical schools nor generally available in ... hospitals" (Eisenberg et al., 1998, p. 1569). However, this type of objective definition is problematic. See Low (2004) for a detailed discussion of this issue.

Complementary therapy: Can be defined from the lay perspective as use of both alternative and allopathic health care, where one system is not seen as superior to the other (Pawluch et al., 1998). However, this is not the only available definition. See Low (2000) for a full review of the concept.

Kinesiology: A therapeutic approach that incorporates elements of healing touch, energy work, nutritional counselling, detoxification therapy, and creative visualization (Low, 2001).

Reiki: A therapy that affects healing through the transmission of universal energy (Low, 2001).

Stigma: An aspect of identity that devalues the person's social worth (Goffman, 1963).

ENDNOTES

1. Portions of this chapter have been previously published in *Using Alternative Therapies: A Qualitative Analysis*, 2004, Toronto: Canadian Scholars' Press, and in the journal *Evidence-Based Integrative Medicine*, 2003, 1(1), pp. 65–76.
2. I am grateful to the Parkinson's Disease Society and the Faculty of Health and Community Studies, De Montfort University, for their generous funding of this research. Most of all, I would like to express my thanks to the people living with Parkinson's disease who participated in the interviews. In doing so they generously gave of their time and expertise.

REFERENCES

Blumer, H. (1969). *Symbolic interactionism: Perspective and method*. Upper Saddle River: Prentice-Hall Inc.

Cassee, E. (1970). Deviant illness behaviour: Patients of mesmerists. *Social Science and Medicine, 3,* 389–396.

Clarke, J.N. (1996). *Health, illness, and medicine in Canada* (2nd ed.). Oxford: Oxford University Press.

Cobb, B. (1958). Why do people detour to quacks? In E.G. Jaco (Ed.), *Patients, physicians, and illness* (pp. 283–287). New York: The Free Press.

Corbin, J.M., & Strauss, A.L. (1990). Grounded theory research: Procedures, canons, and evaluative criteria. *Qualitative Sociology, 13*(1), 3–21.

CMAJ. (1991). One in five Canadians using alternative therapies, survey finds. *Canadian Medical Association Journal, 144*(4), 469.

Dunfield, J. (1991). Consumer perceptions of health care quality and the utilization of non-conventional therapy. *Social Science and Medicine, 43,* 149–161.

Eisenberg, D.M., Davis, R.B., Ettner, S.L., Appel, S., Wilkey, S., Van Rompay, M., et al. (1998). Trends in alternative medicine use in the United States, 1990–97: Results of a follow-up national survey. *Journal of the American Medical Association, 280*(18), 1569–1575.

Feigen, M., & Tiver, K. (1986). The impact of alternative medicine on cancer patients. *Cancer Forum, 10,* 15–19.

Freidson, E. (1970). *Profession of medicine: A study of the sociology of applied knowledge*. Chicago: University of Chicago Press.

Fulder, S. (1996). *The handbook of alternative medicine* (3rd ed.). Oxford: Oxford University Press.

Furnham, A., & Smith, C. (1988). Choosing alternative medicine: A comparison of the beliefs of patients visiting a general practitioner and a homeopath. *Social Science and Medicine, 26,* 685–689.

Goffman, E. (1959). *The presentation of self in everyday life*. Garden City, NY: Doubleday Anchor Books.

Goffman, E. (1963). *Stigma: Notes on the management of spoiled identity*. Upper Saddle River: Prentice-Hall.

Health Canada. (2001). *Perspectives on complementary and alternative health care*. Ottawa: Health Canada Publications.

Illich, I. (1975). *Medical nemesis: The expropriation of health*. Toronto: McClelland & Stewart.

Leech, P. (1999). *Complementary medicine, RSM.* Paper presented at the conference Primary Care Groups and Complementary Medicine: Breaking the Boundaries, Department of Complementary Medicine, University of Exeter, Exeter, UK.

Low, J. (2000). Alternative, complementary, or concurrent health care? A critical analysis of the use of the concept of complementary therapy. *Complementary Therapies in Medicine, 9,* 105–110.

Low, J. (2001). *Lay perspectives on the efficacy of alternative and complementary therapies: The experiences of people living with Parkinson's disease.* Division of Health Studies, Faculty of Health & Community Studies, De Montfort University, Leicester, UK.

Low, J. (2004). *Using alternative therapies: A qualitative analysis.* Toronto: Canadian Scholars' Press.

Lyotard, J.F. (1990). The post-modern condition. In J. Alexander & S. Seidman (Eds.), *Culture and society: Contemporary debates* (pp. 330–341). Cambridge: Cambridge University Press.

Monson, N. (1995). Alternative medicine education at medical schools: Are they catching on? *Journal of Alternative and Complementary Therapies, 1,* 168–171.

Moore, J., Phipps, K., & Marcer, D. (1985). Why do people seek treatment by alternative medicine? *British Medical Journal, 20,* 28–29.

Murray, J., & Shepherd, S. (1993). Alternative or additional medicine? An exploratory study in general practice. *Social Science and Medicine, 37,* 983–988.

Northcott, H. (1994). Alternative health care in Canada. In S.B. Bolaria & H.D. Dickinson (Eds.), *Health, illness and health care in Canada* (pp. 487–503). Toronto: Harcourt Brace.

Pawluch, D., Cain, R., & Gillet, J. (1998). *Approaches to complementary therapies: Diverse perspectives among people with HIV/AIDS.* Unpublished research report. Hamilton, ON: McMaster University.

Prus, R. (1997). *Subcultural mosaics and intersubjective realities: An ethnographic research agenda for pragmatizing the social sciences.* Albany: State University of New York Press.

Ramsey, C., Walker, M., & Alexander, J. (1999). *Alternative medicine in Canada: Use and public attitudes.* Fraser Institute Publications, Public Policy Sources #21.

Saks, M. (1995). *Professions and the public interest: Medical power, altruism and alternative medicine.* London: Routledge.

Sharma, U. (1992). *Complementary medicine today: Practitioners and patients.* London: Routledge.

Sharma, U. (1993). Contextualizing alternative medicine: The exotic, the marginal, and the perfectly mundane. *Anthropology Today, 9,* 15–18.

Yates, P., Beadle, G., Clavarino, A., Najman, J., Thomson, D., Williams, G., et al. (1993). Patients with terminal cancer who use alternative therapies: Their beliefs and practices. *Sociology of Health and Illness, 15,* 199–216.

PART 2C

DOING AND RELATING

Chapter 21

Negotiated Order and Strategic Inaction in Television Coverage of the Olympics

Josh Greenberg, Graham Knight, Margaret MacNeill, and Peter Donnelly

INTRODUCTION

There now exists a well-established body of research on the news media that demonstrates how news production involves continuously negotiating demands, obstacles, and pressures, such as financial imperatives, time limits and access to news sources, occupational interests and aspirations (for example, claims to expertise and autonomy on the part of journalists), and rituals of objectivity that serve both organizational and occupational legitimacy (e.g., Ericson, Baranek, & Chan, 1987). These factors, which condition the relative freedom journalists enjoy over the gathering, preparation, and presentation of news, are generally external to the specific content of any given news story. They function as both constraint and challenge, delineating the range of legitimate decisions and courses of action available to journalists while providing a potential inducement for innovation. Like the real world events and interactions that news represents, the outcome of any particular news story can never be fully determined; it is dependent on the context in which all these factors are enacted in relation to one another. The organization of news production is, in other words, a *negotiated order* (Strauss, 1978, 1993).

We apply the negotiated order perspective to a particular instance of news organization, that of television sports, in order to understand what transpires when attempts are made by organizational management to renegotiate production practices. Sports news production is of particular interest to the study of organizational negotiation because while sports reporters tend, like politics, business or crime reporters, to rely on routine sources (i.e., athletes, spokespersons, and

---

Box 21.1

"In general, [news] production is far from chaotic at anything other than a superficial level. Its rationale is to aim at control and prediction, while those who work the system celebrate its relatively rare contingencies" (Schlesinger, 1978, p. 87).

organizations with deep roots in the commercial sports world) for the bulk of their raw material (Lowes, 1997), **interpretive latitude** is generally greater for sports journalists than for journalists in other areas of news production. This is particularly true in the case of *international* sporting events where the emotional resonance of national identity can be allowed to inflect news coverage with positive as well as negative angles (MacNeill, 1996; Silk, 1999).

This chapter reports on the negotiation of structural conditions at a local television station—identified by the pseudonym MTVS—in its coverage of the 2000 Sydney Olympic Games. MTVS was the focus of research interest because of two particular challenges it faced in reporting the Olympics. Firstly, MTVS is a station with a unique mandate. It is a multilingual, multicultural broadcaster serving primarily minority ethno-linguistic communities with daily news broadcasts in Italian, Portuguese, and Cantonese, and weekly community-oriented programming in other languages. Because of this multicultural mandate, the question of how MTVS would negotiate the potentially competing national identities of its viewers was at issue. Secondly, MTVS did not hold the broadcast rights for the Olympics, and was severely restricted in the amount and type of Olympic footage it was permitted to use. The Canadian Broadcasting Corporation (CBC), in concert with The Sports Network (TSN), held the Canadian rights to broadcast primary television coverage of the Sydney Olympics. Non-rights holders such as MTVS were seriously limited in the type of programming they could show and when they could show it. Infractions of these access rules could make the station liable to considerable financial penalty.

The primary focus of our study was to see whether these conditions were accepted by newsroom staff as a constraint or treated as a challenge and opportunity for innovation. There were divergent perspectives between the station management and the sports production team over the import and weighting of these conditions, and these viewpoints were informed as much by past experience as immediate self-interests. While station management defined the broadcasting rules as constraining, it also recognized that "getting around" the regulations offered a challenge and opportunity for the sports crew to do something different by exploiting the station's identity and forte as a local broadcaster to create original, community-based coverage directed at the different ethno-linguistic audiences it served. The sports crew, on the other hand, acknowledged this opportunity but invoked the rules and regulations, as well as current working conditions, as an effective constraint in order to maintain control over the news-making process. Despite management's intentions of manoeuvring around the legal restrictions with innovative coverage, the station failed in the end to produce the kind of creative reporting that was originally hoped

Box 21.2

"The critical feature for understanding social order and social change is the communication process through which meaning is established" (Altheide, 1988, p. 341).

for. To understand this failure we have to recognize not only how the process of negotiation is socially situated, but also how organizational hierarchies create different, competing interests and aims that can invert formal relations of power and interact with and counteract one another as much by inaction as action.

THEORETICAL FRAMEWORK: NEGOTIATED ORDER

At the heart of the "negotiated order" framework is an understanding that social organization and order are inconceivable without some form of negotiation between individuals and groups. Rules and regulations, market forces, occupational hierarchies, working ideologies, and other "characteristics that appear to be stable features of organizational life" (Maines & Charlton, 1985, p. 277) are not treated as forces that *determine* the course of social action (Altheide, 1988). Rather, they are considered to be meaningful only insofar as social actors in specific contexts can enact them as a means of coordinating action and interaction over time. Social organization thus entails a relationship between certainty and ambiguity that delineates ongoing attempts to create order by way of a mutually agreeable definition of the situation. This definition of the situation is achieved through ongoing interaction, and functions as the basis on which subsequent action and inaction are realized. This has two implications. On the one hand, it is questionable if a fully shared definition can ever be reached. What is more plausibly achieved is only ever a definition that the parties can abide by for present and practical purposes. On the other hand, the relation between certainty and ambiguity implies that organization and order should be seen to be only "loosely coupled" (Thomas, 1984) with the broader social context because that context itself is constituted by an infinite array of other ongoing action situations that are subject to similar processes of negotiation.

The relation between certainty and ambiguity also impinges on the functioning of authority and hierarchy in news organizations. Editors and producers exercise formal authority over decisions concerning story assignment, story angles, and, in some cases, even the selection of sources that journalists should consult. Because editors and producers also operate in a context of competing constraints, pressures, expectations, interests, and aims, this authority may constrain the range of action choices for reporters and production staff, but it does not determine these choices in a finite way. In the immediate situation of news gathering reporters have to confront **contingencies**, such as the unavailability of preferred sources or the lack of technical resources and time, which enhance their autonomy by necessitating improvisation and innovation (Luhmann, 2000). In responding to contingencies reporters have to rely on their stocks of practical and experiential knowledge and their familiarity with the story topic, its scene, and cast of characters. Prospective angles may expire and new angles may emerge during the news-gathering process as new information comes to light or news sources generate new uncertainties and possibilities. Faced with operational imperatives such as the need to meet deadlines, fill airtime or newspaper space, or avoid disruptive conflict, the authority of editors and producers over nominal subordinates (reporters) becomes provisional.

Like most organizations, news media constantly transact with their environments (the fields of politics, health, education, sports, etc.). Definitions of the situation are provisional inasmuch as they are shaped by the overlap and permeability of news organizations and their environments that are unavoidable to the extent that these environments are the news media's primary sources of raw material. While sport, for example, is a routine field of news coverage, the particular focus (which sports, which teams, which athletes, etc.) varies from newscast to newscast.

Despite this overlap and permeability, it is useful to distinguish between external and internal conditions that shape organizational performance. Internal factors, such as the division of labour between reporters and editors, or professional interests, values, and aspirations, are often taken for granted and function in a relatively routine way. External conditions, such as the need to maintain the kind and size of audience that will attract advertisers and revenue, are normally more transparent and function in a relatively stable and predetermined fashion. What is important is that internal and external conditions impinge on different actors in different ways and in different contexts. For some they may operate primarily as constraints or pressures; for others they may provide the opportunity for strategic advantage and the exercise of power or influence. In negotiating a practical definition of the situation, actors are also negotiating a balance of advantage and power in the pursuit of interests and aims that may or may not converge with explicit organizational goals.

METHODOLOGY

Prior to the commencement of the Sydney Olympics, MTVS management agreed to allow a researcher (the first author) to spend time at the station observing the news staff during the Games, and to conduct open-ended, semi-structured interviews with selected personnel at the end of the period of fieldwork. Given the minimal time available for fieldwork, the researchers agreed that **in-depth ethnography**, an approach to qualitative research aimed at achieving total immersion into the field of study, would be the most appropriate method of observation. The first author spent approximately 60 hours in the field, shadowing the sports coordinator, his assistant, one of the segment producers, and the three sports anchors during the main production periods, and conducting open-ended interviews with all of the sports production crew as well as with staff not directly involved in the Olympics news.

For the most part, the researcher maintained the "observer" role; however, his understanding of the broadcast regulations and knowledge of the Olympics also made him a source of information for the production crew at various times (cf. Silk, 1999). For example, on a couple of occasions, the sports coordinator and sports editor did not follow the previous day's events and asked the researcher what he felt were the most interesting and/or important events and outcomes of the day. Had anything spectacular happened? What were the visuals like? While adopting a "participant-observer" role poses methodological limitations in terms of potentially influencing the field of observation, it was also indicative of the production team's comfort level with the researcher's presence and their willingness to communicate openly with him (Silk, 1999, p. 116). As we will see below, however, this also provided clues as to the production team's tactics in negotiating the structural conditions it faced.

Semi-structured interviews were conducted by the first author with the news director, sports coordinator, the assistant to the sports coordinator, one of three segment producers, and one of the three sports reporters. The purpose of the interviews was to explore the attitudes of participants to the access regulations, the news values used to select among the available and allowable footage, the options available to the production crew in "getting around" the regulations, and the perceived levels of success and/or failure in doing so.

CONSTRAINT AND OPPORTUNITY: LAWS, MARKETS, AND ORGANIZATIONAL DYNAMICS

Negotiating the conditions of coverage meant first and foremost ensuring that all sport staff at MTVS understood what the regulatory requirements entailed. On September 5, 2000, two weeks before the opening ceremonies, the station received an official, seven-page fax from CBC Television containing the following information:

> CBC has acquired the exclusive broadcast access rights to the 2000 Sydney Olympic Games for Canada. CBC's exclusivity extends to all aspects of the Games. This includes: all athletic competitions (training, preliminary, qualifying and final rounds), exhibitions and demonstrations, the Opening and Closing Ceremonies, all award and other official ceremonies and all of the events, performances, exhibitions and activities staged at the Olympic venues or in other areas controlled by the Sydney Organizing Committee for the Olympic Games, including the Olympic Athletes Village, the competition sites and the practice venues.

MTVS management immediately produced its own in-house version of the broadcast guidelines and circulated copies to all members of the station's sports production crew. The news director met with each of the segment producers and the sports coordinator four weeks before the start of the Games to explain the rules and convey the importance of adhering to them closely. This was followed up with an additional meeting the week before the Games to go over the rules again and clear up any possible concerns or misunderstandings. It was then up to each segment producer and the sports coordinator to ensure that all other members of the production team were comfortable with what they could and could not show. Reproducing the access rules was significant because past violations of Olympic broadcast access regulations by the station indicated that management did not want to be penalized again. As the sports coordinator noted, "[We] had been reprimanded a few years ago during [the] Nagano [Winter Games] … [I]t is really important to stay in line this time around" (Interview, October 3, 2000).

Operating within the parameters of the regulations proved to be a significant challenge not only from a procedural viewpoint, but also because it impinged directly on other operational requirements, particularly the need to attract audiences. The possibility of lost market share as regular viewers turned to the CBC, TSN, or other non-rights broadcasters for their Olympic coverage, if even only for a short period of time, was of considerable concern. This concern manifested itself primarily in normative rather than financial terms. It was the *fairness* of the regulations, rather than simply their effects, that figured prominently. This was a point of view that was held particularly strongly by station management. As the news director put it,

> ... I work in a private business. [MTVS] is a privately run company, so I understand how difficult it is to bid for these rights and how difficult it is to break even, never mind make a profit. At a time of government cutbacks to funding for the CBC, I can see the tremendous pressure there is to break even. I'm sure they [CBC] had a very large team in Sydney, which must have cost them a lot of money. The rights must have cost them a lot of money too. There's a great deal of pressure to deliver a certain number of viewers to the advertisers who invested a huge deal in this project of theirs. So from a business angle, I can understand things ... A public broadcaster operating as a private business, that's where my conflict resides ... [T]his is the broadcast that's paid for by taxpayers and government subsidies.

For the station management, the main contention was that competition was being unfairly skewed, and this provided compelling grounds on which to rationalize the possibility of failure and displace blame elsewhere.

MTVS was in competition not only with the CBC for audience/market share and advertising revenue but also with broadcasters from the home countries in each of its three main language areas whose telecasts were available via direct satellite feed or specialty cable services. There was nothing in the regulations *per se* to prevent viewers from obtaining satellite feeds from other countries whereas, in theory, the broadcasting regulations did apply to small specialty channels in Canada. In practice, however, it was unlikely that infractions of the regulations would be penalized given the insignificant market share of these specialty channels and the cost of surveillance and litigation on the part of either the IOC or CBC/TSN. This was a market reality understood by the news director: "I don't want to speak for the CBC, but if I were them, I'd probably want to make sure that the bulk of my audience was watching my program and not the programs of my competitors. I don't know if they think of the Chinese specialty services as competition. Theirs [the Chinese specialty channels] is a much smaller audience, and if those audiences were getting a re-cap of how the Chinese athletes were doing, that probably didn't affect the CBC's audience reach. So, for that reason, it probably wasn't worth their while to go after them" (Interview, September 20, 2000).

Nevertheless, the news director was still frustrated that MTVS was following the regulations closely while others were not. He was clear that he did not enjoy the idea of being "taken for a sucker," adding that "[we owe it to our viewers] to provide them with the news and information they want, otherwise they will go elsewhere" (Interview, September 20, 2000).

In addition to the broadcast regulations and market considerations, there were also conditions internal to the news station and its organizational culture that complicated its ability to produce original programming. Two interrelated factors stood out as particularly significant: human resources and news-gathering resources. Human resources factored into the situation in two respects, each of which represented a different operational viewpoint in the organizational hierarchy. Firstly, the station faced the difficulty of finding qualified journalists who had both a "nose for news" and necessary language skills. While this issue was not a conscious concern for the sports staff, it was particularly salient for the news director as it undermined the ability of the station to perform creatively:

> When we hire people, we look for language skills first. The first thing we want is someone who can understand another language and translate that into English, and vice versa. That's always the first thing. Then, we look for journalism skills ... Then we look for broadcasting skills ... I can count on the fingers of one hand the good reporters I've got. The rest are all people who are translators or rewriters who are here because of their linguistic ability and are trying to learn the skills to be a good journalist or broadcaster. So, that's what I manage. I manage a multicultural, multilingual newsroom that really spends more time in rearranging the information already available. So that's why I get frustrated about the lack of initiative in finding new things ... I try to stimulate creativity and independent thinking. But at the same time, we've got to do all this other stuff: this information management and translation we do every day (Interview, September 20, 2000).

As the news director's remarks indicate, the strength of the station's identity as a multicultural, multilingual broadcaster was, therefore, also a source of weakness, as the need for linguistic diversity and skill generally took precedence over hiring on the basis of journalistic ability and experience.

Secondly, and primarily from the viewpoint of the sports staff, the sports section was viewed as less important than other news areas, and received lower priority in the allocation of resources and staffing support. The two problems compounded one another as the lack of resources made it even more difficult to attract and retain staff with both linguistic and journalistic skills and experience. The view among those working in the sports department was that there was generally a lack of commitment on the part of station management to staff the department adequately, and this served as a disincentive to be creative and proactive.

> Interviewer: "What has been the biggest challenge so far?"
> Sports Coordinator: "The problem...[is]...lack of resources, but in particular lack of manpower ... the big number at [MTVS] is politics, not sports ... hell, sports isn't even considered a real department most of the time ... There are too many problems specific to the station."
> Interviewer: "What kinds of problems? Can you be specific?"
> Sports Coordinator: "Resources. Not enough cameras, not enough reporters. No will or cash to [do] anything about it. How's that?"

Of the six production team members in the sports department, only two were full-time employees and another (the assistant to the coordinator) was on loan from another department in the station. One of the effects of having a small staff was that much of the news-gathering responsibility fell onto the shoulders of a small number of people, in particular the sports coordinator. The lack of resources and the demanding workload, in turn, affected motivation and morale. For the sports coordinator, it translated into a determination to maintain the status quo: "Was I going to come up with this stuff out of thin air? No. Was I going to do extra [work]? Why should I? Just do the basics and be consistent. That's the way I do things 'cause there's no point in doing it any other way" (Interview, October 3, 2000).

The staffing problem was clearly linked to a broader problem of limited news-gathering resources. There was a hierarchy of topic importance in which sports came last after international politics, business, local politics, and entertainment. As indicated by the sports coordinator above, sports issues were always given the least consideration when it came to resource allocation such as travel expenses, cameras and microphones, and station vehicles. When other events or issues emerged unexpectedly (such as political conflict in Yugoslavia or the death of former Canadian Prime Minister Pierre Trudeau, both of which occurred during the Olympics), equipment or materials already allotted to sports would, if necessary, be reallocated elsewhere. It also meant that if these issues or events were significant in terms of either their political or economic impact, the amount of time allotted to the sports component of each broadcast would be reduced.

At first blush it seems that the problems the sports team faced—restrictive access rules, insufficient human and material resources, low overall station priority—were interpreted and enacted as constraints rather than opportunities. We would interpret the situation somewhat differently, however. These constraints were treated as an opportunity, but as an opportunity to continue as usual, i.e., to remain effectively *inactive* in terms of initiating original or innovative coverage. This *strategic inaction* reflected the effect of working in a context where organizational support and recognition were in relatively short supply. It also represents the situated interests of the production team in maintaining the status quo in the face of prospective changes that would intensify the work process, but do so without necessarily yielding additional resources or recognition. The sports crew used the compelling effect of the constraints they faced as an opportunity not to renegotiate existing practices in a new direction that, by implication, would have created greater demands on their time and effort. The challenge they faced was to resist these demands, and this meant enacting the structural conditions of the job and specific situation as an opportunity to be constrained rather than as an opportunity to effect change.

For management the problem went beyond the structural constraints of regulations and limited resources. It was also clearly a problem with competence, skill, and motivation on the part of the production team. While the news director did recognize the constraining effect of these factors on programming options, he saw the main problem as a lack of initiative on the part of his staff. In response to our question for his general thoughts on the station's performance, the news director indicated that the production was "mediocre at best," adding his "disappointment" with the unwillingness of his staff to "get into the community." Overall his feeling was one of frustration: "I do feel frustrated because, yes, we do have structural constraints, absolutely, but I think that some of our people, if they were truly interested in being sports journalists, they would have done something. If they, you know, seen the opportunity that it was … It's extremely frustrating for me when sports people, or people on sports assignment, need to take a few hours at the beginning of their shift to find out what the hell is going on. You know, that's not acceptable" (Interview, October 5, 2000).

The constraint that management faced was the ability of the sports team to enact the challenges of the situation. While each side recognized the viewpoint of the other, the sports crew's definition of the situation prevailed. It did so because they could claim effectively that the combination of constraints they faced eliminated any realistic room to manoeuvre, constraints whose legitimacy and effect management in part conceded. As the station manager admitted, "there wasn't much preparation, to be honest" (Interview, October 5, 2000). The rationalization of failure did not, however, prove insurmountable. The news director had already framed the bigger picture at the outset in terms of the unfairness of having to compete against a broadcaster whose funding came from the taxpayer, not from competitive market success. The smaller scale picture of day-to-day performance (or lack of it) was framed retrospectively as a problem of personal shortcomings and motivation in the face of challenging conditions. At both levels, blame could be largely displaced elsewhere.

STRATEGIC INACTION AND THE REVERSIBILITY OF POWER

The negotiated order perspective, with its emphasis on agency, temporality, and the indeterminacy and permeability of structures, tends to emphasize negotiation over order inasmuch as it sees negotiation as the process and order as the outcome. The case of MTVS, however, indicates that order and negotiation are interchangeable as goals and means. The fact that the sports crew's definition of the situation succeeded over the news director's might seem to suggest that order (established routines) prevailed over negotiation (innovation). What we would argue, however, is that the order of established routines was the means that organizational subordinates (reporters) used to negotiate their own goal of inaction and lack of initiative in their interaction with organizational superiors (station management). This reversal of the relationship between order and negotiation points to the *reflexive* character of negotiation; that is, the way that negotiation itself can be negotiated. Manoeuvring around the legal restrictions in the way that the news director desired would, from the viewpoint of the sports crew, have resulted in a more constraining work situation. It would have intensified the demands on workload in a context where the necessary organizational resource support was absent or contingent at best.

The hierarchy of roles and authority in the newsroom functioned as the context in which this struggle over negotiation took place. The reflexive character of negotiation can be understood only if we recognize that situational conditions are constraining in different ways and to different extents, and this depends on one's position and power in relation to the position and power of others. Negotiating a definition of the situation entails managing the tensions that competing interests imply and the constraining effect these can be made to have. Constraints not only restrict and limit options for feasible courses of action; they can also intensify the demands that are made on what might be called an actor's "stock of resources," i.e., the knowledge and know-how acquired through past experience. As courses of action are restricted, resources are depleted or rendered ineffectual. In both respects, however, constraints are relational and are implicated in the strategic nature of social interaction where realistic possibilities are competitively distributed.

Organizational research has recognized for some time that subordinates can exercise effective, informal power through their ability to acquire resources such as practical knowledge (*inter alia* Crozier, 1964). These resources are deployed to preserve or enhance autonomy, but in a way that constrains the range of options available to others. The constraining effect that social structures have represents the way that structures embody differential power relations and the unequal capacities for social agency resulting from these relations. As the power of subordinates demonstrates, power can sometimes be subverted and power relations reversed. The ability of the MTVS sports team to resist and neutralize the news director's desire for innovative reporting was an example of this kind of strategic reversal of power. It did not rest on the acquisition of special knowledge so much as on an ability to mobilize an array of conditions (legal requirements, limited material resources and labour, low institutional priority) as a means to justify the status quo. This resistance did not entail a different course of action so much as inaction in the face of management's wishes. It did not entail open, active defiance or confrontation but rather localized tactics of evasion and indifference. Original coverage was accepted by the sports staff as desirable in theory, but implementation was constantly deferred on the grounds of contingencies and limitations about which little could realistically be done with the resources at hand. There was no alternative plan that the sports staff was attempting collectively to implement, simply a reliance on established routines. In contrast to the news director, who felt obliged to concede the constraining effect of actual conditions—lack of resources, lack of advanced preparations and organizing—the sports staff only had to concede the reasonableness of someone else's ideal. They were able, therefore, to mobilize constraint as a means to justify inaction.

CONCLUSION

MTVS did not produce any original Olympic coverage; it relied on rebroadcasting visual images of the games supplied by the CBC over which it dubbed voice-over commentary that was produced in-house. The routines of sports production remained effectively undisturbed; no new production order was negotiated into place. Rather than seeing this as simply the upshot of structural constraints imposing their power on social actors striving to generate new forms of social order, we would argue that the situation was more complex. To be effective, constraints have to be enacted, even in the passive sense of being taken as obvious in their meaning and irresistible in their impact. The enactment of constraints is implicated in the strategic nature of social interaction, particularly in negotiating a practical definition of the situation that enables all parties to agree on courses of action and inaction, and which provides actors with the means to accommodate themselves to and rationalize undesirable as well as satisfying outcomes. To the extent that interaction continues, failure is only ever partial. Constraints are turned into resources in the protection and pursuit of competitive or conflictive interests. They can be deployed as assets to enhance an actor's general stock of resources as well as to deplete the resources of others whose interests diverge or contradict. Constraints can be used not only to negotiate social order but also as an opportunity to negotiate the process of negotiation itself.

While the failure to produce local Olympic coverage was clearly a frustration for the news director, its impact, like the Games themselves, was nonetheless short-lived (though practical lessons were learned that may be applied next time). What made the Olympics such an important news topic—its high cultural (and even political and economic) profile as the premier global sporting spectacle and an event that is intensely concentrated in time and space, occurring only once every four years—allowed in the end for the significance of this instance of organizational failure to deflate quickly once the Games themselves were over.

GLOSSARY

Contingencies: These are disturbances in a social system that disrupt the flow of information necessary for action and change to occur. In the context of organizational activity, contingencies can be understood as "operational irritants" that open up the opportunity to negotiate how a job gets done. While contingencies pose a challenge to organizational action and interaction, they also create new opportunities to initiate innovation and change.

In-depth ethnography: This approach to qualitative fieldwork emphasizes the total immersion of the researcher as a participant-observer into the fieldwork setting. While this approach can be used in any instance where the researcher wishes to unpeel the layers of an organization's culture, it is particularly useful when there is very limited time available for research.

Interpretive latitude: Based on the premise that journalists do not report but interpret reality. Journalism is about storytelling and this means that, because of constraints on time and space, reporters can only ever tell some aspects and perspectives of events. In interpreting reality, journalists have some leeway in terms of what information is to be included and how it is to be emphasized.

Negotiated order: Defined as the sum of an organization's rules and policies, agreements, understandings, pacts, contracts, and other working arrangements. A negotiated order emerges from the actions and interactions of individuals operating within an organizational setting that is itself an outcome of broader rules, regulations, procedures, norms, and expectations.

Strategic inaction: Refers to calculated decisions by organizational subordinates to rely on standardized routines instead of enacting opportunities to innovate. Inaction is "safe" and "effective" when exercised in the short term (in the longer term it can become potentially dangerous to job security), and tends to rely on tactics of evasion and indifference as opposed to a strategy of action and change.

REFERENCES

Altheide, D. (1988). Mediating cutbacks in human services: A case study in the negotiated order. *The Sociological Quarterly, 29*(3), 339–355.

Crozier, M. (1964). *The bureaucratic phenomenon*. Chicago: University of Chicago Press.

Ericson, R.V., Baranek, P., & Chan, J. (1987). *Visualizing deviance: A study of news organization*. Toronto: University of Toronto Press.

Lowes, M.D. (1997). Sports page: A case study in the manufacture of sports news for the daily press. *Sociology of Sport Journal, 14*(2), 143–159.

Luhmann, N. (2000). *The reality of the mass media* (K. Cross, Trans.). Stanford: Stanford University Press.

MacNeill, M. (1996). Networks: Producing Olympic ice hockey for a national television audience. *Sociology of Sport Journal, 13*(2), 103–124.

Maines, D.R., & Charlton, J.C. (1985). The negotiated order approach to the analysis of social organization. *Foundations of interpretive sociology: Original essays in symbolic interaction, Supplement 1* (pp. 271–308). Greenwich, CT: JAI Press.

Schlesinger, P. (1978). *Putting reality together*. London: Constable.

Silk, M. (1999). Local/global flows and altered production practices: Narrative constructions at the 1995 Canada Cup of soccer. *International Review for the Sociology of Sport, 34*(2), 113–123.

Strauss, A. (1978). *Negotiations*. San Francisco: Jossey-Bass.

Strauss, A. (1993). *Continual permutations of action*. New York: Aldine de Gruyter.

Thomas, J. (1984). Some aspects of negotiated order, loose coupling and mesostructure in maximum security prisons. *Symbolic Interaction, 7*, 213–231.

ACKNOWLEDGEMENTS

The authors would like to thank the Social Sciences & Humanities Research Council of Canada for funding the research from which this chapter stems.

Chapter 22

Advancing in the Amateur Chess World

Antony J. Puddephatt

INTRODUCTION

While there are numerous studies on social mobility in the social sciences, very little attention is ever paid to the actual "doing" of improvement and achievement, in particular work or recreational settings. Indeed, while structural conditions may provide constraints or allowances for certain people as they pursue various career progressions, researchers ought not to lose sight of the ability for people to "make do," and, working within these limitations, construct lines of action that they perceive will get them ahead. Indeed, as Prus (1997) argues, a focus on people's actual day-to-day activities as they attempt to progress in their social worlds will help to draw trans-situational parallels between various social settings, such that a generic model of "developing a proficient self" (p. 173) may be generated.

Working from the perspective of symbolic interactionism (Blumer, 1969; Prus, 1996), this chapter explores the process by which players in the amateur chess subculture attempt to develop proficiency in the course of their careers. In so doing, I will highlight those features of career advancement that are unique to chess, but I will also try to extend these concepts to other related social arenas. As such, I hope to work towards a generic model of how people develop proficiency and assess their accomplishments in everyday life.

METHODS AND DATA

The data for this study draws on open-ended interviews with 21 amateur chess players, participant-observation in field settings between September 1999 and January 2003, and my own experiences with the game. I interviewed beginning-level recreational players to competitive-style tournament players, from 21 to 70 years of age. Interviews ranged from half an hour to four hours in length. All interviews took place in whatever setting the respondents deemed comfortable, and were then tape recorded, transcribed, and coded into analytic categories. All respondents signed consent forms that ensured anonymity and confidentiality, and outlined ethical ramifications. The respondents understood that they could refuse to answer any questions asked, and that they could curtail the interview at any time.

The participant-observation was conducted at two university-based chess clubs and two city clubs from two medium-sized cities in Ontario, Canada. The university clubs tended to be less competitive and more social in character. At the city level, the clubs usually hosted tournaments rated by the Chess Federation of Canada (CFC). Participant observation involved chatting with members of the clubs, playing friendly games, observing, and getting involved in tournament play. After a day or night spent at a given location, I would return home to write down my observations as field notes. I would code the notes, and then file them into the same conceptual categories as the interviews. All names and places have been changed to ensure anonymity and confidentiality.

THE CHESS SUBCULTURE

I consider the chess subculture to encompass anyone who plays the game, from professional chess players, to club players, to those people who have only a minimum working knowledge of the game. For the purposes of this study, a chess subculture may involve two friends gathering at a coffee shop for a weekly game, or a more organized club that may receive recognition from the national chess organization of the CFC. Those people playing CFC-rated events are expected to play timed games, adhere closely to the rules of the game, and hold chess ratings to measure their level of play. These chess ratings are readjusted and re-evaluated as more tournaments or matches are completed. Top players at the national level may go on to participate in international competitions, sanctioned under the internationally recognized Fédération Internationale Des Échecs (FIDE).

Prus and Dawson (1991) illustrate the multiple meanings that shopping activity may have for various people. By interviewing shoppers, it was found that the perspectives taken towards shopping activity are often very diverse. Eldon Snyder's (1994) work on competitive versus recreational shuffleboard players also highlights the different meanings with which players of different levels approach and perceive the game. Stebbins (1991) notes that one of the major differences between recreational and serious leisure practices is that, in the latter, participants tend to define the activity more as work. In chess, the seriousness with which players view the game also varies widely. For example, while serious players put a lot of emphasis on strict adherence to the rules, quiet, hard work, and competition, recreational players take these issues more lightly.

The importance placed on competition differs depending on the amount players have invested in the game. Only the more serious players in my sample would bother to spend time practising, reading, and improving their play. For casual players, studying to improve is "too much like work" and, as such, they are not interested in investing the time and energy required: "I want to have fun with chess all the time, and I don't want to make it too much of an important thing in my life" (m, 23). As such, this article is focused on the more competitive players as those who put more emphasis on, and thus participate in, activities to improve play. Since most serious, competition-oriented players place a great deal of emphasis on improving in relation to others in their home club, a brief description of the status hierarchies observed in chess clubs is in order.

THE RATING SYSTEM: STATUS IN THE AMATEUR CHESS WORLD

Any player who is involved with a CFC-sponsored chess club, or attends CFC-rated tournaments, is also assigned a chess rating corresponding to the player's skill level. Roughly speaking, the numbers range from under 500 (an absolute beginner), to 1,200 (a weak club player), to 1,600 (an intermediate club player), to 2,000 (an expert), to 2,300 (a master), to over 2,500 (a grandmaster). This hierarchy of ratings goes far beyond a mere designation of chess skill alone. High-rated players often exhibit a great deal of self-confidence in their interactions at the club meetings. Conversely, low-rated players often feel stigmatized, and seem to act with less confidence. As such, a **status hierarchy** is enacted in the club that is based largely on the skill level of the players. As such, weak players will often engage in self-deprecating humour, such as: "The way I play, this game shouldn't take you too long" (m, 64). Over time, less-skilled players routinely act deferential to those at a higher level. The president of a local chess club illustrates the negative side of this: "I swear to god, I am getting so sick of this elitist attitude at the club. For god's sake, the six of them will only play at their own little corner of the room, and not talk or bother with anyone. They call people's moves "primitive" and all of that business. You know, in the club, they are so superior and important compared to the rest of us. Greg, I swear to god, pretends he doesn't know who I am. He has stopped me to ask my name about five times. I say to him, 'I am Fred Perdue'—I am the president of the goddamned club! But, since I am a lower-rated player, no, he doesn't even know my name (m, 70)."

Thus, chess skill is something players must "wear around with them," and as such, losing to lower-rated players can be quite embarrassing to those who invest a great deal of time in the game. Orrin Klapp (1964) developed the notion of the "**dramatic encounter**" to encompass any social activity in which people's reputations or identities are put in a position to be judged by others. Probably due to the rather pronounced hierarchies within which the players are situated, chess games can be grounds for quite consequential dramatic encounters. If, for example, an upset occurs, especially in front of a peer audience, a "hero" (the low-rated underdog) and a "fool" (the unexpected loser) are quickly designated. Depending on how lopsided the upset is, and the way in which the players and audience interpret and react to the event, such encounters can have serious imputations for a player's identity. Not only will the losing player be judged negatively by the audience in question, he or she may also stand to lose several rating points as a result of the loss. As these ratings measure a player's status, and the progress in his or her career in chess, it is akin to being demoted, and as such, carries a stigma. Due to this potential risk, many players will want to avoid playing weaker players at all: "The whole thing is, for me, is to get over a 1,600 rating. I just want to get to 1,600. Because then, at the weekend tournaments, you're not caught playing some ding-dong that doesn't even know how to play. Because, you don't want to lose to him, that's the problem! I go to work and they make fun of me all the time, because they know I've lost to these little kids—they joke to me, "So, did you lose this week to the kid in the high chair again?" So, the bottom line is get into the higher divisions, and then even if you lose, you're still able to maintain at least some level of dignity (laughs)" (m, 38).

Players' skill in chess is monitored constantly with every match and tournament they play. There are permanent identity imputations at stake in every encounter. Judging by the importance of these ratings in players' designation of others, there is often quite a premium on improving play. Of course, most players frequenting a chess club are motivated to improve in the game for intrinsic reasons as well, but this is beyond the scope of this discussion.

DEVELOPING SKILL: ADVANCING IN THE CHESS WORLD

This section considers how players practice skills and gather knowledge in chess in an effort to improve play. This is inspired in large part by Prus's (1997, p. 173) call to study the generic processes associated with "developing proficiencies" and "achieving accomplishments" in social life. Prus insists on the necessity of

---

Box 22.1: "Kids Like It 'Cause It's Fun": Canadian Native Children Learning Chess

Several Aboriginal schools report that playing chess has taken off as a favourite activity in their communities. It can be played in every season, the setup cost is minimal, and no gym, groomed field, or expensive equipment is required. Any simple location with tables and chairs will do, and these days, computers provide instruction and a sense of community. You can play against remarkable software programs or opponents from around the world. Numerous studies have been done that prove chess helps students improve academically. It is rich in problem-solving techniques and improves a child's ability to think rationally.

"There's a tendency to treat chess as some kind of highbrow amusement, but when you look at chess internationally, it's second only to soccer in the number of participants," said Toronto teacher and chess player, Roger Langen. He convinced Toronto's York school board to make chess a part of the math curriculum in Grade 3. "By the time a child is age eight, he or she is ready to take on chess. At this age, children can learn in a way adults will never know."

Aboriginal involvement in chess is also on the rise, representing 20 percent of the Northern Ontario team at the Canadian Youth Championships. "It's a dream of mine to bring chess to all the remote communities in Northern Ontario," said events coordinator John Rutherford. "I want to get a good representation from all the communities. The interest and talent is there."

Source: From "'Kids Like It 'Cause It's Fun': Canadian Native Children Learning Chess," by J. Davis, 2001, *Wind Speaker, 19*(5), p. A18.

studying the detailed processes of skill development and achievement across myriad social situations in order to understand this abstract process in its generic form. Players attempt to develop and advance in chess using a wide variety of resources. In general, the larger process of skill development involves: (1) working towards goals, (2) monitoring progress, and (3) readjusting these goals in light of the progress made.

Working towards Goals

Players who are dedicated to reaching their goals are usually willing to work hard to achieve them. Although this is often described as somewhat laborious (Stebbins, 1991), I found that players often get a lot of fun and enjoyment out of learning. In short, it appears to be a source of recreation for many of those who study, offering significant intrinsic rewards. I have subdivided this larger process of working towards goals into three categories. They are: (1) engaging the chess literature, (2) learning from others, and (3) learning through trial and error.

Engaging the Chess Literature

The various books available on chess cover topics as wide ranging as opening play, middle game, endings, strategy, pawn structure, tactics and combinations, collections of games, chess psychology, checkmating, diagram exercises, and so on. As such, chess can be said to represent an extensive body of **esoteric knowledge**. Much like in the academic world, the literature on chess is almost exclusively produced and consumed by those inside the subculture. Another parallel to academics is that players will usually start with beginner or introductory books, and then move on and study more specialized treatments. As well, new knowledge is constantly being produced, such that the game is continually evolving in new dimensions.

Although many people think that strong chess skill is a function of intelligence, players indicate that success in chess seems to be more closely related to the amount of knowledge players have amassed. For this reason, the accumulation of knowledge in chess is highly regarded, and is often treated as the most important activity towards improving play. Much of the literature in chess is highly specialized. In the case of chess openings, it is possible to obtain books on the basic principles of all openings, books that catalogue all known opening routines, and then more specialized books that dissect and explore variations within one specific opening line. In one lifetime, it is impossible for any player to synthesize all of the knowledge available for study.

While it is common for players to focus on literature that is more directly attuned to the technical elements of chess, some players read books to help them cope with the stress experienced in the game. I myself have read books on chess psychology in an effort to improve. Much like literature on sports psychology, these books illustrate how players can make the best of their talents by staying strong mentally, and taking advantage of an opponent's weaknesses (see Benko & Hochberg, 1991). Some of the literature provides chess diagrams, which are like puzzles for the player to solve. A pre-set board position is presented, and the player tries to figure out the best move for a particular end result. Thus, working through a series of chess diagrams is akin to solving math problems in school. By applying principles known from theory, applications of concepts are practised. While some exercises are solved on the spot, others contain ideas that must be absorbed and sifted through over time. In short, puzzles provide a kind of training ground for players to test vague theoretical concepts in simulated game situations.

Chess literature provides players with new ideas, perspectives, and approaches to the game. Books may carry general strategic advice, or more concrete tactical exercises. They may contain introductory-level material for those beginning the game, or incredibly advanced, in-depth, and specialized explorations into certain specific configurations that may emerge. As such, chess is not only a game, but also an extensive and ever-emergent body of esoteric knowledge.

Learning from Others

Much like other activities, such as hustling and magic (Prus & Sharper, 1991), gambling (Lesieur, 1976), coordinating wedding events (Chester, 1995), ballet dancing (Dietz, 1994), role-playing games (Fine, 1983), and training to become medical students (Haas & Shaffir, 1994), a great deal of chess skill is learned from other more experienced practitioners. While people may develop ideas based largely on independent sources, they will also gather together in small groups to share this knowledge with others. This is very much akin to academic conferences, whereby scholars condense and simplify their hard work, allowing others easier access to the information, in return for the same offering from their colleagues. Younger children or very serious up-and-coming players have been known to hire private chess coaches in an effort to accelerate their advancement. At clubs, it is common to see the advanced senior players helping younger or weaker players on an informal basis. Thus, for the willing listener, membership in a chess club often greatly increases a player's rate of advancement.

When people are willing to share information, and players are reasonably receptive to advice, learning from other players can be highly valuable for improving play: "I sat down with Doug Stephens and he helped me to calm down in openings and showed me all the little tricks to get him in 12 moves, so he helped me out quite a bit, mostly with the openings. We sat down a couple of times at coffee shops and just went over stuff" (m, 42).

For some players, learning from others represents the major source for new ideas. Thus, chess knowledge is both intersubjectively constituted and shared. Whether players learn directly from others, by watching games, by reading literature, or by playing, players always draw from the pool of knowledge provided by other players. Ideas that seem to be fostered independently are almost always extensions of previous principles, or adjustments to problems that others have presented. It is for this reason that chess knowledge represents a body that is constantly growing and evolving from a community context, shaped by the particular problems raised, and addressed through the intersubjective process.

Learning through Trial and Error

In game situations, players draw upon all of the resources that are available to them. Thus, the knowledge they have gained in books or from other people, and the skills that they have developed through solving exercises and trying simulated situations may be utilized to play the best game possible. However, many ideas and concepts (e.g., opening routines, tactical strategies, etc.) are worked out in the context of ideal situations, and therefore may not work perfectly in actual games. Thus, games provide the ultimate medium where ideas and skills can be re-evaluated, refined, reshaped, or dropped by testing them for their actual viability. Through a process of trial and error, notions that seem good in theory are put to the test.

Many of the less serious players comment that learning from the available literature is boring. As such, learning through practice (playing out actual games) is preferred. More often than not, players learn what not to do in games through a process of elimination. Making mistakes in games are telling lessons for players as they begin to learn how to avoid the game's pitfalls: "Yeah, I get ideas sometimes, and usually there's something that I left out, and people capitalize on that, and I get screwed because I will have totally opened myself up. So you learn really fast what doesn't work. You tend to learn a lot more by screwing up than succeeding" (m, 22).

Once having learned what not to do in certain situations, the more "correct" moves in given scenarios begin to take form. The idea that knowledge forms emerge through the ongoing reflective activity of the trial and error process has been stressed time and again in the **pragmatism** of Mead (1934). Nevertheless, the extension of this important notion to other learning contexts (e.g., academics and specialized occupations) is noteworthy.

More advanced players tend to stress that trying out new ideas in the context of informal practice games, or against the computer, is very important for a player to grow. Thus, players will use this medium to try out more unorthodox ideas, despite the probability of failure. Since computer programs are fairly reliable in that they always play the most "objectively correct" move, players are less able to get away with ill-founded plans. Thus, the computer provides a good testing ground for new opening routines, ideas, and strategies. Beyond this, by watching the moves, players can take on the role of the computer in an effort to pick up new strategies (Mead, 1934): "One thing I'll do sometimes is set my computer to the highest attack level, and I'll play black. And I'll just play, game after game, trying to defend against what the computer does. It helps you with your defence because you're trying to fend off a pretty intense attack, but more importantly, you get to watch what white does, like how it attacks. It gives you ideas for what you can do" (m, 38).

By watching the tactics employed by the computer, players are able to pick up and formulate new ideas. By trying to copy various ideas demonstrated by the computer, players are able to expand their repertoires and learn some of the more accepted and objectified approaches to the game.

Box 22.2: Cross-cultural Considerations in Studying Chess

It is important to note that this study is focused on the process of advancement within a Canadian context. In Canada, there are no formal chess schools, it is not a part of the required curriculum, and there is little national support for our top players. Certainly, in countries such as Russia and China, the experience of advancement for many players would be more organized and bureaucratic in nature.

To illustrate these cross-cultural differences, Owen (2003) observes that Texas University in the United States has a chess department that offers full scholarships. In countries such Greece, Brazil, Venezuela, Italy, and Israel, chess is a part of the national curriculum. The Moscow Institute for Physical Culture in Russia offers a university program in chess, which has given rise to some of the world's top players (IntChess Asia, 2004). It is also worth noting that the Russian international chess team is highly regimented in their learning. As Richards (1965) notes, the team engaged in gruelling physical exercise for weeks, did hours of practice drills per day, and spent months pouring over their opponents' games. This activity would take place in a highly disciplined and organized manner, under the close watch of a team of coaches.

These rather drastic cross-cultural differences found in nations with a more institutionalized program for chess development would entail the need for a far different theoretical and methodological approach to studying the social process of advancement. Since the infrastructural support for chess development in Canada is relatively weak, the process of development here is more of an individual or small group process, as I have illustrated in this chapter. However, where there are more formal institutions in place, the advancement process would be better studied in light of the relevant institutional and organizational structures.

Monitoring Progress

Mead (1934) described the ability for people to become objects unto themselves through the process of role-taking. As such, an individual is able to make judgments about himself or herself in relation to the world of the other. Monitoring one's progress in chess requires that players take themselves and others into account to gauge their development. Throughout their careers, it is inevitable that players will either surpass their expectations or fall short of them. Prus (1997) has identified two elements of this larger process: (1) appreciating accomplishments, and (2) dealing with limitations.

Appreciating Accomplishments

By comparing one's present-day self with an older self, players may assess improvements made over time. The following player recollects his previous limitations, which helps to validate his current level of play: "I can remember tournaments where individuals beat me, who I would never even consider a challenge now, but they just destroyed me" (m, 22). Players also seem to find it important to mark their progress in tangible ways, through such things as individual victories or achievements. Without these markers, a player's improvement is more difficult to assess: "It comes down to the individual victory more so, it's not like one day I looked around and said 'Hey, I'm better than all these players.' There are certain landmarks, like beating my father, and drawing with that master" (m, 24).

The key here is that the skill level of the player is probably about the same before the game as it is afterwards. However, it is the use of a tangible marker that allows the player to "realize" (rightly or wrongly) that his or her skills have improved.

Appreciating improvements in one's level of play serves to inspire players to continue or intensify their careers as chess players, at any level of play, by providing an emotional boost: "Oh, it's amazing, when you beat somebody who you could never beat before, it's the greatest high in the world, kind of thing, it's like, climbing a mountain" (m, 21). While reflecting on success seems to be a strong motivator for continued development, the flip side, dealing with limitations, often has the opposite effect.

Dealing with Limitations
When development in chess is slow, many of the players actively implement strategies to cope. Other players, who face the fact that they are not developing as they would like, choose to step away from the game: "I'll move away from chess for a while. I've done that from time to time. So if I hit a plateau, I usually just step away from it, and instead of playing, I just try and be observant" (m, 38).

Players often need time after experiencing slumps to regain a positive attitude. A similar notion is discussed in Lesieur's (1976) study of gamblers. He explains that gamblers take time out, or lessen their involvements in gambling, because they are "sick of losing," and they need to "tone down" their losses. Perhaps unfortunately for many gamblers, these players eventually lose these negative feelings, and, with the encouragement of their peers, take up their gambling routines again. Chess players operate in much the same fashion. Once players hit a "bad streak," they step away from the game in order to regain a more positive attitude.

(3) Re-evaluating and Readjusting Goals
In evaluating their progress, players may adjust their original goals. If they are doing better than expected, players may decide to take on loftier goals that are now defined as more realistic. On the other hand, if progress is slow, players may refocus their pursuits on lesser, more attainable goals. Thus, players change their original aspirations for success in the game, and refocus on that which is easier to attain: "When I started I thought I would be a master in a couple of years. But as you play and you start to realize your own ability, you realize you're not a prodigy in the game, but rather that it's something that will require work, then you realize, okay, and you sort of set your standards a bit lower" (m, 24).

On the other hand, players contest that too much realism can be an obstacle to obtaining success: "There's got to be a certain vanity in your game, aside from a belief, and a confidence in your abilities" (m, 24). Either way, by setting goals lower, or keeping them more open-ended, players are able to progress at a more natural pace without the associated negative feelings.

Some players will hold fast to their original goals, and adapt their work regime accordingly, in an attempt to compensate for slow progress. Thus, negative signals that indicate a player's regression (such as a loss or a reduction in rating) are used to justify a more intensive work regime: "I suppose I just redouble my efforts after something like a loss, it kind of challenges me to get more into it, and play more because I should be at this level, in my head, so, if I'm not, I should work harder to get there" (m, 21). Thus, depending on the seriousness with which players view the game, the amount of personal investment, and their rate of progress, players adjust their goals and work ethic accordingly.

CONCLUSION

This study has examined how amateur players attempt to advance through the hierarchy of the competitive chess world. The identity imputations associated with a player's skill can be paralleled with occupational status in professional occupations and other similar pursuits. We can see that the motivation for taking initiatives to develop proficiency may be linked not only to the intrinsic rewards of acquiring new skills, but also to the social prestige gained through acquiring higher status in relation to others in the community.

Learning chess very much represents a "hands-on" process. The Platonic vision of simply applying preformed ideas to given situations is certainly not supported here. As players apply the knowledge gained through literature, and other more skilled players, this information is recast dialectically between the pure form of the idea and the practical exigencies that emerge in play. As such, chess represents a craft in that things must be reflexively worked out, reshaped, and generated through experience. Skills and knowledge do not evolve strictly in relation to what is read in books and learned from others, but more importantly in the ongoing activities of the players in generating ideas emergently through practice (see Mead, 1934). Further, improvement cannot be monitored without reference to concrete markers given from experience. In social pursuits of all sorts, it is often the case that people look for cues in an effort to measure their development with respect to a particular set of skills.

While this in no way presents an absolute model for the "doing" of career advancement, I hope to have provided some key insights into this issue as a generic social process (Prus, 1996). More importantly, I hope that this study paves the way for future research that would examine similar processes of advancement as they are enacted in various social, leisure, or occupational spheres. This approach might be best applied to those whose advancement is deemed especially problematic. For example, what is it like for a minority group member trying to advance in a competitive job market? What strategies do they use to overcome the various structural obstacles imposed on them? Through a closer investigation of people's efforts to improve in myriad situations, a deeper understanding of the specific issues at stake becomes possible (e.g., Wiseman, 1970). As such, particular situational problems can be identified and addressed, and an overly deterministic (and pessimistic) view of social advancement can be overcome.

GLOSSARY

Dramatic encounter: Any social event in which an actor's performance holds direct identity imputations stemming from the judgment of others.

Esoteric knowledge: A set of information that is highly specialized and sought after, most particularly by those of a specific social membership.

Platonism: The philosophy of Plato, which asserts that ideal forms of knowledge are eternal and unchanging, and can be understood only through reason rather than experience and observation.

Pragmatism: The 20th century American philosophy that holds that meanings of ideas are generated through the practical consequences of human action.

Status hierarchy: A public and asymmetrical distribution of social prestige within a given social sphere.

REFERENCES

Benko, P., & Hochberg, B. (1991). *Winning with chess psychology*. New York: David McKay Company, Inc.

Blumer, H. (1969). *Symbolic interactionism: Perspective and method*. Berkeley: University of California Press.

Chester, T. (1995). *The processes and problematics of coordinating events: Planning the wedding reception*. Paper presented at the Ethnographic and Qualitative Research Conference, McMaster University, Hamilton, Ontario.

Dietz, M.L. (1994). On your toes: Dancing your way into the ballet world. In M.L. Dietz, R. Prus, & W. Shaffir (Eds.), *Doing everyday life: Ethnography as human lived experience* (pp. 66–85). Toronto: Copp Clark Longman, Ltd.

Fine, G.A. (1983). *Shared fantasy: Role playing games as social worlds*. Chicago: University of Chicago Press.

Haas, J., & Shaffir, W. (1994). The development of a professional self in medical students. In M.L. Dietz, R. Prus, & W. Shaffir (Eds.), *Doing everyday life: Ethnography as human lived experience* (pp. 188–202). Toronto: Copp Clark Longman, Ltd.

IntChess Asia. (2004). IntChess Asia Home Page. Available at http://www.intchessasia.com

Klapp, O. (1964). *Symbolic leaders: Public dramas and public men*. Chicago: Aldine Publishing.

Lesieur, H. (1976). *The chase*. New York: Anchor.

Mead, G. Herbert. (1934). *Mind, self and society*. Chicago: University of Chicago Press.

Owen, G. (2003, June 24). Chess prodigy, 7, quits school in row over truancy. *The Times*, 5L, p. 6.

Prus, R. (1996). *Symbolic interaction and ethnographic research*. New York: State University of New York Press.

Prus, R. (1997). *Subcultural mosaics and intersubjective realities*. New York: State University of New York Press.

Prus, R., & Dawson, L. (1991). Shop til you drop: Shopping as recreational and laborious activity. *Canadian Journal of Sociology*, 16(2), 145–164.

Prus, R., & Sharper, C.R.D. (1991). *Road hustler: Hustlers, magic, and the thief subculture*. New York: Kaufman & Greenberg.

Puddephatt, A.J. (2003). Chess playing as strategic activity. *Symbolic Interaction, 26*(2), 263–284.

Richards, D.J. (1965). *Soviet chess*. Oxford: Clarendon Press.

Snyder, E. (1994). Getting involved in the shuffleboard world. In M.L. Dietz, R. Prus, & W. Shaffir (Eds.), *Doing everyday life: Ethnography as human lived experience* (pp. 85–96). Toronto: Copp Clark Longman, Ltd.

Stebbins, R. (1991). *Amateurs: On the margin between work and leisure*. Beverly Hills, CA: Sage.

Wiseman, J. (1970). *Stations of the lost: The treatment of skid row alcoholics*. Englewood Cliffs, NJ: Prentice-Hall.

ACKNOWLEDGEMENTS

I would like to thank Robert Prus for his encouragement and guidance throughout this study. I would also like to thank Karen Kusch, Irene Pugliese, and William Shaffir for their editorial comments on various drafts.

Chapter 23

Singing Out and Making Community:
Gay Men and Choral Singing

Roy Cain

INTRODUCTION

Like a lot of Canadians, I am an amateur choral singer. I have sung in community choirs over a number of years. The choirs with which I have the most experience are large ensembles of about 100 people. The choirs typically had somewhat more women than men, and there were always a number of gay members in the tenor and bass sections. The gay men in the choirs tended to form friendships with each other, creating a small group of friends within the larger choir. A gay chorister myself, I always appreciated these groups. We would chat together before rehearsals, and we might spend time together during breaks and, occasionally, after rehearsals. Like several others I know, I have made close and enduring friendships with other gay men through my choral singing. Even if it was not my intention in joining these groups, my membership in choirs ended up being an important means to develop my social life. In speaking to others, I realized that the choirs often played similar roles in the lives of its gay members. As well, several of my choir friends talked about how singing helped them come out as gay and to integrate into gay social worlds. Clearly there was more going on here than simply people coming together to sing music.

My personal experience in choirs led me to consider the role of community choirs in the personal and social lives of gay men. Choral singing seems to play a particularly important role in the lives of many gay men and lesbians. Gay and lesbian choruses exist in a number of communities across North America. These organizations can be important sites for social and community organizing (Morris, 1999; Roma, 1992; Sudderth, Eder, & Staggenborg, 1995), and they are often prominent organizations in local gay and lesbian communities. These musical groups can play an important role in building self-esteem, creating a sense of community, and educating the community-at-large (Hilliard, 2002). Most gay men and lesbians, however, probably sing in choral groups that are predominately heterosexual in membership, like the ones in which I sang, and which are examined in this chapter. An examination of gays who sing in predominately heterosexual community choirs presents some interesting opportunities for better understanding the intersections of gay and non-gay social worlds, and to understand how such mixed settings can play a role in gay identity and in the development of social ties between gay men. Gay choristers, for example, need to manage their identities, interact in ongoing ways with non-gay members, make decisions about the disclosure of their sexual preferences, and establish ties to other gay members. A detailed examination of this area of leisure and community involvement contributes to the small literature on friendship and leisure among gay men (e.g., Herkma, 1998; Messner, 1992; Nardi, 1992, 1999) and helps to shed light on how some gay men organize their social lives, find friends, and, for some, come to see themselves as gay.

METHOD

In the tradition of qualitative social research (Lofland & Lofland, 1986), I began the project with a general interest that was grounded in my own personal experience as a chorister. I started the study with a few general questions: what leads some men to want to sing in a choir, did they consider singing in a gay identified choir, did their involvement in singing have any relationship to their gay identities, and in what ways did their singing contribute to the development of their social lives. To examine such questions, I interviewed 12 gay men in two large choirs in the Toronto area. Interviews were tape recorded and transcribed verbatim. They were analyzed using a grounded theory approach (Glaser & Straus, 1967), looking for common themes across interviews.

Each of the two choirs that are the focus of this paper has about 100 members. I would estimate that somewhere from one-quarter to one-third of the tenor and bass sections were gay men. Ages of the 12 respondents varied from 30 to 61. All had sung in community choirs for at least five years. One respondent had been singing in the same choir for about 50 years, having joined in 1948. Ten of the 12 respondents in this study were amateur musicians. At the time of their interviews, they were employed in a diverse range of occupations, none of which had anything to do with music performance: an administrator of an arts organization, a painter, an insurance underwriter, a computer programmer, an office worker, a lawyer, among others. Two respondents were professional musicians. One was a paid church music director, although he sang in the community choir as an unpaid member. The other was the artistic director of one of the two choirs in this study. A gay man himself, this respondent spoke about his own experiences in choral music, and about the gay men in his choir. It should be noted that this chapter focuses on the experience of gay men, as there were few lesbians in the two choirs examined in this study. To my knowledge, there were only one, maybe two, lesbians in each of the choirs I studied. These women spent no time with the informal groupings of gay men.

SINGING AND IDENTITY

Respondents in this study came to singing at various points in their lives. Some were young adults when they first started singing in a choir, whereas others were well into their forties and fifties. Some had already established an extensive social life as gay men, while others went through the early stages of coming out as gay while in choirs. Most respondents made a point of saying in their interviews that their decision to join a choir had nothing to do with being gay, and no one said that they joined as a way of redefining their sexual identity or meeting other gay men. Consistent with Goffman's (1963) description of how people with **discreditable identities** can come together as a way of consolidating a positive sense of themselves, choirs played an important role in the coming out process of several respondents. Despite changes in social attitudes about gay sexuality in recent decades, coming out can still be very difficult. One man described his history in these terms: "I had this homosexual problem, that's how I understood it. I had no friends who knew ... I went through a whole lifetime of wishing that I hadn't been born. I didn't have any close friends to express this to, or my family, my brothers, anybody. I kept it to myself. And it bothered me so bad, the things that I did, I became extremely guilt ridden in my life. And I really had a very bad image of who I was ... I couldn't understand why they called it 'gay' because I thought it was the most ungay thing in the world to be homosexual."

Singing in a choir provided respondents, such as this man, with their initial connections to other gay men. For the first time, they saw gay men who were seemingly happy and well adjusted, and well accepted by others. Seeing others was important in changing their negative images of gays as sad or sick. The opportunity to watch how non-gay choristers dealt with gay members seemed particularly useful to respondents. Seeing other gay men interact with supportive non-gays helped respondents early in their coming out process to see that a gay identity does not automatically mean that others will reject them: "The conductor was an openly gay man, which everyone knew, and they all adored him and thought he was great. And he just seemed to be himself ... No one talked about it. But I thought that that man seemed to be happy with himself, and he's going on in life all right, and everything's okay." Seeing others in this non-gay environment interact as openly gay men held out the mundane and unexceptional possibilities that they might imagine for their own lives.

These social connections seemed crucial for those who were particularly isolated when they joined. One 60-year-old man talked about how isolated he was prior to singing in the choir. His contact with other gay men was largely through clandestine sexual contacts: "The sexual experiences that I had were always with anonymous people because I didn't want people to know my bent. So it was always with complete strangers." Another man, aged 68, had been married for 29 years at the time of his interview. He, too, described a very secretive involvement in gay worlds. These men had no gay friends and had never really talked to anyone about being gay. They only came to develop ongoing social relationships with other gay men through their singing. One recalled an evening when a group of gay men went for a drink following a rehearsal: "That was the first time that I had the friendship of a group of gay men. That was the first time—I had never been to a bar before, much less a gay bar. I had never been there. That was the first little clutch of people where 'I'm gay, you're gay, we don't have sex in common, but we have lots of other things in common.' We could talk about our jobs or whatever and still be open. I felt great. It was great."

These new friends provided respondents with important support early in their coming out process. Other gay men often play an important **socialization** role for individuals coming to see themselves as gay (Weinberg & Williams, 1974). A couple of respondents took advantage of this newly discovered resource to seek out information and support. Choir members can play the role of mentor, giving advice on a wide range of topics. One man described how he used a choir friend for advice and information: "My thoughts to him were 'I want to know what it is like to actually live as a gay man. How do you relate to your partner? How do other people treat you?' All those things. 'Are you involved in strictly gay activities? How do people in the church choir treat you? The minister?' These are all fears that I had myself. I had never seen it. He was very good. Very helpful ... From that point on, I slowly started to be more comfortable about trying to be myself."

Another respondent recalled his first contact with another gay man. When he was in his early twenties, he sat next to an older man in the choir: "As I was talking to him he would intimate quite clearly that he was a gay person, and because I was dealing with it myself, I was sort of drawn to him and wanted to ask him some questions. I needed his advice ... You know, 'I'm gay as well, but I have no knowledge of what life as a gay man is like ...' I lacked the social skills, or felt that I lacked the skills to cruise a man and to make other friends in a gay milieu, and he helped me out with that. [Q: How did he help?] He talked to me about what the culture was, and once I understood the culture and what the rules were, it was easier."

Support during difficult periods of the coming out process was available from other choristers. One man was very appreciative of the support he received from both gay and non-gay choristers when he was first coming out and struggling with his marriage: "People would come up to me and say it was all right. They'd say, 'I know what the problem is, and it's perfectly all right. I just want you to know that I care about you and I love you and I think a lot of you, and I'm here if you ever want to talk.' People would come up and do this and they weren't gay people ... And it made me feel better just knowing they knew and that they felt that way still. I had always had the feeling that I would be tremendously rejected if this knowledge ever came out, but here I was finding that people would accept it and it was okay. It was fine. It gave me more confidence to keep going until—here I am."

Choral singing facilitated respondents' decisions to come out in other ways. For at least two men, singing provided a reason to be out of the house. Singing provided one man with a way to "find himself" apart from his life as a married man: "I think part of it was I needed to get out on my own. Not to search out gay activity, but I needed to get out and become an individual in my own right. I seem to have been so enmeshed in my church activities and my family activities and my children's lives, that I felt I was a little lost as a person. Music was one way out."

Involvement in the choir can help structure or pace the coming out process. Because choirs meet weekly, respondents who are coming out can take gradual risks, taking small steps at a time. In this way, the coming out process is structured into weekly segments. Small hints or cues can be introduced to reveal slowly to others that they are gay. One man recalls:

I would at first worry that the whole group knows I'm gay, but I just let myself go and did my thing. And I thought, if I want to wear bright socks or a little bit flashy clothes, I don't care. That was part of expressing myself. I had been very conservative. I would wear things to the choir and think, people could tell. It was a statement on my part to the whole choir. When I went to the choir I would wear a brilliant buttercup yellow T-shirt. Or a sort of rainbow-coloured shirt. I made sure my jeans were tight. It was an expression, saying that I'm gay and that's okay. I'm sure people picked up on it. They didn't say anything much, but I slowly got comfortable. People still treated me just fine. I don't know if they thought, 'Oh look what he is wearing this week!' They may not have even noticed. I don't know. But I noticed, and it was how I was feeling about it. I was making a statement. An increasing statement. It was subtle at first, then I got bolder.

Singing in a group facilitates disclosure in other ways. By associating with gay choristers who are more open, other choristers sometimes assumed that respondents were gay as well. This means that a direct disclosure was not necessary, as people simply came to their own conclusions: "I know that when I first joined the choir several people concluded I am gay because I tended to hang out with a long-standing member who was widely suspected to be gay." The behaviour of knowing others may also signal to people that an individual is gay: "A number of gay people from the choir came to one of my [art] shows and they flooded in there. They were just hanging on me, hugging me. And I thought, 'Everybody knows now!' The choir was actually a great help to me in coming out. A big help."

So for several respondents in this study, choirs were important in helping them come to terms with their sexual identity. However, choirs played a different role in the lives of most of the men with whom I talked. Rather than facilitating their coming out process, choral singing played an important role in extending and deepening their social networks with other gay men.

THE SOCIAL STRUCTURE OF SINGING

Choirs are often highly regimented, and the organization of the choral experience is one that, in many ways, is not conducive to the development of social ties. While choirs vary in their degree of discipline, punctuality is typically stressed. Choristers can be chastised by conductors for arriving late for a rehearsal and disrupting others. Attendance is taken at rehearsals, and too many "unexcused" absences can lead to choristers being asked to withdraw from the choir. Talking during rehearsal time is frowned upon. Choristers are typically expected to dress in carefully prescribed ways for public performances. In classical community choirs, such as the ones in this study, men are often expected to wear black suits or tuxedos; women's attire may be a similar kind of uniform, often a white blouse and a long black skirt. Choristers are also expected to act in highly prescribed ways. During performances, they may be required to file onto the stage, silently, row by row. They are told to hold the music with the same hand, open their scores on cue, and avoid excessive movement while singing. The idea is to blend in, to be part of the larger group, and to not draw attention onto themselves.

Box 23.1: Golden Harmony

Why all the fuss about choral music? For all the developments in symphonic and operatic music in recent decades, choral singing remains the most pervasive musical activity in the country, whether in churches, schools or concert halls ... I interviewed a number of [people] to learn their views on the continuing popularity of one of the most basic of musical activities. Here are some of their thoughts:

Lydia Adams [conductor of the Elmer Iseler Singers, in Toronto]: "Whatever happens in people's lives, within five minutes of starting to sing, all that goes away. The voice can be a very powerful thing ..."

Noel Edison [conductor of the Toronto Mendelssohn Choir, Toronto]: "The human connection is very important in singing. Singing is direct, with no instrument in between. And it is therapeutic. Many of my singers have been helped through major handicaps, such as cancer, and have been rejuvenated through singing in a choir ..."

Jon Washburn [founding conductor of the Vancouver Chamber Choir]: "Choral singing is a team sport. You do it with other people and enjoy a collective satisfaction when it works. By way of contrast, the life of a soloist is rather lonely ..."

Francine Labelle [arts publicist and long-time choral singer]: "Certain singers are meant to be choral singers. You have to be willing and able to control your vibrato and blend your voice with others. It's like sharing a meal. Besides, I get stage fright, so I don't want to be a soloist ..."

Source: From "Golden Harmony," by William Littler, February 22, 2004, *The Toronto Star,* p. D1.

Despite such regimentation, there are other characteristics that facilitate social connections between choristers. Even for those respondents who had a pre-existing network of gay friends prior to their involvement in singing, choirs provided an opportunity to meet other people. One man, aged 36, identified that singing has been important to him socially: "Certainly when I look back to the stronger friendships that I've had since I've been out, I would have to say that they were all generally people that I met through singing." Choirs bring together people with a shared interest in music. Members often select choirs on the basis of the kind of musical repertoire they sing, so the people who are brought together generally share an interest in a similar kind of music. This common interest forms a basis for relationships: "You share a major interest, which is music and performing. And, I've always thought that the best way to make friends is to have hobbies and activities where you're going to meet people with similar interests to yourself." Another man noted, "There tend to be certain patterns of interest. It's unusual—forget sexuality for a moment—to find a male in a choir who spends the rest of his time swilling down beer and watching sports on TV and riding a motorbike. It just doesn't fit—it doesn't matter whether you're gay or straight. So, I think what it is, is that there are certain patterns, or certain types of makeup of people that, chances are, if you like choral singing, you'll find other areas that overlap as well."

There are weekly rehearsals through much of the year. Coming together on a regular basis means that relationships can develop in a slow and paced fashion. There is a continuity of relationships in so far as choristers come back week after week for rehearsal. Like several others, the following respondent compared his experience in meeting gay people through choirs and through other venues, such as gay bars: "You see the same people week after week. You get a chance to get to know them better. If I met someone in a bar, I might see him one Saturday night and then not see him again for months, depending on how our going out intersected. Choirs provide an opportunity for a little bit of continuity in a relationship that is starting off. You get to know people, and you get to talk to them a bit, and you get to find out what their week has been like, and you talk about other things."

Most of the rehearsal time together is activity-focused. There is little time for discussion, so choristers can spend time with new friends without having to worry about keeping conversation going. One man noted how this helps to minimize the awkwardness of early friendships: "There is no sense of being stilted or thrown together ... whereas in a bar, if you are going to stand and talk to one another, there are lots of pregnant pauses, 'What will I say to this guy?'" Because there is a common interest, there is easy content for discussion, when it can occur. Choirs are not sexually charged environments, which helps avoid some of the tensions and awkwardness that might occur in other gay-identified venues. In a bar, if one were to stand and talk too long to a stranger, questions might be raised about sexual intentions. This sometimes happens in choirs, but unlike bars, contact in choirs continues week after week, so it is easier to overcome early awkwardness and to nurture a non-sexual relationship: "I realized one man was interested in me, but I was not interested in him, so I made sure that he understood that ... I made sure that I didn't put myself in a situation where he might be led on or whatever. But after that it sort of developed that we formed a friendship."

Respondents stated that relationships between gay choristers are almost always non-sexual. This observation is consistent with Attinello's (1994) analysis of gay choirs, where he notes, "Actual liaisons are extremely few, and the socialization of new members involves a dramatic shift in which other chorus members become 'just sisters,' and inappropriate for most sexual contact" (p. 319). A respondent expressed this sentiment: "In fact, if anything, if it happens, it's downplayed. The camaraderie is important. In truth, if there were sexual encounters, it's not something that's advertised. It's something that people would keep to themselves." The structure of choral relationships seems to facilitate friendships, but the same structure may create barriers to the formation of sexual liaisons. One respondent noted: "If I am looking for a date or for sex, I can go other places to find it. I wouldn't go to a choir. [Question: Why is that?] It's slower [laughs]. I haven't got all day! ... I don't think gay men go to a choir because it provides them with the opportunity to meet other men. I think there are other opportunities to meet men and have sex with them that you wouldn't go to the trouble of joining a choir to meet men or have relationships with them."

People have to take certain personal risks in singing. For most choristers, to sing is to risk embarrassment, particularly when auditioning or engaging in a challenging activity like sight reading a new piece of music. For many, singing feels riskier than other kinds of musical performance. According to Attinello (1994), "Instrumentalists are able to objectify their skill as a function of time and work, external to their personal worth; the vocalist is constantly returning to the problem of judging the way he expresses himself through speech, which is identified closely with the social persona" (p. 322). This sense of risk taking helps to solidify bonds between people. Annual auditions help draw choristers together in the face of a common challenge, as do the anxious conversations backstage prior to a concert. A quote from one of the respondents in Drew's (1997) study of karaoke singers applies equally well to choristers: "It's like being shipwrecked together. You all join forces, you don't even know anybody, but you join forces because you're stronger that way" (p. 460). This shared sense of vulnerability seems to help to break down interpersonal defences and create a sense of camaraderie.

Choral singing requires a certain degree of teamwork and co-operation. At a bare minimum, singing in a choir means submitting to basic rules, such as showing up on time or not talking during rehearsals. Choir members have to sit and stand on the conductor's command, and basically do what they are told. For some respondents, that was one of the joys of singing: "Taking direction and being told what to do as part of a large group was kind of a nice break from work, where I was always having to make decisions and always having to give direction and also show a lot of initiative. The lovely thing about choir practice was that you had to pay attention—and you should go home and practise—but in truth, this was not a place to show a lot of initiative."

In less obvious ways, people have to work together musically to blend their voices; choral singing requires individuals to sing as part of the group, not as soloists. Having to co-operate in these ways helps people connect with each other. One respondent suspected that this was true, but he was careful not to overstate this factor: "It would be wonderful for me to do some rhapsodic thing about how the voice, and the discipline needed to sing with a group, creates some kind of special thing that bonds people. It well may, but I really haven't a clue about that." Even if they do not particularly get along, people are obligated to work things out enough to function as a section and as an ensemble. One respondent spoke of his dislike of one of the members of his section: "I find his personality is not to my liking, but you have to admit that at the end of the day we are both there to make music, so we'll have to get along and make the best of it, and work well together."

Respondents sometimes described benefits to choir singing that were perhaps less obvious. One man, who thought his choral singing had nothing to do with how he saw himself as a gay man, concluded by the end of the interview that it had played an important, but subtle role. He said he came to appreciate the importance of his gay friendships through singing: "It wasn't until I was well into probably my thirties that I actually began to see that I liked having other gay friends. It was special to me to have them and it was because there was this special connection that there isn't with other friendships. Other friendships bring different things. One of the contributing factors [to this realization] was, in fact, the choirs ... I think, in that sense, it was one of the things that helped me realize that I had something to celebrate when we came together as a group."

Box 23.2

Choral singing is a popular leisure activity. Choirs Ontario, an organization that promotes choral music in the province, has a membership of over 300 choirs and 400 individuals who support choral music. Their website states, "Our overall reach of members of member choirs is some 20,000 residents of Ontario. And, in turn, each of those choirs presents on average three concerts a year to a total audience of more than half a million people" (Choirs Ontario, 2004). And while this chapter examines gay men who sing in non-gay community choirs, there are a large number of gay and lesbian choruses throughout North America, Europe, and Australia. GALA Choruses, the Gay and Lesbian Association of Choruses, is an association of LGBT (lesbian, gay, bisexual, and transgendered) choral groups. According to its website, the association has over 185 member choruses, which range in size from four to 240 singers. Its member choruses are made up of over 10,000 singers (GALA Choruses, 2004).

CONCLUSION

Involvement in leisure activities, such as singing, can play important **social roles** in people's lives (see Stebbins, 1992), yet the connection between their involvement in choirs and their identities and social lives was not immediately apparent to most respondents in this study. Almost all of the respondents started their interviews unclear of the links between their involvement in choirs and their gay lives. As they began to talk, all of the men spoke of the gay friends they have made through choirs, and several talked about how the choirs helped them identify as gay and integrate into gay social worlds. The reluctance or inability of respondents to see the links between their gay lives and their singing may be indicative of the degree to which we compartmentalize our lives. Gay identity is often seen by gays and non-gays alike to be simply a matter of sex; in our heterosexist culture, it is easy to overlook the many other ways that sexual identity can permeate people's social lives. This study helps to illustrate the often subtle ways that gay identification can shape people's relationships with gay and non-gay others and how they perceive themselves.

The structure of choirs facilitates forming social relationships between choir members, but it does not do so equally: gender and sexual orientation continue to play important roles. Respondents in this study were consistently more likely to form ties to other gay men than to lesbians. Most were largely unaware of lesbian choristers, although in both choirs, there were at least a couple of women. This divide is, perhaps, due in part to seating arrangements. In choirs, people need to sit in sections: tenors sit with tenors, sopranos sit with sopranos. In other words, the men sit with men, and the women sit with women. This leads to a high degree of gender division in that choristers are most likely to connect to those who are seated nearby. But the lack of connection between lesbians and gay men—which was consistent across interviews—was nothing particular to their involvement in choirs. Most respondents simply did not know any lesbians in their lives. Yet, gendered seating arrangements do little to nurture ties to heterosexual men. Few respondents reported any significant relationship to non-gay men in the choirs. A distance seems to enter quickly into relationships with heterosexual men. So while they can sing in the same choir and share the same leisure activity for years, the differences can sometimes be so great as to lead respondents to say, "I've never understood why straight men would sing with a choir." While the non-gay environment of the choirs was important in bringing the gay choristers together, the pattern of social relationships in the choirs largely mirrored those in the rest of respondents' lives.

Despite the divisions that were often reproduced in the context of the choirs, interviews indicate that there are benefits to singing in a mixed environment. Respondents had the opportunity to see other choristers interact with and accept openly gay men. They were able to experience something that Goffman (1963) observed years ago about the relationships between **"the discredited"** and others—that known difference is often treated as irrelevant. Beyond that, several received active support from non-gays, and a number of men, particularly those who were fairly new to the coming out process, negotiated new boundaries between their gay and non-gay lives. All this suggest that ongoing research into the points of intersection between people's gay and non-gay lives might yield useful and interesting theoretical insights about the organization of gay worlds. A similar approach could be very useful in understanding the social life of other groups. For example, studying the points of intersection between disabled and non-disabled people could bring into sharper relief the features of the social lives of those living with physical disabilities. In this way, we can see how the sociological study of a leisure activity can provide useful insights into the interactions and the organization of different social worlds.

GLOSSARY

Discreditable identity: A term used by Goffman to refer to a stigmatized identity that, if known to others, might lead to rejection or disapproval of the individual.

Discredited identity: A term used by Goffman to refer to a stigmatized identity that is known to others and that might lead to rejection or disapproval of the individual.

Social role: A set of behaviours and expectations associated with a social status; the role is not fixed, but negotiated between individuals.

Socialization: A process by which people learn the various attributes of a social group (behaviour, customs, values), and a process by which people learn to see themselves as members of a social group.

Social structure: The relationship of people to each other that guides behaviour and interaction within the group.

REFERENCES

Attinello, P. (1994). Authority and freedom: Toward a sociology of the gay choruses. In P. Brett, E. Wood, & G. Thomas (Eds.), (315–346), *Queering the pitch: The new gay and lesbian musicology*. New York: Routledge.

Choirs Ontario. (2004). Retrieved on November 1, 2004, from www.choirsontario.org/companyinfo.html

Drew, R. (1997). Embracing the role of amateur. *Journal of Contemporary Ethnography, 25,* 449–468.

GALA Choruses. (2004). Retrieved November 1, 2004, from www.galachoruses.org

Glaser, A., & Straus, B. (1967). *The discovery of grounded theory*. Chicago: Aldine.

Goffman, E. (1963). *Stigma: Notes on the management of spoiled identity*. Englewood Cliffs, NJ: Prentice-Hall.

Herkma, G. (1998). "As long as they don't make an issue of it ...": Gay men and lesbians in organized sports in the Netherlands. *Journal of Homosexuality, 35,* 1–23.

Hilliard, R. (2002). The San Francisco gay men's chorus: A historical perspective on the role of a chorus as a social service." *Journal of Gay & Lesbian Social Services, 14,* 81–96.

Lofland, J., & Lofland, L. (1986). *Analyzing social settings*. Belmont, CA: Wadsworth Publications.

Messner, M. (1992). Like family: Power, intimacy, and sexuality in male athletes' friendships. In P. Nardi (Ed.), *Men's friendships* (pp. 215–237). Newbury Park, CA: Sage.

Morris, B. (1999). *Eden built by Eves: The culture of women's music festivals*. Los Angeles: Alyson Books.

Nardi, P. (1992). Sex, friendship, and gender roles among gay men. In P. Nardi (Ed.), *Men's friendships* (pp. 173–185). Newbury Park, CA.: Sage.

Nardi, P. (1999). *Gay men's friendships: Invincible communities*. Chicago: University of Chicago Press.

Pronger, B. (1990). *The arena of masculinity: Sports, homosexuality, and the meaning of sex*. New York: St. Martin's.

Roma, C. (1992). Women's choral communities: Singing for our lives. *Hotwire* (January), 36–39, 52.

Stebbins, R. (1992). *Amateurs, professionals and serious leisure*. Montreal: McGill-Queen's University Press.

Sudderth, L., Eder, D., & Staggenborg, S. (1995). The National Women's Music Festival. *Journal of Contemporary Ethnography, 23,* 485.

Weinberg, M., & Williams, C. (1974). *Male homosexuals: Their problems and adaptations*. New York: Oxford University Press.

Chapter 24

For Better and for Worse:
Psychological Demands and Structural Impacts on Gay Servicewomen in the Military and Their Long-Term Partners

Lynne Gouliquer and Carmen Poulin

INTRODUCTION

In society and in the military in particular, many factors impede the ability of homosexual individuals to maintain long-term relationships. Militaries are conservative institutions, pervasively heterosexual, and predominantly male enclaves (Connell, 1995). In addition, most militaries around the world tightly regulate the sexuality of their members by discriminating against homosexuals (Gouliquer, 1998). During the last 30 years, however, lesbian, gay, bisexual, and transgendered (LGBT) people have challenged prejudicial practices and discrimination within and outside the military.

In 1989, Lieutenant Michelle Douglas was released from the Canadian Armed Forces for homosexuality, and subsequently filed a suit against the military for discrimination. In 1992, the Supreme Court of Canada found the military in violation of the Charter of Rights and Freedoms regarding its policy on homosexuality. Consequently, the Canadian military ended its sanctioned discrimination against homosexuals (Department of National Defence, 1992) and thus began a series of changes that would dramatically affect the lives of its homosexual members.

In 1991, the Canadian Armed Forces officially recognized heterosexual common-law relationships and granted them the same social-medical family benefits as married couples (Harrison & Laliberté, 1994). It took until 1996, however, for military policy to grant homosexual couples the same right. This change occurred only after the civilian sector had extended these benefits to homosexual couples (CANFORGEN 055/97, 1997). This last change meant that lesbian and gay service members finally gained access to family benefits. To exercise this right, however, required coming out officially to the military bureaucracy. Even today, many choose not to do so. Research indicates that men are more reluctant than women to officially come out (Gouliquer, 2003). For those coming out, access to family benefits is reported as the motivating factor (Gouliquer, 2001).

While access to these benefits has now been secured, other forms of discrimination persist for gays and lesbians. In May 1999, the Supreme Court of Canada struck down the long-standing heterosexual definition of a spouse. As a result, hundreds of Canadian laws require revision ("Gay Rights," 1999). Currently, the right of same-sex couples to marry is being debated and pursued.

These events are paradigmatic shifts, yet we know very little about the impact they had on military members, either gay or straight. In a series of life-history interviews, we investigated the ability of gay military servicewomen and their partners to maintain long-term relationships.

Box 24.1

We interviewed 10 military lesbians and six partners who had been in a relationship for a minimum of three years, or had gone through one posting together. For reasons of confidentiality, pseudonyms have been used. Pseudonyms were also discontinued between quotes, further protecting participants' identities. Specific dates, locations, and identifying details may have been changed. While the meaning has not been compromised, all quotes have been edited to ease comprehension and readability.

We paid particular attention to the ways in which the military milieu affected and organized these relationships, and the cognitive processes used by these women to make sense of their reality. While the Canadian military makes similar demands on both gay and heterosexual service members and their families, the present study highlights the unique realities faced by military lesbians and their partners.

We begin this chapter by describing the epistemological framework underpinning our study.

Box 24.2

Epistemology is simply a way of knowing (Harding, 1991). It is a set of assumptions regarding the acquisition and creation of knowledge, and influences what is accepted as knowledge (Ramazanoglu, 2002). The epistemology we espouse influences the entire research process.

Source: From "Recherche sur la Violence Familiale: Contribution des Différentes Epistémologies," by C. Poulin and L.R. Ross, 1997, *Criminologie, XXX*(2), p. 17.

Next, we present a brief overview of the military context as it specifically relates to homosexual members. In the results section, we discuss relationship maintenance behaviours of lesbians in the context of the military lifestyle. We focus on particular military events: postings and attached-postings. We refer to these as "**organizational moments**."

The effect of organizational moments is highlighted by examining four themes pertinent to the maintenance of long-term partnerships for gay servicewomen and

Box 24.3

Organizational moments are ordinary events, regularly occurring in the every day. They structure activities and thought processes, but their meaning is based on the needs of the institution. In the context of this study, organizational moments draw their meaning from the goals of the Canadian military and organize the lives of those people who are directly (e.g., service members) and indirectly (e.g., military wives or children) involved.

their partners: (1) supportive social networks, (2) coming out to families of origin, (3) searching for equity as a maintenance behaviour, and (4) career issues. The themes of communication and shared time are also important for maintaining relationships and will be discussed when examining the effects of attached-postings. The chapter concludes with a discussion of possible directions for future research, and assesses the practical implications of such research on homosexuals in the military.

EPISTEMOLOGY, METHODOLOGY, AND METHOD OF THE STUDY

All research is based on particular assumptions. The assumptions shaping our approach are grounded in feminist standpoint theory (Harding 1987, 2004; Sprague, 2001), institutional ethnography (Smith, 1987), and cognitive psychology's **schema** theory (Bem, 1993).

Similar to Marxism, **feminist standpoint epistemology** recognizes experience as a way of knowing, and values the knowledge of the oppressed over that of the oppressor (Hartsock, 1987). According to standpoint epistemology, the oppressed have experiential knowledge of their own reality, but must also understand the oppressor's reality in order to survive. Thus, the oppressed develop a bifurcated (Smith, 1987) or multiple (Ladson-Billings, 2000) consciousness. Moreover, the oppressed have less investment in maintaining the status quo, and in providing partial or distorted descriptions (Harding, 1991; Sprague, 2001).

Box 24.4

For example, to find out about the daily operation of a large factory, we could seek this information from two distinct sources. The owner or managers provide official rules and regulations (which could be in the form of a written text), and the information that corresponds to the knowledge needed to manage the activities of the factory. If we ask the workers, however, these informants also know the official rules and regulations, but, in addition, provide a description of the daily experiences of working in the factory. If our interest is in the everyday operation of the factory, or more specifically, the ways the official rules and regulations are translated into the actual daily activities, then in all likelihood the workers could provide a version closer to the truth (i.e., the oppressed in a Marxist framework).

The epistemological framework selected also guides the choice of the methodology (Ussher, 1996). Institutional ethnography (Smith, 1987) is a methodology that seeks to uncover and explain the institutional **"relations of ruling"** that give meaning and direction to the everyday experiences of the women.

Box 24.5

The relations of ruling represent a socially pervasive, taken-for-granted, powerful, and complex structure of organized practices that control and regulate the everyday life (Smith, 1987). For example, we assume that the world is heterosexually organized and is a place where everyone has access to marriage. Laws and social practices support these assumptions and organize our lives accordingly.

Institutional ethnography, therefore, is a feminist standpoint methodology that directs us to start with women's stories (in our case, gay servicewomen and their partners): their social experiences of their institutional reality.

Individuals also engage in sense-making practices or schema formation and modification to deal with their social reality.

Box 24.6

Schema theory suggests that, in order to make sense of reality, we construct and utilize cognitive maps (i.e., schemata). With schemata, we efficiently process information being received by the senses (Holland, 1985). In other words, individuals collectively create meaningful concepts (e.g., masculinity, stereotypes) from the patterns and associated meanings derived from the information received through the senses (e.g., conversations, images, practices). Thus, schemata are socially available units of cognitively organized networks of information, which facilitate communication and sense making (Bem, 1993). As such, schemas help us psychologically cope with our realities.

In the context of a patriarchal institution such as the military, organizational moments typically complicate the social and psychological realities of women. These complications represent institutional instances where "individual psychologies intersect with social ideologies" (Khayatt 1992, p. 77). In other words, individuals engage in sense-making processes to deal with the institutionally created complications. Readily available schemata are routinely employed, but often modified to fit individual realities (Ryan & Bernard, 2000). When the socially available schemata do not correspond with an individual's experience, confusion, contradictions, and struggle result. What is of particular interest to us is how women resolved these complications.

The goal of the present study, therefore, is to identify the nature of the schemata present when a lesbian makes sense of an organizational moment. Institutional ethnography provides the methodology for elucidating the relations of ruling that shape the realities of Canadian gay servicewomen and their partners; whereas exploring organizational moments leads us to understand their psychological realities and coping strategies.

HOMOSEXUALITY AND THE CANADIAN MILITARY

The military is a distinct community where separateness from civilian society is emphasized through the wearing of uniforms, the use of a language heavily infused with jargon, and the application of an additional but separate set of laws for its members. Because of its insular nature, the military organizes its members' work and leisure activities and, in many ways, their personal lives. These practices psychologically and physically secure the commitment and support of the soldiers and their families (Loomis & Lightburn, 1980).

Until 1992, the Canadian military investigated and released many military women for homosexuality (Gouliquer, 2000). The investigations were disruptive, demeaning, and psychologically difficult for gay servicewomen as Chantale's quote (servicewoman, eight-year relationship) exemplifies. "One of the girls ... the SIU threatened her with release from the military and said that they had photographs of her in bed with a woman who was underage ... [S]he was very upset and was interviewed many, many times. The SIU was trying to break into the 'circle.' They knew that there were a lot of us that were friends and maybe that is why people were individually targeted ... I knew that it was a witch hunt ... and there was [another] girl ... [T]his investigation followed her to Borden and she eventually took her release under the pressure. Karrie also took her release; the girl that ... they said they had photographs [of her]." Militaries have tried for many years without success to eliminate lesbians and gays from their ranks. Despite past and present discrimination, however, lesbians remain an integral part of the Canadian military and, like their civilian counterparts, they form romantic long-term liaisons.

RELATIONSHIP MAINTENANCE BEHAVIOURS OF MILITARY LESBIAN COUPLES

In the next two sections, we examine two specific types of organizational moments of military life—postings and attached-postings. Postings are military-imposed relocations, which usually involve the soldier and his/her family changing where they live. Attached-postings are displacements of short duration (usually six or more months), during which time only the military member leaves. Once the particular tasking is completed, she or he returns to her/his family. These organizational moments have implications for all military members who are in relationships, but the impacts are often more salient and poignant for lesbians.

POSTINGS

For the Canadian soldier, a posting is integral to military life. Based on institutional requirements and ideology, soldiers are regularly, and for extended periods of time, ordered to move to other military locations across the country and around the world. Ultimately, soldiers are obliged to obey and consequently must relocate with their families. Postings clearly tap into the military-comes-first schema, and accordingly the soldiers and their families come second. Postings sever family members from their established social networks, jobs, and possibly their culture. Isabelle (servicewoman, 4.5-year relationship) describes the impact of a posting order: "When she heard that I was posted [to English Canada], she left [the relationship]. She was scared, she didn't even know how to say yes in English ... It was considered a really bad posting. There is nothing to do [in Shilo]. It's Anglophone everywhere. It's only hunting. It's in the woods. It's still a semi-isolated base."

Against the rigid backdrop of the military structure and ethos, the partner's life is perceived as flexible and shapeable in the name of military requirements. Eileen (partner, 10-year relationship) describes the impact of the first posting she underwent, and draws on a traditional schema of a committed relationship to make sense of her experience: "I had to quit school if we were going to have a committed relationship. It was 'put up or shut up' time. She moved out east. I had to figure out what I was going to do. So I spent four months earning some money because Gander is not a place that your spouse can get a job, and yeah, I moved. But for four months, I worked my butt off, just saved money ... Paid off debt. Paid off everything, and quit school. And January or December I moved to Gander."

Supportive Social Networks

Lesbians engage in many of the same relationship maintenance behaviours as heterosexual couples (Hass & Stafford, 1998). However, as Hass and Stafford suggested, seeking out supportive environments is a conscious strategy for lesbians and gays. Given the military's past history of witch hunts, and its practice of periodically posting service members, establishing and maintaining supportive social networks becomes most salient for lesbians in the Canadian military. Kelli-jo (partner, 9.5-year relationship) describes how she and her partner actively sought positive social contexts after a posting to Petawawa: "We missed the reinforcement [of being with other lesbians], but we would go to Toronto on the weekends, and we would visit friends when we were in Kingston, and certain [other social] events would happen, so we would find reinforcement elsewhere, but not in Petawawa itself."

Women in the Canadian military represent about 10% of the soldiers; thus, lesbians represent an even smaller proportion. When postings are to an isolated region or a different culture, lesbians' experience of marginalization will be intensified. In addition, the military socializes its members to look inward for their social support. Given these factors, military lesbians and their partners face structural, and sometimes cultural, challenges establishing supportive and affirming social networks of any kind.

Coming Out to Family

Making a relationship public to a social network is essential if such a network is to affirm and support the relationship. In the case of gays and lesbians, making a relationship public implies coming out. The family is the primary social network utilized by heterosexual couples to positively affirm their relationships. This is not necessarily the case for homosexuals, as we cannot assume that families provide a positive and affirming atmosphere for homosexual relationships. Because homosexuality is not the norm and is generally viewed negatively, seeking support within the family always first involves the stress and process of coming out. In the context of the military, this theme was salient for a number of our interviewees, especially the civilian partners of servicewomen. Frances (partner, three-year relationship) speaks about the familial code of silence. This is a schema that informs and directs family members (i.e., their thoughts and behaviours) to keep hidden the truth around perceived shameful matters, in this case Frances's homosexuality: "I was raised a very strict Catholic, and my mother would just shudder every time she saw a [gay] pride parade: 'Oh, I'd die if any of my kids were like that' ... It [my being gay] was never spoken 'til the day my mom had passed away ... She knew, but it was never spoken about."

For a number of these women, postings also precipitated coming out to their families. The timing of events did not typically correspond to their needs in terms of this coming out process. If the women had been partnered with a military serviceman, their numerous moves would have required no explanation. Thus, not being able to draw on the traditional heterosexual couple schema (i.e., the woman follows the man, and sacrifices her career and social networks), these women often invented stories rather than come out.

While seeking affirmation and support from the family is a habitual undertaking for heterosexual couples, in the case of gay people, it is clear from our interviews that this is complicated by the need to come out. Participants, especially the partners of military lesbians, are often cast into these emotionally highly charged events as a result of military postings. Socially available schemata related to these events do not help them make sense of the stress they experience.

Equity as a Maintenance Behaviour

Hass and Stafford (1998) identified a preoccupation with equity as a means to maintaining a long-term relationship in the gay and lesbian population they studied. In our present work, this theme emerged often and taps into two socially available schemata: (1) the independent lesbian schema; and (2) the traditional heterosexual couple, where the woman is dependent-on-the-husband schema. Mary's comment (partner, one-posting relationship) regarding officially coming out to the military taps into these two social schemata: "I would just rather keep it separate [the relationship from the military]. I don't want to be 'a dependant' in the military. I'd rather just 'be' because that's what it would be, military personnel and their 'dependants' no matter [what my social status might be]."

Unlike heterosexual women, lesbians cannot hold on to the gender schema that suggests women will find a husband to take care of them financially (Bunch, 1987). Although women tend not to earn as much as men (Statistics Canada, 2000), the partnership schema common to lesbian relationships is infused with independence and employment outside the home. Consequently, finances tend to represent a major concern for gay servicewomen's partners. Power dynamics and equity issues that accompany financial independence are also underlying concerns. This is exemplified by Gia's quote (partner, one-posting relationship) as she describes her reality: "The stability is gone. I don't make enough money to live on my own so it's like, [if we broke off], all of a sudden I'm out on the street. [Interviewer: So what would happen if Barb and you did break off?] I'd probably move back home ... If it happened tomorrow ... everything would fall apart. But I'd probably end up going back home." As discussed above, the familial support system plays a major role in lesbians' lives. The significance of and reliance on the family of origin was echoed in many of the interviews conducted.

Drewry Lehr (1999) suggests that military wives are now more likely to have employment than previously. The majority of the civilian lesbian partners in the present study did find jobs, but these were poorly remunerated, and few managed to have a career. Further, regardless of their financial situation, all civilian partners raised financial status as a salient relationship issue. Given the emphasis lesbian culture places on financial equity as a maintenance behaviour in long-term relationships, partners of servicewomen were creative in their ability to "make the best" of a challenging situation. All couples discussed finances openly, but not all of them found a satisfactory resolution to the inequality. There is no question that postings, as organizational moments, limit the ability of the civilian partner to take the necessary steps to further her career needs. Franky's discussion (partner, three-year relationship) of a previous long-term relationship illustrates this point: "We had a very rough go. When I agreed to move out there with her, I agreed 50/50, right down the middle. [But] it was impossible for me to keep it 50/50. I had just bought a car because I had to commute. I was spending however much on gas. You are paying your rent, everything else, and there are phone bills, because I'm calling home."

Career Issues

Among the lesbians we interviewed, two possible paths were encountered with respect to careers. The first path was to live the relationship at a distance. Only one couple we interviewed succeeded thus far in such an undertaking. The second path, as some of the previous quotes suggest, involves one partner giving up her career or work in favour of the relationship. When both women were in the military, one partner would give up her military career to facilitate moves and support the other woman's military career. For example, when Lori (partner, 10-year relationship) found out that her military partner was about to have their child prematurely, she took her release from the military to be able to return home early from an overseas posting. "She was on a maternity leave, and she was due to have the baby. She was by herself and so I said, 'I'm not going to wait. I'm going to put in my release now' ... 'Cause I couldn't bring her with me or say, 'You know, we are partners.' 'Cause I could not use that [her pregnancy] as an excuse 'cause if I was gay, then they would know Tammy was as well, and her career would be over."

Some of the women we interviewed had never been in the military and chose to follow their servicewomen partners. In addition to distancing themselves from family and sometimes their language and culture, the loss of their civilian social network of lesbian friends was most salient for this group.

ATTACHED-POSTINGS

Attached-postings, such as peacekeeping missions, take military members away from their homes for extended periods of time. Many of the women in this study endured separations, and frequently this involved the servicewomen going to foreign countries under stressful situations (e.g., Bosnia).

Sharing Time and Tasks

The two most frequently reported maintenance behaviours in long-term relationships are sharing tasks (mundane chores such as washing dishes) and sharing time together or being in each other's presence (Dainton & Stafford, 1993). Dainton and Stafford suggest that "for many couples merely being together ... is central to the maintenance of their relationship" (p. 267). Attached-postings organize couples' lives in such a way that partners must struggle with the fact that they cannot easily share tasks or share time together. Cali's frustration (partner, eight-year relationship) was a common experience. "There is that aspect, just sitting there laughing and talking, sharing things from the day, maybe watching something on TV, or something in the news and then talking about it ... Now you are the one running around doing all of the bill paying, not the two of you ... You are doing it all ... Keeping everything running, keeping animals happy ... [I]f I forget to pick something up, I can't just pick up the phone and say, 'Can you do this on the way home from work?' ... So it is just the little things. But the big factor is the loneliness."

Communication

In addition, Hass and Stafford (1998) reported on the importance of communication among long-term same-sex couples. As mentioned above, the Canadian military features a history of overt discrimination towards homosexuals and especially lesbians, and a privileging of an exclusively heterosexual culture. During an attached-posting, and depending on where the military member is sent (e.g., Afghanistan), communication between a lesbian couple can be rendered nearly impossible. Even in the best of times, it can be difficult because of the lack of privacy, and the military's limitation on the duration and number of phone calls allowed. "She is in a house with nine guys. Before, they had little rooms that they could go into [to make their phone calls]... It's hard to keep up the communication end of things when you only have 15 minutes to talk ... You don't want to bring up the little things because you feel like you are wasting time, but yet you don't want to bring up the big things because you think, well, this is something that is going to take a lot longer than 15 minutes to discuss. And then you sit there and you are like, we have nothing to talk about" (Jessica, one-posting relationship).

Consequently, the ability of long-term partners to maintain communication, or share time together, especially when the military lesbian is on an attached-posting, is greatly reduced. No matter how frustrated the partner is, the servicewoman is obliged to go, epitomizing the "military-comes-first" schema. When both partners are in the military, the frequency of attached-postings is doubled, further reducing the ability of partners to engage in primary maintenance behaviours.

To help them psychologically and socially deal with postings and attached-postings, soldiers and their families are able to draw upon a repertoire of social schemata. These schemata generally consist of traditional ideas concerning gender roles. Two powerful socially available schemata function in the context of the military. First, a soldier is assumed to be heterosexual and male. Lesbian military members have to make adjustments to this schema with respect to their sexual orientation and gender within a historical context where lesbians were ferreted out. Second, the "traditional-heterosexual-couple" schema assumes that domestic tasks are the woman's primary responsibility, whereas the man provides the majority of the income for the family. Lesbian partners and heterosexual women who do not buy into this script are faced with choosing between their careers and their relationships. Choosing the relationship may require them to modify their schema of themselves with respect to the balance between dependence/independence they have or wish to have in their relationship. The military-comes-first schema regarding postings must also be modified for lesbians: Coming out to the family of origin may have to be integrated into this schema in order to justify a move, especially if this represents leaving a good work position or a course of study.

CONCLUSION

We have discussed some of the specific effects of the military's organizational moments, such as postings and attached-postings, on lesbians' long-term relationships. This sheds light on the impact the military lifestyle has on lesbians' ability to create social networks, come out when they are ready to do so, pursue career goals, establish equity in their relationships, share time together, and maintain communication. We analyzed some of the complications that emerged when socially available schemata do not correspond to military lesbians and their partners' everyday reality, and how they modified these schemata where possible in order to engage in sense-making processes.

One of the differences between homosexual and heterosexual couples is cultural: Lesbians, for instance, have their own culture. While some Queer theorists argue that no single lesbian culture exists (Gamson, 2000), there is evidence indicating that many aspects that typically define a culture—such as common symbols, music, literature (Penelope & Wolfe, 1993), and experiences based on sharing a particular marginalized identity (Brown, 1989)—are in fact shared among lesbians. The military also represents a distinct culture with values and traditions. Investigating the interaction between the lesbian and military cultures seems relevant when trying to understand maintenance behaviours in long-term relationships. As Poulin (2001) suggested, the lesbian and the military cultures make overlapping demands on their members, but more often compete with each other. Most importantly for long-term relationships, this competition seems to interfere with the ability of lesbian servicewomen and their partners to engage in relationship-maintenance behaviours, and often deprives them of affirming contexts. Psychologically, they must adjust the socially available schemata: They need to manage and integrate elements related to their family of origin values (e.g., attitudes towards heterosexual versus same-sex couples), and those of the general population; sort out lesbian norms (i.e., traditional heterosexual model of female dependence versus the independent lesbian model); and grapple with a military ethos (i.e., commitment, allegiance, and obedience).

FUTURE RESEARCH

The present research represents an examination of the maintenance behaviours of lesbian partners in long-term lesbian relationships in the military milieu. In the first instance, it seems important to us to further our analysis and systematically examine differences and similarities between the general civilian community and the military population with respect to maintenance behaviours in both heterosexual and homosexual couples. Do these groups utilize the same or different maintenance strategies, and what are the gender differences? Are they equally successful despite their differing social realities? Do long-term, long-distance relationships in the civilian world differ from those in the military community? Data collection to address some of these questions is presently underway.

At this time, however, we are most interested in understanding the impact of the military, as a total institution (Goffman, 1960), on the particular maintenance behaviours used by homosexual versus heterosexual individuals. We also seek to understand how, in this milieu, lesbians make sense of their everyday experiences and what schemata they utilize to cope with the contradictions in their lives. The importance of better understanding the impact of such an institution lies in its ability to inform us with respect to policy changes that need to take place. Given the policy changes that have already taken place in the Canadian military context with respect to the decriminalization of homosexuality, the present research represents a unique opportunity. It allows us to gain an understanding of the potential such changes can have on the homosexual population, their everyday lives, and psychological coping strategies.

GLOSSARY

Epistemology: A theory of knowledge, especially with regard to its method and validation; a way of knowing; a set of assumptions regarding the acquisition and creation of knowledge, which influences what is accepted as knowledge.

Feminist standpoint epistemology: A way of knowing grounded in the different features of women's social situations.

Organizational moments: Ordinary events, regularly occurring in the every day, that serve institutional needs but typically complicate the lives of marginalized individuals.

Relations of ruling: A socially pervasive, taken-for-granted, powerful, and complex structure of organized practices that control and regulate the everyday life.

Schema: Cognitive maps or structures for interpreting the world; psychological organization of cognitions used to efficiently process sensory information.

NOTE
The order of authorship was determined randomly as both authors contributed equally.

REFERENCES
Bem, S. (1993). *The lenses of gender: Transforming the debate on sexual inequality*. New Haven, CT: Yale University Press.

Brown, L. (1989). New voices, new visions: Toward a lesbian/gay paradigm for psychology. *Psychology of Women Quarterly, 13*, 445–458.

Bunch, C. (1987). Learning from lesbian separatism. In C. Bunch (Ed.), *Passionate politics: Feminist theory in action* (pp. 182–191). New York: St. Martin's Press.

CANFORGEN 055/97. (1997). *Relocation, isolated post, and military foreign service regulations — Same-sex partner benefits*. National Defence Headquarters, Ottawa, Ontario, Canada.

Connell, R.W. (1995). *Masculinities*. Berkeley: University of California Press.

Dainton, M., & Stafford, L. (1993). Routine maintenance behaviours: A comparison of relationship type, partner similarity and sex differences. *Journal of Social and Personal Relationships, 10*, 255–271.

Department of National Defence. (1992). *Change to CF sexual orientation policy*. News Release/Communiqué AFN, 57/92. Ottawa: National Defence Headquarters.

Drewry Lehr, D.D. (1999). Military wives: Breaking the silence. In F. D'Amico & L. Weinstein (Eds.), *Gender camouflage: Women and the US military* (pp. 117–131). New York: New York University Press.

Gamson, J. (2000). Sexualities, queer theory, and qualitative research. In N.K. Denzin, & Y.S. Lincoln (Eds.), *Handbook of qualitative research*, 2nd ed. (pp. 347–365). London, UK: Sage Publications, Inc.

Gay rights suit poses challenge to 58 federal laws. (1999, January 8). *The Toronto Star*, p. A1.

Goffman, E. (1960). Characteristics of total institutions. In M.R. Stein, A.J. Vidich, & D.M. White (Eds.), *Identity and anxiety: Survival of the person in mass society* (pp. 449–479). Glencoe, IL: Free Press.

Gouliquer, L. (2000). Negotiating sexuality: Lesbians in the Canadian military. In B. Miedema, J.M. Stoppard, & V. Anderson (Eds.), *Women's bodies, women's lives: Health, well-being, and body image* (pp. 254–277). Toronto: Sumach Press.

Gouliquer, L. (2001). What gay servicewomen can tell us about the gender order. *Proceedings of feminisms challenge the traditional discipline*. McGill Centre for Research on Teaching and Women.

Gouliquer, L. (2003). *Post-1992: The Canadian military and homosexuality*. Experiences of Foreign Militaries Roundtable, Don't Ask, Don't Tell: 10 Years Later Conference, Hofstra University, Hempstead, New York (September 18–20).

Gouliquer, M.L. (1998). *A menace to the gender order: The management of lesbian sexuality in the Canadian Military*. Unpublished MA research paper, McGill University, Montreal, Canada.

Harding, S. (1987). *Feminism and methodology*. Bloomington, IN: Indiana University Press.

Harding, S. (1991). *Whose science? Whose knowledge? Theorizing from women's lives*. Ithaca, NY: Cornell University Press.

Harding, S. (Ed.). (2004). *The feminist standpoint theory reader: Intellectual and political controversies*. New York: Routledge.

Harrison, D., & Laliberté, L. (1994). *No life like it: Military wives in Canada.* Toronto: James Lorimer & Company Publishers.

Hartsock, N. (1987). The feminist standpoint: Developing the ground for a specifically feminist historical materialism. In S. Harding & M. Hintikka (Eds.), *Discovering reality: Feminist perspectives on epistemology, metaphysics, methodology, and philosophy of science* (pp. 283–310). Dordrecht: Reidel/Kluwer.

Hass, S.M., & Stafford, L. (1998). An initial examination of maintenance behaviours in gay and lesbian relationships. *Journal of Social and Personal Relationships, 15*(6), 846–855.

Holland, D. (1985). From situation to impression: How Americans get to know themselves and one another. In J. Dougherty (Ed.), *Directions in cognitive anthropology* (pp. 389–411). Chicago: University of Illinois Press.

Khayatt, M.D. (1992). *Lesbian teachers: An invisible presence.* New York: State University of New York Press.

Ladson-Billings, G. (2000). Radicalized discourses and ethnic epistemologies. In N.K. Denzin and Y.S. Lincoln (Eds.), *Handbook of qualitative research,* 2nd ed. (pp. 257–277). Thousand Oaks: Sage Publications.

Loomis, D.C., & Lightburn, D.T. (1980). Taking into account the distinctness of the military from the mainstream society. *Canadian Defence Quarterly, 10*(2), 16–21.

Penelope, J., & Wolfe, S.J. (1993). *Lesbian culture: An anthology.* Freedom, CA: The Crossing Press.

Poulin, C. (2001). The military is the wife and I am the mistress: Partners of gay service women. *Atlantis, 26*(1), 65–76.

Poulin, C., & Ross, L.R. (1997). Recherche sur la violence familiale: contribution des différentes épistémologies. *Criminologie, XXX*(2), 7–25.

Ramazanoglu, C. (2002). *Feminist methodology: Challenges and choices.* Thousand Oaks: Sage Publications.

Ryan, G.W., & Bernard, H.R. (2000). Data management and analysis methods. In N.K. Denzin & Y.S. Lincoln (Eds.), *Handbook of qualitative research,* 2nd ed. (pp. 769–802). London, UK: Sage Publications, Inc.

Smith, D.E. (1987). *The everyday world as problematic: A feminist sociology.* Toronto: University of Toronto Press.

Sprague, J. (2001). Comment on Walby's "Against epistemological chasms: The science question in feminism revisited: Structured knowledge and strategic methodology." *Signs, 26,* 527–536.

Statistics Canada. (2000). *Women in Canada, 2000: A gender-based statistical report.* Ottawa: Ministry of Industry.

Ussher, J.M. (1996). Premenstrual syndrome: Reconciling disciplinary divides through the adoption of a material-discursive epistemological standpoint. *Annual Review of Sex Research, 7,* 1053–2528.

ACKNOWLEDGEMENTS

The authors wish to thank Bev Brazier, Sarah MacAulay, and Bette Brazier for feedback on an earlier draft.

Critical Thinking Questions

1. Consider a social group to which you belong. It can be a religious group, a hockey team, a group such as Amnesty International, or a group of Women's Studies or Kinesiology majors. What would an outsider need to know about the unique perspective that you bring to your understanding of the world that would make sense of your participation in that group and the decisions you have made about how to live your life or spend your time? Do you think that an outsider could ever completely "get it"? What steps might an outsider, genuinely interested in capturing the insider perspective on your group, take in order to achieve that goal?

2. Consider a situation where you feel that people may be making a negative judgment about who you are based on your appearance (size, disfigurement, tattoo, hair style, etc.), behaviour (riding a motorcycle, biting your nails, taking or not taking illegal drugs, etc.), or beliefs (on vegetarianism, gun control, feminism, or globalization, etc.). What strategies do you use to try to neutralize these negative judgments? How are these strategies similar to, or different from, those used by the hackers (Kleinknecht), smokers (Kellner), adoptive mothers, adoptees, biological mothers of adopted children (March), obese women (Joanisse), ex-politicians (Shaffir & Kleinknecht) and complementary therapy users described in the previous chapters?

3. In this book and elsewhere, Robert Prus argues that the advantage in focusing on generic social processes is that we can take a series of case studies about groups that do not appear to have much in common and identify parallel social processes playing themselves out in each instance. Consider the papers in the section on constructing identities. The papers deal with, among others, smokers, adoptive mothers, obese women, ex-politicians, and people who use complementary therapies. What would you say these groups share in common? What parallels or generic social processes can you identify? What generalizations can we make, based on these readings, about how social actors construct and manage identity? Consider the papers that focus on constructing perspectives.

What generalizations can we make, based on these readings, about how social actors construct perspectives?

4. Chapter 1 provides an extended discussion of "developing relationships" as a generic social process. The reading in Chapter 24 is about relationships—among gay servicewomen in the military. In what ways do the activities of these gay servicewomen reflect the generic social processes Prus identifies? Consider your own relationships. How do these generic social processes play themselves out in your relationships?

5. If you were asked to conduct an ethnographic study, what group would you think about studying and what questions would you be interested in asking about that group? How would you collect data? Are there any particular problems, either ethical or methodological, that you anticipate confronting? Would access be a problem? Do you foresee any difficulties establishing rapport? How would you attempt to resolve these problems?

RELEVANT WEBSITES

Each of the following sites offers useful information about where to find ethnographic studies similar to those published in this volume.

1. <www.ucpress.edu/journals/si/edsub.htm>
   Site for *Symbolic Interaction,* the official journal of the Society for the Study of Symbolic Interaction.
2. <www.sagepub.com/journal.aspx?pid=225>
   Site for the *Journal of Contemporary Ethnography.*
3. <www.nova.edu/ssss/QR/index.html>
   An online journal dedicated since 1990 to the publication of papers based on qualitative and ethnographic research.
4. <http://qualitative-research.net/fqs/fqs-eng.htm>
   A German/English peer-reviewed interdisciplinary online journal for qualitative research.
5. <www.kluweronline.com/issn/0162-0436/>
   Site for *Qualitative Sociology.*
6. <www.ucpress.edu/journals/sp/>
   Site for *Social Problems,* official journal for the Society for the Study of Social Problems.

Contributors' Biographies

Michael F. Atkinson is Assistant Professor in the Sociology Department at McMaster University. His sociological interests revolve around issues in research methods, masculinity, body modification, sports violence, and figurational sociology. His current ethnographic research projects include studies of men's cosmetic surgery, criminal violence in Canadian ice hockey, and the use of body-building supplements in exercise figurations. In addition to his book *Tattooed: The Sociogenesis of a Body Art* (2003, University of Toronto Press), his recent publications include: "Tattooing and Civilising Processes: Body Modification as Self-Control" (2004, *Canadian Review of Sociology and Anthropology*), and "The Civilizing of Resistance: Straightedge Tattooing" (2003, *Deviant Behavior*).

Katherine Bischoping is Associate Professor in Sociology at York University. She teaches qualitative and quantitative methods to undergraduates, and interviewing techniques and survey research methods at the graduate level. She is a University-Wide Teaching Award winner whose current research includes identifying effective videos for use in sociology classrooms. Other publications include: "Selecting and Using Course Readings: A Study of Instructors' and Students' Practices" (2003, *The Canadian Journal of Higher Education*); a co-edited paper, "Talking about Silence: Reflections on Racial Issues in a University Course on Genocide" (2001, *Reflective Practice*); and "Toward a Social Psychological Programme for Improving Focus Group Methods of Developing Questionnaires" (1999, *Journal of Official Statistics*, with Jennifer Dykema).

Bette L. Brazier is a Ph.D. candidate in Clinical Psychology at the University of New Brunswick, Fredericton. Her primary research interests are in the areas of violence against women, the socio-political influences in the lives of First Nations women, and the role of attachment in grief outcomes. Bette is a Clinical Associate at the Royal University Hospital in the Department of Clinical Health Psychology in Saskatoon, Saskatchewan. She is currently working towards the completion of her dissertation, which examines the impact of intimate partner violence among First Nations women in Canada.

Roy Cain is Professor in the School of Social Work and Director of the Health Studies Programme at McMaster University. Much of his research examines social and community services for people living with HIV/AIDS. As a member of the HIV/ AIDS Social Research Group at McMaster, he has completed a longitudinal study of how people with HIV manage their health and health care. The research group has published a number of papers on complementary and alternative therapy use among people living with HIV and AIDS. His current research interests focus on mental health concerns among Aboriginal people living with HIV.

Andrea L. Cashmore works in insurance at Hope and Harder in St. Catharines, Ontario. She has a keen interest in social justice research and actively promotes equality for women and sexual minorities in her community.

Catherine Chiappetta-Swanson is Assistant Professor in the Sociology Department at McMaster University. Her teaching and research interests include issues in health care, bioethics, family, gender, reproductive technology, bereavement, and international adoption. Her current qualitative research focuses on the area of bereaved parents and self-help support. Her most recent publications are "Secrecy, Integrity, Agency: Nurses and Genetic Terminations" (2002, *The Journal of Clinical Ethics*), and "Dignity and Dirty Work: Nurses' Experiences in Managing Genetic Termination for Fetal Anomaly" (Forthcoming, *Qualitative Sociology*). She is also a professional consultant for Bereaved Families of Ontario Halton/Peel and serves as the Chairperson of their Professional Advisory Committee.

Peter Donnelly is Director of the Centre for Canadian Sport Policy Studies at the University of Toronto. He is the former President of the North American Society for the Sociology of Sport, and is currently Editor of the *International Review for the Sociology of Sport*. He has published widely in the area of sport sociology in Canada and North America generally.

James Gillett is Assistant Professor in the Sociology Department and Health Studies Programme at McMaster University. He is a member of the McMaster HIV/AIDS Social Research Group. James's teaching and research interests are in the areas of health, media, and sport. He is currently completing a longitudinal study examining approaches to health among people with HIV/AIDS. James's recent publications include "The Challenges of Institutionalization for AIDS Media Activism" (2003, *Media Culture and Society*) and "Media Activism and Internet Use by People with HIV/AIDS" (2003, *Sociology of Health and Illness*).

Lynne Gouliquer left the Canadian Military, after serving for 16 years, to pursue graduate studies at McGill University, Montreal, Quebec, Canada. Her primary research focus is the interplay between institutions, gender, sexuality, and identity. In 1998, she completed her master's thesis, entitled "Negotiating Sexuality: Lesbians in the Canadian Military." Currently, she is pursuing her Ph.D. and exploring women's soldiering experiences as negotiated within the Canadian military.

Josh Greenberg is Assistant Professor in the School of Journalism & Communication at Carleton University. His current research involves a multi-phase study of news coverage of the voluntary sector in Canada, and the communication strategies and activities of charities and non-profit groups. His research interests are in the areas of news and public policy, media strategies, media constructions of social problems, social movements, and public relations. Published work appears in *Voluntas, Journalism Studies, Communication and Critical/Cultural Studies, Management Communication Quarterly, Canadian Review of Sociology & Anthropology, Racial & Ethnic Studies,* and *Canadian Journal of Communication.*

Andrew D. Hathaway is a scientist at Toronto's Centre for Addiction and Mental Health, and a Sociology instructor at McMaster University. Specializing in the study of deviance, social problems, and moral regulation, his current research centres on illicit drug use patterns and correlates, and analysis of the debates informing legal-political and health policy responses. His recent articles include: "A Tale of Two Stimulants: An Analysis of Newspaper Coverage of Cocaine and Tobacco in Canada" (2004, *Canadian Journal of Communication*), and "Cannabis Effects and Dependency Concerns in Long-Term Frequent Users: A Missing Piece of the Public Health Puzzle" (2003, *Addiction Research and Theory*).

Leanne Joanisse recently completed her Ph.D. in Sociology at McMaster University. Her dissertation focused on women's experiences of weight loss surgery and its impact on their identities, health, and relationships. Her research interests include obesity stigma, body work, and feminist qualitative research methods. She currently works as an independent researcher for the Cardiovascular Obesity Research and Management Group at the Hamilton General Hospital in Hamilton, Ontario.

Florence June Kellner is Professor in the Sociology and Anthropology Department, Carleton University, and Research Associate for the Canadian Centre on Substance Abuse. Recent publications include a chapter on research ethics in *Walking the Tightrope,* and (with Patricia Begin and Irene Smolik) an FAQ on cannabis and driving. Most of her work has been in the area of the epidemiology of alcohol use and alcohol problems. Her current research involves analyses of the Canadian Addictions Survey and review of Canada's policy on alcohol.

Katharine Kelly is Associate Professor of Sociology at Carleton University where she has worked in the area of youth crime and marginal youth for the past eight years. She was co-investigator in the first national study of dating violence in Canada. Katharine Kelly and Mark Totten are the authors of "When Children Kill: A Social-Psychological Study of Youth Homicide" (2002, *Broadview Press*).

J. Scott Kenney is Assistant Professor in the Sociology Department at Memorial University of Newfoundland. He completed his undergraduate and professional education at Dalhousie University, where he obtained his B.A. (1984) and LL.B.

(1987). After practising law for several years, he completed an M.A. (1993) and Ph.D. (1999) in Sociology at McMaster University. He conducted research at Dalhousie as a SSHRC Postdoctoral Fellow (1999–2000), and taught at St. Mary's University (2001–2004) before taking up his current appointment. Professor Kenney's interests include law and criminal justice, deviance, victimology, the sociology of health, social theory, social psychology, and the sociology of emotions.

Steven Kleinknecht is a doctoral student in the Sociology Department at McMaster University. His research interests lie in the study of qualitative methods, subcultures, deviant behaviour, online interaction, and social problems. Studying people's everyday lived experiences using a symbolic interactionist framework and adopting an ethnographic approach appeal to him the most. His recent research includes the study of the hacker subculture, ex-politicians, and online qualitative methods. He has also worked as a research analyst at the Department of Justice Canada, where he has written on issues pertaining to restorative justice, juvenile delinquency, and cybercrime.

Graham Knight is Associate Professor in the Sociology Department at McMaster University. His academic interests lie primarily in the area of media sociology, and he has recently been involved in research projects on media coverage of the Olympics, and the role of communications media in the development of the anti-sweatshop movement and the campaign against Nike. His recent publications have appeared in *Journalism Studies, Communication and Critical/Cultural Studies*, the *European Journal of Communication, Critical Sociology*, and *Studies in Political Economy*. His future research plans include a study on the growth of the public relations industry and its relationship to globalization.

Lynne Lohfeld is Assistant Professor at McMaster University in Clinical Epidemiology and Biostatistics and a faculty member with PERD (Programme for Educational Research & Development), providing expertise in qualitative research methods. Dr. Lohfeld received her Ph.D. in Medical Anthropology at the University of Connecticut. She has recently completed a three-year investigation of the needs of family and informal caregivers. She has also conducted Rapid Assessment Procedure research with the World Health Organization dealing with acute respiratory infections in Turkey. Current studies include program evaluation of McMaster University's medical school curriculum, and improved services for immigrant women, critically ill neonates, and abused elders.

Jacqueline Low is Assistant Professor in the Sociology Department at the University of New Brunswick. Among her areas of research specialization are alternative and complementary health care, chronic illness and disability, deviant behaviour, and qualitative research methods. Among her most recent publications are: *Using Alternative Therapies: A Qualitative Analysis* (2004, Canadian Scholars' Press), "Managing Safety and Risk: The Experiences of People with Parkinson's Disease

Who Use Alternative and Complementary Therapies" (2004, *Health*), and "Lay Assessments of the Efficacy of Alternative/Complementary Therapies: A Challenge to Medical and Expert Dominance?" (2003, *Journal of Evidence-Based Integrative Medicine*).

Margaret MacNeill is Associate Professor and the Director of the Centre for Girls' and Women's Health and Physical Activity at the University of Toronto. She was the first researcher to conduct an ethnographic study of the Olympic Games in 1988, a study that won the top journal article award from the *Sociology of Sport Journal*. Her current ethno-semiotic research projects include: knowledge engagement in activity mentoring programs, youth understanding of health and fitness, gender and televised health communication, and contested nationalisms produced in Olympic broadcasting.

Karen March is Associate Professor in the Sociology and Anthropology Department at Carleton University. She has published a book on adopted adults' experience with biological family contact entitled *The Stranger Who Bore Me* and is currently writing a book on the biological mothers' experience. Her research interests include personal and social identity, motherhood, the body, and perceptions of family and family relationships. Together with Charlene Miall, she has recently completed a Canada-wide study of community attitudes towards adoption, parental roles, and adoptee-birth family contact.

Charlene Miall is Professor in the Sociology Department at McMaster University. She has published papers on involuntary childlessness; community attitudes towards infertility, adoption, and new reproductive technologies; and social policy. More recently, she has published "The Exxon Factor: The Role of Corporate and Academic Science in the Emergence and Legitimation of a New Global Model of Sequence Stratigraphy" (2002, *Sociological Quarterly* with Andrew Miall of the University of Toronto). This paper examines the social production of scientific knowledge, demonstrating the importance of human interpretations and reputations in legitimating ideas in the absence of data or independent proof.

Kristin L. Newman is a Ph.D. student in Psychology at the University of New Brunswick, Fredericton. Her teaching and research interests include qualitative research methods, the psychology of women, and social justice among diverse groups. She recently completed a comprehensive paper in which she examined body image disturbance and eating disorders among gay men. Her dissertation project investigates the daily lives and psychologies of New Brunswick mothers of children with autism spectrum disorders.

Dorothy Pawluch is Associate Professor in the Sociology Department at McMaster University. Her research and teaching interests lie in the areas of sociology of health, deviance and social problems, work and occupations, and social psychology. Her previous publications include: *The New Paediatrics: A Profession in Transition* (1996, Aldine de Gruyter), and a series of papers on HIV/AIDS with Roy Cain and James Gillett, including "Lay Constructions of HIV and Complementary Therapy Use" (2000, *Social Science and Medicine*). She is a member of the McMaster HIV/AIDS Social Research Group.

Carmen Poulin is Professor of Psychology and Women Studies at the University of New Brunswick, Fredericton. In addition to her research on gays and lesbians in the military, her present research focuses on sexualities, women in transition from abusive relationships, and the psychological impact of institutional and social practices on marginalized groups. She has recently published in a special edition of *Women & Psychology* on women and disabilities, a paper entitled, "Part-Time Disabled Lesbian Passing on Roller Blades, or PMS, Prozac, and Essentialising Woman's Ailments." Her most recent publication, with L. Gouliquer, is entitled "Translating Theory into Methodology: The Intersection of Sociologies and Psychologies Meetings of the Canadian Psychological Association, St. John's, Newfoundland" (2004).

Robert Prus is Professor in the Sociology Department at the University of Waterloo. As a symbolic interactionist and ethnographer, he intends to connect social theory with the study of human action in a very direct, experientially engaged (community life-world) sense. He has authored or co-authored several books that focus on the ways that people make sense of and engage the situations in which they find themselves. These include *Road Hustler* with C.R.D. Sharper; *Hookers, Rounders, and Desk Clerks* with Styllianoss Irini; *Making Sales*; *Pursuing Customers*; *Symbolic Interaction and Ethnographic Research*; *Subcultural Mosaics and Intersubjective Realities*; *Beyond the Power Mystique*; and *The Deviant Mystique* with Scott Grills. At present, Dr. Prus is tracing the developmental flows of pragmatist thought from the classical Greek era (c. 700–300 B.C.E.) to the present time and is attending to the study of human knowing and acting in a number of areas of Western social thought—including rhetoric, poetics, religious studies, ethno-history, education, politics, and philosophy.

Antony J. Puddephatt is a Ph.D. candidate in the Sociology Department at McMaster University. His areas of interest include science and technology, ethnographic research, and sociological theory. He has published a paper that examines decision making in chess as a socially contingent process, "Chess Playing as Strategic Activity" (2003, *Symbolic Interaction*). More recently, he has drawn on the work of George Herbert Mead in an effort to extend the constructionist study of technology in "Mead Has Never Been Modern: Using Meadian Theory to Extend the Constructionist Study of Technology" (Forthcoming, *Social Epistemology*).

Gillian Ranson is Associate Professor in the Sociology Department at the University of Calgary. Her research interests include gender, families and work;

and methodological and ethical issues in qualitative research. Current projects include a study of couples with children who are dividing up paid work and family responsibilities in non-traditional ways. She is also a co-investigator in an international study of information technology workplace relations. Recent publications include "Beyond 'Gender Differences': A Canadian Study of Women's and Men's Careers in Engineering" (2003, *Gender, Work and Organization*), and "Men at Work: Change—or No Change?—in the Era of the 'New Father'" (2001, *Men and Masculinities*).

William Shaffir received his Ph.D. from McGill University. He is a Professor in the Sociology Department at McMaster University. He has authored books and journal articles on Hassidic Jews, professional socialization, and field research methods. He has studied the conversion experiences of newly Orthodox Jews as well as those who have drifted from the ultra-Orthodox fold. Studies he is currently conducting focus on ex-politicians and how they rationalize and cope with defeat at the polls, the professionalization of members of corporate boards, and the management of racial diversity in institutionalized settings.

Christina Sinding is Assistant Professor, cross-appointed to Health Studies and Social Work at McMaster University. She conducts research on illness experience, informal and formal care, and innovative research representation. Recent publications include "Informal Care—Two-Tiered Care?" (2004, *Journal of Sociology and Social Welfare*), "Disarmed Complaints: Unpacking Satisfaction with End-of-Life Care" (2003, *Social Science and Medicine*), and "Exposing Failures, Unsettling Accommodations: Tensions in Interview Practice" (2003, with Jane Aronson, *Qualitative Research*). She is co-author with Ross Gray of *Standing Ovation: Performing Social Science Research about Cancer* (2002, AltaMira Press). Her current research explores the experiences of marginalized women who have had cancer.

Linda L. Snyder is Assistant Professor in Social Work at Renison College, University of Waterloo. Her research has focused on matters of diversity, poverty, and social justice, in particular the potential of women's employment initiatives to address poverty and the comparison of Canadian and Latin American endeavours. Her most recent publications are "Communities in Cooperation: Human Services Work with Old Order Mennonites" (2004, *Journal of Ethnic and Cultural Diversity in Social Work*), and "Collective Outcomes and Social Mobilization in Chilean and Canadian Employment Initiatives for Women" (2004, *International Social Work*).

Karen Szala-Meneok is Assistant Professor at the School for Rehabilitation Sciences at McMaster University. She teaches in the evidence-based practice program and is Senior Research Associate with the Canadian Longitudinal Study on Aging. Karen received her Ph.D. and her M.A. in Anthropology from McMaster University and Memorial University of Newfoundland. She conducts action-based research with family caregivers and Aboriginal people in Labrador. Other research interests include qualitative research methodology, and ethics governing human subject research. She continues to pursue her interest in health of First Nations peoples with whom she has worked for over two decades.

Mark Totten is author of *Guys, Gangs and Girlfriend Abuse* (2000, Broadview Press) and is Director of Research at the Youth Services Bureau of Ottawa. He has worked in clinical settings with high-risk young people and families for 20 years. Over the past couple of years, he has led a series of national school-based studies on adolescent bullying, sexual harassment, racism, restorative justice, and literacy.

Anne Wright is a psychologist with clinical and research interests that include combined mental health and substance misuse problems, homelessness, and offending behaviour. She obtained her Ph.D. at the University of Bath, and her past research has examined living with schizophrenia, quality of life and depression, the assessment of anger, and post-lingual deafness. Recent publications include "Changes in the Quality of Life of Patients Taking Anti-Depressant Medication in Primary Care: Validation of the WHOQOL-100" (2001, *British Journal of Psychiatry*, with Professor Suzanne Skevington).

Copyright Acknowledgements

Index

Alexander, Bruce, 68–69
allopathy, 275, 283
almost complaints, 183–84
alternative therapies, 283. *See also*
   complementary therapies
amateur chess world
   Aboriginal children and, 303
   advancing in, 303–9
   appreciation of accomplishments, 307–8
   chess literature, 304–5
   chess subculture, 301–2
   competition, 301–2
   cross-cultural considerations, 307
   data, 300–301
   dramatic encounter, 302
   esoteric knowledge, 304
   goals, 304–6
   learning from others, 305
   learning through trial and error, 306
   limitations, dealing with, 308
   methods, 300–301
   mistakes, 306
   monitoring progress, 307–8
   rating system, 302–3
   re-evaluation and re-adjustment of
     goals, 308–9
   skill development, 303–9
   status, 302–3
   status hierarchy, 302
ambiguities, 17, 69
anonymity, unsought, 151
anti-intellectualism, 148
anticipating encounters with others, 19
Aquinas, Thomas, 9
argot, 214, 220–22, 223
Aristotle, 10
aromatherapy, 279
assertive outreach, 95, 100
Association of Professional Engineers,
   Geologists, and Geophysicists of
   Alberta, 105
associational explanations, 7–8
assumptions, 21
Atkinson, Michael F., 30, 66–76, 339
attached-postings, 331–32
Augustine, 9

authenticity, quest for, 20–23
avoiding the other, 278–82
awkward phrasings, 142–44
AZT, 190

B
bariatric surgery, 248. *See also* weight loss
   surgery
Becker, H.S., 27
biases, 27
bifurcated consciousness, 325
biological kinship, 39–40
biological kinship group, 244, 246
birth mothers, 47–48, 242–43
Bischoping, Katherine, 34, 141–54, 339
Blumer, Herbert, 14, 18, 158
body image, 249, 258
Brazier, Bette L., 159, 200–211, 339
Bush, George W., 152

C
Cain, Roy, 159, 163, 189–99, 312–22, 340
Canadian Armed Forces, 323. *See also* gay
   servicewomen
Canadian Council of Natural Mothers
   (CCNM), 242
cancer deaths, 177
care-giving roles, 192–94
care in the community, 91, 100
career, 100
career-builder research model, 55, 61
Cashmore, Andrea L., 159, 200–211, 340
causes, 9
charismatic leadership, 135
chess. *See* amateur chess world
Chess Federation of Canada, 301
chess literature, 304–05
Chiappetta-Swanson, Catherine, 158,
   166–76, 340
Chile. *See* dual perspectives
Choirs Ontario, 320
choral singing. *See* gay men and choral singing
Cicero, 9
claims making, 73
classic or full PAR model (cPAR), 57, 58*f*, 62
collaborative research, 56